XHTML For Dummies

KT-523-147

Cheat Sheet

Golden Rules of XHTML

- Always nest correctly.
- Always include ending tags for non-empty elements.
- Empty elements must follow the syntax `<empty />`.
- Attribute values must always be quoted (you can use single or double quotation marks as long as you're consistent in the type you use).
- Element and attribute names must be lowercase.
- Attributes must always have a value.
- All XHTML documents must begin with a DOCTYPE declaration.
- The root element, `<html>`, must include the XHTML namespace.
- You must use include the `<html>`, `<head>`, `<title>` and `<body>` elements in your document (for frameset documents, the `<body>` element must be replaced by the `<frameset>` element).
- Script and style elements found in the head of a document should be wrapped in CDATA sections.

Layout and Structure Elements

Element	Name	Function
`<!DOCTYPE>`	Document type	Specifies the version of XHTML used in the document
`<address> - </address>`	Attribution information	Lists author contact information
`<body> - </body>`	Body	Defines or indicates a document's body
`<div> - </div>`	Logical divisions	Marks divisions in a document
`<h1> - </h1>`		
`<h2> - </h2>`		
`<h3> - </h3>`		
`<h4> - </h4>`		
`<h5> - </h5>`		
`<h6> - </h6>`	Headings	Identifies first-level through sixth-level headings
`<head> - </head>`	Head	Indicates a document's head
`<html> - </html>`	HTML document	Identifies an (X)HTML document
`<meta />`	Meta-information	Describes aspects of the page's information structure, contents, or relationships to other documents
`<span> - </span>`	Localized style formatting	Applies style to subparts of a paragraph
`<title> - </title>`	Document title	Briefly describes document information
`<!-- - -->`	Comments	Inserts comments; which are not displayed by browsers

For Dummies®: Bestselling Book Series for Beginners

BESTSELLING
BOOK SERIES

XHTML For Dummies®

Cheat Sheet

Text Layout Elements

Text TagsElement	Name	FunctionAdds structural information to text
`<abbr> - </abbr>`	Abbreviation	Identifies expansion for an acronym
`<acronym> - </acronym>`	Acronym	Indicates an acronym
`<blockquote> -</blockquote>`	Quote style	Sets off long quotations or citations
` `	Force line break	Forces a line break in the on-screen text flow
`<cite> - </cite>`	Citation markup	Marks distinctive text for citations
`<code> - </code>`	Program code text	Used for code samples
`<del> - </del>`	Deleted text	Identifies sections of a Web page that deleted in revision
`<dfn> - </dfn>`	Defined term	Emphasizes a term about to be defined in the text
`<em> - </em>`	Emphasis	Emphasizes enclosed text
`<ins> - </ins>`	Inserted text	Identifies Web page sections inserted in revision
`<kbd> - </kbd>`	Keyboard text	Marks text to be entered by the user at the keyboard
`<p> - </p>`	Paragraph	Breaks text into content blocks
`<pre> - </pre>`	Preformatted text	Keeps spacing and layout of original text in mono-spaced font
`<q> - </q>`	Quotation markup	Marks a short quotation within a sentence
`<samp> - </samp>`	Sample output	Indicates sample output from a program or script
`<strong> - </strong>`	Strong emphasis	Provides maximum emphasis to enclosed text
`<sub> - </sub>`	Subscript	Renders text smaller and slightly lowered
`<sup> - </sup>`	Superscript	Renders text smaller and slightly raised
`<var> - </var>`	Variable text	Marks variable or substitution for some other value

Text Style Elements

Presentation ControlsElement	Name	Text presentation tagsFunction
`<b> - </b>`	Bold text	Produces bold text
`<basefont />`	Base font	Specifies the base font color, typeface, and size
`<big> - </big>`	Big text	Makes text larger
`<center> - </center>`	Centered text	Centers enclosed text
`<font> - </font>`	Font appearance	Sets the size, color, and typeface of text
`<hr />`	Horizontal rule	Draws a horizontal line across the page
`<i> - </i>`	Italic	Produces italic text
`<s> - </s>`	Strikethrough	Produces text that has been struck with a line through it
`<small> - </small>`	Small text	Makes text smaller
`<strike> - </strike>`	Strikethrough	Produces text with a line through it
`<tt> - </tt>`	Teletype text	Produces a typewriter font
`<u> - </u>`	Underlined text	Underlines enclosed text

...For DUMMIES

References for the Rest of Us! ®

BESTSELLING BOOK SERIES

Are you intimidated and confused by computers? Do you find that traditional manuals are overloaded with technical details you'll never use? Do your friends and family always call you to fix simple problems on their PCs? Then the *...For Dummies*® computer book series from IDG Books Worldwide is for you.

...For Dummies books are written for those frustrated computer users who know they aren't really dumb but find that PC hardware, software, and indeed the unique vocabulary of computing make them feel helpless. *...For Dummies* books use a lighthearted approach, a down-to-earth style, and even cartoons and humorous icons to dispel computer novices' fears and build their confidence. Lighthearted but not lightweight, these books are a perfect survival guide for anyone forced to use a computer.

> *"I like my copy so much I told friends; now they bought copies."*
>
> — Irene C., Orwell, Ohio

> *"Quick, concise, nontechnical, and humorous."*
>
> — Jay A., Elburn, Illinois

> *"Thanks, I needed this book. Now I can sleep at night."*
>
> — Robin F., British Columbia, Canada

Already, millions of satisfied readers agree. They have made *...For Dummies* books the #1 introductory level computer book series and have written asking for more. So, if you're looking for the most fun and easy way to learn about computers, look to *...For Dummies* books to give you a helping hand.

IDG BOOKS WORLDWIDE

XHTML™

FOR

DUMMIES®

by Ed Tittel, Chelsea Valentine, and Natanya Pitts

IDG Books Worldwide, Inc.
An International Data Group Company

Foster City, CA ◆ Chicago, IL ◆ Indianapolis, IN ◆ New York, NY

XHTML™ For Dummies®

Published by
IDG Books Worldwide, Inc.
An International Data Group Company
919 E. Hillsdale Blvd.
Suite 400
Foster City, CA 94404
www.idgbooks.com (IDG Books Worldwide Web Site)
www.dummies.com (Dummies Press Web Site)

Library of Congress Control Number: 00-103397

ISBN: 0-7645-0751-6

Printed in the United States of America

10 9 8 7 6 5 4 3 2 1

1O/QY/QZ/QQ/IN

Distributed in the United States by IDG Books Worldwide, Inc.

Distributed by CDG Books Canada Inc. for Canada; by Transworld Publishers Limited in the United Kingdom; by IDG Norge Books for Norway; by IDG Sweden Books for Sweden; by IDG Books Australia Publishing Corporation Pty. Ltd. for Australia and New Zealand; by TransQuest Publishers Pte Ltd. for Singapore, Malaysia, Thailand, Indonesia, and Hong Kong; by Gotop Information Inc. for Taiwan; by ICG Muse, Inc. for Japan; by Intersoft for South Africa; by Eyrolles for France; by International Thomson Publishing for Germany, Austria and Switzerland; by Distribuidora Cuspide for Argentina; by LR International for Brazil; by Galileo Libros for Chile; by Ediciones ZETA S.C.R. Ltda. for Peru; by WS Computer Publishing Corporation, Inc., for the Philippines; by Contemporanea de Ediciones for Venezuela; by Express Computer Distributors for the Caribbean and West Indies; by Micronesia Media Distributor, Inc. for Micronesia; by Chips Computadoras S.A. de C.V. for Mexico; by Editorial Norma de Panama S.A. for Panama; by American Bookshops for Finland.

For general information on IDG Books Worldwide's books in the U.S., please call our Consumer Customer Service department at 800-762-2974. For reseller information, including discounts and premium sales, please call our Reseller Customer Service department at 800-434-3422.

For information on where to purchase IDG Books Worldwide's books outside the U.S., please contact our International Sales department at 317-596-5530 or fax 317-572-4002.

For consumer information on foreign language translations, please contact our Customer Service department at 1-800-434-3422, fax 317-572-4002, or e-mail rights@idgbooks.com.

For information on licensing foreign or domestic rights, please phone +1-650-653-7098.

For sales inquiries and special prices for bulk quantities, please contact our Order Services department at 800-434-3422 or write to the address above.

For information on using IDG Books Worldwide's books in the classroom or for ordering examination copies, please contact our Educational Sales department at 800-434-2086 or fax 317-572-4005.

For press review copies, author interviews, or other publicity information, please contact our Public Relations department at 650-653-7000 or fax 650-653-7500.

For authorization to photocopy items for corporate, personal, or educational use, please contact Copyright Clearance Center, 222 Rosewood Drive, Danvers, MA 01923, or fax 978-750-4470.

Trademarks: XHTML is a trademark of Terje Nordehaug. For Dummies, Dummies Man, A Reference for the Rest of Us!, The Dummies Way, Dummies Daily, and related trade dress are registered trademarks or trademarks of IDG Books Worldwide, Inc., in the United States and other countries, and may not be used without written permission. All other trademarks are the property of their respective owners. IDG Books Worldwide is not associated with any product or vendor mentioned in this book.

is a registered trademark under exclusive license to IDG Books Worldwide, Inc., from International Data Group, Inc.

About the Authors

Ed Tittel is a full-time writer/trainer who manages a small gang of technoids at LANWrights (Austin, TX), a wholly owned subsidiary of LeapIt.com. Ed has been writing for the trade press since 1986, and has worked on over 100 books. In addition to this title, Ed has worked on more than 30 books for IDG Books Worldwide, including *Windows NT Server 4.0 For Dummies, HTML 4 For Dummies,* 3rd Edition, *XML For Dummies,* 2nd Edition, and *Networking with NetWare For Dummies*, 4th Edition.

Ed teaches for Austin Community College, NetWorld + Interop, and the Internet Security Conference. He also trains on and writes about Novell and Microsoft certification curricula and certification exams. When Ed's not busy doing all that work stuff, Ed likes to travel, shoot pool, and wrestle with his indefatigable Labrador retriever, Blackie.

Contact Ed by e-mail at etittel@lanw.com.

Chelsea Valentine is a Webmaster, writer, and trainer at LANWrights, Inc., where she maintains the company Website and related training sites, oversees LANWrights online training efforts for Austin Community College, and pitches in on books as her busy schedule permits. So far, she's contributed to four IDG Books Worldwide titles since returning to LANWrights in early 1999: *The Hip Pocket Guide to HTML 4.01*; *XML For Dummies*, 2nd Edition, *HTML 4 For Dummies*, 3rd Edition, and to this book as well.

In her spare time, when she's not listening to her boyfriend Sam perform, or acting as his muse, Chelsea's idea of a good time is sitting (yeah, that's right, just sitting), with nothing at all on her mind.

Contact Chelsea by e-mail at chelsea@lanw.com.

Natanya Pitts is a writer, trainer, and Web guru in Austin, Texas. She works as a freelance courseware developer for various organizations, including NotHarvard.com. Her primary activities are development and maintenance of Web sites, and consulting with organizations about how they develop their Web presences and Web based training efforts. She also teaches Web related classes in the Austin Community College Webmaster Certification program.

Natanya has authored, co-authored, or contributed to more than a dozen Web and Internet related titles, including *XML For Dummies*, 2nd Edition, *The XML Black Book,* and *XML In Record Time*. Ms. Pitts has also taught classes on HTML, Dynamic HTML, and XML at several national conferences (including MacWorld, Networld + Interop, and HP World), as well as at the NASA Ames Research Center.

Contact Natanya by e-mail at natanya@io.com.

ABOUT IDG BOOKS WORLDWIDE

Welcome to the world of IDG Books Worldwide.

IDG Books Worldwide, Inc., is a subsidiary of International Data Group, the world's largest publisher of computer-related information and the leading global provider of information services on information technology. IDG was founded more than 30 years ago by Patrick J. McGovern and now employs more than 9,000 people worldwide. IDG publishes more than 290 computer publications in over 75 countries. More than 90 million people read one or more IDG publications each month.

Launched in 1990, IDG Books Worldwide is today the #1 publisher of best-selling computer books in the United States. We are proud to have received eight awards from the Computer Press Association in recognition of editorial excellence and three from Computer Currents' First Annual Readers' Choice Awards. Our best-selling *...For Dummies®* series has more than 50 million copies in print with translations in 31 languages. IDG Books Worldwide, through a joint venture with IDG's Hi-Tech Beijing, became the first U.S. publisher to publish a computer book in the People's Republic of China. In record time, IDG Books Worldwide has become the first choice for millions of readers around the world who want to learn how to better manage their businesses.

Our mission is simple: Every one of our books is designed to bring extra value and skill-building instructions to the reader. Our books are written by experts who understand and care about our readers. The knowledge base of our editorial staff comes from years of experience in publishing, education, and journalism — experience we use to produce books to carry us into the new millennium. In short, we care about books, so we attract the best people. We devote special attention to details such as audience, interior design, use of icons, and illustrations. And because we use an efficient process of authoring, editing, and desktop publishing our books electronically, we can spend more time ensuring superior content and less time on the technicalities of making books.

You can count on our commitment to deliver high-quality books at competitive prices on topics you want to read about. At IDG Books Worldwide, we continue in the IDG tradition of delivering quality for more than 30 years. You'll find no better book on a subject than one from IDG Books Worldwide.

John Kilcullen
Chairman and CEO
IDG Books Worldwide, Inc.

Eighth Annual Computer Press Awards ≥1992

Ninth Annual Computer Press Awards ≥1993

Tenth Annual Computer Press Awards ≥1994

Eleventh Annual Computer Press Awards ≥1995

Authors' Acknowledgments

Because XHTML is the latest and greatest version of HTML (we explain this in Chapter 1), this book might be considered the seventh edition *HTML For Dummies*. Therefore, we'd like to start our acknowledgements by thanking our many readers for making this book a success. We'd also like to thank them and the IDG Books Worldwide editorial team for the feedback that drives the continuing improvement of this book's contents. Please, don't stop now — tell us what you want to do with XHTML, and how we can help you.

Let me go on by thanking my sterling co-authors, Natanya Pitts and Chelsea Valentine, for their efforts on this revision. I am eternally grateful for their ideas, their hard work, and their experience in reaching an audience of budding Web experts.

Next, we'd like to thank the great teams at LANWrights and IDG Books for their efforts on this title. At LANWrights, my fervent thanks go to Mary Burmeister, for her services and the time spent on this book. I'd also like to thank Bill Brogden for his outstanding programming efforts. At IDG, I must thank our collaborator of many years, Pat O'Brien, for his extraordinary efforts, and Ted Cains, Donna Frederick, Sheri Replin, and the editorial team for their marvelous way with our words. Other folks we need to thank include Kristy Nash and Her Fabulous PLTs for their artful page layouts, Wes Menzel for his painstaking trials, and Heather Dismore and the Heather Dismore Media Chorus for their CD production panache. IDG's Steve Hayes demonstrated extraordinary insight and taste by hiring us again for this edition.

Finally, I'd like to thank my parents, Al and Ceil, for all their support over the years, and my sister, Kat, and her family for keeping me plugged into the family side of life. I must also thank my faithful Labrador companion, Blackie, who's always ready to pull me away from the keyboard — sometimes literally — to explore the great outdoors.

Ed Tittel

For Sam, Mom, Dad, Austin, MaryMary, Nat, Ed, Dawn, Bill, Kim, Michael, Amy, Kate, Cameron, Jenn, Nik, Chris, and Karl: "Why is 6 afraid of 7?" "Because 7 8 9, silly. . ."

Chelsea Valentine

First and foremost, I'd like to thank my co-author Ed Tittel for giving me the opportunity to work on this book. It's been fun! In addition to being a great co-author, you've been a great friend. Special thanks to my beloved husband Robby, and my lovely daughter, Alanna. All things are easier because you are a part of my life. Thanks to my parents, Charles and Swanya, for always believing in me and supporting me. And thanks to my furry fuzzball Gandalf for keeping me company while I work.

Natanya Pitts

Publisher's Acknowledgments

We're proud of this book; please register your comments through our IDG Books Worldwide Online Registration Form located at `http://my2cents.dummies.com`.

Some of the people who helped bring this book to market include the following:

Acquisitions, Editorial, and Media Development

Project Editor: Pat O'Brien

Acquisitions Editor: Steven Hayes

Copy Editors: Ted Cains, Donna Frederick, Sheri Replin

Proof Editor: Dwight Ramsey

Technical Editor: Wes Menzel

Permissions Editor: Carmen Krikorian

Associate Media Development Specialist: Megan Decraene

Editorial Manager: Rev Mengle

Media Development Manager: Heather Heath Dismore

Production

Project Coordinator: Amanda Foxworth

Layout and Graphics: Amy Adrian, Joe Bucki, Tracy K. Oliver, Jill Piscitelli, Erin Zeltner

Proofreaders: Laura Albert, Corey Bowen, John Greenough, Susan Moritz, Charles Spencer, York Production Services, Inc.

Indexer: York Production Services, Inc.

General and Administrative

IDG Books Worldwide, Inc.: John Kilcullen, CEO

IDG Books Technology Publishing Group: Richard Swadley, Senior Vice President and Publisher; Walter R. Bruce III, Vice President and Publisher; Joseph Wikert, Vice President and Publisher; Mary Bednarek, Vice President and Director, Product Development; Andy Cummings, Publishing Director, General User Group; Mary C. Corder, Editorial Director; Barry Pruett, Publishing Director

IDG Books Consumer Publishing Group: Roland Elgey, Senior Vice President and Publisher; Kathleen A. Welton, Vice President and Publisher; Kevin Thornton, Acquisitions Manager; Kristin A. Cocks, Editorial Director

IDG Books Internet Publishing Group: Brenda McLaughlin, Senior Vice President and Publisher; Sofia Marchant, Online Marketing Manager

IDG Books Production for Branded Press: Debbie Stailey, Director of Production; Cindy L. Phipps, Manager of Project Coordination, Production Proofreading, and Indexing; Tony Augsburger, Manager of Prepress, Reprints, and Systems; Laura Carpenter, Production Control Manager; Shelley Lea, Supervisor of Graphics and Design; Debbie J. Gates, Production Systems Specialist; Robert Springer, Supervisor of Proofreading; Trudy Coler, Page Layout Manager; Troy Barnes, Page Layout Supervisor, Kathie Schutte, Senior Page Layout Supervisor; Michael Sullivan, Production Supervisor

Packaging and Book Design: Patty Page, Manager, Promotions Marketing

◆

The publisher would like to give special thanks to Patrick J. McGovern, without whom this book would not have been possible.

◆

Contents at a Glance

Cartoons at a Glance

By Rich Tennant

page 159

"We're here to clean the code."

page 63

"We're much better prepared for this upgrade than before. We're giving users additional training, better manuals, and a morphine drip."

page 9

"Before the Internet, we were only bustin' chops locally. But now, with our Web site, we're bustin' chops all over the world."

page 249

page 357

"OK, I think I forgot to mention this, but we now have a Web management function that automatically alerts us when there's a broken link on The Aquarium's Web site."

page 387

"It says, 'Thank you for downloading Gumpton's Compression Utility shareware. Should you decide to purchase this product, send a check to the address shown and your PC will be uncompressed and restored to its original size.'"

page 315

Fax: 978-546-7747
E-mail: richtennant@the5thwave.com
World Wide Web: www.the5thwave.com

Table of Contents

Introduction

. . . .

*W*elcome to the wild, wacky, and wonderful possibilities inherent in the Web. In this book, we introduce you to the mysteries of the Extensible Hypertext Markup Language (XHTML) that's taking over the world from the original Hypertext Markup Language (HTML), that's used to build Web pages. Our goal is to initiate you into the still-select, but rapidly growing, community of Web authors.

If you've tried to build your own Web pages before but found it too forbidding, now you can relax. If you can chew gum or pull up your socks in the morning, you too can become an XHTML author. (No kidding!)

When we first wrote this book, we took a straightforward approach to the basics of authoring documents for the Web. In this edition for a new generation of Web page designers, we went after the best of old and new. We've kept the amount of technobabble to a minimum and stuck with plain English as much as possible. Besides plain talk about hypertext, XHTML, and the Web, we include lots of examples, plus lots of detailed instructions to help you build your very own Web pages with minimum muss and fuss.

We also include a peachy CD with this book that contains XHTML examples from the chapters in usable form — plus a number of interesting widgets that you can use to embellish your own documents and astound your friends. For this edition, we've added discussions of important topics that have come increasingly to the fore (though not yet to the putting green) in the last few years. Finally, the CD also includes the magnificent and bedazzling source materials for the *XHTML For Dummies* Web pages, which you might find a source of inspiration and raw material for your own use! And we carry on a time-honored tradition upheld by the computer industry generally and IDG Books Worldwide in particular:

Anything silly you might read herein is *a feature, not a bug*!

About This Book

Think of this book as a friendly, approachable guide to tackling terminology, and taking up the tools of XHTML to build readable, attractive pages for the Web. Although XHTML isn't hard to learn, it does pack a welter of details. You'll need to wrestle them into shape while you build your Web pages. Some sample topics you find in this book include:

- Understanding where the X in XHTML comes from
- Understanding XHTML's roots (and split ends) (or the HTML in XHTML)
- Using XHTML elements and attributes
- Designing and building Web pages with XHTML
- Managing XHTML style and layout
- Creating interesting XHTML page layouts

Although at first glance it might seem that building Web pages requires years of arduous training, advanced artistic abilities, and intense meditation, take heart: It's not true! If you can tell somebody how to find your office, you can certainly build a Web document that does what you want it to. The purpose of this book isn't to turn you into a particle physicist (or, for that matter, a particle physicist into a Web site); it's to show you all the design and technical elements you need to build a good-looking, readable Web page, and give you the know-how and confidence to do a great job!

How to Use This Book

This book tells you how to use XHTML 1.0 to get your page up and running on the Web. We tell you what's involved in designing and building effective Web documents that can bring your ideas and information to the whole online world — if that's what you want to do — and maybe have some high-tech fun communicating them.

All XHTML code appears in monospaced type like this:

```
<head><title>What's in a Title?</title></head>...
```

When you type XHTML tags or other related information, be sure to copy the information exactly as you see it between the angle brackets (< and >) because that's part of the magic that makes XHTML work. Other than that, you find out how to marshal and manage the content that makes your pages special, and we tell you exactly what you need to do to mix the elements of XHTML with your own work.

The margins of a book don't give you the same room as do the vast reaches of cyberspace. Therefore some long lines of XHTML markup, or designations of Web sites (called *URLs,* for *Uniform Resource Locators*), may wrap to the next line when we present them here. Remember that your computer shows such wrapped lines as a *single line of HTML,* or as a single URL — so if you're typing in that hunk of code, keep it on a single line. Don't insert a hard return if you see one of these wrapped lines. We'll clue you in that the URLs supposed to be all one line by breaking the line at a slash (to imply "but wait, there's more!") and slightly indenting the overage, as in the following silly example:

```
http://www.infocadabra.transylvania.com/nexus/plexus/lexus/
          praxis/okay/this/is/a/make-believe/URL/but/some/
          real/ones/are/SERIOUSLY/long.html
```

With HTML, you could type your tag text as uppercase, lowercase, or both. However, with XHTML, all tags and attributes must be in lowercase. (Tags lifted from HTML must be entirely in lowercase; character entities must be typed exactly as they appear in Chapter 14 of this book.) Do yourself a favor: please, enter all XHTML tag text in lowercase only. Those of you who own previous editions of the book for HTML may see this as a complete reversal of our earlier instructions. That it is! But the makers of XHTML, the World Wide Web Consortium (or W3C), have changed the rules of this game, so we change our instructions to follow their requirements.

Three Presumptuous Assumptions

They say that making assumptions makes a fool out of the person who makes them and the person about whom those assumptions are made (and just who are *They,* anyway? We *assume* we know, but . . . never mind). Even so, practicality demands that we make a few assumptions about you, our gentle reader:

- ✔ You can turn your computer on and off.
- ✔ You know how to use a mouse and a keyboard.
- ✔ You want to build your own Web pages for fun, for profit, or because it's your job.

In addition, we assume you already have a working connection to the Internet, and one of the many fine Web browsers available by hook, by crook, by download from that same Internet, or from the attached CD. You don't need to be a master logician or a wizard in the arcane arts of programming, nor do you need a Ph.D. in computer science. You don't even need a detailed sense of what's going on in the innards of your computer to deal with the material in this book.

If you can write a sentence and know the difference between a heading and a paragraph, you're better off than nine out of ten playground bullies — *and* you can build and publish your own documents on the Web. If you have an active imagination and the ability to communicate what's important to you, even better — you've already mastered the key ingredients necessary to build useful, attractive Web pages. The rest is made up of details, and we help you with those!

How This Book Is Organized

This book contains seven major parts, arranged in a peculiar and pleasing order (to us, anyway): All seven parts contain four or more chapters or appendixes, and each chapter or appendix contains multiple modular sections. Any time you need help or information, pick up the book and start anywhere you like, or use the Table of Contents and Index to locate specific topics or key words.

Here's a breakdown of the parts and what you find in each one.

Part I: Getting Cozy with XHTML

This part sets the stage and includes an overview of and introduction to the terms, techniques, and metalanguages (not a language about metals, but rather, a language used to describe other languages) that make XHTML do its thing. Of course, you also get introduced to the Extensible Hypertext Markup Language to which this book is devoted, and various software components and text files that make it so powerful and effective a tool for communication online.

XHTML documents, also called *Web pages,* are the fundamental units of information organization and delivery on the Web. Here, you also discover what XHTML is about and how hypertext can enrich ordinary text. Next, you examine XHTML's roots in HTML and XML, the two markup languages that combine to create XHTML. After that you learn what's involved in converting old-fashioned HTML into new-fangled XHTML, after which you take a bracing plunge into the XHTML specification that describes this crazy ball game!

Part II: Getting Started

XHTML mixes ordinary text with special strings of characters, called *markup,* used to instruct browsers how to display XHTML documents. In this part of the book, you find out about markup in general, and about the structure of XHTML in particular (including how we structure it in this book). After that, you tackle your very first XHTML document, so you can practice what we preach. Next, you'll find an overview of the many XHTML elements and attributes, along with explanations of what they do and how they work. Then, we tell you all about XHTML and style sheets, to help you understand how to manage how text and graphics look when displayed on a Web page. After that, you participate in the dissection and analysis of a basic XHTML page, so you can see what it's made of and how all its pieces fit together (don't worry — we promise there's no smell of formaldehyde nor sharp-edged instruments involved).

By the time you finish Part II, expect to have a good overall idea of what XHTML is, what it can do, and how you can use it yourself.

Part III: The Building Blocks of XHTML

Part III takes the elements and attributes covered in Part II and explains them in greater detail to help you design and build commercial-grade XHTML documents. This includes working with XHTML element and attribute syntax and structures, plus working with the kind of document controls you need to build complex Web pages. After that, you find out how to make the most of XHTML links and graphics, how to build a variety of lists, and how to include all kinds of keen symbols in the text that appears on screen in your Web pages.

Part IV: Taking XHTML to the Next Level

Part IV adds elegance and *savoir faire* to the basics covered in Part III. By the time you read these chapters, you can build complex Web pages of many different kinds. You also find out how to organize textual and graphical data into a variety of tables, how to create and use clickable images called image maps to help users navigate your Web site, how to work with data input tools called forms, and how to break your display into individual on-screen areas called frames to improve your readers' access to Web document contents and functions.

Part V: Advanced XHTML Topics

In this part, you go a little beyond the built-in capabilities that XHTML 1.0 delivers to its users, to examine some interesting facilities that sometimes show up in Web pages — but not always. This includes working with Java, scripting, and multimedia, but also understanding how modularization of XHTML functions lets you include only the kinds of bells and whistles you want in your Web pages, without also having to include a chrome kitchen sink. You also learn about how to put the X in XHTML — that is, the extensible part — defining and using your own customized markup to extend the functionality and structure in your XHTML documents. Part V also covers how to work with events and objects to make your documents more interactive, and how to build real-world XHTML solutions today, covering a range of potential applications from maintenance manuals to writing books.

Part VI: The Part of Tens

In the penultimate part of this book, we sum up and distill the very essence of what you now know about the mystic secrets of XHTML. Here, you have a chance to review the top do's and don'ts for XHTML markup, to rethink XHTML document design, to identify and locate some cool XHTML tools, and to find and fathom the best of the many XHTML information resources available online.

Part VII: Appendixes

The last part of this book ends with a set of Appendixes designed to sum up and further expand on the book's contents.

By the time you make it through all the materials in the book and on the CD, you should be pretty well equipped to build your own Web documents and perhaps even ready to roll out your own Web site!

Icons Used in This Book

This icon signals technical details that are informative and interesting, but not critical to writing XHTML. Skip these if you want (but please, come back and read them later).

This icon flags useful information that makes XHTML markup, Web page design, or other important stuff even less complicated than you feared it might be.

This icon points out information you shouldn't pass by — don't overlook these gentle reminders (the life, sanity, or page you save could be your own).

Be cautious when you see this icon. It warns you of things you shouldn't do; the bomb is meant to emphasize that the consequences of ignoring these bits of wisdom can be severe.

Text marked with this icon contains information about something that's on this book's CD-ROM.

Where to Go from Here

This is the part where you pick a direction and hit the road! *XHTML For Dummies* is a lot like the *1001 Nights:* It almost doesn't matter where you start out; you'll look at lots of different scenes and stories as you prepare yourself to build your own Web pages — and each story has its own distinctive characteristics, but the whole is something to marvel at. Don't worry. You'll get it handled. Who cares if anybody else thinks you're just goofing around? We know you're getting ready to have the time of your life.

Enjoy!

Part I
Getting Cozy
with XHTML

"We're much better prepared for this upgrade than before. We're giving users additional training, better manuals, and a morphine drip."

In this part . . .

This part includes an introduction to the Extensible Hypertext Markup Language, a.k.a. XHTML; it explains the terms and concepts that make XHTML work. We also cover the fundamental and enduring relationship between the Hypertext Markup Language (HTML) and XHTML, along with the basic principles of well-formedness and validity. We also explain how to convert old-fashioned HTML into XHTML, and take you on a behind-the-scenes tour of the XHTML specification that defines the rules for this peculiar and fascinating game.

Chapter 1

Welcome to XHTML!

*A*s its name suggests, XHTML is a re-engineered version of the original Hypertext Markup Language, or HTML. XHTML has been cleaned up and made open-ended to get it ready for the 21st century, but is otherwise exactly the same as HTML 4.0. In fact, as XHTML's precursor, HTML was designed and developed by Tim Berners-Lee in the early 1990s and is what led to the explosion of the World Wide Web as we know it today.

HTML has been through some serious changes since it made its debut. Why its developers found it worthwhile — even absolutely necessary — to put an X in front of HTML is a story worth knowing.

The X Marks a Whole New Spot!

From its humblest beginnings, extensibility played no role in the definition of HTML. When Tim Berners-Lee began formulating what was to become known as HTML, he was solely creating a simple way for scientists to exchange papers and other information across a network.

Soon after HTML became available outside its development environment at CERN (the *Conseil Européen pour la Recherche Nucléaire,* or the European Center for Nuclear Research) in 1992, it was used in ways that Tim never anticipated. Since 1992, HTML has gone through four major revisions and numerous minor ones to accommodate the strange changes its users have put it through.

The force that has driven HTML through its changes has been the need to extend and expand what HTML does. In this way, HTML meets increasingly sophisticated needs for information access and display on the Web. But accommodating change has remained an ongoing source of activity at every step.

X marks the Web site

If you doubt the deep and abiding relationship between HTML and XHTML, consider the role of current specifications in defining HTML and XHTML. An industry group called the World Wide Web Consortium (W3C) maintains the official standards that govern HTML and XHTML. The W3C maintains a pointer to the current HTML and XHTML specification at its Web site. That particular Web page resides beneath the W3C's Technical Reports (TR) page at this Uniform Resource Locator, or URL (which is the online address for this specific document):

```
www.w3.org/TR/html/
```

At this URL, the specification is entitled "XHTML 1.0: The Extensible HyperText Markup Language: A Reformulation of HTML 4 in XML 1.0." It's no surprise that another valid address for that same document is:

```
http://www.w3.org/TR/xhtml1/
```

The joys of extensibility

Adding "X" to "HTML" is throwing in the towel on the constant pressure to update HTML. That's because "X" means *extensible*. XHTML opens the closed world of HTML so users can extend and expand its capabilities.

What that X means to you

Two important clues about the future of HTML are hidden in the information about the HTML and XHTML specifications:

- ✔ The current version of HTML is XHTML 1.0.

  In other words, XHTML and HTML are much the same thing.

- ✔ The subtitle of the XHTML 1.0 specification is "A Reformulation of HTML 4 in XML 1.0."

Basic Rules for XHTML

Fundamentally, XHTML (and even, HTML) can be explained as follows:

- ✔ XHTML consists of plain-text characters in a simple text file that describes an *HTML document*.
- ✔ XHTML documents include two kinds of character data:
  - • Sequences of plain-text characters that represent the *content* of an XHTML document.

Content is what people want to read (or see) when they look at XHTML documents online.

- Sequences of special text characters, called *markup,* that describe content, to control how content appears and behaves.

  Markup determines how documents are structured, how they behave, and how they appear. Markup elements also point to external data — such as graphics or multimedia files — that appear on Web pages.

✔ When viewed through the right kind of software — usually a Web browser, or a special-purpose editor of some kind — XHTML markup is interpreted.

Nevertheless, this markup controls how XHTML content appears when it's viewed on a computer (or represented in other forms, for someone who's visually impaired and uses a text-to-speech translator to "hear" Web documents, or someone who reads from a Braille device, instead of seeing that content on-screen).

Thus, understanding XHTML means understanding XHTML markup, and what that markup does to the real content within XHTML documents. A good definition for XHTML markup is *a sequence of special characters that identifies certain text as part of an XHTML document's description, structure, or behavior, rather than as part of that document's content.*

Want a simple way to recognize XHTML markup in the source code for an XHTML document? Watch for anything that occurs between two special characters

✔ < (less-than sign or left angle bracket), which indicates where markup starts

✔ > (greater-than sign or right angle bracket), which indicates where markup ends

Other "special characters" in XHTML's markup cast

There are other special characters that appear in XHTML documents that signal the browser or other software to take special action. These characters include the ampersand (&) and semi-colon (;), which mark the beginning and end of special strings of characters called *entities* that must be interpreted before they can be displayed. Entities are described in Chapter 14 of this book. Entities make normally unprintable characters appear on Web pages, or force control characters — such as the < and > that surround markup, for example — to appear on Web pages.

The following bit of XHTML text denotes the title of an XHTML document:

```
<title>This is a sample document title</title>
```

In fact, the title of an XHTML document appears on the title bar in a Web browser, rather than in the document body itself, as shown in Figure 1-1.

Figure 1-1:
Some XHTML markup doesn't appear in the document window. `<title>` text appears in the window's title bar.

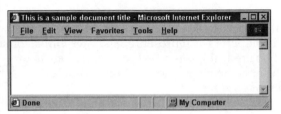

Markup elements often travel in tandem

When XHTML content needs some particular treatment, or belongs to a particular part of a document's structure — its title, for example — such content is enclosed between a pair of *markup elements* (an opening and closing tag). For a document title, the `<title>` markup (opening tag) appears just before the text that becomes a document's title, and the `</title>` (closing tag) markup appears just after that very same text. In other words, the markup string `<title>` signals the beginning of the title, whereas the markup string `</title>` signals its end. This is all part of the syntax and structure for markup languages, which we cover in this chapter, in the section titled "XML Syntax and Rules in General."

Some specific HTML features that impact XHTML include these:

✔ HTML consists of a specific, predefined set of *markup elements* (also sometimes called *tags*) — we use the term element unless specifically referring to the opening and closing tags of an element.

✔ To be completely correct in form and structure, HTML documents require certain elements to be present in a specified order.

　　• HTML *syntax* defines the proper expressions that elements take.

- HTML *structure* defines the proper ordering and sequencing for such elements.

  Structure also decides which elements legally appear within other elements, and which elements can appear only once, as opposed to those that can appear more than once.

The following section of this chapter explains markup terms and concepts in more detail. But for now, it's safe to say that the predefined markup found in the HTML 4.0 specification is more or less the same markup that XHTML recognizes. However, this similarity is subject to changes required to make the language extensible.

Markup Defined and Explained

If you take a look at a typical HTML document inside a Web browser, what you see is the HTML content from that document, as subject to the HTML markup that's also contained in the same document. You aren't normally able to see that markup, however, unless you look at the source code for the document itself.

The technology that underlies both HTML and XML is the same. It's a *metalanguage* — a language designed for defining other languages — known as the *Standard Generalized Markup Language,* or SGML. Most of the terminology and concepts that govern XHTML originate from SGML.

There are those who argue that to be a true XHTML wizard, you must also be an SGML expert. We say, "It just ain't so!" You can speak XHTML fluently without tackling SGML directly.

Behind the veil: Viewing HTML source code

When it comes to seeing what's really inside an HTML document, Web browsers provide techniques to let you look at raw, unadulterated HTML code, instead of its effects. For Internet Explorer, this consists of selecting the **View** menu entry in the program's title bar and then selecting the **Source** entry that shows up in the pull-down menu that results. For Netscape Navigator, choose the **View** menu entry as before, but select the **Page Source** entry that shows up in the resulting pull-down menu instead. If you're both lazy and clever, you can simply right-click a Web page and selecting either **View Source** (Internet Explorer) or **View Page Source** (Navigator) in the pop-up menu that appears.

On the other hand, if you use an HTML or XML editor such as FrontPage, Dreamweaver, Clip!, or your own favorite tool of choice, just open the document file itself to see the source code in its regal majesty. In that case, just use the **File⇨ Open** command to get right to it!

Although markup items, such as `<title>` and `</title>`, are called tags in some places, SGML calls these items *elements*. In fact, the pair of tags `<title>` and `</title>` are both parts of the `title` element; `<title>` is the opening tag and `</title>` is the closing tag of that element.

Some HTML elements occur as *singletons* — that is, there is no closing tag to the element to match the opening tag. The horizontal rule element `<hr>` that draws a line across the display area in a document is an example. In XHTML terms, this is called an *empty element,* because it has no separate closing part.

Empty elements take the form `<element />`. The reason empty elements take this form is because in XML, all empty elements must end with the `/>` characters. What makes these elements uniquely XHTML is that *a space precedes the slash and the right angle bracket*. This allows older HTML browsers to recognize the original HTML element without choking on the XML-ized version of the closing part. Thus, the XHTML version of the empty horizontal rule, which appears as `<hr>` (no space or slash) in HTML, normally appears as `<hr />` in XHTML.

Sometimes, XHTML elements include additional information inside them to qualify, quantify, or otherwise amplify on those elements. A good example is the `<img>` element, used to place a graphical image into a collection of text. Such images reside in files that do not appear in the XHTML source code for a document, but occur in the `<img>` element by naming an external graphics file.

Thus, you can point to an image by including the markup `<img src="logo.gif">` in the source code for an HTML file. Because the image element is empty, that markup in an XHTML file is `<img src="logo.gif"/>`.

- ✔ The `src="logo.gif"` part of this markup tells the Web browser that the source for that image is a file named `logo.gif` in the same directory where the current Web document lives.

- ✔ The `src` markup is an *attribute* of the image element, because it identifies the source for the image data to be associated with a graphical element.

In general, attributes help elaborate on the behavior of specific markup elements and supply specific values to be associated with such elements. For the image element, the `src` attribute is essential, because it points to the graphics file for the image that is to be displayed when this markup is encountered and rendered inside a Web browser or XHTML-aware editor.

Elements represent specific terms or capabilities in a markup language. Often, you enclose content within a pair of tags to control its impact or how it appears. In that case, elements consist of an opening tag that takes the general form `<tag>` in markup, followed by the enclosed content, and concluded by a closing item that takes the general form `</tag>`. On the other hand, empty elements include no content, but often provide special functions (such as `<hr>` in HTML or `<hr />` in XHTML, that draws a horizontal rule) or that point to external content (such as ⟨img⟩ in HTML or ⟨img /⟩ in XHTML), which invoke placement of an image. Some elements take attributes (such as src for the image element) that augment their behavior (in this case, src points to the file where the invoked graphical image resides).

Basic XML Terms and Concepts

Because HTML is closed and predefined, all its markup elements are known in advance, which allows Web browsers not only to handle any and all known HTML elements, but also to make certain assumptions about document structure. For instance, the definition of HTML requires that all documents include this sequence of elements:

```
<!DOCTYPF HTML PUBLIC
  "-//W3C//DTD HTML 4.01 Strict//EN"
  "http://www.w3.org/TR/html4/strict.dtd">
<html>
  <head>
<!-- This markup permits arbitrary comments -->
  <!-- to appear in HTML and XML documents.   -->
  <!-- The head section defines a document's  -->
  <!-- title, and can describe its contents.  -->
  </head>
  <body>
  <!-- Inside the body element is where real  -->
  <!-- document content appears. Comment text -->
  <!-- appears only in source code views.     -->
  </body>
</html>
```

Nevertheless, you can omit any or all of these elements from an HTML document. The document still looks like the more complete version when displayed in a modern browser, such as Internet Explorer.

However, because XML markup is completely open-ended and entirely arbitrary, you can't assume anything about the structure of XML documents. Likewise, it's impossible for XML-aware browsers or other XML-enabled software (such as editors or content development tools) to be forgiving with slightly misformatted text. They have no predefined idea of

✔ What they can or should forgive

✔ When elements are missing from an XML document

✔ When explicit syntax rules are broken

Although XHTML is a re-engineered version of HTML, the "X" in "XHTML" stands for XML. Where syntax, structure, and rules are concerned, the "X" in "XHTML" beats the "HTML" part, hands down!

XML Syntax and Rules in General

As a special case of XML, XHTML is entirely governed by rules and requirements, and makes no assumptions on how to fix incorrect documents, or how to complete incomplete ones. This puts more onus on the humans who develop such documents to do things correctly.

To be more specific, XML (and XHTML) documents impose these requirements on their creators:

- All documents must adhere to a formal set of rules for the markup that they contain. Normally, such markup is completely defined in *a meta-document* (a special kind of document that defines another document's structure and syntax), or such markup is completely defined in a `<!DOCTYPE` section within the document itself.

  Any XHTML document must be associated with an explicit Document Type Definition (DTD), or it must be associated with the XHTML namespace. Likewise, any customized markup created to extend the base set defined for XHTML must also be explicitly defined as well. Both DTDs and namespaces are described in detail later in this chapter. Many XML documents include references to namespaces and DTDs, further customized by their own local definitions for new markup, or redefinitions of existing markup.

- All valid documents can include only markup that's defined in their governing meta-document or namespace. In other words, the only legal markup is markup that is explicitly defined somewhere, be it in the `<!DOCTYPE` section of a document itself, in a DTD, or from a namespace. The concepts that define what makes a document valid are covered in Chapter 2 of this book.

- Whenever DTDs, DOCTYPE declarations, or namespaces are associated with XML (or XHTML) documents, those documents must abide by the syntax and structure that's defined in their associated meta-document(s). Interesting ways in which XML (and XHTML) differ from HTML include these:

  - All elements are case sensitive. If a DTD, namespace, or DOCTYPE information calls an element `<UpToDate>` it can't appear as anything but `<UpToDate>`. Thus, `<UptoDate>`, `<UPTODate>`, and anything else that doesn't match `<UpToDate>` exactly becomes unrecognizable.

  - Any values assigned to attributes *must* be enclosed in quotation marks (single or double). Thus, `<img src="logo.gif">` is legal, as is `<img src='logo.gif'>`, but `<img src=logo.gif>` is not. This is a big change from HTML, which enforced a "quotation rule" only loosely and quite inconsistently.

In XHTML, all attributes must have associated values, so that carryovers from HTML, such as the `checked` attribute associated with forms markup, must appear as `checked="checked"` and cannot appear simply as `checked` (as it can in HTML).

- All elements must close properly, which means that all non-empty elements must begin and end with opening and closing tags. Therefore, when an XHTML paragraph opens with the `<p>` tag, it must close with the `</p>` tag (which is seldom used, and not required in HTML).

  Likewise, all empty tags must close properly. For most forms of XML, this means empty tags end with `/>`; for XHTML this is often preceded by a space for backward compatibility with older browsers that recognize HTML but not XHTML.

- Finally, all markup elements must nest properly. The easiest way to describe what this means in English is to say that you must close the nearest element that's open (looking to the left) before closing any other open element. Thus, the markup `<q>This is <strong>not acceptable!</strong></q>` is correct because it closes the nearest element `<strong>` before it closes the more distant `<q>` element. But the markup `<q>This is <strong>not acceptable!</q></strong>` is incorrect because it closes the more distant `<q>` element before closing the nearer `<strong>` element.

The most succinct way of stating the requirements for XML (and XHTML) documents is "the rules always apply." No exceptions, no cheating, no slack. None of the *laissez-faire* notions of "let the browser figure it out" that let us get away with murder when using HTML! We've learned — and we confess, the hard way — that this tight adherence to the rules is the hardest thing about transitioning from HTML to XHTML!

The great thing about working with XML and XHTML documents is that you usually create them using special-purpose editors that understand these rules, and apply them on your behalf. In fact, such editors are set up to make it difficult (and sometimes, downright impossible) to break the rules that govern the documents you build inside them. (See Chapter 26 for more details on some of the editors we like.) Believe us when we tell you that this is a real blessing!

Defining XML (And XHTML) Documents

The preceding section covers the basic rules and regulations for the mechanics of XML and XHTML markup and syntax. It also covers the questions of what constitutes markup, and how markup must appear within XML and XHTML documents. What it doesn't address is how elements are ordered, for instance:

- ✔ Which elements appear first
- ✔ Which elements follow
- ✔ Which elements appear inside other elements

This set of rules for precedence, sequence, and inclusion in turn defines the rules for legal document structure. The markup that defines those rules appears in

- ✔ Document Type Definitions, or DTDs
- ✔ Namespaces
- ✔ DOCTYPE markup at the start of such documents

Any of these items can appear, or be referenced, in any XML and XHTML documents!

Rules have benefits

Confused? Don't be! Although this idea that a well-defined set of rules for what may appear in a document may be hard to get used to, HTML has worked this way all along in the background. The biggest benefit of HTML's closed set of predefined markup is the ability it confers on software developers to employ their complete and perfect knowledge about that markup to encode the document descriptions in the software they build.

The rules that DTDs, namespaces, and DOCTYPE code state also prescribe these document behaviors for XML and XHTML documents:

- ✔ The order in which markup elements appear
- ✔ Which elements may appear inside other elements (unless explicitly allowed or required, one element may not occur within another)
- ✔ Which elements (and attributes for elements) are mandatory, and which are optional
- ✔ What kinds of content data may be associated with specific elements

More details about DTDs and DOCTYPE code for XHTML are covered in Chapter 21, which covers what's involved in extending XHTML documents to incorporate new markup. Appendix B is specifically devoted to an overview of DTDs and the markup that appears within them. Finally, we cover the XHTML namespace in the last section in this chapter.

Rules make a difference

The biggest difference between HTML and XHTML, in fact, is that XHTML requires software developers to demand and read the rules they plan to follow when interpreting the documents their software reads, rather than simply following a fixed set of assumptions. In some ways, this makes their jobs harder because they must read those rules and internalize them before they can apply them to a document. But it also makes their jobs easier because they can write more compact code that knows how to build and apply arbitrary sets of rules on the fly, rather than building a large and complex — but fixed and inflexible — set of rules into their code.

The biggest benefit of these rules is huge, however. With a well-defined set of rules that a computer understands exists, the right program determines whether any document adheres to those rules. In layman's terms, this means that software can check any XHTML document, and only has to "digest" those documents that don't make it "puke." Although this analogy may be unappetizing, there are profound benefits in being able to make sure a document is legal before trying to display it, rather than waiting until something blows up in the middle of processing its content.

The XHTML Namespace

Some of you may be following the news and discussions about ongoing XML developments. If so, you may have noticed certain XML gurus arguing about namespaces recently, in much the same way that medieval pundits argued about the number of angels that could dance on the head of a pin. These abstruse matters aside, do not fret, because the basics of namespaces are really quite simple . . .

A namespace is a powerful tool. In XML, a *namespace* simply allows you to refer to the tags and semantics for some particular, well-defined type of XML document. In other words, a namespace is a succinct way to refer to a well-known XML document type inside another XML document without going through the rigmarole of defining and declaring the well-known document type's markup in a DTD. Because there's an XHTML namespace defined, this is emphatically true for XHTML documents. It's not an overstatement to say that namespaces are another great benefit of the X in XHTML!

To expand on our main topic, you should recognize that XHTML tags and elements occur within an XHTML namespace. This namespace requires a unique name to identify it — a name that won't be used for anything else. And what kind of name has been designed from the ground up to be unique? A Uniform Resource Locator (URL), of course. Therefore, a namespace usually takes a URL as its value (see the code example at the end of this section, for instance).

When a URL is used to identify a namespace, it's used purely as a unique name. Nothing need be physically present at the other end of the URL. A URL is designed to be unique. Furthermore, the domain name part of the URL is guaranteed to be under someone's control. This makes URLs ideal for use as unique names. For example, www.lanw.com is a domain under our control, so we can invent a unique name to use as a namespace, such as www.lanw.com.xml.mynamespace, and be completely sure that nobody else can (legally) use that same name.

If you want to include an element from another XML document type, such as an XHTML document, in your own document type you must inform the XML software that processes your document about this reference. The simplest way is to use the xmlns:somename attribute in the document's primary or root element. The xmlns identifies the attribute as an XML namespace. The somename part of the name can be anything you care to call it. For the XHTML namespace, that name is xhtml (go figure).

Any element or attribute that contains a colon (:) is reserved for use by the W3C. The colon tells software that something is special and noteworthy.

The complete specification for the XHTML namespace in an XHTML document may look like this (notice that it appears by default in the <html> opening tag, because the <html> . . . </html> element is the root element for any HTML or plain-vanilla XHTML document):

```
<html xmlns:xhtml="http://www.w3.org/1999/xhtml">
```

Sometimes, this code is abbreviated as follows (and this is also the way it appears in the XHTML specification, on the assumption that it is the first namespace referenced):

```
<html xmlns="http://www.w3.org/1999/xhtml">
```

Unless you absolutely *must* include a DTD, this kind of namespace reference is the best way to tell the software that's going to process your XHTML where your markup is coming from!

If you try to see where this URL takes you on the W3C's Web site, an error message says access to that document is forbidden. You just have to take our word for it (or read the specification) that this is indeed the current and correct name for the XHTML namespace.

Chapter 2

The XML Connection

*H*eard a lot of loose talk about XML replacing HTML on the Web? This assumes that XML and HTML are the same types of things. However, XML and HTML are two totally different kinds of beasts. XML is in fact a set of rules that tell you how to write a markup language. In nerd talk, XML is known as a *meta-language*. HTML is a language written to the rules of another meta-language called SGML.

The Hot Meta

A *meta-language* lays down the rules that a language must use. If you think of the relationship between HTML, the language, to SGML the meta-language, it's a little like the relationship of English, the language, to the English rules of grammar.

To clear things up, here's a simple example of a short story that you would like to send over the Web:

> *Godzilla fights King Kong*
>
> *Late Breaking News!*
>
> *Godzilla vs. King Kong*
>
> *Tokyo Flattened! Millions die!*

In Tokyo today, Godzilla took on King Kong in an unprecedented slugfest. During the course of the battle, Tokyo was completely destroyed. After the battle, the victorious Mr. Kong was asked his plans. He is reported to have said:

"I am fed up with being a misunderstood overgrown anthropoid. I plan to retire back to Saba and grow bananas."

Saba is the small Caribbean island where Mr. Kong was born.

Mr. Godzilla could not be reached for comment.

Sensational Press reports that there are no immediate plans to rebuild Tokyo.

Here's the story in HTML:

```
<HTML>
<TITLE> Godzilla fights King Kong </TITLE>
<H1>Late Breaking News!</H1>
<H2>Godzilla vs. King Kong</H2>
<H3>Tokyo Flattened! Millions die!</H3>
<P>In Tokyo today, Godzilla took on King Kong in an unprece-
          dented slugfest. During the course of the battle,
          Tokyo was completely destroyed. After the battle,
          the victorious Mr. Kong was asked his plans. He is
          reported to have said:
<BLOCKQUOTE>"I am fed up with being a misunderstood overgrown
          anthropoid. I plan to retire back to Saba and grow
          bananas."</BLOCKQUOTE>
<P>Saba is the small Caribbean island where Mr. Kong was
          born.
<P>Mr. Godzilla could not be reached for comment.
<P> Sensational Press reports that there are no immediate
          plans to rebuild Tokyo.
</HTML>
```

This is a perfectly legal HTML document. If we save it as story.htm and open it in a Web browser, it will probably render perfectly well. However, the tags are not very descriptive of the content, so we can mark it up in XML using elements we create to describe the content. Some of the elements we make up will define the structure of the document, and some will describe the type of information we're conveying; therefore, perhaps a search engine can tell what the content of the document is all about:

```
<mydoctype>
<news-title>Godzilla fights King Kong</news-title>
<news-story type="disaster">
<banner-headline>Late Breaking News!</banner-headline>
<headline><lizard>Godzilla</lizard> vs. <ape>King
          Kong</ape></headline>
<subhead><city country="Japan">Tokyo</city> Flattened!
          Millions die!</subhead>
```

```
<para>In Tokyo today, Godzilla took on King Kong in an
        unprecedented slugfest. During the course of the
        battle, Tokyo was completely destroyed. After the
        battle, the victorious Mr. Kong was asked his
        plans. He is reported to have said:</para>
<quotation>"I am fed up with being a misunderstood overgrown
        anthropoid. I plan to retire back to <island
        location="caribbean">Saba</island> and grow
        <fruit>bananas.</fruit>"</quotation>
<para>Saba is the small Caribbean island where Mr. Kong was
        born.</para>
<para>Mr. Godzilla could not be reached for comment.</para>
<para><agency>Sensational Press</agency> reports that there
        are no immediate plans to rebuild Tokyo.</para>
</news-story>
</mydoctype>
```

As a little experiment, we saved this as an XML file and opened it in Internet Explorer 5. Figure 2-1 shows the result.

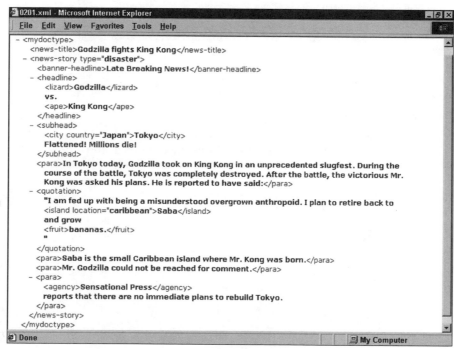

Figure 2-1:
Our story saved with a .xml extension and displayed in Internet Explorer 5.

Right away you'll notice that we have a small problem. There's no styling applied to our document because Internet Explorer 5 does not know how to style our tags. It shows a nice tree view of our XML document that is in fact unique to Internet Explorer 5. Other browsers, such as Opera 4.0 or Netscape 6, just show the text content with no structure or styling whatsoever applied. For an XML document to be displayed correctly, we have to attach a style sheet. (Style sheets are covered in detail in Chapter 8.)

We can save this document as an html file and open it in a browser, but we wouldn't be better off. The browser just ignores all the tags it doesn't understand (which is all of them). The browser would shows the plain text (as shown in Figure 2-2).

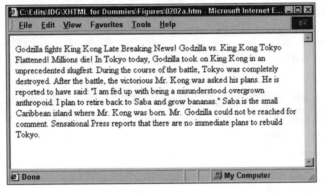

Figure 2-2:
Our story
saved with a
.htm exten-
sion and
displayed in
Internet
Explorer 5.

However, what happens if we replace our structural tags with HTML type tags, and kept our own descriptive tags? Look at the following document, which is also an XML document that uses HTML type tags.

```
<html xmlns="http://www.w3.org/html"
 xmlns:mydoc="http://www.mydoccom/news">
<head>
<title>Godzilla fights King Kong</title>
</head>
<body>
<mydoc:news-story>
<h1>Late Breaking News!</h1>

<h2><mydoc:lizard>Godzilla</mydoc:lizard> vs. <mydoc:ape>King
        Kong</mydoc:ape></h2>
<h3><mydoc:city country="Japan">Tokyo</mydoc:city> Flattened!
        Millions die!</h3>
```

```
<p>In Tokyo today, Godzilla took on King Kong in an unprece-
        dented slugfest. During the course of the battle,
        Tokyo was completely destroyed. After the battle,
        the victorious Mr. Kong was asked his plans. He is
        reported to have said:</p>
<blockquote>"I am fed up with being a misunderstood overgrown
        anthropoid. I plan to retire back to <mydoc:island
        location="caribbean">Saba</mydoc:island> and grow
        <mydoc:fruit>bananas.</mydoc:fruit>"</blockquote>
<p>Saba is the small Caribbean island where Mr. Kong was
        born.</p>
<p>Mr. Godzilla could not be reached for comment.</p>
<p><mydoc:agency>Sensational Press</mydoc:agency> reports
        that there are no immediate plans to rebuild
        Tokyo.</p>
</mydoc:news-story>
</body>
</html>
```

For now, just ignore the colons and take it from us that this is a perfectly legal XHTML document. When we save this as an HTML file and open it in Internet Explorer 5, we get Figure 2-3. It's exactly what we want.

Figure 2-3: A valid XHTML document displayed in Internet Explorer 5.

So the question we should ask isn't whether XML will replace HTML, but whether XML-based documents (including XHTML) will replace SGML-based documents such as HTML? The answer to this is *inevitably,* although HTML 4.0 and its predecessors may be around for a few more years

XML vs. HTML

Table 2-1 shows the differences between XML and HTML. As in the preceding example, this is not a very fair comparison, because we're kind of comparing apples to oranges.

Table 2-1	The Differences between XML and HTML
XML	*HTML*
XML is a meta-language.	HTML is an application of SGML.
In XML you make up your own tags and elements.	In HTML you have to use a predefined set of elements.
An XML document stands by itself.	An SGML document always requires a Documents Type Definition (DTD) for interpretation. (In HTML browsers this DTD is "hardwired" into the browser.)

XML vs. SGML

A much fairer comparison is to compare XML to SGML, as shown in Table 2-2!

Table 2-2	XML Compared to SGML
XML	*SGML*
XML rules are simple.	SGML rules are complex.
XML tags must always have closing tags.	SGML tags need not be closed.
XML tags can never be implied.	SGML tags can be implied, in other words, they do not always have to be written out.
XML documents do not need a DTD; they are quite understandable by themselves.	SGML documents always require a DTD.
Software for parsing XML is easy to write. Most of this software is free.	Software for SGML is difficult to write, and expensive.

A DTD is a document that lays down the rules of a language, such as what can be contained between opening and closing tags, and what attribute an element can take.

The Best of Both Worlds

After making HTML an application of XML, all kinds of good things happen.

If it's broke, don't fix it

Yes you read that heading correctly. Firstly and probably most importantly, XML is draconian in the enforcement of its rules. XML browsers are instructed that *If it's broke, don't fix it.* In other words, if your code isn't perfect, it won't display. This may seem a little difficult at first, until you realize that it's just as easy to write correct code as it is to write incorrect code. In addition, the reason that you were writing bad code in the first place is that you probably didn't realize it was bad code.

Add new tags

The X in XHTML stands for *extensible.* As we saw in the example in the preceding section, it is easy, and perfectly legal, to add your own tags. You can even style the content of your tags if you want to use a style sheet language. (See Chapter 8 for more information on style sheets.)

Write once, read everywhere

In the old days, it was very common for HTML authors to go through a process called *browser sniffing.* They used to write code to discover what kind of browser was asking for their pages, and then, depending on the browser, they would send Netscape pages or Microsoft pages, and so on. This put a tremendous burden on authors because they had to write and maintain several different sets of pages.

If you write a document in XHTML, you only need to write one document, and know that it can be displayed on all different kinds of media, from the desktop, to the TV, to the mobile phone.

Displaying information on multiple types of media is accomplished using a *proxy server*. When a mobile phone asks for your page, it will not go to your server directly, but will route the request through its own server, called a proxy server. This proxy server will convert the author's XHTML page into a form suitable for viewing on a mobile phone.

Using XML tools

One of the design goals of XML was that it should be easy to write software to parse and manipulate it. This has in fact happened. There's now a plethora of tools available for reading, writing, and manipulating XML documents, and most of them are free. Now that you have an XHTML page you can use all these tools to do all kinds of wonderful things to your document. (See Chapter 26 for information on some of these tools.)

Using HTML Tidy

Perhaps you have hundreds of HTML pages already written, and you dread the thought of converting them to XHTML. Not to worry, there's a wonderful tool written by Dave Raggett (who is the lead of the XHTML working group, and one of the main players leading the drive to XHTML) called HTML Tidy that automatically converts your HTML Web pages to XHTML. And the wonderful news is that these pages don't even have to be written in good HTML. For the most part, HTML Tidy will convert your incorrect code to correct code. Now that's neat! You can download HTML Tidy from the W3C site at `www.w3.org/People/Raggett/tidy/`. We also cover HTML Tidy in some detail in Chapter 3.

Being Well Formed

Up until now, we really haven't said any thing about the rules of XML, and how they differ from those of SGML. XML introduced the concept of a *well-formed document* to the world. What does it mean for a marked up document to be well formed? All the document has to do to be well formed is follow some simple rules. First, we look at a list of these rules and then at some examples.

- ✔ A well-formed XML document must contain a single element, called a root element, that encloses the entire document.
- ✔ All non-empty elements must have a closing tag.
- ✔ XML is case sensitive, and these tags must match in case.

- ✔ Empty elements must be of a special form.
- ✔ All elements must nest.
- ✔ All element attributes must have values, and these attributes must be quoted.

What about all these names?

Before going any further, you need to be familiar with some of the names and definitions used in XML.

What is an element?

Before looking at any examples, you need to know what is meant by an element, and what the parts of an element are.

Here is a simple element.

```
<greeting> Hello XHTML!</greeting>
```

- ✔ This element would be known as a `greeting` type element. It consists of an *opening tag, element content,* and a *closing tag.*
- ✔ The opening tag is `<greeting>` and the *opening tag-name* is `greeting`.
- ✔ The *content* of the element is `Hello XHTML!`
- ✔ The closing tag is `</greeting>` and the *closing tag-name* is `greeting`.

Most people would refer to this as a `greeting` element, but to be technically correct it should be referred to as an element of the element-type `greeting`.

Element attributes

Elements can have attributes. An *attribute* gives added meaning to an element. Attributes always have a value. Here's an example of an attribute added to our preceding example.

```
<greeting type= "cordial"> Hello XHTML!</greeting>
```

Empty elements

An empty element is an element that has no content. Here's an example of an empty element in XML:

```
<image source= "mypic.gif" description= "my picture" />
```

Your Refrigerator Is a Browser!

Turning your refrigerator into a browser isn't as far fetched as one may imagine. It's already being done. See it for yourself at www.electrolux.com/screenfridge. The marketing gurus tell us that by 2002, over 80 percent of page look-ups on the Web will be done by platforms other than the traditional computer. Therefore, if you want to be ready to capture this market, move over to XHTML all those people who will be browsing when they make their morning coffee.

Chapter 3

Converting HTML to XHTML

● ●

In This Chapter

▶ Discovering the advantages of XHTML

▶ Converting your HTML to XHTML

▶ Learning the rules

▶ Working with HTML Tidy

● ●

*A*s you sift through the pages of this book (or just this chapter), a little voice in the back of your head is probably whispering softly over and over again, "What about my existing Web pages?" Contrary to popular belief, introducing multiple acronyms is not a conspiracy at the World Wide Web Consortium (W3C) to confuse everyone. And adding XHTML to the list of technologies known on your resume doesn't mean you have to painstakingly recode all your HTML pages. After reading this chapter, you can silence that little voice for good!

If you're anything like us, you have to constantly reinvent your knowledge base to keep on top of the Web learning curve. First came HTML. Easy enough. But then came Java, JavaScript, VBScript, Cascading Style Sheets (CSS), and so on. Ouch!

XHTML is a little different. You don't have to start from scratch because XHTML builds on HTML (and uses the same *Document Type Definition,* or *DTD*). You need to know only a few extra steps to get control of XHTML, and we cover the basics of these steps in this chapter.

Before you go running to call your Web-savvy Grandma, instructing her to update all her HTML pages, you may want to take a peek at the rules involved.

Why are most people converting?

We're not talking religion here; we're talking about that little voice whispering in your head. We may rant and rave about why XML (and therefore, XHTML) may take home the prize, but you need to reflect on HTML briefly. If you're one of the folks who works with HTML (in other words, your audience is the general public), you probably already know that HTML is a presentation language used to create documents for display on the Web. HTML elements define how text should appear in a Web browser. Add HTML markup to some text, add some graphics, throw in some hyperlinks for good measure, and you have an HTML document.

The idea behind HTML was modest. HTML was meant to describe not the page content but rather how that content should be displayed in your browser. Since its introduction to the public, however, HTML has been called on to provide solutions to problems it was never meant to solve. Some of the things HTML wasn't meant to do include the following:

- Tight controls over document display
- Sufficient flexibility to describe different, but specific types of information
- Convey information in a variety of media and formats
- Define complex linking relationships between documents
- Publish a single set of information across a variety of media

Web designers (like us, for example) sometimes catch themselves thinking, "But my heading has to be in two-point Arial and centered in the first third of the page." Pretty artsy, huh? Although this sentiment is a bit exaggerated, it's not far from what Web designers expect their HTML to do, leaving them wondering why HTML doesn't live up to their expectations.

Today's Web designers want to achieve the same formatting control over their Web documents that they have over printed documents. They want what they see on their screens with their browsers to be exactly what any visitor to their sites sees. Two overarching problems prevent Web designers from achieving this control using HTML:

- **HTML lacks fine controls.** First and foremost, HTML doesn't include the mechanisms to maintain fine control. You can't specify the display size of a document or control the size of a browser window. These two variables are affected by a user's screen size and personal preferences. Although HTML 4.0 includes the <font> element to help you manipulate font style, size, and color, users can override your settings with their own.

- **Browser displays vary.** Differences among Microsoft Internet Explorer, Netscape Navigator, Mosaic, HotJava, and other graphical browsers make it impossible to know exactly which browsers and/or platforms display your pages. And you can't realistically test every Web page on every available browser on every platform just to see what your users will see.

But why is XHTML so much better than HTML, you ask? And if you didn't ask, that little voice did — take our word for it. XHTML allows you to do all the things covered in the preceding bulleted lists. Another great thing about

XHTML is that if you already know HTML, you almost know XHTML. The only differences are a few new syntax rules, which are covered in the "Converting to XHTML by Hand" section later in this chapter.

Ringside with HTML and XHTML

If HTML and XHTML were really duking it out, XHTML would be Mike Tyson (no biting, of course) and HTML would be the little person cowering in the corner.

Saying that one language is better than the other is not easy; however. Because XHTML is as easy to code as HTML and provides extra benefits, why not choose the heavyweight? Take a look at some of the reasons we think you were smart to take interest in XHTML:

- **Extensibility:** XHTML can be extended to include new (and by *new* we mean you create your own) elements and attributes.

  With HTML, you have to work within a fixed set of elements, with no variation allowed. Adding new elements and attributes to existing markup creates many new ways to embed content and programming in a Web page. XHTML allows you to mix and match known HTML elements with elements from other languages based on or created with the Extensible Markup Language (XML) or even your own XML language.

- **Portability:** XHTML allows you to adapt to new media without re-creating all your pages, one by one.

  You've probably already heard of digital phones accessing the Web. Just think about those tiny, tiny screens — not to mention zero disk space — downloading huge Flash graphics. Impossible, right? Well, yes. When working with HTML, you have to create a new page for each different type of browser, tailoring that page to fit the specific needs of each browser. XHTML solves this problem, while enabling you to work with that same old trusty element set found in HTML.

Converting to XHTML by Hand

In the previous sections, you found out why you should stop using HTML and why you should start using XHMTL, so now it's time to get started. XHTML and HTML adhere to the same DTD, which means that all the element names are the same. The main difference between HTML and XHTML is that XHTML follows XML syntax rules.

Syntax rules govern the technical side of markup. For example, XML syntax rules state that anything between ⟨ and ⟩ is a tag. The name of that tag is defined in the DTD, but the syntax of the markup is defined by the XML specification. After the name of the tag is defined, it then becomes an element.

The terms *tag* and *element* seem to be everywhere — and they are often used incorrectly!

- A *tag* is a simple little piece of markup — for example ⟨i-am-a-tag⟩.

- After you apply meaning to a tag's name, the tag becomes an element — for example, ⟨html⟩ is an element. The term *element* also refers to the opening tag, the closing tag, and everything in between.

If you're still confused by the words *tag* and *element*, you may want to check out Chapter 7.

If you decide you want to convert your HTML to XHTML by hand, you *must* follow a few rules — and we mean *absolutely must* follow — before your page is ready to don its new XHTML acronym.

XHTML takes backward compatibility into account and provides authors with a couple of easy fixes that allow older browsers to display pages meant to work with the newer generation of browsers. So, the verdict is in, and XHTML is compatible with today's HTML 4 browsers. Can we hear a loud woohoo from everyone, please?

The following sections cover the rules you must follow to convert your HTML document to XHTML.

Nest tags correctly

Overlapping elements — or tags for that matter — is illegal in XML; therefore, you must nest you elements correctly.

Say this with us: *What you open first, you close last.*

If you're scratching your head, here's an example to clear things up. This is correct:

```
<p>What you open <em>first</em>, you must close
      <em>last</em></p>
```

This is incorrect:

```
<p>What you open <em>first</em>, you must close
      <em>last</p></em>
```

Always include optional ending tags

In HTML, you could omit that ending </p> tag. Less typing always sounds good. But this shortcut is now gone, because omitting ending tags is illegal in XML (and therefore XHTML). This does not include *empty elements,* which are forbidden to have a closing tag.

If an element has an optional or required end tag in HTML, you must include the end tag in your XHTML code.

This is correct:

```
<ul>
    <li>list item one</li>
    <li>list item two</li>
</ul>
```

This is incorrect:

```
<ul>
    <li>list item one
    <li>list item two
</ul>
```

Quote attribute values

This rule requires a little more effort. You can use both single (') or double (") quotation marks. We (and the W3C) don't care what kind you choose, as long as you include them (and use the same marks to open and close a quoted string).

Be consistent. Use either single or double quotation marks — don't mix and match. Don't confuse the people who view your source code.

This is correct:

```
<colgroup span="40" width="15">
...
</colgroup>
```

This is incorrect:

```
<colgroup span=40 width=15>
...
</colgroup>
```

Lowercase all element and attribute names

Unlike HTML, XML is case sensitive. You must always use lowercase when using XHTML element names and attribute names.

This does not always apply to attribute values — only attribute and element names. We tell you when an attribute value is case sensitive.

All element and attribute names are declared — and defined — in the XHTML DTD, which is where case decisions are made. Because the DTD declares all elements and attributes in lowercase, you and the rest of the world must follow suit!

This is correct:

```
<input type="checkbox" name="pet" value="cat">
```

This is incorrect:

```
<INPUT TYPE="checkbox" name="pet" value="cat">
```

Attribute name-value pairs cannot stand alone

In HTML, you can find a couple of instances of attributes that are standalone text strings, such as `compact` or `checked`. Standalone text strings are not allowed in XML.

The way to work around this problem is simple: You set standalone attributes equal to themselves. Although this may seem a little silly, it's still another XHTML rule.

This is correct:

```
<input type="checkbox" name="pet" value="cat"
        checked="checked">
```

This is incorrect:

```
<input type="checkbox" name="pet" value="cat" checked>
```

Open and close an element in the same tag

An empty element is an element for which an end tag is forbidden; in other words, it doesn't have a closing tag. In XHTML, you must open and close the element within the same tag. To do this, you include a backslash before the right-angle bracket, like this />, at the end of all your empty elements. For example, `<img src="file.gif"/>`.

Although /> is all that is needed for empty tags to follow legal XML, there's an issue with backward compatibility. To ensure that older browsers can understand this construction, include a space before />.

This is correct:

```
<img src="graphic.gif" />
```

Note the space after the filename and before the trailing />.

This is incorrect:

```
<img src="graphic.gif">
```

Include a DOCTYPE declaration

The DOCTYPE declaration — also known as a *document type declaration* — is what references the DTD. This is not a required rule in HTML, but because you're following XML rules and because you want your page to validate against a DTD, you can't leave it out.

The declaration looks like this:

```
<!DOCTYPE html PUBLIC
        "-//W3C//DTD XHTML 1.0 Strict//EN"
        "DTD/xhtml1-strict.dtd">
```

The DTD must appear before the root element — that is, the `<html>` element — and must follow the previous syntax. Here's a breakdown of the code:

- **Declaration keyword:** `<!DOCTYPE`
- **Type of document:** `html`
- **Public identifier keyword:** `PUBLIC`
- **Public identifier:** `"-//W3C//DTD XHTML 1.0 Strict//EN"`
- **DTD filename:** `"DTD/xhtml1-strict.dtd">`

The previous example is one of the three DTDs you may choose from. Here are the two other options:

```
<!DOCTYPE html PUBLIC
        "-//W3C//DTD XHTML 1.0 Transitional//EN"
        "DTD/xhtml1-transitional.dtd">
```

```
<!DOCTYPE html PUBLIC
        "-//W3C//DTD XHTML 1.0 Frameset//EN"
        "DTD/xhtml1-frameset.dtd">
```

Therefore, you have strict, transitional, and frameset DTDs. The only differences are the in the DTD public identifier and the filename. To read more about your DTD options, visit the XHTML specification at www.w3.org/TR/xhtml1/#normative or see Chapter 4 or Appendix B of this book.

You may be wondering, "What the heck is a DTD?" That is a valid question.

- ✔ DTDs define the grammar for XHTML.

  DTDs are used by XML applications — such as XHTML — to specify rules that apply to the markup of documents of a particular type, including a set of element and attribute declarations.

- ✔ An XHTML DTD describes, in computer-readable language, the allowed names for and behavior of XHTML markup. To read more about DTDs, see Appendix B.

Include an XML namespace within <html>

According to the specification, the root element — <html> — must include the XML namespace using the xmlns attribute. A namespace usually looks like URL, but it really identifies a unique name for a well-known set of predefined elements and attributes (in fact, if you aim a browser at the URL that appears in the next paragraph, you'll find that the corresponding Web address doesn't exist).

A *namespace* simply allows you to refer to the tags and semantics for some particular, well-defined type of XML document. It's a collection of names that can appear in XML documents for element types and attribute names. A namespace is nothing more than a unique identifier, and it should not be confused with a DTD. See Chapter 1 for more information on XML namespaces.

XHTML uses the XHTML collection of names and therefore needs a namespace. It looks like this:

```
<html xmlns="http://www.w3.org/1999/xhtml">
</html>
```

Include the <head> *and* <body> *elements*

That's right, if you want your XHTML documents to be valid, you have to use a couple of familiar structural elements: the <head> and <body> elements — that is, unless you're creating a frameset document. In which case, you must substitute <frameset> for the <body> element. Including the <frameset> element is a must for frameset documents.

XHTML documents adhere to DTDs. The majority of your documents use a *transitional* DTD. But if you're creating a frameset document, you need to reference the *frameset* DTD. The rules governing when you must include the <body> or the <frameset> element are stated in the DTD. To read more about different types of DTDs in relation to XHTML, see Chapter 4.

This is how you must code your glorious works of art:

```
<!DOCTYPE html PUBLIC
          "-//W3C//DTD XHTML 1.0 Transitional//EN"
          "DTD/xhtml1-transitional.dtd">
<html xmlns="http://www.w3.org/1999/xhtml">
<head>
<title>Insert Document Title Here</title>
</head>
<body>
...document content...
</body>
</html>
```

Wrap your script and style elements

The XHTML DTD declares that script and style elements contain character data (like any other text paragraph or heading). However, because script and style elements contain < and &, they are treated as the start of XHTML markup. You need to contain the script or style element within a CDATA marked section to avoid any browser confusion. To end the CDATA section, use the]]> string, like so:

```
<script language="JavaScript" type="text/javascript">
 <![CDATA[
 document.write("<b>We love XHTML</b>");
    ]]>
</script>
```

You can avoid using CDATA sections by referencing external files. For JavaScript, use <script language="JavaScript" src="myscript.js"> </script> to read your script code from a server. For CSS, you can link to an external file using <link href="mystylesheet.css" />. See Chapter 19 for more information on using CDATA with scripts.

Take a look at an example

That sums up all the rules you need to know. Before you pick up the phone to call Grandma, take a look at this rule-abiding example:

```
<!DOCTYPE html PUBLIC
          "-//W3C//DTD XHTML 1.0 Transitional//EN"
          "DTD/xhtml1-transitional.dtd">

<!-- This is our root element with a namespace -->

<html xmlns="http://www.w3.org/TR/xhtml1">
<head>
    <title>LANWrights - Network-Oriented Writing and
          Consulting
    </title>
    <link href="lanwstyle.css" type="text/css"
          rel="stylesheet" />
</head>

<!-- This begins the body of our XHTML document -->

<body>
<div>
    <p><img src="graphics/lanwlogo.gif" width="240"
          height="123" alt="LANWrights" /></p>
    <p><img src="graphics/ntwkori.gif" width="469"
          height="25" alt="Network-Oriented Writing &amp;
          Consulting" /></p>
    <p><img src="graphics/line.gif" width="100%" height="1"
          /></p>
</div>
<div class="description">
    <p>LANWrights, Inc., based in Austin, Texas, is dedicated
          to network-oriented writing, training, and con-
          sulting. Our projects cover the Internet,
          Networking and Communications, and Microsoft
          Certification, among other topics. LANWrights
          seeks to supply accurate, timely information on
          cutting-edge technologies and useful services to a
          wide range of users.</p>
</div>
<div class="line">
    <p><img src="graphics/line.gif" width="100%" height="1"
          /></p>
</div>

<!-- This is our table -->

<div class="table">
<table width="97%" border="0" cellpadding="10">
```

```
<tr valign="top">
    <td width="5%" align="center">
            <a href="books.htm">
            <img src="graphics/books.gif" width="51"
            height="51" alt="The Book Nook" align="right"
            border="0" />
            </a>
          </td>
    <td width="45%">
     <p><a href="books.htm">The Book Nook</a>
     </p>
     <p>Detailed descriptions for all of LANWrights'
            books, sorted by type, including pointers to
            associated Web sites.</p>
    </td>
    <td width="5%" align="CENTER">
     <a href="showcase.htm">
     <img src="graphics/showcase.gif" width="51"
            height="51" alt="Web Technology Showcase"
            border="0" />
     </a>
    </td>
    <td width="45%">
     <p><a href="showcase.htm">Web Technology
            Showcase</a>
     </p>
     <p>Java examples and demonstrations of recent
            adventures on the cutting edge.
     </p>
    </td>
</tr>

<tr valign="top">
    <td width="5%" align="center">
     <a href="training.htm">
     <img src="graphics/training.gif" width="51"
            height="51" alt="Training Center" align="right"
            border="0" />
     </a>
    </td>
    <td width="45%">
     <p>
     <a href="training.htm">The Training Center</a>
     </p>
     <p>Read about or sign up for upcoming classroom
            sessions, demo our online training, and learn
            more about licensing our testing and training
            environments.</p>
    </td>
    <td width="5%" align="CENTER">
     <a href="corporat.htm">
```

```
            <img src="graphics/corporat.gif" width="51"
                height="51" alt="Coporate Services" border="0"
                />
                </a>
        </td>
        <td width="45%">
         <p><a href="lanw.htm">Corporate HQ</a>
         </p>
         <p>Learn more about LANWrights' organization,
                including available services and rates. Read
                staff bios, and find out what's new here.</p>
        </td>
    </tr>

    <tr valign="TOP">
        <td width="5%" align="center">
                <a href="exam.htm">
                <img src="graphics/testprep.gif" width="51"
                height="51" border="0" alt="Certification
                Central" /></a>
                </td>
        <td width="45%">
         <p><a href="exam.htm">Certification Central</a>
         </p>
         <p>Learn about preparing to pass exams required
                for Microsoft, Novell, or Java certifications.
                Covers the Exam Prep, Exam Cram, and CT Guide
                series, including errata and practice
                tests.</p>
        </td>
        <td width="5%" align="middle">
         <a href="overview.htm">
         <img src="graphics/wayfind.gif" width="51"
                height="51" alt="Site Overview" border="0"
                /></a>
        </td>
        <td width="45%">
           <p><a href="overview.htm">Site Overview</a>
           </p>
           <p>A bird's-eye view of our Web site. From
                here, you can jump to any other section or
                page on the site.</p>
        </td>
    </tr>
</table>
</div>
<!-- Whew! That was the end of our table -->

<div class="footer">
<p><br />
<img src="graphics/line.gif" width="100%" height="2" />
</p>
<p class="address">
```

```
<a href="http://www.w3.org/Style/css/">
<img src="graphics/css.gif" align="right" border="0"
          alt="Made With Cascading Style Sheets" />
</a>
URL:<a href="default.htm">http://www.lanw.com/
              default.htm</a>
<br />
Layout, design &amp; revisions &#169; 1997, 1998
<a href="default.htm">LANWrights</a>, Inc.
<br />
<a href="mailto:webmaster←nw.com">Webmaster:</a> Chelsea
          Valentine
<br />
Revised -- February 14, 2000<i>[CV]</i></p>
</body>
</html>
```

After you look at the previous code, you should be able to find some empty elements (<br />) and many closing tags (</p>) — and that is just the tip of the iceberg. As stated previously in this chapter, XHTML has many rules and you must follow all of them for your pages to be valid XHTML.

Converting with HTML Tidy

Many Web designers swear by their trusty old text editor — and gloat about never using software to aid in the process of creating their masterpieces. Although we too are fairly addicted to our text editors, we don't necessarily agree with the "never using software to aid" approach — and neither do the folks at the W3C. David Raggett, a household name at the W3C, has created a tool to help you convert your HTML to XHTML.

Remember back in the day when we all made mistakes when creating — and editing — HTML? David Raggett did too, so he created a simple tool to fix these mistakes automatically and tidy up sloppy editing. The tool is called HTML Tidy, and it's a free utility offered on the W3C Web site. That was then.

Luckily for us, Raggett added some XHTML features to HTML Tidy, so now it can now take a look at your HTML page, clean it up, and then output it in XHTML. It can even help you identify spots where you need to pay further attention when making your pages more accessible to people with disabilities.

To read more about Tidy, visit www.w3.org/People/Raggett/tidy/ and see Chapter 26.

The program itself is not currently a Windows program, unless you download the entire HTML kit for editing. If you're familiar with DOS programs, feel free to download HTML Tidy as a single program and get to work. But if you're like most of us and have been spoiled by Microsoft's GUI Windows interfaces, you may want to visit a Web-based version created by Peter Wiggin. Visit the following URL, enter your URL in the space provided, and then see it magically convert before your very eyes. Here are some hints to remember when using this URL to covert your XHTML:

- Your Web site must be published.
- You must enter the full URL, including the http://.
- You need to view the source to see the corrected XHTML.
- You need to cut and paste the corrected source code into your XHTML document on your Web server.

To convert your pages using Peter Wiggin's HTML Tidy Web-based version, visit http://webreview.com/1999/07/16/feature/xhtml.cgi.

Chapter 4

The XHTML Specification

*I*n this chapter, we introduce you to the concept of a specification and what's in the XHMTL specification. One of the most important parts of the XHTML specification is the Document Type Definition (DTD); therefore, we help you figure out how to read a DTD.

The XHTML specification outlines three flavors of XHTML. You'll find out what they are so you know which one's best for you and your needs. Lastly, we highlight the areas of the specification that we think you need to pay some extra attention to.

What is a Specification?

The Merriam-Webster's Collegiate Dictionary defines a specification as, "A detailed precise presentation of something or of a plan or proposal for something." In other words a specification describes what makes something what it is. Building a specification includes all the plans of the specification and a list of instructions as to how to implement the plans. This includes a list of the materials, what is considered suitable and what is considered unsuitable material, and the amount of care necessary to put the specification together.

In principle, a document type specification is no different. Again, there's a set of plans, the Document Type Definitions (DTDs), as well as a separate document that tells how to execute those plans. The XHTML specification is a good example of a document specification.

What's in the XHTML specification?

The XHTML 1.0 specification can be found at `www.w3.org/TR/xhtml1`. This document consists of a narrative document and a set of DTDs. The narrative document also describes:

- ✔ The need for XHTML
- ✔ Terms used in the specification
- ✔ The differences between HTML and XHTML

In addition, the narrative documents have a set of the appendices that describe the meat of the specification, particularly, the DTDs.

Are you asking me or telling me?

The content of the narrative documents of the specification is divided into two main parts: the so-called normative part and the informative part. The *normative part* of the specification describes what has to be done if a document is to be called an XHTML document, or if a piece of software is going to claim to be XHTML compliant. Normative parts of the specification deal with document conformance, user-agent conformance, as well as the DTDs and element prohibitions.

The *informative part* of the specification is the part that advises the user the best way to go about making an XHTML document or XHTML-compliant software. Users do *not have* to adhere to the suggestions to be in compliance with the specification, although obviously, it's strongly suggested that they do. The informative part of the specification includes guidelines as to how to make XHTML documents viewable in older browsers.

A Little Bit about DTDs

Unfortunately, there's no getting away from the fact that to truly understand a specification, you have to know a little bit about DTDs. This section does not aim to turn you into a DTD guru, but it should give you enough knowledge so you can look at a DTD and understand what's going on. There may come a time when you're stuck as to how to proceed in your document authoring, and all the textbooks you have won't be able to answer your questions. This is the time when being able to con a DTD is really useful. Keep in mind that there are hundreds of thousands of people writing HTML and XHTML documents who wouldn't know a DTD from a hole in the ground, so if you want to skip this section, that's OK. However, for those of you who don't want to just follow the herd, here it is.

What is a DTD?

DTD stands for Document Type Definition. A DTD is to a document specification what the plans of a building are to a building specification. In other words, a DTD is the starting point to obtain detailed knowledge of how to put your product together.

The DTD is the formal document that explains which elements and attributes are allowed in a document, and what each of these can or cannot contain. The DTD is written in a special kind of syntax that is clear and precise. The following sections introduce you to this syntax using illustrations and examples taken from the *XHTML Strict DTD,* which can be found at `www.w3.org/TR/xhtml1/DTD/xhtml1-strict.dtd`.

What's in a DTD?

There are essentially four kinds of content allowed in a DTD:

- ✔ Comments
- ✔ Element declarations
- ✔ Entity declarations
- ✔ Attribute declarations

Comments

Comments in a DTD are just like comments anywhere in an XML (hence, XHTML) document. Everything between `<--` and `-->` is a comment. Of course, comments cannot be nested. Here's what a comment looks like:

```
<!--This is a comment-->
```

Element declarations

An *element declaration* defines the content that can appear in an element. It takes the following general form:

```
<!ELEMENT element name (allowed content)>
```

For example, the root element of an XHTML document is the `<html>` element. Here's how it's declared in the DTD:

```
<!ELEMENT html (head, body)>
```

This says that the `<html>` element can contain one `<head>` element followed by one `<body>` element and they must appear in that order.

Here's the element declaration for the `<title>` element.

```
<!ELEMENT title (#PCDATA)>
```

This says that a title can only contain text (that's what #PCDATA means in nerd talk) and can't contain any elements.

Here's the element declaration for the `<meta />` element.

```
<!ELEMENT meta EMPTY>
```

This says that the `<meta />` element cannot contain any content. In fact, a `<meta />` element just uses attributes to give different meanings to the element.

Here's how the `<dl>` (definition list) element is defined:

```
<!ELEMENT dl (dt|dd)+>
```

This tells us that a `<dl>` element can contain either `<dt>` or `<dd>` elements. The pipe stem (|) between them means *or* in DTD syntax. The plus sign (+) after the bracket means that there must be at least one of these elements present, but that each `<dl>` element can contain an unlimited number of `<dt>` or `<dd>` elements. You find out more about what the plus sign means in the section "Defining element content" later in this chapter.

Note that `(dt|dd)+` is different from `(dt+|dd+)`. The first means you can have as many `<dt>` *and* `<dd>` elements as you want; the second means you can have as many `<dt>` *or* `<dd>` elements as you want.

Here's how the paragraph (`<p>`) element is defined:

```
<!ELEMENT p %Inline;>
```

This tells us that the paragraph element can contain content defined by the `Inline` parameter entity, described in the following section.

Entity declarations

DTDs can contain what are known as *parameter entity* declarations. The general configuration for a parameter entity declaration is as follows:

```
<!ENTITY % entity name "entity content">
```

Now, whenever this entity is referenced using the following syntax

```
%entity name;
```

It's as if the content of the entity is put where the reference is. Here's how this works in practice. Here's the element declaration for the paragraph element again:

```
<!ELEMENT p %Inline;>
```

When the `Inline` entity declaration is found, the following is seen:

```
<!ENTITY % Inline "(#PCDATA | %inline; | %misc;)*">
```

Note the `inline` entity starts with a lower case i. Remember that XML is case sensitive; therefore, `Inline` is different from `inline`. Substituting this, the paragraph element declaration becomes:

```
<!ELEMENT p (#PCDATA | %inline; | %misc;)*>
```

Note how there's nesting of these entities. Looking up `inline` and `misc` (in the DTD) we find:

```
<!ENTITY % inline "a | %special; | %fontstyle; | %phrase; |
        %inline.forms;">
<!ENTITY % misc "ins | del | script | noscript">,
```

So the paragraph declaration now becomes:

```
<!ELEMENT p (#PCDATA | a | %special; | %fontstyle; | %phrase;
          | %inline.forms; | ins | del | script |
          noscript)*>
```

After resolving the `special`, `fontstyle`, `phrase`, and `inline.forms` entities (go to the DTD to look these up), we finally see that our original paragraph declaration

```
<!ELEMENT p %Inline;>
```

resolves to

```
<!ELEMENT p
      (#PCDATA | a |br | span | bdo | object
       | img | map | tt | i | b | big | small
       | em | strong | dfn | code | q | sub
       | sup samp | kbd | var | cite | abbr
       | acronym |input | select | textarea
       | label | button | ins | del | script
       | noscript)*>
```

This tells us that the paragraph element can contain all these elements as well as text. The * after the closing parenthesis tells us that it can contain as many or as few of these elements as is desired.

When text can be mixed with elements as element content, we say that an element can contain *mixed content*. A declaration for mixed content must always take this form:

```
<!ELEMENT element name  (#PCDATA| element1 name|element2 name
          etc..)*>
```

You can see how parameter entities make it easier to handle the content of DTDs, and you can also see how much work you may have to do to resolve some of the element's content.

Defining element content

The syntax of the element declaration tells us, and more importantly, any browser or other software that is checking a document, all about the allowed content of the element. It not only dictates which child elements the element can contain, but also how many of them are allowed, and whether they have to be in a strict order or whether they can be in any order.

You've already seen an example of strict ordering in the `<html>` element:

```
<!ELEMENT html (head, body)>
```

When a comma (,) separates the element, the elements have to be in that order, and they both have to occur. In other words, the following is the only acceptable configuration:

```
<html>
 <head>
 head content
 </head>
 <body>
 body content
 </body>
</html>
```

However, in this example, the pipe stem means either/or:

```
<!ELEMENT dl (dt|dd)+>
```

Therefore, this and numerous other combinations are all acceptable:

```
<dl>
  <dt>some text here</dt>
</dl>
<dl>
  <dd>some text here</dd>
</dl>
<dl>
```

```
   <dd>some text here</dd>
   <dd>some text here</dd>
   <dt>some text here</dt>
</dl>
<dl>
   <dt>some text here</dt>
   <dd>some text here</dd>
   <dt>some text here</dt>
</dl>
```

In the previous examples, where the element declaration is:

```
<!ELEMENT dl (dt|dd)+>
```

dt and dd are grouped together in parenthesis, and followed by the plus sign (+). When elements are grouped together by parenthesis, any symbol outside the parenthesis applies to all the elements contained with in them.

If you look at the previous code in this chapter, you probably noticed a couple extra symbols, such as the plus signs (+), stars (*), and question marks (?). These symbols indicate how many times an element or an element group can or must appear. If there's no symbol after an element or element group, that element or group can only appear once, and more importantly must appear at least once. Table 4-1 shows what the symbols mean.

Table 4-1   Giving meaning to element declaration symbols

Symbol	Name	Description
?	question mark	If there is a ? after the element or group, that element can appear only once, or not at all. In other words, the element or group is optional.
+	plus sign	If there is a + after the element, the element or group must appear at least once, but after that, it can appear as many times as wanted or needed.
*	asterisk	If there is a * after the element or group, the element or group can occur not at all or as many times as needed or wanted.

Here's the element declaration for the table element:

```
<!ELEMENT table
    (caption?, (col*|colgroup*), thead?
    , tfoot?, (tbody+|tr+))>
```

Here's how you would decipher this code:

✔ The elements and groups are separated by commas, so they must appear strictly in this order.

✔ The first element is the `caption` element. The question mark (?) tells us that this is an optional element. However, there can be no more than one caption.

✔ The element group (`col*|colgroup*`) tells us that you can either have as many `col` elements as you want, *or* as many `colgroup` elements as you want, but you cannot mix them.

✔ The `thead` and `tfoot` elements are optional.

✔ The element group (`tbody+|tr+`) is not optional. This tells you that a table must contain at least one `tr` element or as many `tr` elements as you like *or* at least one `tbody` element or as many `tbody` elements as you like.

Note that if the DTD author had written (`tbody|tr`)+, you could mix and match as many `tbody` *and* `tr` elements as you wanted.

Attribute declaration

An *attribute declaration* defines what kind of attribute is allowed on an element, the type of attribute it is, and the allowed value of the attribute. An attribute declaration takes the general form:

```
<!ATTLIST element name
    attribute name attribute type allowed values
    >
```

Each attribute declaration can have several entities, and indeed an element can have several attribute declarations. The XHTML DTD uses parameter entities in its attribute declarations. Here's the attribute declaration for the paragraph element.

```
<!ATTLIST p
  %attrs;
  >
```

And here's what it looks like if we expand it. Now you can see the DTD for all the entity values:

```
<!ATTLIST p
    id          ID        #IMPLIED
    class       CDATA     #IMPLIED
    style       CDATA     #IMPLIED
    title       CDATA     #IMPLIED
    lang        NMTOKEN   #IMPLIED
    xml:lang    NMTOKEN   #IMPLIED
```

```
dir            (ltr|rtl)        #IMPLIED
onclick        CDATA            #IMPLIED
ondblclick     CDATA            #IMPLIED
onmousedown    CDATA            #IMPLIED
onmouseup      CDATA            #IMPLIED
onmouseover    CDATA            #IMPLIED
onmousemove    CDATA            #IMPLIED
onmouseout     CDATA            #IMPLIED
onkeypress     CDATA            #IMPLIED
onkeydown      CDATA            #IMPLIED
onkeyup        CDATA            #IMPLIED
>
```

The various values that an attribute can take are determined by the attribute types. Of the attributes listed in the previous code, all of them are #IMPLIED, and only four of them take value types other than CDATA, which means that the values of these attributes can contain text of any kind:

✔ **ID:** First of all, note that the first attribute name listed is id. This attribute is of the type ID. In documents, as in real life, ID's are designed to be unique, which means that the value placed on an attribute of the type ID must be unique throughout the document. There are also constraints on the make up of the value. The value of an attribute of the type ID must start with a letter (a-z or A-Z), a colon (:), or an underscore (_) and can contain no white space.

A parser checks for the uniqueness of the value of an id attribute and throws an error if it finds two id attributes with the same name.

Note, in particular, that the constraints put on the value of an id attribute mean that it cannot start with a number. Thus <div id="123"> is illegal, whereas <div id="a123"> is legal.

✔ **NMTOKEN:** The lang and xml:lang elements are attributes of the so-called NMTOKEN type. This type of attribute has constraints on the make up of its value. These constraints are exactly the same as for an attribute of the type ID. Namely, the value of an attribute of the type NMTOKEN must start with a letter (a-z or A-Z), a colon (:), or an underscore (_) and can contain no white space.

✔ **(ltr|rtl):** The dir attribute is what is known as an enumerated attribute. The actual values it can take are spelled out, namely (ltr|rtl), which means that the only legal value it can contain is ltr or rtl.

The allowed value of an attribute tells us whether an attribute must be used, whether the attribute is optional, whether it has a default value, or whether it has a fixed value.

The allowed values for all these paragraph element attributes is #IMPLIED, which means that the attribute does not have to be present on the element. The other allowed values are #FIXED and #REQUIRED and we discuss them later in this section.

The xml:lang attribute is a special kind of attribute. It's not, in fact, part of the XHTML specification, but has been borrowed from the XML specification. The colon (:) tells us that it belongs to a different namespace, and the xml before the colon tells us that it belongs to the XML namespace (we cover this in Chapter 1).

Another example of a borrowed attribute is found in the attribute declarations of the pre element. This time, it's the space attribute that is borrowed from the XML namespace:

```
<!ATTLIST pre
  %attrs;
  xml:space (preserve) #FIXED 'preserve'
  >
```

This attribute's also an enumerated type of attribute with a single allowed value. The #FIXED allowed value tells us that this attribute must always be present, and it must always take the fixed value of preserve.

Some attributes are required. In other words, if a document author leaves an attribute out, the parser signals an error. The following extract from the img attribute list illustrates where an attribute is required. This means that all img elements must take an src and an alt attribute:

```
<!ATTLIST img
  %attrs;
  src          %URI;          #REQUIRED
  alt          %Text;         #REQUIRED
  . . .
>
```

The following example of an attribute from the attribute list of the form element completes the roundup of attribute types. Here the method attribute is of the enumerated type, and a default value is declared. If the author of a document does not specify a method attribute in his or her document, the parser does it for him or her, and automatically assigns it a value of get:

```
<!ATTLIST form
  . . .
     method       (get|post)      "get"
  . . .
     >
```

This attribute is particularly important in XHTML, because 99.9 percent of the time, you want to use the post value. The get value is the default value for historical reasons, and who are we to argue with tradition?

This brief trip around DTDs probably won't make you an expert, but hopefully it will give you enough knowledge to be dangerous, and more importantly, enough knowledge to let you know when some one else is talking nonsense.

The Three Flavors of XHTML

All the examples from the previous section were taken from just one DTD, the so-called *strict DTD*. The strict DTD, in fact, does not contain any styling elements or attributes and is the version of XHTML used by both puritans and purists. These noble individuals would have us use style sheets for all our styling needs. (We cover style sheets in Chapter 8.) There are however two other flavors of XHTML: *loose* DTD, and the *frameset* DTD.

Although most of us pay lip service to rigorousness and purity, the fact is that most of us, as in real life, slip from these lofty heights. The loose DTD allows us to use elements, such as the `<font>` element (most of us could live without that). It also allows things such as the `align` attribute, which allows us to center our elements, and although this can be done perfectly well with style sheets, most of us use this attribute from time to time.

The frameset DTD allows us incorporate several pages in a single frame. We cover frames in Chapter 18.

For the gory (uh, glory) details on the various types of DTDs, your best source, as always, is the W3C Web site: go to `www.w3.org/TR/xhtml1/#dtds`.

Specification Highlights

The meat of the specification is in fact contained in the DTDs, but there are a lot of other interesting things in the XHTML specification. In this section, we take you through a guided tour of the parts of the specification that we think are most important and the most helpful for you, they are:

- ✔ Section 3: The Normative Definition of XHTML 1.0
- ✔ Section 4: Differences with HTML 4
- ✔ Appendix B. Element Prohibitions
- ✔ Appendix C. HTML Compatibility Guidelines.

The normative definition of XHTML 1.0

This section of the specification provides a definition of a strictly conforming XHTML document, and also defines what is required of a user agent to be a conforming user agent.

Four things are required for a document to be a strictly conforming XHTML document:

- The document must validate against one of the three DTDs (strict, loose, or frameset).
- The root element of the document must be the `<html>` element.
- The root element of the document must designate the XHTML namespace (more on this in Chapter 1 and later in this chapter).
- There must be a DOCTYPE declaration using the formal public identifier, and this doctype must reference a copy of the DTD that the document validates against.

Are you valid?

Anyone using XHTML is strongly urged to validate all documents against a DTD. If your documents are online, you can visit the W3C site and use one of its validators found at www.w3.org. Alternatively, you can use an XML validator and validate your document against your own copy of the DTD.

You can find copies of all three DTDs on the CD.

Getting to the root of the matter

All valid XML documents must have a root element, and in the case of XHTML, this root element must be the `<html>` element. You may think this statement is redundant, because if a document validates against a DTD, surely it has to have `<html>` as a root element. Surprisingly, this is not the case. The following minimal document validates against the DTD:

```
<p>A paragraph</p>
```

The reason for this has to do with the very nature of XML. You can always validate a strict subset of an XML document type against the main DTD.

What's in a name?

We cover namespaces in Chapter 1, but a word or two about namespaces is in order here. One of the main advantages of XHTML is that it can be extended to include elements from other document types, including your own. One way to do this is to use namespaces. In an XHTML document, we need to inform the browser or processor that every element that does not contain a colon belongs to the XHTML namespace. You do this by putting a namespace declaration in the root element. Here's how you do it:

```
<html xmlns= "http://www.w3.org/1999/xhtml">
```

For now, the best thing to do is adopt a *monkey see, monkey do* approach, and just put this attribute and its value on each namespace. The same attribute and value covers all three flavors of DTDs.

Going Public

Like HTML, all XHTML documents should have a public identifier. This identifier varies with each flavor of DTD. Here's the identifier for all three flavors of DTDs:

```
<!DOCTYPE html
    PUBLIC "-//W3C//DTD XHTML 1.0 Strict//EN"
    "DTD/xhtml1-strict.dtd">

<!DOCTYPE html
    PUBLIC "-//W3C//DTD XHTML 1.0 Transitional//EN"
    "DTD/xhtml1-transitional.dtd">

<!DOCTYPE html
    PUBLIC "-//W3C//DTD XHTML 1.0 Frameset//EN"
    "DTD/xhtml1-frameset.dtd">
```

There's both a public reference and a reference to a copy of the DTD. Although it's acceptable to put the address of the copy of the DTD that resides on the W3C site, this is probably not a good idea. The problem is that if millions of user agents try and look up a single site, a *denial of service* situation will arise. It's better to cache a copy of the DTD on your own site, and reference these URL's.

The black art of white space

The other interesting things to notice in Section 3 of the XHTML specification are the instructions to browsers on how they're supposed to handle white space.

White space consists of spaces, tabs, and line breaks. In XML all these are recognized and rendered. However, in XHTML white space is collapsed, except in those elements where the attribute `xml:whitespace` is given a value of `preserve`. The elements that can be given this attribute are the `<pre>`, `<style>`, and `<script>` elements.

Here's what you need to know about white space in XHTML:

- Remove all white space surrounding block elements.
- Inside a block element, remove all leading and trailing white space.
- Convert all tabs and line feed elements to spaces.
- Convert sequences of white spaces into single spaces.

What's different about XHTML

Section 4 of the XHTML specification details the differences between HTML and XHTML. We cover these details in Chapter 2. However, if you read Section 4 of the XHTML specification and Chapter 2, you may notice an eerie similarity in wording. Rest assured that this is not plagiarism. It's just that the same author wrote both these items.

To summarize the difference between XHTML and HTML are as follows. In XHTML:

- ✔ All elements must be strictly nested.
- ✔ All element and attribute names must be in lowercase.
- ✔ End tags are required in all non-empty elements.
- ✔ All attributes must be quoted.
- ✔ Attribute values cannot be minimized.
- ✔ Empty elements must end with `/>`.
- ✔ Leading and trailing white space in attribute values will be stripped. Although most HTML browsers in fact do this, it's not a requirement of HTML.
- ✔ Script and style elements need to be escaped using `<![CDATA[` sections. The problem here is that XML does not allow an elements content to be declared as CDATA (SGML does). So theoretically, XHTML parsers may choke if they find < and & in script or style elements. In practice, this does not happen; however, authors of scripts and style sheets are encouraged to put them in external files.
- ✔ In SGML, it's possible for writers of DTDs to exclude certain content from elements using DTD syntax. This is not possible in XML, so in XHTML, element exclusions are referenced in a separate part of the specification (Appendix B — of the spec, not this book). This will be looked at below.
- ✔ In HTML the `name` attribute of certain elements is meant to be unique. In other words, it's meant to behave as if the attribute was declared as being of an `ID` type. However, XML only allows each element to have one attribute of the type `ID`. Because every element in XHTML can take an `id` attribute, this means that the `name` elements cannot be declared in the DTD to be of the type `ID`. However, Section 4 of the XHTML specification instructs user agents to treat the `name` attributes of certain elements as if they were of the type `ID`.

I'm sorry you can't go here!

As we mention in the previous section, SGML DTD syntax allowed DTDs to specifically exclude some kinds of content. XML does not have this provision. Although it would be possible to write a DTD in XML that could mimic the exclusions of SGML, the convolutions necessary to do this would make the DTD almost unreadable.

For this reason, the authors of the XHTML specification decided to just add a normative section outlining the exclusions. This is found in Appendix B of the specification, which can be summarized as follows:

- ✔ An `<a>` element cannot contain other `<a>` elements.
- ✔ A `pre` element cannot contain `<img>`, `<object>`, `<big>`, `<small>`, `<sub>`, or `<sup>` elements.
- ✔ A `<button>` element cannot contain `<input>`, `<select>`, `<textarea>`, `<label>`, `<button>`, `<form>`, `<fieldset>`, `<iframe>`, or `<isindex>` elements.
- ✔ A `<label>` element cannot contain other `<label>` elements.
- ✔ A `<form>` element cannot contain other `<form>` elements.

HTML compatibility guidelines

The last part of our quick tour through the specification looks at Appendix C, the compatibility guidelines. These guidelines tell authors how to write XHTML documents so they can be viewed in older HTML browsers, and yet are still valid XHTML. Some of the tips are quite arcane, but there are a few important ones that all authors should be aware of.

Leave out the XML declaration.

All XML documents can start with a version declaration

```
<?xml version= "1.0" ?>
```

Browsers should ignore it because it should look like an unknown element. Unfortunately, browsers don't always do the correct thing, and this version declaration may display on down-level HTML browsers, so leave it out.

Watch that empty element!

In XML, an empty element must take a special form, for example `<hr/>` and `<br/>`. Unfortunately, this form may cause older browsers to throw a fit. Luckily, the cure is quite simple. Just put a space before that forward slash, like so `<hr />` and `<br />`.

Embedded style sheets and scripts

Whereas the last two tips allow for the writing of documents in down-level browsers, this tip allows you to write documents for future, yet to be invented browsers, a process known as future proofing. You are free to embed style sheets and scripts in your XHTML document, but if a strictly conforming XML parser reads your document, it will probably interpret your ampersands and less than signs as entities and opening angle brackets. To avoid this and several other problems, you're urged wherever possible to place your scripts and style sheets as external rather than embedded documents.

Part II
Getting Started

The 5th Wave   By Rich Tennant

"We're here to clean the code."

In this part . . .

In this part of the book, we describe the structures and functions that XHTML documents can deliver, along with the XHTML markup that makes Web pages possible. Next, we show you how to build your very first XHTML page by hand. After that, we explore the details of XHTML markup, as we document its many elements and attributes. Then, we explain how to use style directives to control how XHTML content and graphics appear when displayed on a computer. This part of the book concludes with a detailed anatomy lesson on the structure that's proper for a well-built XHTML document, and throw in the basics of good document design, so you learn about good structure and content in one single lesson!

Chapter 5

Behind the Scenes of XHTML Documents

XHTML is really nothing more than a set of markup elements that you use to describe a document's content. XHTML looks a lot like HTML and is almost as easy to use. But before you jump into XHTML development, you can benefit from knowing a bit about what goes on behind the scenes in XHTML documents.

In this chapter, you find out that XHTML is founded in hypertext, as HTML is, but that XHTML separates content from display. You also get a look at how some of the most popular Web browsers deal with XHTML and what other uses XHTML can have. Finally, you gain access to all the XHTML elements and their attributes in one place so you can get a handle on how to use XHTML to build Web pages — and more.

Hypertext Is Part of the Name

XHTML is simply HTML that starts with an *X*, which means two basic things:

✔ XHTML is an Extensible Markup Language (XML) vocabulary (hence the *X*).

✔ XHTML is a hypertext-based markup language (hence the *HTML*).

One of the great things about XML is that you can create your own elements. However, the freedom to build an element and use it to describe just about any content comes with some fairly serious side issues, including how to display or process your content without an available tool that knows what to do with custom elements.

The architects of XML realized early on that although there's a great need to extend the Web with customized elements, the need for standard Web pages that everyday Web browsers can read and display still exists. XHTML provides the solution to this dilemma, and does it in the context of XML.

What this means to you is that you shouldn't treat XHTML much differently from XML. XHTML is a bit stricter than HTML (as discussed in Chapter 3), but in the end, you're still building documents that are served over the Internet from Web servers to Web browsers. These documents are linked to one another using hypertext, and they still include nontextual media, such as graphics, Java applets, and multimedia files.

When you learn XHTML, you learn more than just which element does what. You learn a bit about markup theory, a bit about XML, and a bit about style. Even with these other things to think about, try not to forget that XHTML documents are founded on hypertext just as HTML documents are. You want to take full advantage of hypertext media as you create XHTML documents.

Style Sheets Separate Content from Display

Although XHTML builds on the same basic principals as HTML, be aware of this fundamental difference: XHTML seeks to separate content from display; HTML does not. This separation of content and display is a function of XHTML's origin as an XML vocabulary. One of the goals of XML, as described in Chapter 1, is to keep the directions that guide the final look and feel of a document totally separate from the markup that defines its content. The biggest advantage to separating content from display is that you can build a single document with XHTML for display on a variety of devices, from standard Web browsers to mobile phones to Web TV. This isn't a particularly new activity, but an XHTML implementation with style sheets is easier, faster, and more straightforward than other approaches.

With HTML, when you build a single Web page, you can't make it look good in multiple browsers. Also, the same HTML document that you use for a standard Web site would definitely not look good on a mobile phone's tiny display. The only real solution when using HTML to create a document that looks good in a variety of different environments is to build multiple versions of the same page, each tailored to some specific browser or device. This isn't necessarily a problem when you have five or ten pages on your site; but when you have 5,000 pages, managing multiple versions can turn into a maintenance nightmare.

Separating content from display solves the multiple-browser, multiple-device problem. You use XHTML to build a single document that doesn't include any information about how the document should appear. Instead, you use XHTML elements simply to identify the different pieces and parts of your documents — paragraphs, headings, lists, tables, and so on. Then, you can build a series of style sheets tailored to each browser or device where you want to deploy that document. You can create one style sheet for Web browsers, one for personal digital assistants (PDAs), and another for mobile phone displays.

Each style sheet meets the particular needs of each device. The Web browser style sheet may use lots of colors, different font sizes and styles, and even a set of frames. PDA and mobile phone style sheets, however, must be sensitive to the small screen sizes and limited colors available on both these devices. These style sheets must use a simpler layout, fewer fonts, and eschew graphics to make information as accessible as possible.

Although you have three different style sheets, you still have only one base document and one set of content. Any changes you make to your content need apply to a single XHTML document. And as a bonus, you can apply one style sheet to a whole slew of XHTML documents, which means that you can build one style sheet to direct the display of thousands of Web pages on a particular device.

The benefits of style are myriad, and we're huge believers in the benefits of separating content from display. Chapter 8 covers style sheets in more detail and shows you how to build style sheets to go along with your XHTML documents.

XHTML and Web Browsers

XML is the latest technology craze, and XHTML is the future of HTML. Although this is all well and good, reality must intrude at some point. This forces you to step back and evaluate XHTML's real-world implementation issues. In a nutshell, you must know how XHTML works with current Web browsers!

The developers of XHTML designed it to work as well as possible with older browsers. Really, the biggest difference between XHTML and HTML is that XHTML has to follow a few more rules than HTML. Here are some of the most important rules:

- ✔ Always identify XML documents as XML documents.
- ✔ Always use a closing tag with every opening tag (unless it's an empty tag, of course).
- ✔ Always mark empty elements with a slash (/) before the greater-than sign (>).
- ✔ Always nest elements properly — in other words, close first what you opened last.
- ✔ Always put quotation marks around attribute values.
- ✔ Always use lowercase for your elements and attributes.

Chapter 3 covers these rules in greater detail. If you aren't already familiar with the rules and regulations of building XML documents, read Chapter 3 before you try to build any XHTML documents. You'll be happier in the end, we promise!

If you look at these basic rules for XHTML documents, you can see that they aren't earth shattering and they don't cause you to build pages that confuse current Web browsers.

However, one of these rules may cause some older browsers to choke on your XHTML: *Always identify XML documents as XML documents.* In practice, this rule means that all XHTML documents start with this bit of code:

```
<?xml version="1.0" encoding="UTF-8" ?>
```

This snippet of code is a declaration that identifies the document as an XML document. Some older browsers won't know what to do when they see this identifier, so instead of ignoring it and moving on to the next line in the page, the browsers stop displaying the page altogether. The browsers that do this are limited to 2.0 and 3.0 versions browsers of various types.

The best litmus test for how a browser handles XHTML is to attempt to display an XHTML document. Of course, you may want to test browsers before you begin building XHTML, so you can look at other people's XHTML pages. The W3C's HTML Home Page is written in XHTML. To test how a browser handles XHTML, visit www.w3.org/MarkUp/. Most browsers can deal with this page perfectly; therefore, the way is clear for you to start building XHTML pages now.

Beyond Browsers: The Many Uses for XHTML Documents

You can use XHTML for more than just building Web pages for delivery to a user's desktop PC. The Internet and Web are branching out, and you can create content for delivery to a whole host of new devices, including the following:

- ✔ Handheld and mobile devices
- ✔ WebTV
- ✔ Web appliances

Flip on the TV and you see the airways littered with ads for mobile phones and PDAs to provide wireless Web access. WebTV has been around for a while and is becoming more popular. Smart appliances — refrigerators, VCRs, ovens, and even toasters, to name a few — are being built for Web-based access and control (we kid you not!). Because XHTML is display independent, you can build XHTML pages that work on any or all these devices — as long as those devices recognize XHTML and know what to do with it.

A good example of using both Web and handheld devices to deliver content is the RedGorilla Web-based time tracking tool at www.redgorilla.com. RedGorilla provides a Web-based environment for individuals and organizations to set up and track projects, billable hours, and invoices. Figure 5-1 shows the standard Web interface to track time spent on a particular project.

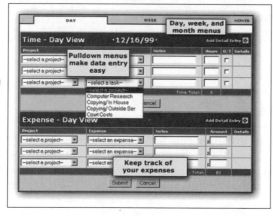

Figure 5-1:
The RedGorilla Web interface for time tracking.

This interface is just right if you're sitting in front of a desktop PC with a Web browser and Internet connectivity. But what if you're at a client site without a PC or a browser, and you want to access your project and time records? That's why RedGorilla also offers Palm and mobile phone interfaces, as shown in Figure 5-2.

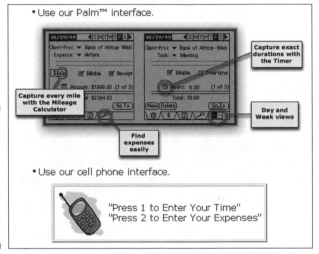

Figure 5-2:
The
RedGorilla
Palm and
mobile
phone time
tracking
interface.

This kind of approach to Web content delivery takes full advantage of the different devices people use for communication — PCs, PDAs, and mobile phones — and recognizes that users need Web access when they aren't at their computers. Because XHTML is display-independent, you can build a single set of Web documents for display on a variety of different devices to keep you connected with your users wherever they go. Ahhh, the beauty of XHTML!

XHTML Element List

The chapters in Parts III and IV of this book take a close look at different sets of XHTML markup, such as list and table markup. Even though we cover the majority of the XHTML elements in detail in these other chapters, you should find a general element reference that covers all the XHTML elements in one place valuable.

Table 5-1 lists all the XHTML elements, along with a brief description and the attributes for each element. The elements are organized into categories — as specified in the XHTML DTDs themselves — and the last column of the table lists the chapter that includes more detailed information about each element.

Bookmark this section for quick and easy reference. Even the most seasoned Web developer forgets which attributes go with each and every element. Find that info here!

The three flavors of XHTML revisited

As Chapter 4 discusses in greater detail, three different versions — or flavors — of XHTML have been defined:

- **XHTML Transitional:** The version of XHTML that's most like HTML 4.01. This flavor of XHTML includes presentation-oriented elements, such as the `<font>` and `<center>` elements. Use this version of XHTML to build Web pages compatible with older browser versions.

- **XHTML Strict:** This version of XHTML truly separates display from content. This flavor contains no formatting-oriented elements, and works well with Cascading Style Sheets (CSS).

- **XHTML Frameset:** This version of XHTML includes frame markup. Use it to create framed sets of Web pages (popular for many kinds of Web sites).

All three flavors of XHTML have a large number of elements in common, but some elements occur in one flavor but not others. Table 5-1 specifies which flavors of XHTML each element belongs to: *transitional, strict,* or *frameset.* Those elements that belong to all three flavors are identified as *all.*

A word about attributes

XHTML has four sets of attributes that are common in a variety of elements. Rather than repeating these particular attribute collections, all three XHTML DTDs combine these common attributes into four different well-recognized sets:

- **Core attributes:**
  - `id`
  - `class`
  - `style`
  - `title`
- **Internationalization attributes:**
  - `lang`
  - `xml:lang`
  - `dir`

✔ **Events attributes:**

- onclick
- click
- onmousedown
- onmouseup
- onmouseover
- onmousemove
- onmouseout
- onkeypress
- onkeydown
- onkeyup

✔ **Standard attributes:** Includes the other three attribute sets: core, internationalization, and events.

The attribute column of Table 5-1 lists all the attributes for each element and refers to these attribute sets in this way:

✔ **Core attributes:** *core*

✔ **Internationalization attributes:** *internatl*

✔ **Events attributes:** *events*

✔ **Standard attributes:** *standard*

Chapter 7 covers element and attribute structure and how you use the two together to describe content.

Table 5-1		The XHTML Element List			
Category	*Tag*	*Description*	*Attributes*	*DTD*	*Chapter*
Document Structure	html	document element	*internatl*	all	10
			xmlns		
Document Head	head	document header	*internatl*	all	10
			profile		
	title	document title	*internatl*	all	10
	base	document base url	href	all	10

Category	Tag	Description	Attributes	DTD	Chapter
			target		
	meta	document meta data	*internatl*	all	10
			http-equiv		
			name		
			content		
			scheme		
	link	link to other documents	*standard*	all	8
			charset		
			href		
			hreflang		
			type		
			rel		
			rev		
			media		
			target		
	style	internal style sheet	*internatl*	all	8
			type		
			media		
			title		
			xml:space		
	script	internal script	charset	all	19
			type		
			internatl		
			src		
			defer		
			xml:space		

(continued)

Table 5-1 *(continued)*

Category	Tag	Description	Attributes	DTD	Chapter
	noscript	script alternative text	*standard*	all	19
Frames	frameset	set of frames	*core*	frameset	18
			rows		
			cols		
			onload		
			onunload		
	frame	frame in a frame set	*core*	frameset	18
			longdesc		
			name		
			src		
			frameborder		
			marginwidth		
			marginheight		
			noresize		
			scrolling		
	iframe	floating frame	*core*	transitional, frameset	18
			longdesc		
			name		
			src		
			frameborder		
			marginwidth		
			marginheight		
			scrolling		
			align		
			height		
			width		

Category	Tag	Description	Attributes	DTD	Chapter
	noframes	frame alternative text	*standard*	transitional, frameset	18
Document body	body	document body	*standard*	all	10
			onload		
			onunload		
			background		
			bgcolor		
			text		
			link		
			vlink		
			alink		
	div	block level container	*standard*	all	10
			align		
Paragraphs	p	paragraph	*standard*	all	11
			align		
Headings	h1	first level heading	*standard*	all	11
			align		
	h2	second level heading	*standard*	all	11
			align		
	h3	third level heading	*standard*	all	11
			align		
	h4	fourth level heading	*standard*	all	11
			align		
	h5	fifth level heading	*standard*	all	11
			align		
	h6	sixth level heading	*standard*	all	11
			align		

(continued)

Table 5-1 *(continued)*

Category	Tag	Description	Attributes	DTD	Chapter
Lists	ul	unordered list	*standard*	all	13
			type		
			compact		
	ol	ordered list	*standard*	all	13
			type		
			compact		
			start		
	menu	menu list	*standard*	transitional, frameset	13
			compact		
	dir	directory list	*standard*	transitional, frameset	13
			compact		
	li	list item	*standard*	all	13
\			type		
			value		
	dl	definition list	*standard*	all	13
			compact		
	dt	definition list term	*standard*	all	13
	dd	definition list description	*standard*	all	13
Address	address	addressing information	*standard*	all	11
Horizontal Rule	hr	horizontal rule	*standard*	all	11
			align		
			noshade		
			size		
			width		

Category	Tag	Description	Attributes	DTD	Chapter
Preformatted Text	pre	preformatted text	*standard*	all	11
			width		
			xml:space		
Block-like Quotes	block-quote	lengthy quote	*standard*	all	11
			cite		
Text alignment	center	centered text	*standard*	transitional, frameset	11
Inserted/ Deleted text	ins	inserted text	*standard*	all	11
			cite		
			datetime		
	del	deleted text	*standard*	all	11
			cite		
			datetime		
Anchor	a	hyperlink	*standard*	all	12
			charset		
			type		
			name		
			href		
			hreflang		
			rel		
			rev		
			accesskey		
			shape		
			coords		
			tabindex		
			onfocus		
			onblur		

(continued)

Table 5-1 *(continued)*

Category	Tag	Description	Attributes	DTD	Chapter
			target		
Inline Elements	span	generic inline element	*standard*	all	12
	bdo	bi-directional override	*core*	all	12
			events		
			lang		
			xml:lang		
			dir		
	br	line break	*core*	all	12
			clear		
	em	emphasis	*standard*	all	12
	strong	strong emphasis	*standard*	all	12
	dfn	definition	*standard*	all	12
	code	code	*standard*	all	12
	samp	sample text	*standard*	all	12
	kdb	keyboard text	*standard*	all	12
	var	variable	*standard*	all	12
	cite	citation	*standard*	all	12
	abbr	abbreviation	*standard*	all	12
	acronym	acronym	*standard*	all	12
	q	inline quotation	*standard*	all	12
			cite		
	sub	subscript text	*standard*	all	12
	sup	superscript text	*standard*	all	12
	tt	teletype text	*standard*	all	12
	i	italicized text	*standard*	all	12
	b	boldfaced text	*standard*	all	12

Category	Tag	Description	Attributes	DTD	Chapter
	big	bigger text	*standard*	all	12
	small	smaller text	*standard*	all	12
	u	underlined text	*standard*	transitional, frameset	12
	s	strike through text	*standard*	transitional, frameset	12
	strike	strike-through text	*standard*	transitional, frameset	12
	basefont	base font size	id	transitional, frameset	12
			size		
			color		
			face		
	font	font specifics	*core*	transitional, frameset	12
			internatl		
			size		
			color		
			face		
Object	object	embedded objects	*standard*	all	19
			declare		
			classid		
			codebase		
			data		
			type		
			codetype		
			archive		
			standby		
			height		
			width		

(continued)

Table 5-1 *(continued)*

Category	*Tag*	*Description*	*Attributes*	*DTD*	*Chapter*
			usemap		
			name		
			tabindex		
			align		
			border		
			hspace		
			vspace		
	param	object/applet parameter	id	all	19
			name		
			value		
			valuetype		
			type		
Java applet	applet	embedded java applet	*core*	transitional, frameset	19
			codebase		
			archive		
			code		
			object		
			alt		
			name		
			width		
			height		
			align		
			hspace		
			vspace		
Images	img	embedded image	*standard*	all	12
			src		

Category	Tag	Description	Attributes	DTD	Chapter
			alt		
			name		
			longdesc		
			height		
			width		
			usemap		
			ismap		
			align		
			border		
			hspace		
			vspace		
Client-side maps	map	image map information	*internatl*	all	16
			events		
			id		
			class		
			style		
			title		
			name		
	area	image map area	*standard*	all	16
			shape		
			coords		
			href		
			nohref		
			alt		
			tabindex		
			accesskey		
			onfocus		

(continued)

Table 5-1 *(continued)*

Category	Tag	Description	Attributes	DTD	Chapter
			onblur		
			target		
Forms	form	form container	*standard*	all	17
			action		
			method		
			name		
			enctype		
			onsubmit		
			onreset		
			accept		
			accept-charset		
			target		
	label	form element label	*standard*	all	17
			for		
			accesskey		
			onfocus		
			onblur		
	input	form input element	*standard*	all	17
			type		
			name		
			value		
			checked		
			disabled		
			readonly		
			size		
			maxlength		
			src		
			alt		

Category	Tag	Description	Attributes	DTD	Chapter
			usemap		
			tabindex		
			accesskey		
			onfocus		
			onblur		
			onselect		
			onchange		
			accept		
			align		
	select	drop down list	*standard*	all	17
			name		
			size		
			multiple		
			disabled		
			tabindex		
			onfocus		
			onblur		
			onchange		
	optgroup	select list option group	*standard*	all	17
			disabled		
			label		
	option	select list option	*standard*	all	17
			selected		
			disabled		
			label		
			value		
	textarea	large text box	*standard*	all	17

(continued)

Table 5-1 *(continued)*

Category	Tag	Description	Attributes	DTD	Chapter
			name		
			rows		
			cols		
			disabled		
			readonly		
			tabindex		
			accesskey		
			onfocus		
			onblur		
			onselect		
			onchange		
	fieldset	form elements group	*standard*	all	17
	legend	field set label	*standard*	all	17
			accesskey		
			align		
	button	form button	*standard*	all	17
			name		
			value		
			type		
			disabled		
			tabindex		
			accesskey		
			onfocus		
			onblur		
	isindex	search field	*core*	transitional, frameset	17
			internatl		

Category	Tag	Description	Attributes	DTD	Chapter
			prompt		
Tables	table	table container	*standard*	all	15
			summary		
			width		
			border		
			frame		
			rules		
			cellspacing		
			cellpadding		
			align		
			bgcolor		
	caption	table caption	*standard*	all	15
			align		
	thead	table group header	*standard*	all	15
			align		
			car		
			caroff		
			valign		
	tfoot	table group footer	*standard*	all	15
			align		
			car		
			caroff		
			valign		
	tbody	table group	*standard*	all	15
			align		
			car		
			caroff		
			valign		

(continued)

Table 5-1 *(continued)*

Category	Tag	Description	Attributes	DTD	Chapter
	colgroup	column grouping	*standard*	all	15
			span		
			width		
			align		
			car		
			caroff		
			valign		
	col	table column	*standard*	all	15
			span		
			width		
			align		
			car		
			caroff		
			valign		
	tr	table row	*standard*	all	15
			align		
			car		
			caroff		
			valign		
			bgcolor		
	th	table row header	*standard*	all	15
			abbr		
			axis		
			headers		
			scope		
			rowspan		
			colspan		
			car		

Category	Tag	Description	Attributes	DTD	Chapter
			caroff		
			align		
			valign		
			nowrap		
			bgcolor		
			width		
			height		
	td	table row cell	*standard*	all	15
			abbr		
			axis		
			headers		
			scope		
			rowspan		
			colspan		
			car		
			caroff		
			align		
			valign		
			nowrap		
			bgcolor		
			width		
			height		

Chapter 6

My First XHTML Page

● ●

In This Chapter

▶ Finding tools for building XHTML documents

▶ Identifying your audience

▶ Mapping out your content

▶ Planning a style sheet

▶ Building a simple XHTML document

● ●

XHTML documents are simply Hypertext Markup Language (HTML) documents that conform to the basic rules of XML. You build XHTML documents in the same way you build HTML documents — combining text, elements, and attributes. Of course, because all XML documents must play by a specific set of rules (that is, they must be well formed), all XHTML documents must also be well formed. Your XHTML documents should also conform to the XHTML specification, so your documents are not only well formed, but also valid. In addition to making sure your documents play by XML's rules, you need to put all the same forethought and analysis into your XHTML documents that you would put into HTML documents.

XHTML-Savvy Tools

A good tool can be your best ally in building a document. Even if you're new to the world of Web development, you'll quickly figure out that this is true. A plethora of existing HTML development tools, as well as a rapidly growing field of XML tools, strongly support this claim.

Today, you have trouble finding tools designed specifically to make writing XHTML easier. Instead, you choose from an array of HTML- or XML-editing tools:

✔ You can use a standard HTML editor, such as Dreamweaver or FrontPage, to build HTML documents and convert them to XHTML using HTML Tidy. Chapter 3 includes everything you need to know about this process.

After you convert HTML documents to XHTML, validate them against the XHTML Document Type Definition (DTD) at `http://validator.w3.org` and make necessary corrections to them by hand in a plain-text editor, such as Notepad.

✔ You can use one of the many DTD-driven XML editors to build your pages. Most of these editors apply a DTD, such as the XHTML DTD, to guide your document-building.

We prefer XML editors because

✔ Many HTML editors don't generate valid HTML, so you must clean up any XHTML document you convert from HTML. Then, you must validate that document against the XHTML DTD. This process is time consuming and a bit frustrating — trust us, we've tried it!

✔ If you want to make changes to an XHTML document built with an HTML editor, you must make them by hand or make them in the editor and repeat the entire conversion process. Because XHTML syntax is just different enough from HTML to make things interesting, some HTML editors spit out error messages when they see XHTML. (You know they do that just to make life a bit more difficult for you, don't you?)

✔ XML editors are designed to build XML documents, and XHTML documents are a form of XML. A good XML editor gives warnings if you fail to put quotation marks around an attribute value, or forget to mark an empty element with a closing slash (/). Many XML editors read a DTD and warn you if you try to create markup that breaks the DTD's rules.

Well-formedness and validity are important issues in XHTML. Your documents *will* break if they aren't well formed. They also break if they aren't valid. Most XML editors help make your documents well formed and valid. Therefore, in our not-so-humble opinions, an XML editor is the right tool for this job.

We expect to see XHTML support emerging in upcoming releases of certain HTML editors. If you have a favorite HTML editor and hope to use it to build XHTML, visit that vendor's Web site and see if they have anything to say about support for XHTML. And drop them an e-mail to let them know that you'd like to see XHTML support in the next version their product.

Finding an XML editor

XML editors come in many flavors, with varying price tags. Editors are available for just about every operating system, including UNIX and the Mac OS, but Windows is the most prevalent. You can spend nothing and download a freeware editor or spend over a thousand dollars on high-end XML software. We've found that, although freeware tools get you by, you're better off spending a few dollars to buy a commercial editor if you plan to build more than a few XHTML documents.

If this is your first foray into XML, you probably don't have a dozen different XML editors lying around on your desktop waiting to be used. Of course, because XHTML documents are just text, you can use any application that generates text — from Microsoft Word to SimpleText — to build your documents. But we believe that if you can find tools better suited for the job, you should use them.

One of our favorite XML editors is CLIP!, reasonably priced at $99.95. CLIP! includes a variety of tools to help you build any XML document — with or without a DTD — inside an intuitive interface. We show you how CLIP! deals with XHTML later in the chapter. CLIP!'s biggest drawback is that it runs only on Windows. You can find CLIP! at www.t2000-usa.com.

Java is the programming language of choice for many XML editors. To run any of these editors, you need a copy of a Java Runtime Environment (JRE), which is available from www.javasoft.com. Before you download and install a Java-based XML editor, read the installation instructions on the vendor's Web site and find out what version of the JRE you need to install and if it's packaged with the editor.

There a couple of excellent online resources for XML software:

- ✔ XMLSoftware.com at www.xmlsoftware.com/editors/ lists most of currently available editors with brief descriptions and pointers to product Web pages. What we like most about this site is that the platform information for each editor is included in its description. If you're looking for an editor to run on some particular platform, you can easily skip those editors that don't support your chosen platform and spend your time investigating those that do.

- ✔ Robin Cover's SGML/XML public software page at www.oasis-open.org/cover/publicSW.html focuses primarily on freeware and shareware tools, so the list is more limited than the one at XMLSoftware.com. But you can be guaranteed that anything your find on Cover's site won't cause you to dig very deep into your wallet.

The biggest hassle in evaluating software is not the 30-day evaluation period, but the length of time it takes to download a 6 or 8MB file over a slow Internet connection. To make it easier for you to find an XML editor to meet your needs, the CD that comes with this book includes trial versions of a variety of commercial XML editors, as well as freeware and shareware editors. We encourage you to install them, play with them, and then keep — and, of course, pay for, if necessary — the ones you like best.

How XML editors handle XHTML documents

Most XML editors are DTD-agnostic — they work with any properly written XML DTD, including the XHTML DTD. Any XML editor makes sure that your XHTML documents are well formed, but you make sure they're valid, too. Check these tools:

- **An XML editor that reads DTDs and validates against them.** Most do, but some don't. Make sure any editor you choose works with DTDs.

- **The XHTML DTD.** Actually, three different XHTML DTDs exist, as described in Chapter 5, so you need to decide which to validate against. We use the XHTML Transitional DTD most frequently because it's very compatible with HTML 4.0. The XHTML DTDs are available for download at www.w3.org/TR/xhtml1/#dtds.

Each XML editor has its own command to open a DTD for validation. Check each editor's help files for exact instructions on loading a DTD. In our experiences with XML editing software, we haven't had much difficulty getting DTDs up and running, and we're notorious for not reading documentation.

The following two sections show you how two different XML editors display an XHTML document and enable you to validate and work with the document.

CLIP! XML Editor

The CLIP! XML Editor from Techno2000 has three different views for any given XML document:

- **Text Mode:** Displays the entire text of an XML document.

  Text Mode acts much like a standard text editor. You can see markup and text, which are displayed in different colors so you can tell them apart.

- **Structure Mode:** Displays a tree of the elements in an XML document.

  Structure Mode gives you a totally different view of the XHTML document — as a tree of related pieces and parts (usually called nodes).

> ✔ **Document Type Definition:** Displays the DTD for a document; this view is not available if a DTD isn't associated with the document.

There are advantages to being able to look at an XHTML document's structure. You can see how the different elements of your document relate to one another and expand and collapse different elements to hide document text, or you can just examine elements by themselves. This is particularly nice when you're trying to view a large document.

Because CLIP! reads the XHTML DTD while it displays the document, it actually interprets the DTD and guides you in your document development. When you click an element in the tree, the *Component Manager* to the right of the main window shows you which elements you can legally nest inside that element. The *Interaction Manager* beneath the main window has several tabs that show you which attributes you can use with an element, store content for an element, show you the results of a search you perform on elements and attributes, and display any validation warnings.

The Structure Mode and Text Mode in CLIP! don't automatically update when you make a change to one or the other of the views. You have to click a button to build XML from the elements you add to the Structure Mode or validate the document to have new items in the Text Mode appear in the Structure Mode view.

If you're familiar with a DTD, such as XHTML, you can use the Text Mode for most of your coding work and then use the Structure Mode to check your work. However, if you're not familiar with a DTD, try working in Structure Mode to learn the DTD's ins and outs and then view the document in Text Mode to see the final markup. Either way, CLIP! is a great tool for working with any XML document, and because it reads in a DTD, you can use it to build well-formed and valid XHTML documents as well.

XMetaL 1.2

XMetaL from SoftQuad, the makers of HoTMetaL, sits more in the mid-range price zone. Weighing in right around $500, it's definitely an investment in a software tool. SoftQuad is an established organization and its HTML editor is a good tool, so you can count on future releases of XMetaL and good tech support.

XMetaL's approach to document display is a bit different from the one you saw in CLIP!, providing you with three different display options:

> ✔ **Normal:** Displays document text without the markup around it.

> ✔ **Tags On:** Displays document text and markup.

> ✔ **Plain Text:** Displays a document in the same way a text editor would.

In the real world, the terms tag and element are still used interchangeably; therefore, the Tags On display really displays what we call elements in this book.

The nice thing about XMetaL's different views is that you can see as little or as much information about the markup in your document as you want.

The Normal display is great if you want to edit text independent of markup. All the views allow you to have the tags window open on the right of the screen. In this window, you can toggle between two tabs: Used and All. The Used tab shows all the elements you've used so far in the document. The All tab builds an element list based on your DTD (XHTML, in this case) and is context sensitive so that it shows only those elements you can legally use based on the location of your cursor in the document. If your cursor is within the `<head>`...`</head>` element, the only element listed on the All tab is the `<title>`...`</title>` element. This feature helps you build valid documents.

The Tags On display allows you to see both your text and your markup but keeps the two separate. If you hold your mouse over a tag, you see what attributes you set for the tag, and if you right-click the tag, you get a pop-up menu with a variety of options, including inserting an element and inspecting the attributes associated with the tag.

The Plain Text display looks like a typical text editor, but it has a variety of features you won't find in any old editor. The context-sensitive attribute lists and tag lists on the right side of the screen still display as you move your cursor from tag to tag. This view also lets you hack every last detail of your XHTML document yourself.

In addition to the different views and tag-related tools, XMetaL has the following features:

- Built-in validation
- A tag-aware, spell-checking tool
- Tools for building basic style sheets

If you're going to be doing large amounts of XHTML work, you may want to consider an investment in XMetaL.

CLIP! and XMetaL are two examples of the standard XML editors that you can use with XHTML. Before you do much more work with XHTML, take the time to find an editor that you like; it can make your page-building activities much more productive and help you avoid every-day human error (well, for the most part).

Defining Your Audience

In high school English class, you probably learned that the first question you always ask when you start to write anything is "Who is the audience?" This basic question is at the core of all decisions you must make about what information to place on a Web page and how it should be displayed. Before you begin tagging text and worrying about interface design, you need to identify your audience and make it the target for all subsequent page-building work you do.

Nearly everyone who picks up on Web design wants to charge right out and build "killer" Web pages on the fly — an easy way to kill a Web page before it even gets to fly. If you worry too much about the wrong stuff — graphics, multimedia, and other jazzy effects, for example — you loose track of both your audience and your content. Then all your hard work will be for naught.

The first thing you need to figure out is who will be visiting your Web page. You want to create pages that people can use, enjoy, and want to revisit. If you don't know who's going to visit your Web site and what they expect to find when they get there, why build it in the first place?

Now, don't get us wrong. Many folks out there don't really care who visits their sites. Many pages on the Web are personal pages — not so fondly referred to as *vanity* pages — that don't contain much content of interest to everyday people. Although vanity pages are great tools for people learning to create Web sites, they really don't make for the best Web presence.

If you have more serious reasons for building your Web site and hence have some substantial content to offer your readers, then you're on your way to building a good page. When thinking about your audience, ask yourself these questions:

- Who do you want to attract to your site?
- How can you attract them and keep them there?
- How can you emphasize your site's message?

Of course, to get accurate answers to these questions, you need the resources to do market research — which many people don't have. Therefore, you have to rely on your good judgment and make educated guesses about what visitors want on your site. The fact that you're even thinking about your audience as you build your pages will make your site user-centric and much more prone to success.

You can find out a great deal about your audience without spending anything more than time. Identify your target audience and then begin visiting their favorite haunts in both the real world and in cyberspace. Listening to live conversations and reading print conversations can give you lots of insight into how the members of your audience think, what they like, and what they don't like.

After you have a sense of your audience's needs and wants, you need to ask yourself these questions:

- ✔ How does your content address their needs and wants?
- ✔ Is there a clear niche in their world that my content can fill?
- ✔ How can you hook them into your content and fill the niche? In other words, how can you be different from everyone else out there trying to fill the same niche?

If you can answer these questions, you're almost ready to deliver real content to real users. You can have a great understanding of XHTML, build perfectly formed and valid documents, and still have a Web site bomb if you can't identify your users and figure out how your content relates to them.

Mapping the Content

If you decide to use XHTML to build a Web page and you've thought long and hard about who your audience is and how you can help them, you probably have a handle on how your page will take shape and what its content will be. As your content and your page move from an amorphous idea to concrete code, always keep in mind what you want the page to do for you and for your audience.

To get your page to speak your users' language (well enough for effective emphasis), you must be fairly fluent in two languages: your native tongue and XHTML. Therefore, you should call upon the basic writing skills laid before you long ago. The first of these skills is to create an outline before you start writing (or creating XHTML).

One of the great benefits of outlining an XHTML page, in addition to organizing your thoughts and content, is that the outline gives you a good idea of what elements you'll use and what kind of links you need to make to other pages on your site and on other Web sites. The code you need to write to build your page literally flows from the outline, and therefore, you have fewer reworks and changes. As you organize your content, try these techniques:

- ✔ Identify the major topics and elements.
- ✔ Consider how your major topics relate to one another.
- ✔ Surf the Web to find other resources that relate to your topics.

- ✔ Identify graphics and other multimedia that compliment your content.

- ✔ Sketch out different navigation schemes that can help users move through your content effectively and efficiently.

- ✔ Use your outline as a blueprint that you can refer to as you write your XHTML code.

After you build an outline of your content — keeping your audience in mind the entire time, of course — you're ready to think about the look and feel of your page. XML strives to separate form from content, so you should use a style sheet to drive the form of your pages and not formatting elements, such as the `<font>` element. Because style sheets work hand in hand with markup, you want to plan your style sheet in advance and tweak it as you go along.

Planning Style Sheets

Although XHTML markup tells everything about your content, a style sheet tells everything about how your content should look. Because you know your audience, how your content meets their needs, and the outline your content, you should have a good idea of how you want that content to look when your audience sees it. This is a great time to plan that look and feel because it has a big impact on how you use XHTML to describe your content.

We don't go into details about how to build a style sheet in this chapter. Instead, we devote all of Chapter 8 to discussing style sheet conventions and usage. For now, your biggest concern is to think about how you want your pages to look, not how you're going to make them look that way.

The way you arrange your content is influenced by your audience and your goals for the page. You may want your page to influence people or to educate them, or you may want to build a site where visitors can shop or access services. The ultimate goal of your page dictates much of your page's look and feel. Here are some tips to help you narrow down how you want your page to look:

- ✔ If you want to build an e-commerce or services page, try to grab user's attention with eye-catching visuals and a sharp look. Navigation is extremely important on these sites because people want to find information quickly, and when they do decide to buy, they want to be able to make purchases easily.

- ✔ If you want to build an educational site, reduce the number of graphics and other multimedia and focus on the content. Your visitors don't want to be distracted. They want to get to the heart of the matter.

If you have a good idea of the goal of your page, you can sketch out a basic look and feel for it. You can use a page layout program to play with element positions and colors. You can also use a good WYSIWYG HTML editor, such as Dreamweaver, to build an HTML template for your page to see how it looks in a Web browser. Many WYSIWYG tools also have built-in support for style sheets so that you can build a framework for your style sheet as your build your mock HTML page and use that framework as a basis for your final XHTML style sheet.

No matter how stylistically complex or simple you want your page to be, thinking about look and feel before you dive into code development can save revision time in the long run. If you have a framework for your style sheet, you can update it and revise it as you go along, making the building of the final style sheet a much quicker process.

A Simple XHTML Document

The title of this chapter is "My First XHTML Page," and we don't want to end without helping you build your first XHTML page. Here's some sample code for the quintessential first exercise for any coding activity:

```
<?xml version="1.0" encoding="UTF-8" standalone="yes"?>
<!DOCTYPE html SYSTEM "../DTDs/xhtml1-transitional.dtd">
<html>
  <head>
    <title>My First XHTML Document</title>
  </head>
  <body>
    <h1 align="center">My First XHTML Document</h1>
    <hr/>
    <p>This is my first XHTML document. It looks very
        much like other HTML documents.</p>
  </body>
</html>
```

Open your favorite text editor — or download one of the XML editors we discuss in this chapter — and type this code into it.

The great thing about XHTML is that most browsers display it in the same way they do HTML. Although you may not want to convert all your old HTML documents to XHTML, consider developing all your new ones in XHTML because XML is the direction in which the Web is heading.

Chapter 7

Elements and Attributes

. . . .

In This Chapter

▶ Scrutinizing XHTML element syntax

▶ Categorizing XHTML elements

▶ Keeping up with attribute rules

▶ Understanding common attributes

. . . .

*I*f you want a no-holds-barred look at XHTML markup, you've come to the right place. In this chapter, we talk some serious turkey about XHTML syntax to make sure that you can keep up with all the gory details. We also establish some categories for what XHTML can do and then group markup elements into meaningful categories (to make them easier to use and eventually master).

XHTML Rules and Regulations

In addition to the formal syntax for XHTML that we use throughout the book (because XHTML is a very finicky language), the markup language itself has some general properties that are worth covering before you encounter the elements directly.

You may already know quite a bit about XHTML syntax and layout. If you do, yeehaw! However, you also need to know quite a bit of additional information, some of which we touch on in the following sections. This additional information includes a discussion of some goofy characters and such that aren't part of XHTML itself, but that are necessary to explain XHTML formally.

Whitespace

XHTML element names must be contiguous. In other words, you can't insert extra blanks within an element name or you end up confusing the browser — not to mention your readers.

This requirement means that `</body>` is a valid closing tag for a document body, but that none of the following is legal:

```
</b ody>
</bod y>
</bo dy>
```

We hope that you get the idea: Don't use blanks (spaces) inside element names, except where you use a blank space deliberately to separate an element name from an attribute name (for example, `<img src="picture.gif">` is legal, but `<imgsrc="picture.gif">` is not).

When assigning values to attributes, however, spaces are okay. Therefore, all four of the following variants for this `src` assignment are legal:

```
<img src="picture.gif">
<!@hy In the previous line, there are no spaces before or
        after the = sign @hy>
<img src = "picture.gif">
<!@hy In the previous line, there are spaces before and after
        the = sign @hy>
<img src= "picture.gif">
<!@hy In the previous line, there is no space before the =
        sign, and there is one after the = sign @hy>
<img src ="picture.gif">
<!@hy In the previous line, there is one space before the =
        sign, and none after the = sign @hy>
```

Where one space is legal, multiple spaces are legal. Don't get carried away with what's legal or not, though — try to make your XHTML documents as readable as possible and everything else should flow naturally.

You may have noticed that we snuck some additional XHTML markup into the preceding code example. After each `<img>` element line, we inserted readable XHTML comments to describe what occurred on the preceding line. To open a comment, you use the string `<!@hy`; to end, or close, the comment, you use `@hy>`. See Chapter 10 for more information about XHTML comments.

Defaults

Attributes supply additional information, such as the direction of text (left to right or right to left) or if a table should have a border. Lucky for you, those attributes also have default values. The default of an attribute provides a way for the browser to decide what to assume when an attribute is not supplied for a particular element. For example, the `<table>` element creates a table with a border. The only element you use is the `<table>` element; you get a border free of charge.

Here's another example. You use the `dir` attribute with almost any element to set the text direction to either `ltr` (left to right) or `rtl` (right to left). Having to set the text direction to `ltr` for every element would be extremely tedious. You're in luck — the default for the `dir` attribute is `ltr`. Wow, that saved you lots of work! However, if you wanted to include a language, such as Hebrew, that isn't read from left to right, then you would use the right to left (`rtl`) attribute value. (See Chapter 11 for more information on the `dir` attribute.)

Two different types of default values exist: one that the specification clearly sets and one that the browser sets. If the specification sets a default, the browser follows suit. However, don't jump to too many conclusions, because if the specification does not specify a default, many browsers take it upon themselves to do that for you. Therefore, you should always check your attributes.

Nesting properly

Sometimes, you may want (or need) to insert an element within another element (which is called *nesting*). For example, you have to nest the `<title>` element within the `<head>` element.

On the other hand, you may want a few words within a sentence already marked for special emphasis to be the trigger for a hyperlink. For example, the entire heading "Contact LANWrights" draws the reader's attention if it's in boldface. However, you want only the word *LANWrights* to be hyperlinked to another XHTML document listing relevant contacts. You're in luck. We show you how to do this in the following paragraphs.

When the nesting instinct strikes you, the only rule is to close first what you opened last. For example, the element `<a href="contact.xhtml">` . . . `</a>` provides a way of linking text to another XHTML document. If this phrase occurred within strongly emphasized text, `<strong>` . . . `</strong>`, you have only one correct way to handle it.

First, the following is the incorrect way to handle this hyperlink:

```
<strong>Contact
        <a href="econtacts.xhtml">LANWrights</strong></a>
```

The correct way to handle the hyperlink is like so:

```
<strong>Contact
        <a href="econtacts.xhtml">LANWrights</a></strong>
```

As shown, you close the nested `<a>` element with its mate before you close out the `<strong>` heading. Some browsers may let you violate this rule, but others may behave unpredictably if you don't open and close tags in the correct order. However, regardless of what browsers allow, not closing your tags in the correct order is illegal according to the XHTML specification.

You can't nest all elements within any ol' element. For example, within `<title> . . . </title>`, you specify information that shows up only on a window title, rather than on a particular Web page. Text and layout controls clearly do not apply here (and are cheerfully ignored by some browsers, while making others curl up and die). Note that you have to obey the rules as to which elements you can nest within which elements. On the CD, we've included an interactive tool that magically predicts the allowed children for the element of your dreams. Open the xhtmlfd/xhtml4dum.htm folder and open applet.htm to check it out.

Always look back to the left as you start closing elements you already opened. Close the closest one first, then the next closest, and so on. Check the element details with our interactive tool found on the CD to find out which elements you can nest within your outermost open element. If the element you want to use doesn't appear on the okay list, you cannot legally nest it within the element in question. So, don't even try it! Close what you must close and then open the element you need.

Keeping your elements in the right nests keeps your readers' browsers from getting confused! It also makes sure that you create only good-looking Web pages.

XHTML Elements at a Glance

XHTML elements are code words (or markup) that tell a computer program, such as a Web browser or a word processor, how to format the text in an XHTML document. When a Web browser or a word processor reads an XHTML document, the program determines the formatting by watching for specific markup and punctuation — the program assumes everything else is the actual text of your document.

Browsers and word processors assume that you remember the following rules of XHTML syntax:

✔ Tags use left and right angle brackets, like this:

```
<tag>
```

✔ Nonempty elements must be closed. For example, `<head>` marks the beginning of a document heading block, and `</head>` marks the end. (Note the use of the forward slash before the closing tag name. The forward slash tells the browser that this tag is closing.) You must always include closing tags in nonempty elements.

Your browser considers all the text that occurs between opening and closing tags as the content for that element and handles that text appropriately. Because the majority of XHTML elements work this way, we flag all the possible exceptions when we introduce them.

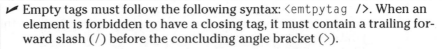

✔ Empty tags must follow the following syntax: `<emtpytag />`. When an element is forbidden to have a closing tag, it must contain a trailing forward slash (/) before the concluding angle bracket (>).

Older browsers do not recognize the XHTML empty tag syntax unless you include a space before the trailing forward slash and angle bracket (for example, `<img src="graphic.gif" />`). Although new browsers don't have a problem with or without the space, older browsers may get tripped up. So be safe and always use the following syntax: `<empty-tag />`.

✔ XHTML elements (and attributes) must be written in lowercase. (Note that most attribute values are not case sensitive but if they are, we tell you.)

XHTML uses the HTML 4.01 Document Type Definition (now known as the XHTML 1.0 DTD or just DTD), which means that tags have already been named for you. When the authors of the DTD named these elements, they chose to use lowercase letters; therefore, you must do that, too.

✔ Elements can sometimes take attributes to do the following:

- Define data sources or destinations
- Specify URLs
- Further specify the characteristics of the text to which an element is applied

To read more about attribute rules and syntax, see the section on attributes later in this chapter.

Tag versus element

You may be confused about the differences between an element and a tag. We throw the terms around constantly throughout the book, and you see the terms used in most XHTML discussions.

So here's the skinny:

✔ A *tag* is just a tag (such as `<head>`)

✔ An *element* includes

- An *opening tag* (such as `<head>`)
- The *content* of the element
- The *closing* tag (or in the case of empty elements, just the empty tag and its content).

An empty element is an element for which an end tag is forbidden; in other words, it doesn't have a closing tag.

When you want to refer to `<head>` . . . `</head>`, you would simply say the `<head>` element. However, when you're referring specifically to the opening tag of the `<head>` element, you would say the `<head>` opening tag.

Throughout this book, the term *element* refers to general usage of XHTML tag names. The term *tag* is used when referring to a single opening or closing tag.

XHTML categories

Okay, you want to know about all these elements we keep twittering about. Gotcha covered:

- ✔ In most of the following chapters of this book, the chapter begins by introducing you to a group of elements; the rest of that chapter shows you how to spin them. If you read straight through from here to the end of the book, you cover the basic everyday stuff first, then the tricky stuff later.

- ✔ Appendix A lists all the standard XHTML elements in alphabetical order. For each element, we tell you what it does.

Before we take you through each XHTML element found in this book, we want to introduce them to you grouped by category. These categories help to explain how and when you can use those elements, and what functions those elements provide:

- ✔ **Document structure:** Document structure elements provide a logical structure for the document. Before any other elements appear, document structure elements must be present. (See Chapter 10.)

- ✔ **Text tags:** Text elements provide a logical structure for content of a document. This structure may or may not alter that content's display properties. (See Chapter 11.)

- ✔ **Lists:** You use list elements to define a variety of different lists, such as bulleted lists and numbered lists. (See Chapter 13.)

- ✔ **Tables:** Table elements define the structure and layout of tables. (A table is where you sit and eat your dinner. Just kidding; a table is data presented in tabular format, with configurable height and width for each entry.) You can use tables to arrange data or to aid page layout and design. (See Chapter 15.)

- ✔ **Links:** Link elements create connections — such as hyperlinks, image links, and links to style sheets — between Web resources. (See Chapter 12.)

- ✔ **Inclusions:** You use these elements to include non-XHTML items, such as Java applets and multimedia files, within Web documents. (See Chapter 19.)

✔ **Style sheet elements:** These XHTML elements define how the browser renders content. Note that users can set browser preferences, such as font settings, therefore, you can't always ensure exactly how the data will be rendered. (See Chapter 8.)

A style sheet tells everything about how your content should look. In other words, it's a template for your document.

✔ **Presentation elements:** Presentation elements alter the display of content by affecting visual properties, such as font styles and horizontal rules. (See Chapter 11.)

✔ **Frames:** Frame elements define and control frames within the display area of a browser. Technically, a single browser window is a framed display. Using XHTML, you can create multiple frames (Web documents) in a single window. (See Chapter 18.)

✔ **Forms:** Form elements control the input of data from a user and transmission of that data to a background Common Gateway Interface (CGI) or similar application, which specifies how browsers send information back to servers. (See Chapter 17.)

✔ **Scripts:** You use these elements to embed programming language scripts into Web documents. (See Chapter 19.)

Attributing Your Sources

An *attribute* is a named characteristic associated with a specific element. In XHTML, the following must happen:

✔ Attributes must take a value.

✔ That value must be enclosed in quotation marks.

You can use either single or double quotation marks; however, we suggest that you be consistent and use one or the other in case someone views your source code. Consistency makes the code look neater to you and your users.

This is how we represent attributes throughout this book: `attribute="value"`. Where `value` is typically enclosed in quotes — single (`' '`) or double (`" "`) — and may be one of the following:

✔ **URL:** A uniform resource locator, `"url"`, (which is an online address a specific document)

✔ **Name:** A user-supplied name, probably for an input field (`"name"`)

✔ **Number:** A user-supplied numeric value (`"number"` or `"%"`)

✔ **Text:** User-supplied text (`"text"`)

✓ **X or Y or Z:** Where the attribute value should be one value chosen from a set of fixed values (which we list with the set value specified; for example, `"top"` or `"bottom"`)

✓ **#rrggbb:** Hexadecimal notation for a color value (`"rrggbb"`)

✓ **Color:** A named color (`"color"`)

There are special cases in which the attribute value is the same as the attribute name, for example `ismap="ismap"`. Setting the attribute to equal itself is necessary for the syntax to strictly adhere to the XML specification and the XHTML DTD.

Common Attributes

In an effort to save trees — and because this is the way the W3C does it — we list three sets of common attributes that are used with more than 60 percent of all the XHTML elements. Instead of repeatedly listing these attributes page after page after page, you'll find a brief description of each one in the following sections.

Core attributes

XHTML's *core attributes* provide several ways to label an element and its content uniquely and to define style information directly to that element's content. These attributes apply to all XHTML elements, without exception:

✓ `id="name"`: A document-wide identifier that you can use to give an XHTML element a unique identifier within a document.

✓ `class="text"`: An attribute that assigns a class name(s) to indicated that the element belongs to a specific class. Multiple elements may be given the same class name(s).

✓ `style="text"`: An attribute that provides rendering information specific to this element, such as the color, size, and font specifics.

✓ `title="text"`: An attribute that defines an advisory title to display additional help. You can generate balloon text around hyperlinks and graphics using this attribute.

Language attributes

XHTML's *language attributes* apply to most elements (especially those that contain text) to identify the language (such as English, French, and so on) in which the content of the element appears and to instruct programs or robots

in what direction to read an element's content. By default, the language setting (and its default direction) from the XHTML prolog (everything from the
document type declaration to the opening body tag) for the document
applies here, if these elements are not used — and they seldom are!

- ✔ `dir="ltr"` **or** `"rtl"`: Indicates the direction the text is read in — left to
  right or right to left (for example, English is read from left to right, and
  Hebrew is read from right to left)
- ✔ `lang="name"`: Specifies the language that the element and its contents
  are written in

Event attributes (a.k.a. intrinsic events)

XHTML's *event attributes* name specific, or intrinsic, events that scripts and
programs must recognize and respond to on a Web page. For example,
`onmouseover` names the event that occurs when an on-screen mouse cursor
travels over a specific object.

With XHTML, numerous intricate event triggers support programming and
scripting on Web pages. When an intrinsic event is tied to an XHTML element,
a script runs when a user acts. The user doesn't have to click a hyperlink.
The user simply performs the event and the script is called.

Because many elements have intrinsic events, remember that intrinsic events
are scripting related. Table 7.1 shows which intrinsic events can be used with
which markup elements.

Table 7-1	Which Intrinsic Events Can Be Used with Which Markup Elements
Intrinsic Events	*Markup Elements*
onrese, onsubmit	\<form\>
onload, onunload	\<frameset\>, \<body\>
onchange, onselect	\<input\>, \<select\>, \<textarea\>
onblur, onfocus	\<button\>, \<input\>, \<label\>, \<select\>, \<textarea\>

(continued)

Table 7-1 *(continued)*

Intrinsic Events	Markup Elements
onclick, ondblclick, onkeydown, onkeypress, onkeyup, onmousedown, onmousemove, onmouseout, onmouseover, and onmouseup	\<a\>, \<abbr\>, \<acronym\>, \<address\>, \<b\>, \<big\>, \<blockquote\>, \<body\>, \<button\>, \<caption\>, \<center\>, \<cite\>, \<code\>, \<col\>, \<colgroup\>, \<dd\>, \<del\>, \<dfn\>, \<dir\>, \<div\>, \<dl\>, \<dt\>, \<em\>, \<fieldset\>, \<form\>, \<h*\>, \<hr\>, \<i\>, \<img\>, \<input\>, \<ins\>, \<kbd\>, \<label\>, \<legend\>, \<li\>, \<link\>, \<menu\>, \<object\>, \<ol\>, \<option\>, \<p\>, \<pre\>, \<q\>, \<s\>, \<samp\>, \<select\>, \<small\>, \<span\>, \<strike\>, \<strong\>, \<sub\>, \<sup\>, \<table\>, \<tbody\>, \<td\>, \<textarea\>, \<tfoot\>, \<th\>, \<thead\>, \<tr\>, \<tt\>, \<u\>, \<ul\>, \<var\>

This cool technology helps you add interactivity to Web pages in a relatively simple way and is well worth exploring after you get your feet firmly planted in XHTML land.

Some browsers, namely Netscape Navigator, support only a small number of intrinsic events.

Rather than include code snippets and screen shots, we want you to see XHTML at work for yourself. So we include some sample code for elements and attributes, whenever possible, on the CD-ROM. Just open the file list in your browser under the Examples section to see how element information is rendered. To view the XHTML, choose View⇨Source (or something similar) in your browser or open the file with a text editor. As you read each chapter of *XHTML For Dummies,* you can identify the examples you want to see.

Deprecated Means Bye-Bye

Throughout this book, many presentational elements and attributes are *deprecated.* Deprecated elements and attributes will be excluded from future versions of the specification. So, deprecating an element or attribute is a polite way of saying, "Hey, stop what you're doing and use style sheets instead!" To read more about using style sheets, see Chapter 8.

The reason elements become deprecated is because the folks at the World Wide Web Consortium (the authors of the XHTML specification) want to separate presentation from function. The best way to do this is to use style sheets for presentation and stick with XHTML for the structure.

Chapter 8

Styling XHTML with CSS

● ●

In This Chapter

▶ Introducing style sheets

▶ Building CSS style rules

▶ Linking style sheets to XHTML documents

▶ Utilizing CSS resources on the Web

● ●

A common theme throughout this book — as well as in the world of XHTML and XML in general — is that markup should not be used to direct layout; you should separate content from formatting whenever possible. This means that much of the focus on XHTML surrounds its descriptive capabilities and the issues of layout and design are left for another mechanism to address (as is right and proper when dealing with markup). The mechanism for specifying layout and design for XHTML documents is *style sheets*.

The gist of how style works on the Web is this: A style sheet's specification combines with users' personal settings to make a Web document display "properly." Of course, the term *properly* has a variety of connotations, but most often refers to the document developer's sense of how the document should be displayed.

Style sheets are important enough that the W3C has devoted an entire section of its Web site to this topic. You can find style sheet information there, plus a collection of links for further study. Look this information up at `www.w3.org/Style/`.

In this chapter, we give an introduction to the concept of style, describe Cascading Style Sheets (CSS), and provide a solid overview of the basics of style sheet syntax so you can see what's going on in any given style sheet.

We don't go into gobs of detail about how to make style sheets of your own in this book. Although style sheet syntax is pretty straightforward, the issues surrounding the development and use of style sheets — browser support, interface design, and platform issues to name a few — are fairly complicated. Not that we think you can't tackle them successfully, but the ins and outs of style sheets are simply too large to go into in a single chapter.

Why Add Style?

If you've worked extensively with HTML, you may be wondering why you need style sheets for XHTML. After all, you don't have to use a style sheet with an HTML document to make it display in a Web browser (although you *can* use style sheets with HTML).

HTML was originally designed to be a simple markup language that didn't include elements to direct display, such as font and text decoration controls. However, early in the history of HTML, developers began clamoring for more and better ways to control the display of their pages in Web browsers. The simplest solution was to add more tags to HTML and that's what happened. Of course, adding formatting tags to HTML pretty much violates the basic premise of markup, but it happened anyway.

XHTML represents a return to the theory of separating content from display. This means that to use XHTML correctly, you should use XHTML tags only for describing your content and use a style sheet to format your content. There are actually several advantages to this path of document development, as the next few sections illustrate.

Adding form to function

XML (and the XHTML vocabulary created according to its specification) is a highly functional language. However, neither XML nor its various vocabularies are intended to describe *how* content should be formatted. Instead, they are designed to describe the *roles* that content plays in a document.

We all know that form is often as important as function and that, more often than not, form supplements function. Take a look at Figure 8-1. It's a plain line of text: 12-point Times New Roman with no bells or whistles. As far as anyone can tell, it's just a bunch of characters.

Figure 8-1:
A plain line
of text
doesn't tell
much about
its function.

Now take a look at Figure 8-2. It's the same line of text, but now it's in 36-point Arial and centered on the page. The size and alignment of the text make its function clearer. Most likely, this line of text isn't just some text but is instead a title for the page or a title for a section.

Figure 8-2:
Text size
and
alignment
give a clue
to the text's
function.

Form and function often walk hand in hand, and you'll have many reasons to closely control the form of your documents so they can convey the function of each and every bit of content. Of course, you could do this with deprecated XHTML tags, but what happens if one document needs to have many forms for a variety of functions? You don't really want to build a whole collection of layouts for one document do you? Read on.

One document, many uses

One of the best things about XHTML is that it's highly portable. You can send one XHTML document from system to system, and even application to application, without changing it. This means you don't need to create multiple versions of your content.

The initial separation of form from function makes XHTML documents even more portable. You can write one XHTML document and then write multiple style sheets for it. You may be thinking why would I want more than one style sheet? The reason is so you can take advantage of the particular mediums you're designing for. For example, you could prepare one style sheet for putting the XHTML document on the Web, another style sheet for printing the XHTML document, and yet a third for displaying the document on a PalmPilot or mobile phone. You still have one document, but you've built four separate displays for it, and you needn't to change the XHTML document at all!

By using XHTML to describe a document's content and style sheets to drive its display, you need only make changes to one document to change all forms of display. After the document is updated, your content is also updated in whatever forms it can be displayed. This means less work for you and improved consistency of content. It's a win-win situation. In fact, it seldom gets much better than this in the topsy-turvy world of markup languages!

A great example of how you can use different style sheets to affect the display of a single document is found at the W3C's core style pages. To further the rapid development and implementation of style sheets, the W3C put together a collection of style sheets that anyone can use (see the "Implementing CSS here and now sidebar"). Figure 8-3 shows how a document called "XML, Java and the future of the Web" looks when the *Steely* style sheet is applied to it.

Are you ready for a totally different version of the exact same document? Check out Figure 8-4 to see how the same document is displayed when the *Modernist* style sheet is applied to it.

There's nothing up our sleeves, really. It's the magic of style sheets that made the same document display quite differently.

Consistency is a good thing

The last section hinted at the fact that a style sheet can help you maintain consistency among documents. A style sheet defines design and layout information for documents. Usually, style sheets also specify fonts, colors, indentation, kerning, leading, margins, and even page dimensions for any document that invokes them.

To see how style sheets promote consistency, step away from the electronic world and into the paper world for a minute. In the publishing world, style sheets are indispensable because they enable numerous people to collaborate. All participants can work at their own systems, independently of other team members. When the pieces of a project are brought together, the final product derives a consistent look and feel (or design and layout, if you prefer "typographically correct" language). That's because a common template — what style sheets are often called in the print industry — ensures a common definition for the resulting document.

Consistency is a highly desirable characteristic in final products for both print and electronic (online) documents. Therefore, the W3C has made a gallant effort to incorporate such consistency on the Web by introducing style sheets. With the use of Web style sheets, an entire site can look nearly the same on every platform, within any browser that supports style sheets. You write one or two style sheets that apply to each and every page, and your worries about consistency are over.

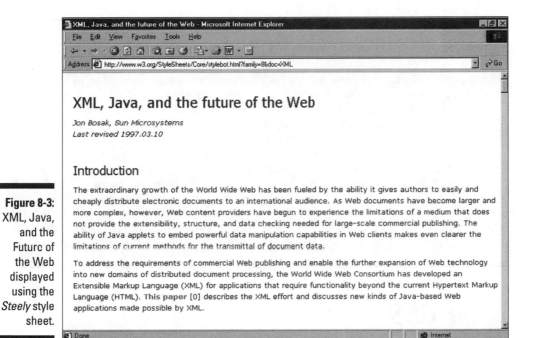

Figure 8-3:
XML, Java,
and the
Future of
the Web
displayed
using the
Steely style
sheet.

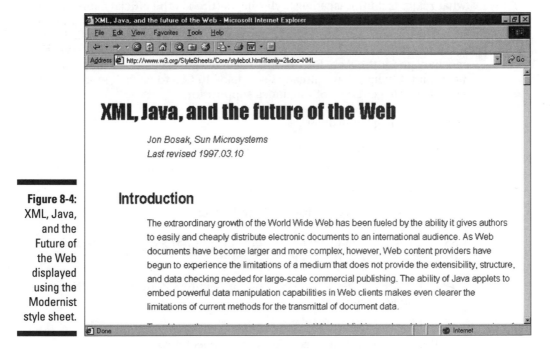

Figure 8-4:
XML, Java,
and the
Future of
the Web
displayed
using the
Modernist
style sheet.

Implementing CSS here and now

So you want to use CSS right now, but you don't have the time to learn a new set of syntax rules. Not a problem! Many of the Web page development tools available, such as Dreamweaver (www.macromedia.com) and HomeSite (www.allaire.com), come with CSS support. There are also a whole bunch of development tools designed specifically for building style sheets. Check out the W3C's list at www.w3.org/Style/CSS/#editors.

If you want a truly slick and quick CSS implementation, visit the W3C's core styles page. The W3C gathered input from the world's foremost style sheet experts and created a pre-built set of style sheets that anyone can use immediately. The W3C Core Styles page at www.w3.org/StyleSheets/Core shows you how to add the style sheets to you pages and provides a nice interface for testing each style sheet before you use it with your pages. If you're looking for a down and dirty way to get started with style sheets, this site is it.

Meet CSS

So if the business of adding form to function is out of the realm of markup, what realm is it in? Cascading Style Sheets (CSS) is the official name for the XHTML style sheet tool. Currently, CSS is in its second version (CSS2); however, the current Web browsers better support the first version of CSS — aptly referred to as CSS1. CSS1 was a good, solid shot at building a style sheet mechanism for the Web. But, as you may have guessed, it was only a preliminary shot. Changes have already been made to CSS to make it more robust — enter CSS2. In general, CSS1 includes support for:

- ✔ Controlling list display
- ✔ Defining background colors and images
- ✔ Directing many aspects of text layout, including alignment and spacing
- ✔ Setting margins and borders
- ✔ Specifying font type, size, color, and effects

CSS2 improves the implementation of many of CSS1's components and expanded on CSS1. CSS2 includes support for:

- ✔ Automatically generating content for counters, footers, and other standard page elements
- ✔ Controlling cursor display
- ✔ Defining aural style sheets for text-to-speech browsers
- ✔ Defining table layout and display

Although CSS2 is the most recent specification, most style sheets of the CSS variety that you see at work on the Web today use the CSS1 specification simply to make them backward compatible. For this reason, and because CSS1 is more effectively supported by browsers — and is therefore more practical to use for real-world development right now — most of our discussions in this chapter focus on CSS1. Rather than exploring the details of CSS1 completely, we discuss its key concepts to help you appreciate its capabilities.

What does cascading mean?

You're probably wondering what the *C* in *CSS* is about. What does cascading mean in the context of a style sheet? No, there aren't waterfalls involved in CSS, although the mental image of a waterfall may help you grasp the ever so important concept of cascading. *Cascading* refers to the ability to apply multiple style sheets to any single document and resolve any conflicting style definitions gracefully. Each cascading style sheet attached to any document carries a weight that identifies how important it is in the grand scheme of style. If one style sheet conflicts with another, the style sheet with the heavier weight — in other words, the one that's higher on the style sheet food chain — takes precedence.

For example, if an individual Web page implements CSS, three style sheets apply to it: the cascading style sheet, the browser's built-in style sheet, and the individual user's preference settings, such as font sizes, styles, and colors. These three style sheets cascade — are applied to — the Web page in this order:

1. **User's preferences**

2. **Cascading style sheet**

3. **Browser's style sheet**

Therefore, if the cascading style sheet indicates that the font size should be 10-point Times but the user has set his or her preferences so all text is displayed in 12-point Garamond, the user's style sheet wins. More often than not, cascading style sheets override a browser's default settings to create pages that look like the W3C's CSS page depicted in Figure 8-5.

That's it for the basics of the *C* in *CSS*. Of course, if you start to apply multiple cascading style sheets to a document, things can get interesting. CSS incorporates a host of mechanisms to handle such an occurrence. If your curiosity gets the better of you, check out the CSS1 specification at

```
www.w3.org/TR/REC-CSS1
```

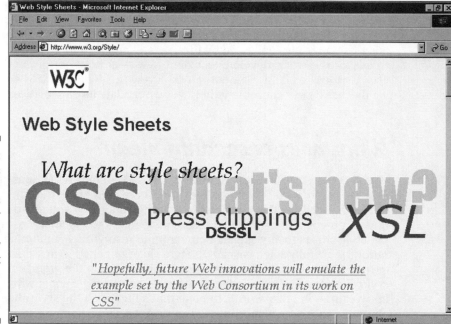

Figure 8-5:
The W3C's
CSS page
overrides
user
settings to
display
colored text
with a
specific
layout.

Internal style sheets vs. external style sheets

When you're working with style sheets, you have two options for where to house them. The first is right inside of the document itself. You simply add the style information in the header of the document and you're done. The benefit of this particular approach is that your style sheet is always right where you can get your hands on it while you're working with the document. However, what if you want to use the same style sheet for a collection of documents? You could cut and paste the style sheet from document to document, but, jeez, what a pain. There has to be a better way.

That better way is to use an *external style sheet*. To put it simply, external style sheets live in their own separate files somewhere on your Web site. Their makeup and structure are no different than an internal style sheet. The only difference is the style sheet isn't housed directly within a document. This approach to style sheet storage means you can link literally thousands of document to a single style sheet. What's even better is if you make a change to an external style sheet, its effect automatically trickles down to every document it's linked to.

The style sheet linking section later in the chapter tells you exactly how to store a style sheet internally or how to link to an external style sheet. And, if you want to have a generic style sheet that applies to all pages on your site and then make style tweaks to individual pages, you can apply both an external and an internal style sheet to any given document.

The Basics of Writing CSS

Enough talk already. It's time to roll up your sleeves and get your hands dirty building a style sheet. Working on the principle that you should jump right into the deep end, we show you a fully functional style sheet.

```
body {margin-left: .3in;
      margin-right: .3in;
      color: black;
      background-color: white;
      font-family: Verdana
      }

h1.staff {color: maroon;
          font-family: Arial;
          }

h1.book  {color: navy;
          font-family: Arial;
          }


h1, h2, h3 {font-family: Arial;}

p.address {font-family: Arial;
           font-size: 80%;}

p.bookhead {color:navy;
            font-family: Arial;
            font-size: 120%;
            }

p.textnav  {font-family: Arial;
            font-size: 80%}

p, ul, ol, li, blockquote {font-family: Verdana}
```

Isn't our style sheet pretty? It's actually a style sheet in use in the real world at the LANWrights Web site. Figure 8-6 shows how this style sheet affects the display of a basic page on the site.

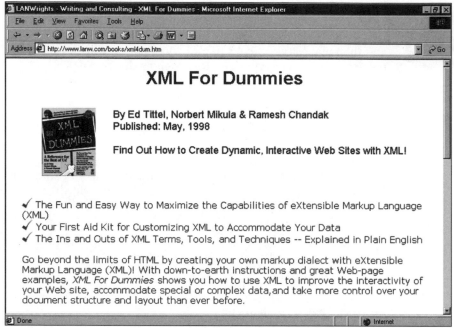

Figure 8-6:
A simple
style sheet
guides the
display
of the
LANWrights,
Inc. Web
site.

As you can see, a style sheet is nothing more really than a collection of style rules that govern the formatting of the various elements in a document. All style rules use the same syntax, so even if you've never seen a cascading style sheet, you can probably guess how to build a basic style rule.

The magic formula for building CSS style rules

All style rules in a cascading style sheet follow the same syntax — or magic formula if you prefer:

```
selector {declaration}
```

The selector identifies the tag to which the style rule applies. The declaration holds all the specifics that the style rule applies to the selector.

We can even break this basic syntax down a bit further:

```
selector {property: value}
```

All declarations consist of `property:  value` pairs. Some of the ones from our LANWrights style sheet include

- ✔ `{font-family: Arial}` to display tag content using the Arial font
- ✔ `{margin-left: .3in}` to set the left margin for each page to .3 inches
- ✔ `{color: navy}` to display book titles using the color navy

All specific CSS properties — and the values they can take — are predefined in the CSS1 and CSS2 specifications. The hardest part of learning CSS is remembering specific property names and their values. The good news is there are all kinds of resources on the Web that do the remembering for you. Check out the last section of the chapter for pointers to those sites.

A quick note about another important CSS term: *inheritance.* Did you note that when we set style rules for the `<body>. . .</body>` element and specified margins, background color, font, and text color, we didn't set them again for each of the other document elements? That's because the body element is the element that contains all other displayed elements inside it. Thus, the style rule we create for the `<body>` element is *inherited* by all other elements that nest within it. This means that after you create a style rule for an element, any other elements it contains are also subject to that style rule.

And that's really all there is to creating a style sheet. You put together a whole bunch of selectors and declarations and poof! — there's a style sheet.

Variations on the magic: Selector specifications

But wait, it can't really be that simple. Not all our selectors in our truly simple style sheet look the same. What about `p.address`? It has an extra period that none of the other selectors use. This syntax tells the application processing the style sheet to look for `<p>` tags with the attribute `class="address"`. If the paragraph doesn't include the proper attribute and value, the style rule doesn't apply to it.

Using selectors means that you can target your style rules more precisely to affect particular groups of tags. In most documents all paragraphs aren't created equal, so you may not want to apply the same style rule to each. The LANWrights style sheet accounts for three different kinds of paragraphs:

- ✔ Addressing information (`p.address`)
- ✔ Publishing information about a book (`p.bookhead`)
- ✔ Text navigation (`p.textnav`)

All other paragraphs have a basic paragraphs style rule applied to them, but these three have their own unique rules. This is a perfect example of form following function. The base element for each kind of paragraph is the same, but CSS recognizes that there are subsets of elements and the best way to attach unique styles to them is to use selectors.

Using the `class=` attribute is just one of the many variations on the selector portion of the magic formula. You can link selectors to different tags based on attribute values, context, type, parent-child relationships, and a variety of other options. The CSS resources at the end of the chapter will tell you all you need to know about how to use selectors to selectively apply style rules to different elements.

Efficiency is good: Combining selectors and declarations

What if you want to assign the same style rule to two different elements? You could retype the declaration or cut and paste it. But then, if you change one instance of that declaration, you must change it in each and every selector where that declaration appears. It's much easier to simply apply one declaration to several selectors. To do so, simply list all of your selectors separated by commas, as in:

```
selector, selector. . . {declaration}
```

The following style rule assigns the same declaration (`font-family: Verdana`) to the `<p>`, `<ul>`, `<ol>`, `<li>`, and `<blockquote>` elements:

```
p, ul, ol, li, blockquote {font-family: Verdana}
```

Along these same lines, you can also combine declarations in a style rule to include a collection of property/value combinations in a single selector. The syntax for this neat trick is to separate your `property: value` combinations with semicolons as in this example:

```
p.bookhead {color:navy;
            font-family: Arial;
            font-size: 120%;
            }
```

Three different declarations — `color: navy`, `font-family: Arial`, and `font-size: 120%` — are assigned to one selector, `p.bookhead`. Combining selectors and declarations makes style sheet maintenance much easier and it helps you group like elements and apply a consistent style to them.

Punctuating CSS rules

Punctuation plays a large role when creating CSS style rules. If you accidentally use a colon instead of a semicolon to separate `property: value` pairs in a declaration, your style sheet will break. Table 8-1 provides a short, but helpful, guide to punctuating CSS properly.

Table 8-1		Punctuation in CSS
Character	**Name**	**What It Does**
.	period	Identifies selector context
,	comma	Separates multiple selectors in a style rule
;	semicolon	Separates multiple property/value combinations in a style rule
:	colon	Separates a property and its value in a declaration

Because punctuation can make or break a style sheet, it's always good to validate your style sheets before you put them to use. The W3C has a CSS validation tool that checks your style sheets to make sure they are syntactically correct. The site `http://jigsaw.w3.org/css-validator/` tests your style sheets with the tool.

Adding Style Sheets to Your Web Pages

To link a cascading style sheet to an XHTML document, use one of the following methods:

- Reference an external style sheet with the `<link>` tag, for example:

```
<link rel="stylesheet" href="url" type="text/css" />
```

  where `rel="stylesheet"` specifies that the link is to a style sheet; `href="url"` points to the style sheet's location; and `type="text/css"` identifies the style sheet as a cascading style sheet.

- Include an internal style sheet directly within an XHTML document between `<style>. . .</style>` tags in the document's header (between the `<head>` and `</head>` tags, in other words).

- Import style rules from an external style sheet into an internal style sheet (between `<style>. . .</style>` tags in the document header) using `@import url(url)`.

✔ Place style information directly within an XHTML element using the style= attribute, for example, `<p style="color: navy; font-family: Arial; margin-right: .5in;">. . .</p>`.

The following code fragment illustrates all four of these methods (refer to the comments to see which is which):

```
<head>
 <title>Linking style sheets</title>

 <!-- the <link> tag links an external style sheet
     to the HTML document -->

 <link rel="stylesheet" type="text/css"
  href="http://www.style.org/css/traditional.css"
         title="Traditional">

 <!-- an internal style sheet resides within
      <style> . . . </style> tags and external style sheets
           can be imported into it with @import -->

 <style type="text/css">
 @import "http://www.style.org/css/swiss.css"
 H1.foo { color: blue }
 </style>

</head>

<body>
 <h1 class="foo">Headline is blue</h1>

 <!-- add style directly to an element with the
      style attribute -->
 <h1 style="color: teal">The heading is teal.</h1>
</body>
```

The Best of CSS on the Web

There's much more to CSS than we can cover in this book, so we provide you with additional resources. Some of the very best resources for discovering more about CSS appear — where else? — on the Web itself. Before you build any serious, complex cascading style sheets, take the time to peruse one or two of them. Our favorites include

- ✔ The W3C's CSS pages at `www.w3.org/style/css`
- ✔ The Web Design Group's CSS tutorials and resources at `www.htmlhelp.com/reference/css/`
- ✔ WebMonkey's CSS tutorials and resources at `www.hotwired.com/webmonkey/stylesheets/`
- ✔ Webreview's CSS articles at `webreview.com/wr/pub/Style_Sheets`

Chapter 9

A Basic XHTML Page

*B*uilding your first Web page should not be scary. The pressure's off; you can build your own simple, but complete, Web page.

Your *look and feel,* which is the way the page looks to the user, combined with your king-sized content, is how your site creates its all-important first impression. The first time a user visits an ugly page with little or no useful content may also be the last time. A Web page is one place where looks and guts matter — fortunately, XHTML gives you a way to describe your content so that it looks great in any Web browser.

Remember that the Web itself is a confusing concept to many users. Your Web pages can be pleasing to the eyes — and an oasis of clarity — if you keep them simple. Everything you can do to make your page "intuitively obvious" to a visitor — and keep it that way — makes your viewers happier and keeps them coming back for more.

The basics of good Web page design are as follows:

✔ Content

✔ Layout

✔ Simplicity

Think of this page as a prototype for future pages. You can always go back to it later and add bells, whistles, or hungry T. Rexes. You can add whatever's needed to make your Web page the one you want — whether for a business, an academic institution, or a government agency.

Page Design from Top to Bottom

The first step in creating an XHTML Web page is to build a basic template. After you build your basic template, you can enhance it with all the flair of a drag queen. To begin the fun, make sure that your first Web page doesn't occupy more than a single screen. This size limit makes a page much easier to edit and test. You can get more than enough information on a single screen and help your audience avoid unnecessary scrolling, all at the same time.

A *single screen* seems like an easy concept, but is it? A single screen is how much information a browser can display on a monitor without scrolling. You've seen movies that are "formatted to fit your screen." Well, you may not know exactly how big every screen is because this amount tends to vary. Don't forget, not all browsers — or monitors — are created equal; if they were, we all may be out of work!

Your users may be running quite an equipment menagerie. Although these differences don't require you to design for lowest-common-denominator sys- tems, we *can* tell you how to avoid one monster mistake: *Don't assume that your users see your page the same way you see it in your browser.*

Testing your pages with a relatively small desktop area (640 x 480 pixels) with several different browsers can help you see your pages through your users' eyes. Getting this view is well worth the time! To find out how to set your monitor's desktop area, consult your operating system's help file or manual.

You may find it helpful to sketch your design ideas on paper first — or on sticky notes! Some designers dust off their favorite graphics program to *mock-up* (that's a techie term for creating a sketch) a model page. Before you get too involved in color schemes, you should sketch — or storyboard — a diagram of your page components.

Figure 9-1 offers one such drawing, showing not only the spatial relationships on the page but also the amounts and locations of the essential breathing room that page designers call *white space*. Although you can leave too much white space on a page, most designers err in the other direction and wind up with far too little, which makes their pages appear cramped and cluttered.

Organize your page so that your viewers can scan through its content quickly and easily. And remember that most people read from left to right, top to bottom. Here are some additional tips:

Title
    Heading

        Text and/or Main Graphic here.

    Body

        Explanation of page purpose.

        Information and primary links.
        Most important graphics, but only
        a couple of large or 3-4 small ones.

        Secondary links.
        Less important graphics.

    Footer

        Author, Date revised, Link to Home
        Page if this isn't, or another page,
        copyright notice if you desire & URL.

Figure 9-1:
A sketch of
basic Web
page layout,
including
white
space.

- ✔ Start with the most important information near the top.

    Important information should be in large type, surrounded by plenty of white space.

- ✔ Follow with less earth-shaking items.

You'll probably never create a standalone Web page; instead, you'll create a group of pages that — when combined — makes an entire Web site. Links are the glue that interconnects a collection of Web pages. Find out more about links in Chapter 12.

Good page design isn't a space-filling contest. You're trying to hit the highlights and invite closer examination — usually of no more than one topic per page. If you have lots of material or more topics to cover, you can easily make more pages and link them to the original.

One good rule comes from professional presenters: *A single screen should convey no more than five pieces of related information.*

What's in a Title?

XHTML files use their titles to give search engines (Yahoo!, Excite, AltaVista, and so on) something to grab and put in an index. For indexing purposes, make sure your title contains the most important information a user needs to know about your Web site, distilled to short-but-sweet. After the title draws your visitors to your Web site, document headings show them around.

XHTML styles, or the users' browser settings, determine the font, page size, and length of line your users see on-screen. Despite the range of possible browsers and monitors, you still have some control over the first impression your page makes. With appropriate content and layout, you can make your pages' titles and headings attractive and informative.

Titles — see and be seen

Think of your Web page's title as a magnet. Web-indexing search engines — the software robots that relentlessly cruise the Web in search of information — use titles to create index records in *their* databases, pointing the way to *your* pages. That means the software robots use your titles to figure out what's on your pages.

Most browsers use titles in the name fields of their *hotlist* or *bookmark* sections, which collect Uniform Resource Locators (URLs) that users want to revisit.

To help people find and read your pages, make your titles as concise and descriptive as possible. Here's how:

- ✔ Try to fit your title on one line.
- ✔ Use an arresting arrangement of keywords to describe the contents of your page (thoroughly knowing your content helps).

Writing a title can be straightforward.

Start with the simple stuff: Type a short list of keywords that describe your page best. Then use them in a sentence. Next, delete all conjunctions, adverbs, and unnecessary adjectives. With a little rearranging, what's left should be a darn good title. Here's an example of constructing a title:

- ✔ **Words:** Band, Pajamacus.
- ✔ **Sentence:** Pajamacus is a band.
- ✔ **Title:** Pajamacus' Band Page.

The following shows this title with some markup around it to describe it as a title:

```
<head>
 <title>Pajamacus' Band Page</title>
</head>
```

This title should fit on one line when viewed by most browsers. Test it with several browsers to see how it looks. If the title is too long, shorten it!

Web browsers display the content between the `<title>` . . . `</title>` tags in the window's *title bar,* not at the top of the page as you may expect. Don't panic when you add a title to your document and don't see it appear automatically on the page. Look to the top of your browser window to see it instead.

Headings — here's the beef

Headings are special little critters, some more immediately visible than others. Many Web pages need a *heading section* after its title and various *paragraph headings* within the body of the document. In the print world — for example, in this book — headings take the form of emphasized text that appears just before particular paragraphs. So while we're at it, a closer look at them is in order.

Headings, along with the title, are the most important text in your Web page. They are the first text that users notice, so they better be good. If headings aren't attractive and instantly informative, users may jump to another page with a single click. Well-written headings hook readers and make them want more.

As with the other parts of your Web page, content is always your king, queen, or big kahuna. Make sure that your headings exhibit consistent, meaningful ties to the paragraphs they introduce, and that they do so throughout your pages. As you mull over and analyze your content, ideas for headings should arise naturally. If they don't, a fresh outline of your content may be just what the doctor ordered.

The neutron-bomb test

A good, strong heading should paraphrase any important concept that you plan to present. If you were to throw away all the text of your document, leaving only the headings, you should be left with a good outline or a detailed table of contents. (Coincidence? We think not.)

If the situation permits, you can make headings humorous and/or refer to a common theme to help catch users' eyes and interest. Try the neutron-bomb test here, too: The outline you're left may be entertaining, but does it still do its job? (Well, okay, we admit to using this approach with the headings in this book; it's one ambitious goal of the whole *For Dummies* series.)

As a quick and (ahem) modest example, Table 9-1 shows some headings in "plain" and "humorous/theme" forms.

Table 9-1	Headings: Plain versus Extra-Crunchy
Plain	*A Bit More Interesting*
Creating Images	Creating Colorful Imagery
Building Paragraphs	Building Strong Paragraphs Easily
Logos and Icons	Eye-Catchers: Logos, Icons, and Other Gems

Web pages give you some creative space, but not an unlimited amount. You have only a few headings per screen or page; make them count. Keep the structure (and the outline level) of similar headings consistent throughout your pages to help keep your users oriented. Although most browsers recognize at least four levels of headings, most well-constructed Web pages use no more than three levels, even for long documents.

Another valuable suggestion is to follow proper outline form. Always use at least two heading levels under a higher heading level. For example, use two heading 2s under a heading 1 and two heading 3s under a heading 2.

The design-versus-information squabble

Although many designers use heading elements for many reasons, the most common of these reasons is for formatting and structure. When you tackle your headings, remember that structure and presentation are increasingly becoming separate issues, so be safe and use headings as a way to add a little structure to your life and leave the presentation to style sheets.

Use heading elements in increments of one and always start with heading 1 (<h1>). Don't start with a heading 2 and then jump to a heading 4. This approach gives your content an ordered, standardized structure and makes it easy for Web crawlers to pick out headings for their indexes. This is a practical, logical, dependable approach, which is typically used for informative articles.

As with most design decisions, the choice is yours. No Web police organization will write you a citation for using only <h3> or <h4> elements. Be sure to experiment with heading elements until you arrive at a combination that looks good, tells it like it is, and accurately reflects the mood and purpose of your page.

Too much emphasized text diminishes the overall effect. Use it sparingly — emphasis works better when it remains exceptional. Using too many headings is like crying "Wolf!" And look, there's another one! And another one!

Document Bodies

The *body* of an XHTML document is the core of a Web page. It stands between the header and the footer. What you put in the body (its *content*) depends on the type and amount of information you want to put online — and give to the audience you want to reach.

Personal Web pages are generally quite different from their business, academic, or government cousins. The most striking differences are in the content and form of their bodies, although the layout for each type may be strikingly similar. The bodies of most personal Web pages contain text for, or pointers to, the following elements:

- **Résumé:** Mostly dense text with a picture
- **Personal history:** Mostly plain text
- **Favorite sports or hobbies:** Text with an occasional picture and links to sports or hobby sites
- **Favorite Web sites:** Lists of links to Web sites

Pretty good, as far as it goes. But if you want to do business with that page, it needs some judicious editing and restructuring with the market in mind. Take, for example, the body of a commercial artist's Web pages:

- **Pictures, pictures, pictures:** Usually small, thumbnail-size pictures that link to much larger versions
- **Credentials:** A page containing a résumé or a list of shows and exhibits, awards, and other professional activities
- **Professional references:** Links to online samples of work on other pages

After you decide what type of information you want to include, you need to decide how to present that information.

The more scrolling required, the slower the experience of reading your Web page becomes. Lots and lots of scrolling means *too much text, already* and your users may fly away to less wordy climates. It's even been said that 90 percent of scrollable pages never get scrolled. Ouch!

So, how much text is enough, but not too much, to put in the body of your page? The answer, my friend, is blowin' in the minds of your viewers. The better you know their needs and interests (not to say attention spans), the better you can gauge how much text to offer them.

Just how much text is okay?

If you've ever transcribed someone else's dictation, you know that even five minutes' worth of speaking equals quite a stack of paper. If you can feel the white space shrinking as you work on your Web page, beware: When most Web surfers want to read pages and pages of dense text, they buy the book or download the file and print it. They don't hang around online with the meter running.

Online reading, almost by definition, means keeping your online writing succinct. Many users (especially those who dial in with slower connections) view great globs of text as a waste of bandwidth. Not that your Web pages have to be as hit-and-run as those 30-second video bites that sell beer during the Super Bowl. But a little realism can't hurt: At the current level of Web development, most users look for fast ways to find the information they want. They don't dig down through too many strata of text to find it. Your job is to give your readers the fast track to the meat in your pages. Help them cut to the chase by using an appropriate page layout — lean, informative text; and a considerate use of navigational tools, such as indexes with hypermedia links.

Composition is a balancing act

The Web-page equivalent of the body beautiful should contain three to five short, well-written paragraphs. Now imagine, if you will, these paragraphs interspersed with moderate-sized headings, enough white space for breathing room, and small graphics to add visual interest. *Readers will probably scan them in their entirety.* And love it.

Judicious use of separators and numerous links to other (relevant!) pages can also give your page design more bang for the buck. The idea is to put nothing on your page that doesn't belong there; the result should be a page that's between one and three full screens long. More may be technically possible, but that doesn't always mean *commonly* possible. Hardly anybody has a 33-inch, high-resolution computer monitor (or a flying car) yet, and neither is probably going to appear any time soon.

Trimming leggy pages

Web page benchmark: For any given page, you should be able to count the screens of text on the fingers of one hand. A page that runs to more than five screens of text (or, for that matter, five screens of URL link lists) can bog down your reader's attention. Split it into multiple pages. If your content ferociously resists being served in short pages, you can still make a long page readable. Try linking a table of contents (TOC) to each section of the page and providing a link back to the beginning of the page from each section. (If your visitor can travel conveniently, the distance won't seem as long.)

This linking structure does add some structural complexity (it's similar to splitting a page into multiple files), and it also offers two considerable advantages:

✔ Your readers can capture the document as a single file.

✔ The XHTML file becomes easier to edit.

You want to balance your convenience (as the page's creator) against the penalty (from the user's point of view) of moving a single large chunk of data — moving it takes time! Links add to a page's usability, but (as with all the parts of a Web page) don't overdo it.

Once again, dear friends, you've reached that risky borderland between content and controls (links to other pages can count as both, especially if you're building a longish Web page). When you have a lot of content, make it approachable by including effective controls, and only essential ones. If you want your page to rock, *content is King* (thank ya vurry much).

See Chapter 12 for more information on linking pages, and for a good example of a TOC in action, check out the W3C XHTML 1.0 Specification site at `www.w3.org/TR/xhtml1/#toc`.

The bottom line on page bodies

The rules for creating great Web page bodies are simple and dandy:

✔ Keep layouts consistent to provide continuity for users.

✔ Provide plenty of white space and headings for easy scanning.

✔ Keep paragraphs short and use them sparingly.

✔ Use meaningful graphics, but only when absolutely necessary.

✔ Make liberal use of hypertext links to additional pages, instead of making your audience scroll, scroll, scroll.

✔ Vary the placement of hyperlink words to provide more visual contrast on the page.

✔ Write meaningful hyperlink text, not *Click here.* (When confronted with a *Click here*, have you ever thought *Oh, yeah? Why should I?* More on this topic later.)

Creating Strong Paragraphs

Web users demand the clearest, most concise text you can muster. Alas, not everyone on the Web is an English professor. For many folks, grammar was a heavy and dolorous subject (and English class was like doing pull-ups in concrete sneakers). Many have never heard of *The Elements of Style* (a slim volume by William Strunk, Jr., and E. B. White) that has eased the pain of writing for generations of students. Nonetheless, two timeless Strunk and White prescriptions are especially healthful for Web page text:

- **Omit needless words.** Doing so doesn't mean getting rid of all the details. Just scrutinize your paragraphs and ask, "What can I throw out?"

- **Make the paragraph the unit of composition.** Writing one paragraph at a time means not getting stuck on a particular sentence or struggling to turn out a whole page at a time. Often a single paragraph is easier to subdue.

All Web surfers must read *some* language — whether Sanskrit, Mandarin, or High Computerese — and clarity promotes accurate communication, whatever the lingo. To this end, follow these eight steps to build better paragraphs:

1. **Create an outline for your information.**

2. **Write one paragraph for each significant point; keep the sentences short, direct, and to the point.**

3. **Edit your text mercilessly, omitting all needless words and sentences.**

4. **Proofread and spell-check.**

5. **Check your page on a variety of hardware and software setups.**

6. **Ask for volunteers to evaluate your work.**

7. **Revise your text, and then re-edit it as you revise it.**

8. **Oh, did we say re-edit. Well, do it again!**

9. **Solicit comments when you publish online.**

Listward, Ho! Using a List Structure

Provided you don't lose them, lists can be useful (laundry, grocery, mailing) or entertaining (how about those "top-ten lists" on late-night TV?). They're also a simple, effective way to call your viewer's attention to specific items on your Web page.

The most commonly used list structure, the *unordered list,* is actually a lot more ordered than just a jumble of vaguely related facts. It implies that several ideas are related without having to assign them a rank or a rigid level of priority (as *numbered lists* normally do). You may know the unordered list by its other name: *bulleted list.*

A bulleted list is handy for emphasizing several short lines of information. The following shows XHTML markup for an ordered list (displayed with Internet Explorer in Figure 9-2).

```
<ul>
<li>Lists can add structure.</li>
<li>They are also very easy to create.</li>
<li>You will learn how to do this in Chapter 13.</li>
</ul>
```

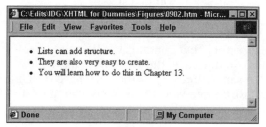

Figure 9-2:
An ordered
list viewed
with
Internet
Explorer.

Although the cardinal rule of page layout is to keep it simple, some information is simply clearer as a list — even a *nested list* (which produces outline formatting, as we explain in Chapter 13). If you use such structures intelligently and sparingly, that's the impression they'll make.

If you're feeling the symptoms of list-o-mania, Chapter 13 presents the different types of XHTML list elements that you can use to purge that urge.

Linking Your Pages

Hypertext links within the body of your pages bring out the power of the Web. To many users, surfing the Web is the ultimate video game. Following links just to see where they go can be interesting and informative.

As a Web page designer and Web weaver, you want users to like your pages well enough to tell others, who tell others, and so on. Therefore, you must provide good links within your own pages and to other Internet resources.

Links come in two flavors — *relative* and *absolute* (also called *full*). Links do their work in two distinct places — respectively, inside your Web site and out on the wider Web.

Relative links (to pages within your Web site)

A typical *relative link* in its native habitat looks like this:

```
<a href="shortcut.html">Jump to a page in your Web site!</a>
```

You can use a link like this one to get around (or show your visitors around) inside your Web site.

How does that link do that?

The URL refers to the directory that contains the Web page itself (which, in turn, calls the reference). In this case, the Web page calls a file (shortcut.html) in the same directory as the current XHTML file (whose address is the current URL). Same Web site, same folder; a relative link keeps you close to home (you know, the place where your relatives are).

In jargonese, we'd say it this way: "The reference is relative to the server's document root plus the path in the file system where the current URL is stored." Got that? (We'd never use such language to order a double mocha latté.)

The tension of extensions

Normally, when you create links to XHTML documents, you'd use the .html extension — all four letters. However, some servers only accept three character extensions, so you can't use .html even if you want to. To add to the confusion, with XHTML you can even use the .xml extension — after all your XHTML document is technically an XML document now. If you opt for the .xml extension, remember that XML is new and not all browsers have caught up yet. Throughout this book, we stick with .html or .htm, because that is what the browsers of today can handle.

Regardless of the number of characters you use in your extensions, remember that file.htm and file.html are *not* the same file but are instead two different files. Always double-check the extension on any file that you link to; be sure the link to it matches the filename exactly. In addition, note that the case of the letters in the filename also matters to most servers, so be consistent when referencing your files.

Here are some typical cross-platform sticky wickets when dealing with .htm or .html:

✔ If a page resides on a DOS machine that requires an ancient and venerable three-character extension, the server's usual habit is to ignore the fourth letter (the l). This habit is okay unless you're moving pages back and forth from a DOS machine to another computer that supports longer extensions. In this case, standardize on .htm and save yourself the grief.

> ✔ If you upload `.htm` files from a DOS or Windows computer to a UNIX server, make sure some kindly technical wizard has taught your server to recognize `.htm` files as valid XHTML files.
>
> ✔ Simple Macintosh text editors (such as SimpleText) don't place default `.htm` or `.html` extensions after a filename. Take heed, Mac Webmasters, always add an `.html` or `.htm` extension onto each and every Web page you create.

In the past, Web servers required the full four-letter `html` extension not only for filenames, but also for the links that called them. Today (ah, progress!), you can use either a four- or three-letter extension (`html` or `htm`) as long as your naming scheme is *consistent*. But before you dash off to change all your extensions, ask your Webmasters or system administrators about how your server really works and what extensions it can see and use.

A bit of advice regarding the overuse of links: Use them only when they convey needed information; use each specific link only once per page. Users can get irritable if each occurrence of a particular word or phrase on a single page turns out to be a link — especially if all those links take them to exactly the same place.

Absolute links (Web world at large)

As useful as relative links can be within single Web site, the whole point of the Web is to establish connections with those realms beyond your own immediate machine. Hence the evolution of the *absolute* (or *full*) link that gives the entire Hypertext Transfer Protocol (HTTP) URL address. A representative of the species looks like this:

```
<a href =
"http://www.lanw.com/xhtmlfd/xhtmlfd.htm">
http://www.lanw.com/xhtmlfd/xhtmlfd.htm</a>
```

You can use absolute URLs for all your links without any noticeable difference in speed, even on a local server. But relative links are shorter to type (which may improve your overall productivity enough so that you can go get that double mocha latté). Whether using relative or absolute links is better is a debate for the newsgroups or your local UNIX users' group. May be worth bothering your Webmaster about, though. After all, who wants to put all that work into a link that doesn't link?

When including absolute URLs for links, we strongly recommend that you go on a little hunting trip first: *Link to the resource and capture its URL with your browser.* Then copy and paste this URL into your XHTML file. Where URLs are concerned, this technique can stop typographical errors before they start.

The links in your XHTML document are what make your site Web-ready. As you create them, you're primarily concerned with the following:

- ✔ The content of the links within your Web site
- ✔ The links' relationships to each another
- ✔ The links' contribution — not only to your own Web site, but also to the wider Web out there

Chapter 12 gets fancy with Web links, roping such evolved critters as image maps.

Choose your hyperlinks with care

Well-chosen hyperlinks enable your users to quickly scan hyperlink text and choose links without having to read the surrounding text. (Surrounding text is usually included only to provide readers with clarification of the link anyway.) Remember that users are in a hurry to scan your pages and quickly pick out important links; unique wording or graphics can aid this process. Make this job easy by using meaningful hyperlinks, and the overall impression left in the reader's mind is *Nice cyberhospitality. I could come here again.* Your home page may have links similar to those shown in Figure 9-3. Notice which words in the sentence are included in the hyperlink text (highlighted and/or underlined). You must click these words to open the link.

Figure 9-3:
Look at the pretty underlined hyperlink!

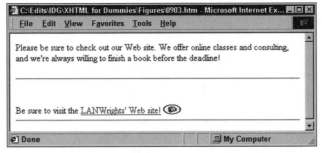

The following XHTML fragment shows the tags that make up the innards of the hyperlink in Figure 9-3.

```
<p>
     Please be sure to check out our Web site. We offer
        online
            classes and consulting, and we're always
        willing to finish a book
            before the deadline!
        </p>
```

```
<hr />
<p></p>
<br />Be sure to visit the
<a href="http://www.lanw.com/">
LANWrights' Web site!</a>
<img src="new.gif" height="17" width="32"
align="top" />
<hr />
```

Keep the text short and the graphics small. And never, ever use the phrase *click here* for link text. ("Why?" you ask. Because your readers may think you're too lazy or uncaring to write more helpful link text. Can't have that!)

To read more about hyperlinks, be sure to read Chapter 12.

Use Those Comments

Do yourself — and everyone that will be taking a peek at your source code — a big favor and *comment* on your XHTML documents, overtly and often, by including text in the file that does nothing more than sit there and explain (to the programmer, editor, or tech-support stalwart) what a particular hunk of the page is supposed to do or why it's there. Comments can also explain the relevance of links or identify information that needs updating. Fast-forward to the future: That joyous noise in the background is you, thanking yourself many times over for this valuable resource.

Most newer browsers ignore comments inside XHTML documents, a trend that is likely to continue. XHTML comment lines are formatted like this:

```
<!@hy comment text @hy>
```

A comment line starts with <!@hy and ends with @hy>. As a general rule, place comments on a line apart from other XHTML text. This way you won't interrupt XHTML text (because browsers *also* ignore any extra spaces — over one — between XHTML elements).

The Basic XHTML Working Draft

As you forge onward through the fog, don't be intimidated by all those weird characters and tag names. After you have the basics of a page down, all you have to do is add a little flare. To give you a head start, take a look at our basic XHTML working draft.

```
<!DOCTYPE html PUBLIC
          "-//W3C//DTD XHTML 1.0 Transitional//EN"
          "DTD/xhtml1-transitional.dtd">
<html xmlns="http://www.w3.org/1999/xhtml">

<!-- Author: The Fonz
     Date Created: May 1, 2000
     Updated: May 15, 2000
-->

<head>
<title>Document Title</title>
<link
</head>

<!-- This begins the body. You may want to include design
          notes to others. -->

<body>

<div>...</div>

<div>...</div>

<div>...</div>

</body>
</html>
```

As you plug away through this book, keep this model in mind.

Chapter 10

Document Structure Elements

● ●

In This Chapter

▶ Creating well-formed XHTML

▶ Following the DTD for valid XHTML documents

▶ Creating XHTML documents from the head down

▶ Describing an XHTML document to robots and search engines

▶ Building XHTML document body

▶ Dividing your XHTML into divisions

▶ Using heading levels

● ●

*B*y now, you may have figured out that XHTML is an application of the Extensible Markup Language (XML). What you may not know is why we think XML is so darn great. Back in the office, fellow colleagues spout off their own views on XML's greatness. Some like XML's portability; others use flashy words like *extensibility*. But if you ask us, you're likely to hear scores and scores about structure. Structure is quite literally the backbone of your XHTML document. You can't create a document without knowing the document structure elements. So, you may want to stick around for this discussion.

If you know HTML, you're already familiar with over half the information in this chapter. But because of some key additions to XHTML, the rules are changed a bit. So, listen up, we have a few rules to share with you.

Sanity through Structure

Structure is wonderful, and we doubt anyone would argue with us on that point. Therefore, structure is very important. But before we tell you about the rules behind structural elements, we need to share two ideas with you:

✔ What we mean when we say structure

✔ What structure may look like

The textbook definition of structure is easy: It's the way something is constructed. What you need to know is what structure means in relation to XHTML. XHTML markup can be loosely divided into three categories:

- ✓ **Stylistic markup:** Defines presentation, such as the <center> element.
- ✓ **Semantic markup:** Defines the content, such as the <cite> element.
- ✓ **Structural markup:** Defines the logical organization of the document, such as the <div> element. (Tada!)

Structural elements enable authors to carve their pages into manageable — and logical — pieces. Now that you know a little about what structure is, here's what it looks like:

```
<!DOCTYPE html PUBLIC "-//W3C//DTD XHTML 1.0 Strict//EN"
        "DTD/xhtml1-strict.dtd">
<html xmlns="http://www.w3.org/1999/xhtml">
    <head>
        <title>My first XHTML document</title>
    </head>
    <body>
        <p>Wow!</p>
    </body>
</html>
```

You can easily decipher the different pieces of the code. The three logical structural separations are as follows:

- ✓ The DOCTYPE declaration that defines the XHTML version
- ✓ The XHTML document head
- ✓ The XHTML document body

Before you find out the details of these logical separations, you need to become familiar with two other XHTML requirements for your document to be structured correctly. For an XHTML document to be *correct*, it needs to be *valid* and *well formed.*

Well-formed documents

For a document to be *well formed*, it must follow the syntax rules outlined by the corresponding specification. If you create an XHTML document, your code must adhere to the XML syntax rules.

Some browsers let you get away with poor syntax, but that doesn't mean it's legal. You should always create well-formed documents. So proceed with caution; we don't want to have to bail you out later.

For more on the syntax rules of a well-formed document, visit Chapters 2 and 7.

Valid and validated documents

Validity is a great way to impress your boss. Well, it's also a great way to impress your browser. A *validator* is a type of software program that performs basic quality control on your HTML documents. Validators check the syntax and structure of a document against a model of what the syntax and structure should be to help developers find and fix errors, omissions, and other gotchas.

Computer geeks like to talk about code as being *valid*. When code is valid, it passes through a validator program as well formed with no errors, follows all the syntax rules of the elements that must be present in a program, and adheres to the rules whenever optional elements appear. Why not do the same with your XHTML documents?

The XHTML specification contains some pesky rules that define what elements can occur where and when. These rules make a document valid. But where do these rules come from? If a document uses a Document Type Definition (DTD) — and XHTML documents do — you must adhere to the rules defined by that DTD. (Oh . . . so that's where those rules come from.)

The DTD defines element and attribute names and behaviors. In other words, the DTD defines naming, hierarchy, and content rules. Here's an example of a DTD rule: "The root element must take the name `html` and the `<title>` element must be the first element after `<head>`."

After you create your valid document, you may want to automate the validating process — and who wouldn't? Where XHTML is concerned, such programs are sometimes still called HTML validators — a throw back from the old HTML days. The ultimate HTML validator comes from — who else — the W3C. You can use the W3C's HTML Validation Service through the Web page at `http://validator.w3.org` to check out your own XHTML documents. And the best thing is *it's free!*

The interesting thing about running your documents through the validator is that you discover that the things a Web browser happily lets you get away with the validator finds fault with — loudly and vociferously, we might add. In other words, most Web browsers are quite indifferent to the requirements built into HTML and cheerfully display so-called XHTML documents that aren't worthy of the name.

DOCTYPE Declaration

In the previous section, you discover that you need to validate your XHTML documents. However, something is missing (and that something is not the red fire engine your mom promised you in the first grade). You can't validate your document without including a *DOCTYPE declaration*.

The point of the DOCTYPE declaration is to reference a DTD. Without pointing to a DTD, how does a person — or a parser — know which DTD to use for validation?

Well, you can't escape it. You're *required* to include a DOCTYPE declaration in your XHTML document. You have three flavors of DOCTYPE declarations to choose from:

- ✔ **Strict:** Use this DTD when you want squeaky-clean markup and want to steer clear of any stylistic markup — we're talking structure only here. The idea is that you would use this with the Cascading Style Sheet (CSS) to get the style you want. Here's the code:

```
<!DOCTYPE html PUBLIC "-//W3C//DTD XHTML 1.0 Strict//EN"
          "DTD/xhtml1-strict.dtd">
```

- ✔ **Transitional:** This is the lazy person's DTD (and the version we use most often). Coincidence? Hmmmm? Nope. Use this DTD when you want to include all the structural markup allowed in the strict DTD, and you want to include stylistic markup (such as the `<center>` element) and/or deprecated elements. Here's the code:

```
<!DOCTYPE html PUBLIC "-//W3C//DTD XHTML 1.0
          Transitional//EN" "DTD/xhtml1-transitional.dtd">
```

- ✔ **Frameset:** This is very similar to the transitional DTD. You use this DTD when your document uses frames. Here's the code:

```
<!DOCTYPE html PUBLIC "-//W3C//DTD XHTML 1.0
          Frameset//EN" "DTD/xhtml1-frameset.dtd">
```

For the time being, anyone concerned with presentation on the Web should use the transitional DTD. Until CSS is uniformly supported by browsers, you can do very little in terms of presentation if you use the strict DTD.

When you sit down to scribble out your first page, always include one of the three DOCTYPE declarations. Don't do it because we say so; do it because the folks at the W3C insist on it. Furthermore, you must place the DOCTYPE declaration before the infamous `<html>` start tag.

XML Declaration

For XHTML, you don't have to learn too much XML if you don't want to; however, you can't shield yourself from XML completely. In this book, you find out everything you need to know about XML in relation to XHTML and even a few extra-tasty bits for you to chew on. The XML declaration is one of those recommended extras. Mmmm, yummy!

The XML declaration has little to do with the XHTML specification and more to do with the XML specification. Hopefully, this fact is already drilled into your brain, but just in case it isn't, here's a reminder: XHTML is an application of XML — meaning that it adheres to the syntax rules outlined in the XML specification. One of the many rules outlined in the XML specification is that including an XML declaration is not necessary, but it is recommended.

Like the W3C, we recommend that you always include an XML declaration. After all, it only takes up one line of text. The XML declaration you're likely to see in most XHTML documents is this:

```
<?xml version="1.0"?>
```

This is a simple example and, as with almost everything in the world of markup languages, you need to make a few decisions before you add just any ol' declaration, such as which attributes to use. Here are the attributes you can include in the XML declaration:

- ✔ `version`: If you decide to use the optional XML declaration, you must always define the `version` attribute. If you decide to include one or both of the optional attributes, the `version` must be specified first.

- ✔ `standalone`: This attribute specifies whether the document has any markup declarations that are defined in an external DTD. Only set the `standalone` to equal `"yes"` — this is case sensitive — if no markup declarations are in external DTDs. Setting it to `"no"` leaves the issue open. In other words, the document may or may not reference an external DTD. This attribute is not commonly used.

- ✔ `encoding`: All XML parsers support 8-bit and 16-bit Unicode encoding corresponding to ASCII. Encoding is how characters are represented as ones and zeros in computer lingo. If you're into programming and you want to designate specific encoding, this is how you would do it. But if you are scratching your head right now, don't worry, this attribute is rarely used.

If you decide to include the two optional attributes, your code looks something like this:

```
<?xml version="1.0" standalone="yes" encoding="UTF-8"?>
```

But for most pages, you can stick with only including the version information.

<!- Comment It Up ->

When you use the comment element, the browser ignores the text between the brackets. You use this element to document your XHTML markup and page structures to make notes for future reference or to provide extra information for others who must read your XHTML code.

You can use comments to temporarily hide sections of a document. Simply adding text between the brackets of comment element keeps the text from being parsed. (However, keep in mind that although a program won't parse the comments, a person who views the source code of your document can still read them.)

<!- . . . -> is legal within all XHTML elements.

Although the results don't appear on-screen, you can enclose any other XHTML elements within the comment brackets: <!- . . . ->. As the preceding tip indicates, this results in "hiding" the enclosed information from your Web browser. Here's an example:

```
<!- This text will not be parsed. ->
```

Remember, the DOCTYPE declaration or comments are not elements — they are just comments and a declaration.

Basic Document Structure Elements

XHTML is strict with its structure, and you have to be, too. That means pay attention as we outline just what can and cannot be used when coding your first XHTML page.

The root element

XHTML requires that you use the root element, <html> . . . <html>, as the document container. Just like with HTML 4, in XHTML, <html> must be the first tag on your page and </html> must be the last tag on your page.

The <html> element — the parent or container element for your document — is the outermost layer of your document's overall structure. All elements must be contained within the opening and closing <html> tags.

Unique Attributes:

```
version="url"
```

The `version` attribute specifies a URL for a DTD to be used to interpret this document, which is usually the same URL that's included in the DOCTYPE declaration. If you follow our recommendations for building valid and well-formed XHTML, this attribute is unnecessary. This attribute is deprecated.

```
xmlns="url"
```

The `xmlns` attribute creates a unique identifier, called an *XML namespace*. When used, it creates a universally unique name for all contained elements and attributes. The predefined XML namespace for XHTML is `http://www.w3.org/1999/xhtml`. To read more about namespaces, see Chapter 1.

Much controversy surrounds the use of namespaces. To keep up with the debate, visit `www.xml.com`.

`<html>` . . . `</html>` is not legal within any other markup elements.

Example:

```
<?xml version="1.0"?>
<!DOCTYPE html PUBLIC "-//W3C//DTD XHTML 1.0 Strict//EN"
          "DTD/xhtml1-strict.dtd">
<html xmlns="http://www.w3.org/1999/xhtml">
 . . .
</html>
```

The document head

Just like humans, every XHTML document should consist of a head and a body. The `<head>` element gives you a way to provide information about the current document, such as its title, keywords for search engines, and other data that is not considered document content. Browsers don't make a habit of rendering elements that appear in the `<head>` as content. This is not to say that the information in the head is not available to users through other mechanisms.

`<head>` . . . `</head>` *Document head block*

The `<head>` . . . `</head>` element is the container for all kinds of information that describes an XHTML document, including the document's title, search engine information, index information, a next-page pointer, and even links to other XHTML documents. The `<head>` . . . `</head>` element and the child element `<title>` are required at the beginning of an XHTML document. Even though many browsers can display documents without a `<head>` . . . `</head>` block, including one is good practice, and required to create a valid, well-formed XHTML document.

Unique Attributes:

```
profile="url"
```

The `profile` attribute defines the location for a metadictionary or profile that defines a set of applicable profile elements.

Example:

```
<head profile="http://www.lanw.com/profile.txt">
```

`<meta />` *Meta-information*

Use the `<meta />` element within the `<head>` element to embed document meta-information (information about information in your document). For example, Internet search engines, such as Yahoo!, Excite, or AltaVista, use Web robots to collect this information and categorize your Web page. The `<meta />` element is an empty element.

Unique Attributes:

```
name="text"
```

The `name` attribute names any of several document properties, including its author, publication date, and so on. If this attribute is left out, the name is assumed to be the value set for `http-equiv`. This attribute is case sensitive.

```
content="text"
```

The `content` attribute supplies a value for some named property or for an `http-equiv` response header. This attribute is case sensitive.

```
http-equiv="text"
```

The `http-equiv` attribute binds the element to a Hypertext Transfer Protocol (HTTP) response header that is sent when a robot or browser queries the page for this information. If the HTTP response header format is known to its requester, its contents can be processed. HTTP header names are not case-sensitive. If `http-equiv` is absent, use the `name` attribute to identify this meta-information; however, the information won't show up within an HTTP response header when requested. (That's why we recommend you use the `http-equiv` attribute to label your site for public consumption.)

```
scheme="schemename"
```

The `scheme` attribute identifies the scheme to use to interpret a property's values. The `scheme` attribute is necessary only when meta-data requires interpretation to make sense. This attribute is case sensitive.

`<meta />` is legal within `<head>`. You can't use any markup elements within `<meta />`; it's an empty element.

Meta-information makes a site's contents more accessible to spiders and robots for automatic indexing. It also makes information more accessible to the programs you use to manage a Web site. No universal `http-equiv` values exist; instead, document designers and robot/agent owners tend to stick to a limited vocabulary of terms. Therefore, when a robot/agent declares its support for a specific `http-equiv` value, it quickly spreads around the Web. Some robots record all meta-information so that specialized or focused data searches can use that information, even if it's not standardized. The Web Robots Pages at `http://info.webcrawler.com/mak/projects/robots/robots.html` can tell you more about how these software programs work and how to use the `<meta />` element to make your site more accessible to them. Also, you can use the Platform for Internet Content Selection (PICS) through the `<meta />` element to identify content, to aid privacy, or to identify intellectual property rights. Details are available at `www.w3.org/PICS/`.

Example:

```
<meta name="Author" content="Ed Tittel" />
```

`<title>` . . . `</title>` *Document title*

The `<title>` . . . `</title>` element encloses the title for an XHTML document, which normally appears in the title bar in the browser's window. By default, the title is set to the XHTML document's filename if you don't specify a title. `<title>` . . . `</title>` is required and legal only within `<head>` . . . `</head>`. You can use only plain text within `<title>` . . . `</title>`, because this text displays only in the browser's the title bar.

Try to come up with a useful title for every XHTML document you write. An accurate, descriptive title helps the many Web search engines and tools to accurately identify or label your content. You should also remember to be consistent when naming your Web site pages.

Unique Attributes:

None

Example:

```
<title>LANWrights' Home Page</title>
```

Two other common elements that appear in the document head are the `<link />` and `<style>` . . . `</style>` elements. Both are used in conjunction with Cascading Style Sheets (CSS) and are covered in Chapter 8.

The document body

The document body contains all the content — or character data — that the viewer sees. You could say that it contains the heart of the matter. And it all starts with the `<body>` element.

`<body>` . . . `</body>` *Document body*

The `<body>` element has only one use: It identifies the body of an XHTML document, which is where the real document content resides. This explicit structure element is required for strictly interpreted XHTML.

Unique Attributes:

```
alink="#RRGGBB" or "colorname"
```

The `alink` attribute sets the color for the active (currently selected) link; colors may be set using a six-digit RGB color code preceded by a pound sign or with a recognized color name; if omitted, the browser picks the color for this link. (See `www.w3.org/TR/html4/types.html#h-6.5` for color names and RGB values.) This attribute is deprecated.

```
background="url"
```

The `background` attribute points to the URL where the document's background image resides. This attribute is deprecated.

```
bgcolor="#RRGGBB" or "colorname"
```

The `bgcolor` attribute sets the background color. You may use a six-digit RGB color code preceded by a pound sign or the name of a recognized color; if omitted, the browser sets the color to white. This attribute is deprecated.

```
link="#RRGGBB" or "colorname"
```

The `link` attribute sets the color for unvisited links, using a six-digit RGB code or a specific color name; if omitted, the browser sets the color (usually to blue). This attribute is deprecated.

```
text="#RRGGBB" or "colorname"
```

The `text` attribute sets the color used for textual data, using a six-digit RGB code or a specific color name; if omitted, the browser sets the color to black (#000000). This attribute is deprecated.

```
vlink="#RRGGBB" or "colorname"
```

The vlink attribute sets the color for links that have already been visited (since the last time the cache was refreshed); if omitted, the browser sets the color to purple (#0033FF). This attribute is deprecated.

Example:

```
<?xml version="1.0"?>
<!DOCTYPE html PUBLIC "-//W3C//DTD XHTML 1.0
          Transitional//EN" "DTD/xhtml1-transitional.dtd">

<!@hy This Example Uses CSS for Presentation @hy>
<html>
<head>
 <title>Working With the Body Element</title>
 <style type="text/css">
   body { background: white; color: black}
   a:link { color: red }
   a:visited { color: maroon }
   a:active { color: fuchsia }
 </style>
</head>
<body>
 ... document body...
</body>
</html>
```

The previous example sets the background to white, the text color to black, the link color to red, the visited link color to maroon, and any active link to fuchsia. Using CSS makes it possible to use the <body> element strictly to define a document's structure. That's because the values that you could set using deprecated attributes for the <body> element are better handled within a Cascading Style Sheet.

More Examples: See file /xhtmlfd/examples/ch10/body.htm.

<base /> *Basis for relative addressing*

Use the <base /> element to define a root-level URL for a collection of Web pages. As long as you put a <base /> element in the <head> section of an XHTML document (which is the only area where it may legally appear), any URLs that occur within the <body> section of the document need to include only as much information as required to navigate from the URL defined in the <base /> itself. The <base> element is not required when building an XHTML document structure. The <base> element is empty.

Unique Attributes:

```
href="url"
```

The href attribute establishes a base URL for the Web document and defines the basis for relative URLs that appear elsewhere within the same document.

With the tag `<base href="http://www.lanw.com" />` in the `<head>` section of a document, any URL in the `<body>` of that document acts as if it is appended to that base. URLs for files in the base directory can take the form `href="file.ext"`, and files in a directory named graphics beneath the `http://www.lanw.com` base directory take the form `href="graphics/file.ext"`. This technique is called *relative addressing*.

```
target="windowname"
```

Use the `target` attribute on framed Web pages to designate that links should be loaded into the window named `windowname`. We cover framed Web pages and use of the `target` attribute in Chapter 16.

Example:

```
<base href="http://www.lanw.com" />
<!- loads linked reference into menu window ->
```

`<div>` . . . `</div>` *Logical division*

`<div>` . . . `</div>` creates distinct, logical divisions within an XHTML document. Use this element to divide a document into separate sections, in which each one can have separate style definitions, including alignment values, font choices, text colors, and so forth. Such assignments apply to everything between the opening `<div>` and the closing `</div>` tags.

Unique Attributes:

```
align="left" or "center" or "right" or "justify"
```

The `align` attribute specifies the default horizontal alignment for the contents within the `<div>` element. The default value depends on the base text direction. For left to right text, the default value equals `left`. This attribute is deprecated.

```
style="text"
```

The `style` attribute is used to insert inline style sheet information and supports all standard XHTML style properties and values, as described in Chapter 8.

Note that the `align` attribute in any element inside `<div>` overrides the `align` value for the `<div>` element itself. You can't use `<div>` in conjunction with `<p>`, because a `<div>` element terminates any preceding paragraph.

Example Using CSS:

```
<div style="align:center">
This text will be centered
</div>
```

The preceding example uses the `style` attribute to introduce style sheet information. Because the `align` attribute is deprecated, we center the text using CSS — the `align:center` property-value pair.

`<span>` . . . `</span>` *Localized style formatting*

This element applies style information to text within a document on an arbitrary basis. (The `<div>` element actually requires dividing a document into separate containers; the `<span>` element lets you select any chunk of XHTML code to which you can apply styles.) Therefore, you should use `<span>` for localized text formatting using the `style` attribute.

Unique Attributes:

```
align="left" or "center" or "right" or "justify"
```

The `align` attribute specifies the default horizontal alignment for contents of the `<span>` element. This attribute is deprecated.

```
style="text"
```

The `style` attribute inserts inline style sheet information and supports all standard XHTML style properties and values, as described in Chapter 8.

`<span>` is an inline division element. It applies no changes to the standard rendering of surrounding content without a `style` attribute definition. Unlike `<div>`, you can use `<span>` within paragraphs, but you can't use it to group multiple elements, as you can with `<div>`.

Example Using CSS:

```
<div>
<p>
<span style="color:red">My Title Is Red!</span>
</p>
<table>
<tr>
<td>Cell 1</td>
<td>Cell 2</td>
<td>Cell 3</td>
</tr>
</table>
</div>
```

In the previous example, we use the `<div>` tags to distinguish a block-level section and the `<span>` element to group inline text. We include inline style sheet information to dictate text color for the information contained by the `<span>` opening and closing tags.

More Examples: See file /xhtmlfd/examples/ch10/span.htm.

`<h*>` . . . `</h*>` *Header levels*

Headers come in different styles and sizes to help you organize your content and make it easier to read. The browser determines the size and display characteristics of any header level. By default, a level-1 heading (`<h1>`) is larger and more pronounced than a level-2 heading (`<h2>`), and so on. Header elements are by no means required in a document, but they help organize its content. Header elements may be numbered from `<h1>` to `<h6>`; however, you seldom find a document with more than three or four levels of headers.

Unique Attributes:

```
align="left" or "center" or "right" or "justify"
```

The `align` attribute sets the alignment of header text on the Web page. The default value depends on the base text direction. For left to right text, `left` is the default. This attribute is deprecated.

Using headings regularly and consistently helps add structure and divisions to your documents. Some experts recommend not using a subordinate header level unless you plan to use at least two of them beneath a parent level. In other words, don't use a single `<h3>` . . . `</h3>` after an `<h2>` . . . `</h2>` pair. This practice follows the outlining principle in which you don't indent unless you have at least two subtopics under any particular topic. Although we think the occasional exception is okay, this guideline is good for XHTML documents.

Example:

```
<h1 align="center">This Level One Header Will Be
          Centered</h1>
```

`<address>` . . . `</address>` *Attribution information*

The `<address>` . . . `</address>` element encloses credit and reference information about an XHTML document, such as the author's name and address, signature files, and contact information. Most browsers display `<address>` element's content in an italic font. The `<address>` element imposes no major layout changes and is not a required XHTML document structure element.

Use the `<address>` element where you want a footer because no there's no `<footer>` element in XHTML. Include this element at the end of any document to supply author contact information for questions or feedback.

Unique Attributes:

None

Example:

```
<address>
<a href="http://www.lanw.com">LANWrights, Inc.</a>,
Webmaster:<a href="webmaster←nw.com">Jane Doe</a>
</address>
```

Pulling It All Together

When you pull an XHTML document together, it looks something like this:

```
<?xml version="1.0"?>
<!DOCTYPE html PUBLIC "-//W3C//DTD XHTML 1.0
          Transitional//EN"
          "DTD/xhtml1-transitional.dtd">
<html xmlns="http://www.w3.org/1999/xhtml">
  <head>
   <title>The model of a well-formed HTML
document</title>
    <base href="http://www.lanw.com" />
     <style>
     body {background-color:pink}
     h1 {font:14pt Times bold}
     p {font: 12 Times; text-align: justify;}
     </style>
     <meta http-equiv="Resource type" content="document" />
     <meta http-equiv="Copyright" content="LANWrights, Inc.
          2000" />
  </head>
<!- ends header portion of the document ->
<body>
<!- begins body portion of the document ->
<div>
  <h1> A Level One Header</h1>
  This is a section of the document.</div>
<div>This is another, longer section of the document.
    <p>Notice, the font size does not drop from the default
          until the first &lt;p&gt; tag. Within this sec-
          tion, we can also add a span section.
    </p>
<span style="font-size: 18pt">
The span text appears in a larger font.
</span>
This text will be back to the original font again, but with
          no line break.
</div> <!- This ends the second division ->
</body> <!- This ends the body of the document ->
</html> <!- This ends the entire XHTML document ->
```

If you flip back to the preceding code and the definitions throughout this chapter as we explain this file line by line, you can form a pretty good picture of what's going on.

```
<?xml version="1.0"?>
```

The XML declaration states that the document adheres to the XML 1.0 specification.

```
<!DOCTYPE html PUBLIC "-//W3C//DTD XHTML 1.0
         Transitional//EN"
         "DTD/xhtml1-transitional.dtd">
```

The DOCTYPE statement identifies that we use a public XHTML definition known as the transitional HTML 4.01 DTD as defined by the W3C, which resides at the URL that appears in the last line in the previous code.

```
<html xmlns="http://www.w3.org/1999/xhtml">
```

The `<html>` tag opens the XHTML portion of the document and continues all the way to the end to the closing `</html>` tag. An XML namespace is used to uniquely identify the contained elements.

```
<head>
```

The `<head>` tag opens the XHTML document header, which contains all kinds of information that describes this document, as you see in the lines that follow all the way through to the `</head>` tag.

```
<title>The model of a well-formed XHTML
document</title>
```

The text between the two `<title>` . . . `</title>` tags defines the title for the resulting XHTML document when viewed in a browser.

```
<base href="http://www.lanw.com" />
```

This `<base />` element identifies the root for all relative URLs in the body of the document as the LANWrights Web server at `http://www.lanw.com`.

```
<style>
body {background-color:pink}
h1 {font:14pt Times bold}
p {font: 12 Times; text-align: justify;}
</style>
```

This section of code defines a set of styles for the entire body of the XHTML document to follow. It sets the page background color to pink, requires level-1 heads to use 14-point Times boldface fonts, and indicates that all text follow-ing the first paragraph marker, ⟨p⟩, should be in 12-point Times, and the text aligned for even right and left margins.

```
<meta http-equiv="Resource type" content="document" />
<meta http-equiv="Copyright" content="LANWrights, Inc.
2000" />
```

These two ⟨meta /⟩ elements are a subset of what you would put on a typi-cal Web page, but they indicate that this file contains an XHTML document in the first line and provides a copyright notice for LANWrights, Inc., in the second line.

```
</head> <!- ends header portion of the document ->
```

This line closes the header portion of the document, followed by an XHTML comment that reinforces this point.

```
<body> <!- begins body portion of the document ->
```

The ⟨body⟩ element opens the content portion of the document. Except for the text between the two ⟨title⟩ . . . ⟨/title⟩ tags in the ⟨head⟩ sec-tion, only text in the ⟨body⟩ . . . ⟨/body⟩ section of an XHTML docu-ment shows up on-screen.

```
<div>
```

This ⟨div⟩ tag opens the first division in the document, which includes the following level-1 header and the text line after that.

```
<h1> A Level One Header</h1>
```

This is a level-1 header that identifies itself as such. You use header levels to identify various levels of structure within a document (or a division within that document).

```
This is a section of the document.</div>
```

The ⟨/div⟩ tag at the end of this line marks the end of the first section of this document and imposes a paragraph break after this line as a consequence.

```
<div>This is another, longer section of the document.
<p>Notice, the font size does not drop from the default until
        the first &lt;p&gt; tag.
Within this section, we can also add a span section. </p>
```

The preceding lines open a new division within the document and show the effects of the `<p>` paragraph style from the `<style>` section in the document header.

```
<span style="font-size: 18pt">
The span text appears in a larger font.
</span>
```

Here, we begin a `<span>` section within a document division, marked by the larger text that appears immediately thereafter. As soon as the `</span>` tag appears to close this section, the font reverts to its original size setting. But because no paragraph break is implied when a `</span>` tag appears, the next line follows immediately, with no line break.

```
This text will be back to the original font again, but
with no line break.
</div> <!- This ends the second division ->
```

The `</div>` tag closes out the second division of the document.

```
</body> <!- This ends the body of the document ->
</html> <!- This ends the entire XHTML document ->
```

The `</body>` tag marks the end of the XHTML document's body, and the `</html>` tag marks the end of the document itself. Notice that comments after the closing tag are perfectly valid (they're ignored by design).

The best way to understand the importance of XHTML's structure elements is to recognize that they define the primary containers for text and other information in an XHTML document.

- DOCTYPE identifies what follows.
- `<head>`, `<title>`, `<meta />`, and `<base />` elements set the stage for what is to come.

Part III
Coding Your First XHTML Page

The 5th Wave   By Rich Tennant

©RICHTENNANT

YOU KIDDING!! TRUE INTERACTIVE CONTENT?! ME CAN'T WAIT, PULL LEVER, OPEN SCREEN!

In this part . . .

Part III is where you roll up your sleeves, and get down and dirty with XHTML. In other words, it's time to tackle a variety of XHTML elements and attributes up close and personal. You begin with the global structure tags that give HXTML documents their form, and that can describe its content. After that, you encounter the presentation tags that allow XHTML to manage fonts and text styles.

From there, it's on to the XHTML tags for links and graphics, as you learn how to reach out beyond the confines of a single source of text to enrich and enliven your Web pages. Then, you tackle various ways to build lists using XHTML, and explore some interesting and offbeat uses for this markup. Your next markup adventure involves the numeric and character entities that XHTML recognizes, that allow you to include many kinds of special characters in Web pages, including alphabets from languages around the world.

Chapter 11

Presentation and Text Controls

● ●

In This Chapter

▶ Understanding document styles versus element controls

▶ Understanding presentation elements

▶ Understanding text elements

● ●

*I*n XHTML, a wide range of elements allows you to manage the way text appears on-screen. These elements govern font selection, text styles, colors, and so forth, and let you control which way text flows on a page (from left to right, right to left, top to bottom, or bottom to top). As a category, these elements allow you to control what the text in your document looks like, which is why we call them *presentation elements*. In this chapter, you encounter a variety of such tools.

XHTML also includes an assortment of elements that allow you to flag the way text appears in a document, based on its content or significance. Unlike the presentation elements, where you operate directly on how the text looks, text elements operate on text to control how its readers interpret its meaning. In this chapter, we take a look at both presentation and text control elements.

Using Presentation or Style Elements

If you want elements to manage text, you came to the right place! This section is chock full of XHTML elements that you can use to manage text. These elements allow you to manage everything from the kind of font you instruct the browser to use for your text — which might be something such as Times New Roman, Courier, Arial, or some other well-known typeface — to the size and weight of the characters chosen from that font. This section also includes a variety of elements for *text styles* (settings such as bold and italic) and other kinds of related items.

Sounds pretty good, doesn't it? But before you take a spin through these elements, stop to consider this: Except for a single element (`<bdo>`) that controls the language choice for a text section and the direction in which text displays, all elements in this chapter create text effects that you can control through styles instead. And, Web designers like style sheets — you will too. See Chapter 8 for more information on style sheets.

Back in the world of XHTML, you need to learn what it means for elements to be deprecated. Almost all the elements in this chapter are deprecated. In ordinary terms, the word *deprecated* refers to something that those in authority disapprove of strongly. In official XHTML-speak, a *deprecated element* is one that is headed for the scrap heap and is probably abandoned when the next release of XHTML is ready.

Therefore, even though these deprecated elements are perfectly legal today and most browsers should display them perfectly, we don't recommend that you use them without pausing to consider that a time may come when these elements no longer work. If your Web pages live only for a short while or you plan to replace your pages with newer versions before the new millennium gets too old, you should be okay.

Just to keep you on the straight and narrow, Table 11-1 lists all the elements in this chapter that are deprecated. Surprisingly, this distinction covers the bulk of the elements covered in this chapter.

Table 11-1	Deprecated Presentation Control Elements in XHTML 1.0	
Element	*What's Deprecated*	*Explanation*
`<basefont />`	Elements and attributes	Selects default font
`<center>`	Element	Centers enclosed text
`<font>`	Element and attributes	Selects typeface, size, and color
`<hr>`	All attributes	Draws horizontal rule
`<s>`	Element	Strikes through enclosed text
`<strike>`	Element	Strikes through enclosed text
`<u>`	Element	Underlines enclosed text

Here's how to interpret the contents of Table 11-1:

✔ If the element is deprecated, it may be phased out with the next release of XHTML. If that element takes attributes, the same goes for them, also.

✔ If all attributes are deprecated, the element remains in effect, but the attributes may be phased out with the next release of XHTML.

✔ If some attributes are deprecated, the element and its other attributes may remain in effect, but the designated attributes may be phased out with the next release of XHTML.

In addition to these deprecated elements, we don't recommend you use the elements shown in Table 11-2, either. The elements in Table 11-2 also produce effects that you can create more easily by using style sheets or style markup in your XHTML documents. (You can find out about this style stuff in XHTML in Chapter 8.) But, because they're not deprecated and we don't recommend their use, we call these elements *nugatory,* which means they're trifling, insignificant, or worthless.

Table 11-2	Nugatory Presentation Control Elements in XHTML 4.01
Element	*Explanation*
`<big>`	Increases font size for enclosed text
`<small>`	Decreases font size for enclosed text
`<tt>`	Uses a monospaced font to make the text look like typewriter text

Because you see these elements all over the place in XHTML code, and because you may prefer to use these elements' quick-and-dirty capabilities from time to time, we have no choice but to tell you about them. Plus, it's better that you hear about them from us than from someone in a dark corner of a seedy nightclub.

Whether you succumb to your base desires to use the `<big>`, `<small>`, and `<tt>` elements, or decide to use style-related markup, remember this: Instead of using these presentation elements, you can use any of the following techniques:

✔ Reference an external style sheet. In such a style sheet, you can select default fonts and manage font sizes, font styles, and even font colors to your heart's content. You can also control margins, spacing before and after text elements, and more.

✔ Create a `<style>` section in an XHTML document's `<head>` section to define the same font characteristics for an entire Web document.

✔ Use the `style` attribute in most XHTML elements to control relevant characteristics only for the text associated with the element in which you're working.

We think that managing text presentation in an XHTML document is best done with style markup using one of the techniques we described previously in this chapter. However, it's your XHTML document, so you can do whatever you like!

Understanding Presentation Control Elements

After you account for all the deprecated elements in Table 11-1 and the nugatory elements in Table 11-2, the only element left is the `<bdo>` element. If you already decided to use style sheet markup with your XHTML documents, you can skip straight to that element in the text that follows. When you finish that element, you're done with this section!

On the other hand, if you want to find out more about the elements you're likely to encounter in most XHTML markup that you may read in other people's Web pages, go ahead and plow through the other elements in this chapter. That way, you know what you're missing if you decide to take the style route, or you know what to look for if you ever decide to go the other way.

`<b>` . . . `</b>` bold text

The `<b>` element indicates that the text between the element's open and close tags should appear in boldface type. You use the `<b>` element to provide specific focus or emphasis on words or phrases in paragraph or body text in an XHTML document. However, style sheets can match the same effects and can better manage character weight and font style. That's why we recommend that you "do it with style" rather than using this element. This element has no unique attributes.

Example:

```
<p>
<b>WOW</b> displays the word "WOW" in bold type.</p>
```

`<basefont />` base font

The `<basefont />` element sets the basic font parameters that are used as the default for any text on a Web page that is not otherwise formatted by a style sheet or by using the `<font>` element directly. This empty element and its attributes are deprecated.

Unique Attributes:

The following code line defines the color for the base font; you can set colors by using a six-digit RGB color code preceded by a pound sign or with a recognized color name; if this attribute is omitted, the browser picks the color for this font. You cannot use additional elements within `<basefont />` because it's an empty element, meaning that it stands alone and may not have a closing tag.

```
color="#RRGGBB" or "colorname"
```

The `face` attribute specifies the base font face; it should be a well-known font family name, such as Times New Roman, Courier, and so forth, or one of the generic Cascading Style Sheets (CSS) font families, such as serif, sans serif, monospace, cursive, or fantasy.

```
face="name"
```

The `size` attribute defines the size of the base font. The value of *number* can be between 1 and 7, inclusive; the default is 3, and 7 is the largest legal value. Relative font size settings (for example, `<font size="+3">`) are set according to this value throughout the document.

```
size="number"
```

Example:

```
<!DOCTYPE html PUBLIC "-//W3C//DTD XHTML 1.0
          Transitional//EN" "DTD/xhtml1-transitional.dtd">

<!-- This Example Uses CSS for Presentation -->
<html xmlns="http://www.w3.org/1999/xhtml">
<head>
 <title>Working With the Body Tag</title>
 <style type="text/css">
   body {color: black; font-size:12pt; font-family:Arial,
         Courier, Courier New}
 </style>
</head>
<body>
 ... document body...
</body>
</html>
```

No exact `<basefont />` equivalent in CSS exists. To set a default font to a page using CSS, all you have to do is define font properties for the `<body>` element.

The previous example is on the CD: /xhtmlfd/examples/ch11/basefont.htm

<bdo> . . . </bdo> bidirectional algorithm

The <bdo> element names the primary language in use on a document and can establish, alter, or reverse the default algorithm used for display direction. For most European languages, this algorithm is left to right and top to bottom; other languages, such as Japanese and Arabic, use a different algorithm.

Unique Attributes:

The lang attribute defines the primary language to be used in the XHTML document where it appears. A list of primary language codes appears in ISO Standard 639a, which you can read online at www.oasis-open.org/cover/iso639-2a.html.

Common language codes include en for English, fr for French, de for German, and so forth.

```
lang="language-code"
```

The dir attribute specifies the direction of text interpretation for languages that read from right to left, such as Hebrew, or for languages whose direction of viewing may be unclear. The default is left to right, so you don't usually need to use this attribute except when you include languages that don't adhere to this display direction.

```
dir="ltr" or "rtl"
```

Example:

```
<bdo lang="he" dir="rtl">
```

<big> . . . </big> big text

The <big> element increases the font of the text enclosed between them to one size larger than the default font size set with CSS or by using the <basefont> element. Because you can handle these effects more transparently using style-related elements, or with an external style sheet, we recommend that you think before using this element. The <big> element has no unique attributes.

Example:

```
<p>The text contained by <big>Big</big> causes the word "Big"
          to be one size larger than the default.</p>
```

<center> . . . </center> centered text

As the name suggests, the `<center>` element centers the text horizontally. The `<center>` element breaks the current line of text and centers the text contained by the opening and closing `<center>` tags on a new line, even if no other markup to control line breaks is used. This element is deprecated and has no unique attributes.

Example:

```
<center>This text shows up centered.</center>
```

<font> . . . </font> font appearance

The `<font>` element sets the size, font, and color of text enclosed between the `<font>` element's opening and closing tags. We recommend that you use style sheets to achieve the effects of this element. This element and all its attributes are deprecated.

Unique Attributes:

The `color` attribute sets the font color; you can set colors by using a six-digit RGB color code preceded by a pound sign or with a recognized color name; if this attribute is omitted, the browser picks the color for this font.

```
color="#RRGGBB" or "colorname"
```

The `face` attribute sets the font face. You can specify a list of font names, separated by commas. If the first font is available on the system, the browser uses it; otherwise, the browser tries the second, and so on. If none of the named fonts is available, the browser uses a default font.

```
face="name, name2, name3"
```

The `size` attribute specifies a font size between 1 and 7 (7 is the largest legal value). A plus or minus sign before the number indicates a size relative to the current size setting. Relative font sizes are not cumulative, so using two `<font size="+1">` elements in a row does not increase relative size by two.

```
size="number"
```

Example:

```
<!DOCTYPE html PUBLIC "-//W3C//DTD XHTML 1.0
         Transitional//EN" "DTD/xhtml1-transitional.dtd">

<!-- This Example Uses CSS for Presentation -->
<html xmlns="http://www.w3.org/1999/xhtml">
<head>
 <title>Working With the Body Tag</title>
 <style type="text/css">
  p {color: black; font-size:12pt; font-family:Arial,
         Courier, Courier New}
 </style>
</head>
<body>
  <p> text affected by CSS </p>
</body>
</html>
```

The previous example is on the CD: /xhtmlfd/examples/ch11/font.htm

<hr /> horizontal rule

The <hr /> element draws a horizontal line across the page, usually one or two pixels wide. Use <hr /> to separate body text from page footers or to separate areas on a Web page. Note also that you can't use any elements within <hr /> because it's an empty element. Some Web browsers (for example, Internet Explorer) accept color as an attribute to this element.

Unique Attributes:

The align attribute draws the horizontal rule left aligned, right aligned, or centered, depending on the align type assigned. The default for the rule is center and for the width of the rule to 100 percent, or the entire width of the display area. Therefore, you can't tell how the rule is aligned unless you use with the size attribute (which is deprecated). The align attribute is deprecated.

```
align="left" or "center" or "right"
```

The noshade attribute draws the outline of the rule without filling it in or providing any 3-D shading effects (which some browsers also do). The noshade attribute is deprecated.

```
noshade="noshade"
```

The size attribute sets the height of the rule in pixels. This attribute is deprecated.

```
size="number"
```

The width attribute sets the width of the rule in pixels or as a percentage of window width. To specify a percentage, the number must end with a percent (%) sign. This attribute is deprecated.

```
width="number" or "%"
```

Example:

```
<p>text of one paragraph</p>
<hr />
<p>text of another paragraph</p>
```

The <hr/> element is used to insert a horizontal rule. If you want to manipulate presentational variables, use CSS. If you look at the previous example in a browser, you would see two — very short — paragraphs separated with a horizontal line.

<i> . . . </i> italic text

The <i> element italicizes all text enclosed between the opening and closing tags. The <i> element takes no attributes. Use italics sparingly for emphasis or effect. Remember that the effectiveness of italicized text fades quickly with overuse. If you set off a citation or quote from a text resource in your document, use the <cite> element instead of the <i> element. The <i> element has no unique attributes.

Example:

```
<p>
<i>Mary</i> displays the word "Mary" in italics.</>
```

<s> . . . </s> strikethrough text

The <s> element causes all enclosed text to appear with strikethrough (a fine line, one pixel wide, drawn through the text). This element is deprecated in XHTML 1.0 in favor of similar style sheet properties. Strikethrough text is difficult to read on a monitor, so use this element sparingly. It's most commonly used to show text that has been removed from earlier versions of a document. The <s> element takes no attributes.

The <strike> element has the same effect as the <s> element, so they may be used interchangeably. However, be consistent and stick with one element for strikethrough text.

Example:

```
<p>
Strike through a text with the <s>strike</s> element.</p>
```

<small> . . . </small> small text

Using the `<small>` element makes the text enclosed within the opening and closing tags one size smaller than the basefont size. Although this element is *not* deprecated, you can use style sheet rules to achieve the same effects. The `<small>` element has no unique attributes.

Example:

```
<p>
Using the <small>small</small> element means that the word
           "small" is displayed at the next smaller font size
           than the default.</p>
```

<tt> . . . </tt> teletype text

Text contained by the opening and closing tags of the `<tt>` element appears in a monospaced (teletype) font, typically some variety of Courier or another sans serif font. Use this element to set off monospaced text, where character position is important, or when trying to imitate the look of line-printer or typewriter output. Teletype is often used to indicate computer output. Two similar but already obsolete XHTML elements of `<kbd>` and `<code>` are sometimes used to indicate user input or existing text, respectively. The `<tt>` element has no unique attributes.

Example:

The following example displays all text, except the word "hello", in the default typeface. "hello" is displayed in a monospaced font.

```
<p>Type <tt>hello</tt> at the command line</p>
```

<u> . . . </u> underlined text

All text enclosed between the opening and closing tags of the `<u>` element are underlined.

Try to avoid this element because most browsers use underlines to empha-size hyperlinks. Underlining may confuse your users, and make them think they see hyperlinks that don't work. The <u> element is deprecated and has no unique attributes.

Example:

```
<p>Don't do <u>that</u>!</p>
```

Remember that the <u> element is deprecated. If you choose to use CSS to underline a line of text, you want to use the text-declaration:underline property value.

Implementing Text Elements

XHTML includes an interesting assortment of elements that permit you to flag the way text appears in a document, based on its content or significance. Unlike the elements in the previous section, where you operate directly on the text's appearance, in this section, you operate on text to control how the text's readers interpret its meaning.

The elements in the following sections allow you to handle quotations from other sources, both long and short, and attribution of those sources, whether visible on the document or hidden in the XHTML source code. These ele-ments also let you apply varying degrees of emphasis to the text in your doc-uments. You can even mark text in one version of a document as deleted from a prior version, or added since that prior version was published.

Perhaps the most confusing — but potentially most powerful — aspect of text control elements is that you can use XHTML markup to distinguish text that originates from a variety of sources, or needs to be input into a com-puter or other text-driven device. In this section, you not only find out how to use these elements, you find out when to use certain elements that may oth-erwise seem indistinguishable from one another.

Separating form from content

We're not trying to confuse you, but we should warn you that numerous ele-ments in this section may produce the same visual effects as the elements in the previous sections. Please understand that the text control elements try to label the content they embrace, whereas the presentation elements simply address the way the text they enclose appears on a Web page.

Consider the following lines of XHTML code:

```
<p>My favorite book,<i>Catcher in the Rye</i>, tells the tale
        of a troubled youth.</p>
<p>My favorite book, <cite>Catcher in the Rye</cite>, tells
        the tale of a troubled youth.</p>
```

Viewed inside a browser, both lines look exactly the same, as long as the defaults are left unchanged. However, the meaning of the <cite> element is different than the <i> element — namely, <cite> indicates clearly that the text that follows it is a citation from a resource of some kind, whereas what follows the <i> could be anything forced into italicized text. Humans and browsers can read significance into the <cite> element and what follows it, whereas the <i> element carries no such weight of meaning for its readers.

The same is true for many other tags covered in this chapter. You can match their appearance quite easily (and perhaps even do so with fewer keystrokes) by using the presentation tags that match their look and feel, but you can't capture the same kind of information with the presentation elements that these text elements can provide.

Using style to emphasize content differences

We recommend the use of the text control elements later in this chapter, but advise against using the presentation elements defined in previous sections. In fact, we recommend that when you must create documents that require the use of multiple kinds of text, that you augment the meaning of these tags with additional changes in their appearance using style markup to under-score their differences.

When creating an online manual for a computer program, you may want to distinguish among three or more kinds of text, such as the following:

- ✔ Text produced by a program to solicit user input
- ✔ Text that the user needs to enter at the keyboard
- ✔ Reports that user input causes the program to emit
- ✔ Error messages that faulty or incomplete user input can provoke

Looking at the previous types of text, you can easily see that it would be beneficial for the users to readily understand the differences between them. Establishing the correct "look and feel" for each of these kinds of text allows you to cue your readers into what they see, and help them separate what the program shows them from what they must input into that program. You can also help them better understand the kinds of information that the program can provide, help them recognize error messages, and take the appropriate action to correct the mistakes that can sometimes cause such error messages to appear.

Text control elements

As you work your way through the text control elements in the following sections, try to associate each element with a specific kind of information. Think of these elements as a way to inform readers of the meaning of the information on the screen, and to separate your thoughts and data from information quoted from other sources. Likewise, some of these elements allow you to clearly separate user input from program output, and even to create distinctions in each of those areas of computer activity as well.

<blockquote> . . . </blockquote> quote style

The `<blockquote>` element sets off large chunks of material quoted from external sources, publications, or other materials. When you quote from an external source (more than one-line long), use `<blockquote>` to offset the text from the left and right margins. Always attribute your sources. For example, use the `cite` attribute to highlight the actual publication, if applicable.

Unique Attribute:

The `cite` attribute provides information about the source of the quote in the `<blockquote>` element. Rendering directions are not provided for this attribute.

```
cite="text"
```

Example:

```
<blockquote cite="XHTML For Dummies, pg. 115">
This optional attribute specifies a URL for processing image
          events ...
</blockquote>
```

*
 force line break*

The `<br />` element forces a line break in XHTML text, immediately after it occurs. This element is useful for creating short lines of text, or for text that must be broken in specific places, such as verse. The `<br />` element is empty.

Unique Attribute:

The `clear` attribute specifies where the line that follows the break should appear. The `left` value inserts space that aligns the following text with the left margin directly below a left-aligned floating image. The `all` value places the following text past all floating images. The `right` value inserts space that aligns the following text with the right margin directly below a right-aligned floating image. The default value is `none`, which does nothing. This attribute is deprecated.

```
clear="left" or "all" or "right" or "none"
```

Example:

In the following example, the `<br />` element breaks the line right after the word Dolly, and places any following text past all floating images on the page.

```
<p>Why, Hello Dolly<br clear="all" /> </p>
```

<cite> . . . </cite> citation emphasis

Use the `<cite>` element to highlight external resource citations for documents, publications, and so forth. The `<cite>` element takes no unique attributes.

Example:

The `<cite>` element sets off a title in a different text style (most browsers render in italics), whereas the rest of the line appears in plain text.

```
<p>Homer's <cite>Odyssey</cite> is the story of an epic jour-
        ney</p>
```

<code> . . . </code> program code text

The `<code>` element encloses programs or samples of code to offset them from normal text. Most browsers use a monospaced font, such as Courier, to set off such text. These tags provide a good way to set off programs, code fragments, or computer output within the body of an HTML document. The `<code>` element has no unique attributes.

Example:

```
<p>Enter the string <code>route print 112*</code> into your
        batch file.</p>
```

Although you may not know what a batch file is, you should know what the `<code>` element does. In the example, `<code>` sets off the string "route print 112*" in a monospaced font. It does not break the line — before the opening `<code>` tag, or after the closing `</code>` tag. To set such text off more emphatically, be sure to precede the opening tag with a `<br />` and follow the closing tag with another `<br />`.

<del> . . . </del> deleted text

Use this lovely little element to mark text as deleted, usually to show changes with respect to a previous version of the Web document in which this markup appears. (This just happens to be our editor's favorite.) This kind of tag is only likely to be used when multiple authors share a single document, and deletions must be explicitly marked for approval or feedback from all parties to the document. This reason is why the timing attributes are so inclusive and specific. Use the companion element <ins> to show where new text is inserted, if necessary.

Unique Attributes:

The following line points to another document that describes why the text was deleted.

```
cite="url"
```

The datetime attribute marks the time when you changed the document. This attribute's value must use the specific format shown to conform to the ISO8601 time/date specification. The abbreviations shown in the following list match the following date and time information:

- ✔ *YYYY:* The year

- ✔ *MM:* The two-digit month — for example, "03" for March

- ✔ *DD:* The day

- ✔ *T:* Indicates the beginning of the time section

- ✔ *hh:* The hour, in military time (0–23 hours), without a.m. or p.m. specifications

- ✔ *mm:* The minute

- ✔ *ss:* The second

- ✔ *TZD:* The time zone

- ✔ *Z:* The Coordinated Universal Time (UTC)

- ✔ *+hh:mm:* The local time that is hours (hh) and minutes (mm) ahead of the UTC

- ✔ *-hh:mm:* The local time that is hours (hh) and minutes (mm) behind the UTC

```
datetime="YYYY-MM-DDThh:mm:ssTZD"
```

Example:

```
<p>The <del cite="http://www.lanw.com/doc/changes.html" date-
        time="2000-05-10T09:36:00-0600">Summary</del>
        References section contains the list of source
        materials. </p>
```

The `<del>` element shows the word Summary with a strikethrough line through the term. You must, however, examine the XHTML source to read the contents of the `cite` and `datetime` attributes for this element. The `date-time` attribute sets the time of the deletion to May 10, 2000, at 9:36 in the morning, six hours behind Coordinated Universal Time (known in the United States as Central Daylight time).

<dfn> . . . </dfn> definition of a term

Use the `<dfn>` element to mark terms when they appear for the first time in a Web document. The text between these opening and closing tags usually appears in italics so users can identify the first occurrence of a term or key phrase. This attribute takes no unique attributes.

Example:

```
<p>An <dfn>element</dfn>, according to the authors of this
        book, is different from the term tag in that it
        references a named opening and closing tag as one
        unit</p>
```

Using the `<dfn>` element sets off the term "element" in italics in most Web browsers.

<em> . . . </em> emphasis

The `<em>` element provides typographic emphasis, usually rendered as italics. Use this element wherever you need to add mild emphasis to body text. Be sure to use sparingly, both in terms of the number of emphasized words and how often text emphasis occurs — you could really wind up confusing your viewers otherwise. This attribute takes no unique attributes.

Example:

```
<p>Pin the <em>tail</em> on the Donkey, not the head</p>
```

The word "tail" is set off in italics in most Web browsers.

<ins> . . . </ins> inserted text

Use this tag pair to mark text that's been added since the prior version of the Web document was published.

Unique Attributes:

The `cite` attribute points to another document that describes why the text was inserted.

```
cite="url"
```

The `datetime` attribute marks the time when you changed the document. This attribute's value must use the specific format shown here to conform to the ISO8601 time/date specification. The abbreviations shown in the following list match the following date and time information:

- ✔ *YYYY:* The year
- ✔ *MM:* The two-digit month — for example, "03" for March
- ✔ *DD:* The day
- ✔ *T:* Indicates the beginning of the time section
- ✔ *hh:* The hour, in military time (0–23 hours), without a.m. or p.m. specifications
- ✔ *mm:* The minute
- ✔ *ss:* The second
- ✔ *TZD:* The time zone
- ✔ *Z:* The Coordinated Universal Time (UTC)
- ✔ *+hh:mm:* The local time that is hours (hh) and minutes (mm) ahead of the UTC
- ✔ *-hh:mm:* The local time that is hours (hh) and minutes (mm) behind the UTC

```
datetime="YYYY-MM-DDThh:mm:ssTZD"
```

Example:

```
<p>The <ins cite="http://www.lanw.com/doc/changes.html" date-
         time="2000-05-10T09:36:00-0600">References</ins>
         section contains the list of source materials.
         </p>
```

The `<ins>` element sets off text that was inserted by underlining the word. In the example above, "References" would be displayed with an underline. To read the contents of the `cite` and `datetime` attributes for this element, you must examine the XHTML source. The `datetime` attribute sets the time of insertion to May 10, 2000, at 9:36 in the morning, six hours behind Coordinated Universal Time (known in the United States as Central Daylight time).

<kbd> . . . </kbd> keyboard text

The `<kbd>` element indicates that text enclosed between the opening and closing tags should be entered at a computer keyboard. The `<kbd>` element changes the type style for all the text it contains, typically into a monospaced font such as that used in character-mode computer terminal displays. Whenever you want to set off text that the user needs to type from the body text, use the `<kbd>` element. This style is different from `<code>`, which indicates existing program text. It's also different from `<tt>`, which indicates computer output. This element has no unique attributes.

Example:

```
<p>Enter <kbd>route print 112*</kbd> to show all routes
          related to networks that begin with 112. </p>
```

Our example sets the text "route print 112*" in a monospaced font. As with the `<code>` element, this element does not force a line break either before the opening `<kbd>` or after the closing `</kbd>` tag. To set off keyboard copy more visibly, use a `<br />` before the opening tag, and another `<br />` after the closing tag.

<p> . . . </p> paragraph

The `<p>` element defines paragraph boundaries for normal text. A line break and carriage return occurs where this element is placed. Use paragraphs to break the flow of ideas or information into related chunks. Each idea or concept should appear in its own paragraph for a good writing style. If you code more than one page, you may become friendly with this element.

Unique Attribute:

The `align` attribute sets the alignment of the paragraph. The `align` type can be `left`, `center`, `right`, or `justify`. The default alignment depends on the base text direction. For left to right text, the default value is `left`. This attribute is deprecated.

```
align="left" or "center" or "right" or "justify"
```

Example:

```
<p>Paragraphs are fun!</p>
```

The preceding example causes a carriage return and line feed at the beginning and end of the enclosed text.

<pre> . . . </pre> preformatted text

Enclosing text within the `<pre>` element forces the browser to reproduce the same formatting, indentation, and white space that the original text contains.

This feature is useful when you want to reproduce formatted tables or other text, such as code listings, especially when other alternatives (such as table-related tags) may not work for all users' browsers.

Unique Attribute:

The value set for width specifies the maximum number of characters per line and allows the browser to select appropriate font and indentation settings. Within a <pre> block, you can break lines by pressing Enter, but try to keep line lengths at 80 characters or less, because <pre> text is typically set in a monospaced font. This tag is great for presenting text-only information, or for reproducing complicated formats where the information is already available in text-only form. This attribute is deprecated.

```
width="number"
```

Not only is the width attribute deprecated, but the width attribute is also not widely supported.

Examples are on the CD: /html4Fd3/examples/ch11/pre.htm

<q> . . . </q> quotation markup

Text contained by the <q> element permits you to highlight short quotations from external resources. When you use a short quote from an external resource, place it within the <q> element. Always attribute your sources. Remember to use the <cite> element to mention the actual publication, if you want that information to appear on your Web document (entries for the cite attribute for <q> appear only in the XHTML source code).

Unique Attribute:

The cite attribute provides information about the source of the quote, but that information is only visible in the HTML source code.

```
cite="text" or "url"
```

Example:

```
<p>
<q cite="Thomas Paine">"Give me liberty, or give me
        death!"</q> is a worthy sentiment. </p>
```

The preceding code does not change text appearance by default in most Web browsers. To add effects, you must use style markup. And, we suggest adding style with CSS!

<samp> . . . </samp> sample output

Use the `<samp>` element for sequences of literal characters or to represent output from a program, script, or other data source. In practice, deciding when to use `<samp>` instead of `<code>` or `<kbd>` is sometimes difficult. We find this element largely superfluous on our Web pages, but you may decide to use it if you have to distinguish among a number of different kinds of output in a document. This element takes no unique attributes.

Example:

```
<p>During the show, the teleprompter read <samp> Superman!
      </samp> at one point.</p>
```

The example causes the word "Superman!" to appear in a monospaced font as part of the body copy. For more separation, add `<br />` tags before and after the `<samp>` element. When using multiple kinds of output in an XHTML document, consider using CSS style properties to change font selections or text colors to help readers distinguish `<code>`, `<kbd>`, and `<samp>` tagged text.

<strong> . . . </strong> strong emphasis

The `<strong>` element places strong emphasis on key words or phrases within normal body text, lists, and other text elements. This element is designed to up the emphasis above the `<em>` element. The `<strong>` element provides the heaviest degree of inline emphasis available in XHTML. This attribute takes no unique attributes.

Overusing the `<strong>` element blunts the effect, so use it sparingly.

Example:

```
<p>Sign it<strong>now</strong>, or I'll call my lawyer. </p>
```

_{. . .} subscript

This element renders enclosed text as a *subscript,* text slightly lower than the surrounding text. This element is most useful when reproducing scientific or mathematical notation. This attribute takes no unique attributes.

Example:

```
<p>H<sub>2</sub>O reproduces the chemical symbol for water
      quite nicely.</p>
```

^{. . .} superscript

This element renders enclosed text as a *superscript,* text slightly higher than the surrounding text. This element is useful for mathematical or scientific notation, footnotes, and when working with foreign languages or proper names. This attribute takes no unique attributes.

Example:

```
<p>M<sup>c</sup>Murray</p>
```

The `<sup>` element moves the "c" in McMurray up from the baseline for other lowercase characters in that line and reduces character size by one level. It's also useful for numerical exponents such as `2<sup>4</sup>` to represent two raised to the fourth power, or the number 16.

<var> . . . </var> variable text

Text enclosed between the `<var>` element is meant to highlight variable names or arguments to computer commands. Use this markup to indicate a placeholder for a value the user supplies when entering text at the keyboard. This attribute takes no unique attributes.

Example:

```
<p>When prompted with the <tt>Ready:</tt> string, enter
        <var>your favorite dog name</var> to begin the
        logon process. </p>
```

This example produces monospace text for the `<tt>` prompt and italics for the `<var>` text. You may want to play with styles to make these tags even more distinctive.

Taking Control of Text On-Screen

If you read the preceding section, with its alphabetical list of text control tags, you noticed the repetitive nature of four elements. In fact, three of these elements produce the same monospaced text; only the `<var>` element looks different — it uses italics by default. These four elements are

- ✔ `<code> . . . </code>`: Display of programs and code fragments
- ✔ `<kbd> . . . </kbd>`: Display of keyboard input
- ✔ `<samp> . . . </samp>`: Display literal character sequence or computer output
- ✔ `<var> . . . </var>`: Display variable names or command arguments, which change with user identity or circumstances

If your Web pages' content requires that you use two or more of the elements in the preceding bulleted list, be advised to use CSS styles properties to alter their appearance somewhat in order to make them a bit easier to tell apart. This alteration could be something as simple as using the nearly ubiquitous `style` attribute when invoking both kinds of text, as the following code example is meant to illustrate. (Please assume, for our sake if not for your own, that this XHTML markup occurs within the context of a well-formed document.):

```
<p>When you want to logon, the program prompts you as fol-
          lows:<br />
<samp>Please enter your favorite color:</samp></p>
<p>
Please enter your favorite color, and then strike the Enter
          key to continue:<br />
<var>your favorite color<var>
<samp>[Enter]</samp>
</p>
<p>For someone who likes green, this produces the following
          output:<br />
<samp>Please enter your favorite color:</samp>
<kbd>Green</kbd>
</p>
```

In a typical Web browser, this code produces the display shown in Figure 11-1. Please notice how difficult it is to separate the various types of text from one another in this display.

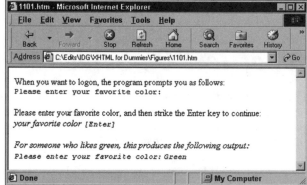

Figure 11-1:
The default appearance of `<samp>` and `<kdb>` look exactly alike.

By adding the following markup to the `<head>` section of the preceding HTML markup, you see a big difference in the version of the same text that appears in Figure 11-2, which follows the markup.

```
<style>
samp {font-family:Courier;
 font-weight:900;
 font-size:14 pt}
var {font-family:Arial;
 font-weight:bold;
 color:teal}
kbd {font-family:Lineprinter;
 font-size:12 pt;
 font-style:italic;
 color:red}
</style>
```

Figure 11-2:
Style sheets
help! With
styles
defined for
`<samp>`,
`<dkb>`, and
`<var>`, the
elements
are easier to
tell apart.

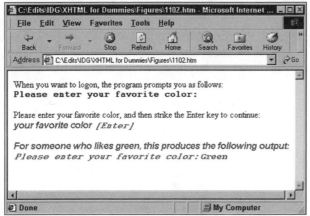

Here, the `<samp>` elements appear in a heavy black Courier font at 14 points, the `<kbd>` elements appear in a 12-point Lineprinter font in red, and the `<var>` elements appear in bold Arial at the default font size in teal. All three elements are now easy to distinguish and even dense text with lots of usage is easy to follow.

The benefit of taking this approach — namely creating a `<style>` section in the `<head>` of the document — comes from its application to all instances of the referenced tags in the `<body>` section. Thus, you can use all three elements as often as you like and the style definitions apply to each instance. You can investigate style markup further in Chapter 8 of this book, but hopefully this example helps explain why we keep pushing this concept!

Chapter 12

Of Links and Graphics

The Web wouldn't be the Web without a way to connect Web pages and other resources. In addition, the Web probably wouldn't be as popular if it wasn't a graphical world with images complimenting the text on most Web pages. In the end, links to other Web pages and embedded graphics have the same basic roots and play a large role in the functionality and overwhelming success of the Web. In this chapter, you find out what links and graphics have in common and what you need to do to add both to your Web pages.

Hyperlinks and Graphics Have a Common Theme

The Web works because documents written in a common language — the Hypertext Markup Language (HTML) or the Extensible Hypertext Markup Language (XHTML) — are exchanged via the Internet with little or no regard for where those documents are housed or what kinds of computers are exchanging the documents. Every document — and every resource for that matter, from Web pages to audio clips — has a unique Web address that is accessible using a standard Uniform Resource Locator (URL). Because the Web is built on commonalities — HTML, XHTML, and Web protocols — it's easy to reference any Web resource.

Web pages and graphics are both Web resources that can be linked to from Web pages as long as you know their unique Web addresses or URLs. When you link to a Web page or a Web graphic, you're really telling a browser to go forth and fetch the resource that lives at whatever Web address you give it. To grab the W3C's XHTML main page, you provide the browser with this URL:

```
http://www.w3.org/TR/xhtml1/
```

To grab the W3C graphic that is on that Web page, you tell the browser to retrieve the resource at this URL:

```
http://www.w3.org/Icons/WWW/w3c_home.gif
```

Both the Web pages that you link to and the images that you embed in your Web pages have unique addresses on the Web. You simply point to those resources and the browser does the rest. You find out how this is done in the following section.

Linking Your Pages

Linked documents on the Web are connected by hyperlinks. A *hyperlink* is simply a bit of text that has a Web address attached to it. When you activate that text in a browser — using a mouse, keyboard, or other device — the browser grabs the document at the Web address and displays it for you. When you're adding hyperlinks to your Web page you need two things:

  ✔ The Web address of the page you want to link to — aka a URL

  ✔ A bit of text or a graphic to attach the address to

Hyperlinks require that you attach the URL to some text or a graphic so that the user has some way of activating the link. Doing so enables the user to see the page at the specified URL. As you learn more about hyperlinks, there are two terms you need to be familiar with:

  ✔ **Linking document:** The document that contains a hyperlink. A user clicks on a link in a linking document to visit the Web resource the link points to.

  ✔ **Linked document:** The document that the hyperlink links to. A user clicks on a link in a linking document to visit the linked document.

Of course, you can link to literally millions of documents on the Web, and the kind of link you make depends entirely on where those documents are housed, as you find out in the next few sections.

Linking to pages within your site with relative links

More often than not, the Web pages on a Web site are all related to each other in some way. The pages usually address a similar subject, and they also usually reside on the same Web server in the same hierarchy of files. Therefore, your Web pages are related to each other in more ways than one.

You want users to be able to move among the Web pages easily; therefore, you build hyperlinks from one page to another. When you build hyperlinks to the Web pages on your Web site, you can take advantage of the fact that you're linking to documents that are part of one big document collection. Web browsers are smart enough to know that if you point to a page by just listing its file name that you are pointing to a file on your own server.

For example, if you point to a file named *help.html* and don't provide any other information about the file's location, the Web browser looks directly back to your Web site and even into the same directory that the linking file resides in. Such links are called *relative links* because the Web browser figures out the location of the linked file relative to the linking file.

Of course, if your Web server has several different folders, you may want to link to a document in one folder from a document housed in an entirely different folder. XHTML provides for this occasion by using standard file-location syntax. For example, two periods and a slash (`../`) means move up one directory, and a slash (`/`) means start at the top of the Web site and work your way down. If you used DOS, this system should be very familiar to you. If not, these examples may help:

- `../../../help.html` instructs the browser to move up three directories from the linking file's directory and look for a file named `help.html`.

- `/docs/help/help.html` instructs the browser to move to the top of the Web site and go down into the `docs` directory, and then to the `help` directory and find the file `help.html`.

- `help/help.html` instructs the browser to look for a folder named help in the linking file's directory and then look inside of that folder for a file named `help.html`.

When you build a hyperlink without specifying the page's full URL, you're building a link that is relative to the linking document. If you move the linking document, your relative links may not work anymore. The moral to this story is to think before you move.

Linking to the outside world with absolute links

Web pages reside on Web servers all over the world. Because of the Web's inner workings, you can link to a Web page on a server in Tokyo from a server in Baltimore, Maryland, and your users wouldn't know the difference. A Web page is a Web page is a Web page. If you're going to link to a Web page that isn't part of your own Web site (in other words, a site that's external to yours), you need to know the page's complete and total Web address. Links made to external Web pages are called *absolute links* because you include the entire URL in the link. The link doesn't depend on any other information to figure out where the page you're pointing to lives. A full-fledged, absolute URL looks like this:

```
<a href="http://www.w3.org">The W3C</a>
```

Linking to a spot on a page

You can build hyperlinks that point to a specific spot on a Web page. To do this, you need two items — a marked spot and a link to the marked spot.

As you find out in the following section, you use the same element (the anchor element) with different attributes to both mark the spot and link to it. When you link to a marked spot, you don't use relative or absolute links. Instead, you use a pound sign (#) followed by the name you gave the spot. Look at the anchor example later in the chapter to see the XHTML code that makes this work. Linking to specific spots on a page is very useful in rather long documents because it helps your users navigate through the content with ease. A great example of linking to spots on a page is the Links portion of the HTML 4.01 specification. Visit it at www.w3.org/TR/html4/struct/links.html to see linking to locations within a document at work.

<a> . . . </a> Anchor

The anchor element describes a bit of text (or a graphic as you learn later in the chapter) to link to another Web resource. The element anchors the address — or URL — of the Web resource to the text in between the open and close anchor tags. Most Web browsers present content described with an anchor element as underlined and colored text so it stands out to users as a hyperlink instead of as plain text.

You can use style sheets to make your hyperlinks appear any way you like, including exactly like the text around the link. Before you make your links blend in with the crowd, remember that most browsers display links differently so as to draw attention to the link. Hyperlinks connect your pages to the rest of the Web so don't hide them from your users. Make hyperlinks stand out in a way that compliments the rest of your site's look and feel.

In addition to using the anchor element to link to another Web resource, you can use anchors to mark a specific spot in a Web page. As described a bit earlier in the chapter, after you mark a specific spot on a page, you can link directly to that spot from a link on the same Web page for from a link on another Web page. The role an anchor element plays — as a link or a marker — depends on what attributes you use with the element. The following lists the unique attributes associated with the anchor element.

Unique attributes:

```
href="url"
```

The `href` attribute points to the URL of a Web resource — usually another Web page — that is linked to the text within the anchor element. The value for `href` can be a complete URL that points to another Web page on an external Web site, a relative URL that points to a Web page on the same Web site, or a pointer to a specific spot on the same Web page.

When you point to a spot on a Web page that you have marked with the anchor element, put a pound sign (#) in front of the spot's name so the Web browser knows to look for a spot instead of a file.

```
name="name"
```

Use the `name` attribute with the anchor element to mark a specific spot on a Web page. When you mark a spot using the anchor element, you don't usually include any text within the anchor element because a Web browser displays that text as a link, even though it's just a marker. Instead, simply place a complete anchor element at the spot you want to mark and don't include any text or other content within it.

```
rel="link type"
```

The `rel` attribute defines what kind of a relationship the current document has to the document the anchor element links to. The attribute's value can be one of several *link types*. The XHTML specification does not predefine particular link types; however, the ones defined in HTML 4.0 and supported by a variety of browsers include:

- ✔ `rel="contents"`: a table of contents
- ✔ `rel="copyright"`: a copyright document
- ✔ `rel="appendix"`: an appendix
- ✔ `rel="help"`: a help document

In the anchor `<a href="toc.html" rel="contents">Table of Contents</a>`, the file being linked to (`toc.html`) is the table of contents for the linking document.

```
rev="link type"
```

The `rev` attribute is similar to the `rel` attribute in that it describes the relationship between the linking document and the resource being linked to. The difference is that the `rev` attribute defines the relationship of the linking document to the linked document. Therefore, the anchor `<a href="white_paper.html" rev="contents">Product White Paper</a>` indicates that the linking document is a table of contents for the linked document (`white_paper.html`).

```
shape="rect" or "circle" or "poly" or "default"
```

Anchor elements can be used in conjunction with the object element to build client-side image maps. The `shape` attribute specifies the shape of an area in an image map that a hyperlink is attached to. See Chapter 16 for more information on image maps.

```
coords="number, number"
```

When you build a client-side image map with the object element and anchor elements, you have to specify the shape of an area in an image map and mark its boundaries. The `coords` attribute defines the coordinates for an area in an image-map. See Chapter 16 for more information on image maps.

```
onfocus="script"
```

Use the `onfocus` attribute to point to a script that the browser should execute when a hyperlink becomes the focus of a browser. Chapter 19 discusses scripts and the attributes associated with them in more detail.

```
onblur="script"
```

Use the `onblur` attribute to point to a script that the browser should execute when a hyperlink looses the focus of a browser. Chapter 19 discusses scripts and the attributes associated with them in more detail.

```
accesskey="character"
```

The `accesskey` attribute sets a single character to act as a shortcut key for the anchor.

```
tabindex="number"
```

Assign a number between 1 and 32767 to the `tabindex` attribute to set an anchor's place in the tabbing order. When a user hits the tab button, the browser moves from link to link in a document. If a value isn't set for `tabindex` for each anchor, the browser moves from top to bottom in the order the links appear. If values are set, the browser moves from anchor to anchor based on the values for `tabindex`.

`charset="`*`character encoding`*`"`

The `charset` attribute specifies which character encoding system the linked resource uses. Visit `ftp://ftp.isi.edu/in-notes/iana/assignments/character-sets` for a complete list of registered character sets. Chapter 14 covers character sets in more detail.

`type="`*`media type`*`"`

The `type` attribute identifies what kind of file the linked resource is. Remember that a URL can be an address for any Web resource, not just HTML pages. Therefore, a hyperlink can point to any one of many varieties of files including audio and video clips, as well as word processing documents. If you're linking to something other than a Web page, it's a good idea to specify what type of resource you are pointing to so that the browser knows what to do with the file after it receives it. If the browser can't process a particular file, it's likely to prompt the user for more information on how to handle the file. You can find a list of the most common file types at `ftp://ftp.isi.edu/in-notes/iana/assignments/media-types/`.

`hreflang="`*`language`*`"`

The `hreflang` attribute specifies what language the linked document is written in. The Internationalization/Localization portion of the W3C site at `www.w3.org/International/O-HTML-tags.html` has more information on language codes.

`target="`*`frame name`*`"`

Usually, a browser opens a hyperlink in the same window as the linking document. However, you can use the `target` attribute to specify that the linked document appears elsewhere. The `target` attribute is most often used with frames to direct a linked document to open in a particular frame. See Chapter 18 for more information on frames and the particulars of using hyperlinks with frames.

The following example shows you how to use some of the attributes we discussed in this section.

Example:

```
<?xml version="1.0"?>
<!DOCTYPE html PUBLIC "-//W3C//DTD XHTML 1.0
          Transitional//EN" "DTD/xhtml1-transitional.dtd">

<html xmlns="http://www.w3.org/1999/xhtml">
<head>
 <title>Hyperlinks</title>
</head>
<body>
<p>
<a href="http://www.w3.org/">This link points to the W3C Web
          site</a>
</p>

<p><a href="home.html">This link points to a file
   named home.html that exists on the same Web site
   as the page that points to it.</a>

<p>
<a href="#footer">Jump to the footer</a>
</p>

<p>
<a name="footer"></a>
This is a footer.
</p>

</body>
</html>
```

Example on CD: See file /xhtmlfd/examples/ch12/a.htm.

Embedding Images

There are entire books and Web sites devoted to the effective (and sometimes ineffective) uses of images. Before you jump into using images on your Web pages, you may want to consult a few of these resources. Some great resources include:

✔ Books

- *Great Web Architecture* by Clay Andres. ISBN 0-7645-3246-4

- *Designing Web Graphics* by Lynda Weinman. ISBN 1-5620-5949-1

- *Designing Web Usability, The Practice of Simplicity* by Jakob Nielsen. ISBN 1-5620-5810-X

📑 Web Sites

- • Webreview.com's Web design articles:
  www.webreview.com/wr/pub/Web_Design

- • Webmonkey's graphics articles:
  http://hotwired.lycos.com/webmonkey/design/graphics/

After you've read up on the ins and outs of incorporating graphics into your Web pages, you can turn to building the code that makes graphics work.

<img /> Image

The image element is an empty element that embeds a graphic in a document. When a Web browser displays a Web page, it displays the graphic wherever the image element is on the page. You want to add your elements where you want your graphics to appear. Like the anchor element, the image element has a variety of attributes that affect the way it acts, and how a browser displays it. As you work more with images, adjust the different attribute values to see how they affect the way a browser displays the image.

Don't forget that the image element is an empty element, so it must always end with a closing slash (/). Also, according to the three XHTML Document Type Definitions (DTDs), the src and alt attributes have to accompany each and every image element that you build if you want your XHTML documents to be valid.

Unique attributes:

```
src="url"
```

The src attribute makes or breaks an image element. This attribute points to the actual graphic that you want to display in your Web page. Just as the anchor element uses the href attribute to point to a Web resource, the image element uses the src attribute to point to a Web resource. Although the href attribute can point to just about any kind of Web resource, the src attribute needs to point to an image saved as a GIF, JPEG, or PNG file. The expansion of those acronyms is Graphics Interchange Format, Joint Photographic Experts Group, and Portable Network Graphics, respectively.

Web graphics are Web resources, so their addresses are URLs just like every other Web resource. You can point to images that reside on your own site using a relative URL or point to external images on someone else's site using a fully qualified URL. This attribute is required:

```
alt="text"
```

Every image that you include on a Web page should have an alternative text description marked with the `alt` attribute. Browsers that don't display graphics use the value of the `alt` attribute to clue a user in on what the image represents. The alternative text should describe the image well, and if the image has a function — such as navigation or information display — be sure to include this in the alternative text. This attribute is required.

```
name="name"
```

Use the `name` attribute to assign a unique name to an image.

```
longdesc="url"
```

Sometimes an image requires a bit of text to describe it accurately. Good examples of this are charts and graphs or complex pictures. If you need to create a long description for an image, save it in an external file on your site in text or HTML format and point to it using the `longdesc` attribute.

```
height="number"
width="number"
```

When a browser loads a Web page, it begins to display the page and its embedded images one at a time as they make their way from the server to the user's computer. You may be able see the text of a page long before the images on the page. If you use the `width` and `height` attributes to specify the exact dimensions of an image (in pixels), the browser can reserve space for the image before it's even downloaded.

If you supply the wrong dimensions for an image, the browser tries to squeeze or stretch the image to fit the specified dimensions. You may be amazed at how distorted a graphic can really become in a Web browser when the height and width are wrong. The best way to find out the exact dimensions of a graphic is to open it in your favorite graphics tool and use the height and width tool to get the specifics.

```
usemap="map name"
```

If an image is an image map, it has a map (contained within the `<map>` element) that specifies which part of the image links to which Web resource associated with it. To point to that markup, use the `usemap` attribute and supply the name of the map that goes with the image. Chapter 16 shows you all you need to know to build image maps.

```
ismap="ismap"
```

Specify that an image is an image map by setting the value of the `ismap` attribute to `ismap`. Check out Chapter 16 for more information on image maps.

```
align="top" or "middle" or "bottom" or "left" or "right"
```

You can set the alignment of an image using the align attribute and one of five predefined values. An image's alignment is set relative to the text and other page elements around it. Therefore, the final display of the image and its surrounding content depends on not only the value of this attribute but also on any other alignments you may have set for surrounding elements.

```
border="number"
```

The border attribute creates a border around an image. The value you set for the attribute determines how many pixels wide the image border will be. If the image is going to have a hyperlink attached to it, you can set the value of border to 0 so that the image won't have a colored border around it. (Colored borders indicate links.) This attribute is deprecated.

```
hspace="number"
```

The hspace attribute sets white space to both the left and right sides of the image. The value you set for the attribute determines how many pixels wide the white space will be. A bit of white space on either side of an image helps set it apart from the rest of the page and keeps text and other content from bumping up against it. This attribute is deprecated.

```
vspace="number"
```

The vspace attribute sets white space above and below an image. The value you set for the attribute determines how many pixels wide the white space will be. This attribute is deprecated.

Example:

```
<?xml version="1.0"?>
<!DOCTYPE html PUBLIC "-//W3C//DTD XHTML 1.0
          Transitional//EN" "DTD/xhtml1-transitional.dtd">

<html xmlns="http://www.w3.org/1999/xhtml">
<head>
 <title>Images</title>
</head>
<body>

 <img src="logo.gif" alt="Corporate Logo"
  align="middle" height="150" width="250" />

</body>
</html>
```

Example on CD: See file /xhtmlfd/examples/ch12/img.htm.

Combining Hyperlinks and Images to Build Clickable Graphics

If you want an image to be a hyperlink on your Web page, never fear. It's easy as pie. You simply combine the anchor and image elements, like so:

```
<a href="home.html">
  <img src="home_button" alt="Home page button" />
</a>
```

When you make a graphic clickable, all you're really doing is attaching a hyperlink to the graphic using the anchor element. Nothing could be simpler. In the end, both hyperlinks and graphics are at the heart of the Web, and you use both on almost every Web page you create.

Chapter 13

Listing Data

● ●

In This Chapter
▶ Using lists effectively
▶ Describing content with list markup
▶ Nesting lists

● ●

*L*ists group similar items together to help folks understand relationships between different pieces of information. A variety of lists have been part of the HTML specification since the original version, 2.0, and the majority of those lists have been carried over to XHTML. In this chapter, you find out about the different kinds of lists supported by XHTML and discover how to group your own information into lists using the XHTML list markup elements.

Using Lists

There's nothing simpler than a list. A list has numbers or bullets and groups items. A list is just a list, right? Actually, that's far from the truth when you're dealing with XHTML. Remember that you use XHTML to describe your content; therefore, when you build a list, you have to describe your list content accurately so browsers and other display devices know how to treat your list items.

The original HTML 2.0 specification included five different kinds of lists:

- Ordered lists
- Unordered lists
- Definition lists
- Directory lists
- Menu lists

Over time, both directory and menu lists have been deprecated (which means they will be left for dead by future versions of XHTML) because they're displayed in exactly the same way as unordered lists — with bullets marking each item in the list. Because the XHTML transitional Document Type Definition (DTD) supports just about every HTML markup element that was ever part of an HTML DTD, both directory and menu lists are alive and well in XHTML. However, because these lists were deprecated in previous HTML specifications, you should consider them deprecated in XHTML and stick with the three main list types: ordered, unordered, and definition.

Ordered lists

An ordered list is just a numbered list. It groups several items and indicates that the order the items are in is important. The item that is first in the list comes before the one that is last, for whatever reason. By default, most browsers display ordered lists using Arabic numbers as list markers, as shown in Figure 13-1. When Arabic numbers simply won't do, you can use a style sheet to make the markers in an unordered list roman numerals or letters.

Figure 13-1:
A basic
ordered list.

To build an ordered list, you need two different elements:

✔ `<ol> . . . </ol>`: The ordered list element is used to specify that your list is an ordered list.

✔ `<li> . . . </li>`: The list item element is used to mark each individual item in the list.

The "List Elements" section later in this chapter gives you the skinny on these two elements and how you use them together to build an ordered list.

Unordered lists

You've probably guessed that an unordered list is a list without order, and therefore, a list without numbers. If you did, you guessed correctly. An unordered list is nothing more than a bulleted list.

As you can see in Figure 13-2, most browsers use a plain, simple black bullet to mark each of the items in an unordered list. If you want to kick things up a notch and use different kinds of bullets in your unordered list, you can use a style sheet to change the list bullet.

To build an unordered list, you need two different elements:

✔ `<ul>` . . . `</ul>`: The unordered list element is used to specify that your list is an unordered list.

✔ `<li>` . . . `</li>`: The list item element is used to mark each individual item in the list.

The "List Elements" section later in this chapter gives you the run down on these two elements and how you use them together to build an unordered list.

Figure 13-2:
A basic
unordered
list.

Definition lists

A definition list is a bit different from either an ordered list or an unordered list. Definition lists show relationships between information in two ways. You use a definition list element to first group one set of information — such as glossary terms. Then, you attach more bits of information to each item in the group — such as multiple definitions for a single glossary term. Figure 13-3 displays a basic definition list. Notice that indentation, rather than list markers, identifies the different list items.

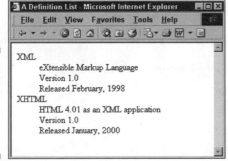

Figure 13-3:
Definition
lists group
information
in more than
one way.

To build a definition list you need three different elements:

- ✔ `<dl>` . . . `</dl>`: The definition list element specifies that your list is a definition list.

- ✔ `<dt>` . . . `</dt>`: The definition term element marks each individual term or item in the list

- ✔ `<dd>` . . . `</dd>`: The definition description element assigns a description (or definition) to each item in the list.

The "List Elements" section later in this chapter provides all the information you need on these three elements and how you use them together to build a definition list.

Although the definition list elements were originally created to describe glossaries and other term-based lists, don't let that stop you from using a definition list creatively. You can use definition list elements to describe just about any kind of related information, from albums and song titles to magazines and articles. By grouping more complex information into definition lists, you help users understand and see the relationships among the different bits of that information.

Deprecated lists

The directory and menu lists that were originally part of the HTML 2.0 specification have been deprecated over time. Most browsers display menus and directories as bulleted lists anyway, so if you think you may want to use one of these elements, try an unordered list instead. Both directory lists and menu lists use the list item element (`<li>` . . . `</li>`) to identify their list items. The directory list identifier element is `<dir>` . . . `</dir>`, and the menu list identifier element is `<menu>` . . . `</menu>`. If you want to know a bit more about these two deprecated list elements, check out the rundown on them in the "List Elements" section.

List Elements

No matter what kind of list you create, you use the same basic formula:

- ✔ Identify the list type (ordered, unordered, defintion)
- ✔ Mark each item in the list

The XHTML list elements help you do both of these things in an easy and fairly predictable way. The best way to learn about lists is to play with list markup. The following element descriptions contain basic but useful examples of list markup and the CD-ROM includes electronic copies of each example. Copy the files on the CD-ROM and play with the elements and content a bit to see how a Web browser processes the elements.

<li> . . . </li> List item

The list item element identifies each item in an ordered, unordered, menu, or directory list. Every item in these lists should be contained within list item elements. List item elements should only be used within a list. Although Web browsers may display a list item element just fine if it's outside of a list (ordered, unordered, menu, or directory), this use of a list item element is not valid.

Unique Attributes:

```
type="disc" or "square" or "circle" or "1" or "a"
          or "A" or "i" or "I"
```

Use this attribute to identify what kind of marker you want to use with the list item: a standard bullet (disc), a solid square (square), a hollow bullet (circle), a lower case letter (a), an uppercase letter (A), a lowercase roman numeral (i), or an uppercase roman numeral (I). This attribute is case sensitive and deprecated.

```
value="number"
```

Use this attribute to specify which number the list item should be marked with. If you specify value="5" and type="a" (lowercase letters), the item is marked with *e* because the letter *e* is the 5th letter of the alphabet. This attribute is deprecated.

Example: See the examples in the following ordered and unordered list element sections.

<ol> . . . </ol> Ordered list

The ordered list element identifies a numbered list and contains list item elements that mark each item in the list.

Unique attributes:

```
type="a" or "A" or "i" or "I"
```

Use this attribute to identify what kind of list number you want to use to mark each item in the list: lower case letters (a), uppercase letters (A), lowercase roman numerals (i), or uppercase roman numerals (I). This attribute is case sensitive and deprecated.

```
start="number"
```

Use this attribute to specify which number the list items should begin with. If you specify value="5" and type="a" (lowercase letters), the list markers start with *e* because the letter *e* is the 5th letter of the alphabet. This attribute is deprecated.

```
compact="compact"
```

Use this attribute if you want the list to be displayed as compactly as possible in the browser. This attribute equals itself because standalone text strings are not allowed in XML. This attribute is deprecated.

Example:

```
<?xml version="1.0"?>
<!DOCTYPE html PUBLIC "-//W3C//DTD XHTML 1.0
         Transitional//EN" "DTD/xhtml1-transitional.dtd">

<html>
<head>
 <title>An Unordered List</title>
</head>
<body>
 <ol>
  <li>The first list item.</li>
  <li>The second list item.</li>
  <li>The third list item.</li>
 </ol>
</body>
</html>
```

Example on CD: See file /xhtmlfd/examples/ch13/ol.htm.

<ul> . . . </ul> Unordered list

The unordered list element identifies a bulleted list and contains list item elements that mark each item in the list.

Unique attributes:

```
type="disc" or "square" or "circle"
```

Use this attribute to identify what kind of list number you want to use to
mark each item in the list: standard bullets (disc), solid squares (square), or
hollow bullets (circle), This attribute is deprecated.

```
compact="compact"
```

Use this attribute if you want the list to be displayed as compactly as possible in the browser. This attribute equals itself because standalone text strings
are not allowed in XML. This attribute is deprecated.

Example:

```
<?xml version="1.0"?>
<!DOCTYPE html PUBLIC "-//W3C//DTD XHTML 1.0
          Transitional//EN" "DTD/xhtml1-transitional.dtd">

<html>
<head>
 <title>An Ordered List</title>
</head>
<body>
<ul>
   <li>The first list item.</li>
   <li>The second list item.</li>
   <li>The third list item.</li>
 </ul>
</body>
</html>
```

Example on CD: See file /xhtmlfd/examples/ch13/ul.htm.

<dl> . . . <dl> Definition list

The definition list element identifies a bulleted list. The definition list element
contains definition term and definition description elements that mark each
item in the list.

Unique attributes:

```
compact="compact"
```

Use this attribute if you want the list to be displayed as compactly as possible in the browser. This attribute equals itself because standalone text strings
are not allowed in XML. This attribute is deprecated.

Example:

```
<?xml version="1.0"?>
<!DOCTYPE html PUBLIC "-//W3C//DTD XHTML 1.0
         Transitional//EN" "DTD/xhtml1-transitional.dtd">

<html>
<head>
 <title>A Definition List</title>
</head>
<body>
 <dl>
  <dt>XML</dt>
   <dd>Extensible Markup Language</dd>
   <dd>Version 1.0</dd>
   <dd>Released February, 1998</dd>
  <dt>XHTML</dt>
   <dd>HTML 4.01 as an XML application</dd>
   <dd>Version 1.0</dd>
   <dd>Released January, 2000</dd>
 </dl>
</body>
</html>
```

Example on CD: See file /xhtmlfd/examples/ch13/dl.htm.

<dt> . . . </dt> Definition term

The definition term element identifies an item in a definition list.

Example: See the example in the earlier definition list element section.

<dd> . . . </dd> Definition description

The definition description element identifies information related to definition terms in a definition list.

Example: See the example in the earlier definition list element section.

<dir> . . . </dir> Directory list

The directory list element identifies a directory list and contains list item elements that mark each item in the list. This element is deprecated.

Unique attribute:

```
compact="compact"
```

Use this attribute if you want the list to be displayed as compactly as possible in the browser. This attribute equals itself because standalone text strings are not allowed in XML. This attribute is deprecated.

Example:

```
<?xml version="1.0"?>
<!DOCTYPE html PUBLIC "-//W3C//DTD XHTML 1.0
          Transitional//EN" "DTD/xhtml1-transitional.dtd">

<html>
<head>
 <title>A Directory List</title>
</head>
<body>
 <dir>
  <li>The first list item.</li>
  <li>The second list item.</li>
  <li>The third list item.</li>
 </dir>
</body>
</html>
```

Example on CD: See file /xhtmlfd/examples/ch13/dir.htm.

<menu> . . . </menu> Menu list

The menu list element identifies a menu list and contains list item elements that mark each item in the list. This element is deprecated.

Unique attribute:

```
compact="compact"
```

Use this attribute if you want the list to be displayed as compactly as possible in the browser. This attribute equals itself because standalone text strings are not allowed in XML. This attribute is deprecated.

Example:

```
<?xml version="1.0"?>
<!DOCTYPE html PUBLIC "-//W3C//DTD XHTML 1.0
          Transitional//EN" "DTD/xhtml1-transitional.dtd">
```

```
<html>
<head>
 <title>A Menu</title>
</head>
<body>
<menu>
  <li>The first list item.</li>
  <li>The second list item.</li>
  <li>The third list item.</li>
 </menu>
</body>
</html>
```

Example on CD: See file /xhtmlfd/examples/ch13/menu.htm.

Nested Lists

You can build some pretty complex documents by simply nesting one list within another. You can nest any kind of list within any other kind of list. For example, you can nest a bulleted list inside another bulleted list, which creates great site maps and outlines. The following shows a portion of the code from the page shown in Figure 13-4, which shows how we use nested lists for a site overview:

```
<h3><a href="books.htm">The Book Nook</a></h3>
  <ul>
   <li><a href="html.htm">HTML &amp; The Web</a>
    <ul>
        <li><a href="books/commerce.htm">Building Web
          Commerce Sites</a></li>
        <li><a href="books/virtwld.htm">Building VRML
          Worlds</a></li>
        <li><a href="books/htmlcgi2.htm">CGI Bible</a></li>
        <li><a href="books/60_java2.htm">Discover
          Java</a></li>
        <li><a href="books/dhtmlbb.htm">Dynamic HTML Black
          Book</a></li>
        <li><a href="books/htmlcss.htm">HTML Style Sheets
          Design Guide</a></li>
        <li><a href="books/hphtml4.htm">Hip Pocket Guide to
          HTML 4</a></li>
        <li><a href="books/html4d4.htm">HTML 4 For
          Dummies</a></li>
        <li><a href="books/mh4d2.htm">More HTML For Dummies
          2nd Edition</a></li>
        <li><a href="books/vcexpl.htm">Visual Cafe for Java
          EXplorer</a></li>
        <li><a href="books/mwg.htm">Web Graphics
          Sourcebook</a></li>
```

```
        <li><a href="books/xml4dum.htm">XML For
        Dummies</a><br />
        <br />
        </li>
    </ul>
</li>
```

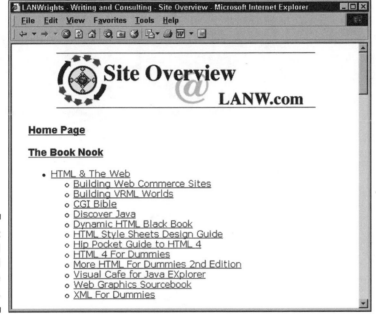

Figure 13-4:
Use nested
lists to build
a site
overview.

Notice how the Web browser indents the nested lists farther from the left
with each nesting? Most Web browsers do this automatically. If you want to
control the look and feel of your nested lists more closely, you can build a
style sheet to control the display.

The most important thing to remember when you're nesting lists is that you
need to completely enclose one list within the other. The maxim "close first
what you opened last" truly applies here. If you remember to do that, your
nested lists work beautifully.

Chapter 14

Adding Character

● ●

● ●

*T*ake a quick look at your keyboard. Notice that it's missing a whole host of characters, such as the copyright symbol and the entire Greek alphabet. If you want to use these kinds of non-ASCII characters in a regular ol' word processing document, you usually have a command or menu item to help you do so (for example, Insert⇨Symbol). In the markup world, things are a bit different. Because XHTML documents are comprised of nothing but ASCII text, you can't just randomly add special characters, such as a bullet or a trademark symbol, into your documents, because they aren't part of the ASCII character set. If you want to add these special characters to your pages, you need to use a special set of markup to do so. It's really not that difficult to do, and this chapter tells you everything you need to know about using special characters in your markup documents.

Entities, Anyone?

The special markup that you use to represent a non-ASCII character in a document comprised entirely of ASCII text is formally an *entity*. An entity is simply a combination of ASCII characters that tells a browser or other processing application which non-ASCII character you want to include in your document. For example, the entity for the copyright symbol is `&copy;`. Instructing a browser to look up entities, such as the degree symbol, with the string `&#176;` may leave you wondering why these contortions are necessary. Here are three important reasons:

✔ Entities allow a browser to represent characters that it may otherwise consider to be markup elements (the characters < and > come to mind immediately).

✔ Entities allow a browser to represent higher-order ASCII characters (those that aren't part of the standard ASCII set you use to build XHTML documents with) or non-ASCII character types, such as ®. Also, these codes support some characters that are even outside the ASCII character set altogether (as is the case with non-Roman alphabet character sets and some widely used diacritical marks).

✔ Entities increase portability of XHTML documents because they ensure that the documents are written in ASCII, which is a language all computers can understand.

In the end, entities let browsers represent a larger range of characters without expanding the actual character set used to write XHTML. This neat trick also helps browsers interpret and display pages faster, which is always a good thing in a world where speed is essential.

As you travel into the land of XHTML character and numeric entities, you encounter strange characters and symbols that you may never use. On the other hand, if your native language isn't English, you can probably recognize lots of diacritical marks, accents, and other character modifications that allow you to express yourself correctly!

Building Entities

Three special characters are part of the code for each and every XHTML entity:

✔ **Ampersand (&):** An & is the first notification the browser receives that the text following the ampersand is a code for a character entity instead of ordinary text.

✔ **Pound sign (#):** If the character after & is a pound sign #, the browser knows that what follows is a number that corresponds to the character code for a symbol to be produced on-screen. This kind of code is called a *numeric entity*.

If the next character is anything other than the pound sign, the browser knows that the string that follows is a symbol's name and must be looked up in a built-in table of equivalent character symbols. This character is called a *character entity*. Some entities can be represented by both character and numeric entities. For example both © and © are codes for the copyright (©) symbol.

✔ **Semicolon (;):** When the browser sees a semicolon (;), it knows that it has come to the end of the entity. The browser then uses whatever characters or numbers that follow (either the ampersand or the pound sign) to perform the correct kind of lookup operation and display the requested character symbol. If the browser doesn't recognize the information supplied, most browsers display a question mark (?) or some other odd character.

A couple of things about character and numeric entities may differ from your expectations based on what you know about XHTML elements and what you may know about computer character sets:

- ✔ Character entities are case-sensitive. This means that À is different from à, so you need to reproduce character entities exactly as they appear in Tables 14-1 through 14-8. This accuracy is one reason we prefer using numeric entities — making a mistake is harder.

- ✔ Numeric codes for reproducing characters within HTML are not ASCII collating sequences; they come from the ISO-Latin-1 character set codes, as shown later in this chapter in Tables 14-1 through 14-8.

If you concentrate on reproducing characters as they appear in Tables 14-1 through 14-8 or copying the numbers that correspond to the ISO-Latin-1 numeric coding scheme, you can produce exactly the right effects on your readers' screens.

You may sometimes encounter problems when trying to represent some of the ISO-Latin-1 character codes in written or printed documentation, as we learned when creating the tables for this chapter in earlier versions of this book (and even a little in this book). Be prepared to obtain some oddball fonts or symbols to help you overcome this problem, especially for the Icelandic character codes! But what you see in this chapter should indeed be what shows up in your browser when you use the codes you see here. If not, please let us know.

Nothing Ancient about the ISO-Latin-1 HTML

The name of the character set that HTML uses is called ISO-Latin-1. The *ISO* part means that it comes from the International Organization for Standardization's body of official international standards. In fact, all ISO standards have corresponding numeric tags, so ISO-Latin-1 is also known as ISO 8859-1. The *Latin* part means that it comes from the Roman alphabet (A, B, C, and so on) commonly used worldwide to represent text in many different languages. The number *1* refers to the version number for this standard (in other words, this version is the first one of this character set definition).

Table 14-1 shows clearly that many more numeric entities exist than character entities. In fact, every character in the ISO-Latin-1 set has a corresponding numeric entity, but not necessarily a corresponding character entity.

As the amount and kind of information presented in Web format has grown, the need for a more extensive character entity set has become apparent.

XHTML 1.0 supports such an extended entity set (not surprisingly the same set supported by HTML 4.0), including:

- ✔ Greek characters
- ✔ Special punctuation
- ✔ Letter-like characters
- ✔ Arrows
- ✔ Mathematical characters
- ✔ Special technical characters
- ✔ Playing card suits

See Table 14-9 for a list of other variants of the ISO-Latin character set (versions numbered 1 through 15, with named variants 1 through 10).

Because XML requires that you have an entity declaration for every entity you want to use in a document, all of the characters supported by XHTML are defined as part of the XHTML Document Type Declarations (DTDs). The entity declarations are divided into three different sets, and you can see them for yourself on the Web:

- ✔ **Latin-1:** www.w3.org/TR/xhtml1/DTD/xhtml-lat1.ent
- ✔ **Special characters:** www.w3.org/TR/xhtml1/DTD/xhtml-special.ent
- ✔ **Symbols:** www.w3.org/TR/xhtml1/DTD/xhtml-symbol.ent

The support for character sets other than Latin-1 was introduced in HTML 4.0, so only browsers that support a full implementation of HTML 4.0 or newer (Navigator 4.0 and Internet Explorer 4.0 and newer versions) can render the character entity codes found in these sets correctly.

The remainder of this chapter includes listings for all the character sets supported by XHTML 1.0 (and consequently HTML 4.0 and 4.01). Tables 14-1 through 14-8 include each character's name, entity and numeric codes, and description. We begin with ISO-Latin-1 because it's fully supported by all current and the majority of older browsers and then continue with HTML 4.0's character sets. We conclude in Table 14-9 with a list of all known ISO-Latin character sets.

Keep in mind that there are some of the characters that even we couldn't get to display correctly because of font restrictions. We really want you to see how the characters look when rendered correctly so we've put together a page on the CD-ROM that duplicates Tables 14-1 through 14-8 so you can see how a browser renders each and every character. Therefore, if you don't see a character in the Char column, try browsing the CD-ROM materials at /examples/ch14/character_sets.htm and displaying it in your browser to see what groovy and cool symbol appears.

As we mentioned a few paragraphs ago, if you want to use a character entity in an XML document you must define it in the DTD. That's why these character sets are all entity declarations in the XHTML DTD. If you're working with other XML vocabularies besides XHTML, you can't just use these entities in your documents and expect them to work. You'll need to consult the vocabulary's DTD to see which entities it supports or declare your own entities in your documents as you build them. For more information on XML structures, such as entity declarations, check out *XML For Dummies,* Second Edition by Ed Tittel and Frank Boumphrey (published by IDG Books Worldwide, Inc.). It tells you everything you need to know about building your own XML documents and DTDs.

Table 14-1	The ISO-Latin-1 Character Set		
Char	*Character*	*Numeric*	*Description*
A-Z (capitals)		A - Z	A is A, B is B, and so on
a-z (lower case)		a - z	a is a, b is b, and so on
0-9 (numerals)		0 - 9	0 is 0, 1 is 1, and so on
			Em space, not collapsed
			En space
			Nonbreaking space
		&#00; - &#08;	Unused
		&#09;	Horizontal tab
		&#10;	Line feed or new line
		&#11; - &#31;	Unused
		&#32;	Space
!		&#33;	Exclamation mark
"	&quot;	&#34;	Quotation mark
#		&#35;	Number
$		&#36;	Dollar
%		&#37;	Percent
&	&amp;	&#38;	Ampersand

(continued)

Table 14-1 *(continued)*

Char	Character	Numeric	Description
'		'	Apostrophe
(		(	Left parenthesis
)		)	Right parenthesis
*		*	Asterisk
+		+	Plus
,		,	Comma
-		-	Hyphen
.		.	Period (full stop)
/		/	Solidus (slash)
:		:	Colon
;		;	Semicolon
<	<	<	Less than
=		=	Equals
>	>	>	Greater than
?		?	Question mark
@		@	Commercial at
[		[	Left square bracket
\		\	Reverse solidus (backslash)
]		]	Right square bracket
^		^	Caret
_		_	Horizontal bar
`		`	Grave accent
{		{	Left curly brace
|		|	Vertical bar
}		}	Right curly brace
~		~	Tilde
		&#127; - Ÿ	Unused

Char	Character	Numeric	Description
			Nonbreaking space
¡	&iexcl;	&#161;	Inverted exclamation mark
¢	&cent;	&#162;	Cent
£	&pound;	&#163;	Pound sterling
	&curren;	&#164;	General currency
¥	&yen;	&#165;	Yen
¦	&brvbar;	&#166;	Broken vertical bar
§	&sect;	&#167;	Section
¨	&uml;	&#168;	Umlaut (dieresis)
©	&copy;	&#169;	Copyright
ª	&ordf;	&#170;	Feminine ordinal
«	&laquo;	&#171	Left angle quote, guillemet left
¬	&not;	&#172;	Not
—	&shy;	&#173;	Soft hyphen
®	&reg;	&#174;	Registered trademark
¯	&macr;	&#175;	Macron accent
°	&deg;	&#176;	Degree
±	&plusmn;	&#177;	Plus or minus
²	&sup2;	&#178;	Superscript two
³	&sup3;	&#179;	Superscript three
´	&acute;	&#180;	Acute accent
>	&micro;	&#181;	Micro
¶	&para;	&#182;	Paragraph
•	&middot;	&#183;	Middle dot
¸	&cedil;	&#184;	Cedilla
¹	&sup1;	&#185;	Superscript one
7	&ordm;	&#186;	Masculine ordinal

(continued)

Table 14-1 *(continued)*

Char	Character	Numeric	Description
»	»	»	Right angle quote, guillemot right
¼	¼	¼	Fraction one-fourth
½	½	½	Fraction one-half
¾	¾	¾	Fraction three-fourths
¿	¿	¿	Inverted question mark
À	À	À	Capital A, grave accent
Á	Á	Á	Capital A, acute accent
Â	Â	Â	Capital A, circumflex accent
Ã	Ã	Ã	Capital A, tilde
Ä	Ä	Ä	Capital A, dieresis or umlaut
Å	Å	Å	Capital A, ring
Æ	Æ	Æ	Capital AE diphthong (ligature)
Ç	Ç	Ç	Capital C, cedilla
È	È	È	Capital E, grave accent
É	É	É	Capital E, acute accent
Ê	Ê	Ê	Capital E, circumflex accent
Ë	Ë	Ë	Capital E, dieresis or umlaut
Ì	Ì	Ì	Capital I, grave accent
Í	Í	Í	Capital I, acute accent
Î	Î	Î	Capital I, circumflex accent
Ï	Ï	Ï	Capital I, dieresis or umlaut
Ð	Ð	Ð	Capital ETH, Icelandic

Char	*Character*	*Numeric*	*Description*
Ñ	&Ntilde;	&#209;	Capital N, tilde
Ò	&Ograve;	&#210;	Capital O, grave accent
Ó	&Oacute;	&#211;	Capital O, acute accent
Ô	&Ocirc;	&#212;	Capital O, circumflex accent
Õ	&Otilde;	&#213;	Capital O, tilde
Ö	&Ouml;	&#214;	Capital O, dieresis or umlaut
×	&times;	&#215;	Multiply
Ø	&Oslash;	&#216;	Capital O, slash
Ù	&Ugrave;	&#217;	Capital U, grave accent
Ú	&Uacute;	&#218;	Capital U, acute accent
Û	&Ucirc;	&#219;	Capital U, circumflex accent
Ü	&Uuml;	&#220;	Capital U, dieresis or umlaut
Ý	&Yacute;	&#221;	Capital Y, acute accent
Þ	&THORN;	&#222;	Capital THORN, Icelandic
ß	&szlig;	&#223;	Small sharp s, German (sz ligature)
à	&agrave;	&#224;	Small a, grave accent
á	&aacute;	&#225;	Small a, acute accent
â	&acirc;	&#226;	Small a, circumflex accent
ã	&atilde;	&#227;	Small a, tilde
ä	&auml;	&#228;	Small a, dieresis or umlaut
å	&aring;	&#229;	Small a, ring
æ	&aelig;	&#230;	Small ae diphthong (ligature)

(continued)

Table 14-1 (continued)

Char	Character	Numeric	Description
ç	ç	ç	Small c, cedilla
è	è	è	Small e, grave accent
é	é	é	Small e, acute accent
ê	ê	ê	Small e, circumflex accent
ë	ë	ë	Small e, dieresis or umlaut
ì	ì	ì	Small i, grave accent
í	í	í	Small i, acute accent
î	î	î	Small i, circumflex accent
ï	ï	ï	Small i, dieresis or umlaut
b	ð	ð	Small eth, Icelandic
ñ	ñ	ñ	Small n, tilde
ò	ò	ò	Small o, grave accent
ó	ó	ó	Small o, acute accent
ô	ô	ô	Small o, circumflex accent
õ	õ	õ	Small o, tilde
ö	ö	ö	Small o, dieresis or umlaut
÷	÷	÷	Division
ø	ø	ø	Small o, slash
ù	ù	ù	Small u, grave accent
ú	ú	ú	Small u, acute accent
û	û	û	Small u, circumflex accent

Char	Character	Numeric	Description
ü	ü	ü	Small u, dieresis or umlaut
ý	ý	ý	Small y, acute accent
þ	þ	þ	Small thorn, Icelandic
ÿ	ÿ	ÿ	Small y, dieresis or umlaut

Table 14-2	Greek Characters		
Char	**Character**	**Numeric**	**Description**
A	Α	Α	Capital letter alpha
B	Β	Β	Capital letter beta
Γ	Γ	Γ	Capital letter gamma
Δ	Δ	Δ	Capital letter delta
E	Ε	Ε	Capital letter epsilon
Z	Ζ	Ζ	Capital letter zeta
H	Η	Η	Capital letter eta
Θ	Θ	Θ	Capital letter theta
I	Ι	Ι	Capital letter iota
K	Κ	Κ	Capital letter kappa
Λ	Λ	Λ	Capital letter lambda
μ	Μ	Μ	Capital letter mu
N	Ν	Ν	Capital letter nu
Ξ	Ξ	Ξ	Capital letter xi
O	Ο	Ο	Capital letter omicron
Π	Π	Π	Capital letter pi
P	Ρ	Ρ	Capital letter rho
Σ	Σ	Σ	Capital letter sigma

(continued)

Table 14-2 *(continued)*

Char	Character	Numeric	Description
Τ	Τ	Τ	Capital letter tau
Υ	Υ	Υ	Capital letter upsilon
Φ	Φ	Φ	Capital letter phi
Χ	Χ	Χ	Capital letter chi
Ψ	Ψ	Ψ	Capital letter psi
Ω	Ω	Ω	Capital letter omega
α	α	α	Small letter alpha
β	β	β	Small letter beta
γ	γ	γ	Small letter gamma
δ	δ	δ	Small letter delta
ε	ε	ε	Small letter epsilon
ζ	ζ	ζ	Small letter zeta
η	η	η	Small letter eta
θ	θ	θ	Small letter theta
ι	ι	ι	Small letter iota
κ	κ	κ	Small letter kappa
λ	λ	λ	Small letter lambda
μ	μ	μ	Small letter mu
ν	ν	ν	Small letter nu
ξ	ξ	ξ	Small letter xi
ο	ο	ο	Small letter omicron
π	π	π	Small letter pi
ρ	ρ	ρ	Small letter rho
ς	ς	ς	Small letter final sigma
σ	σ	σ	Small letter sigma
τ	τ	τ	Small letter tau

Char	Character	Numeric	Description
υ	`&upsilon;`	`&#965;`	Small letter upsilon
φ	`&phi;`	`&#966;`	Small letter phi
χ	`&chi;`	`&#967;`	Small letter chi
ψ	`&psi;`	`&#968;`	Small letter psi
ω	`&omega;`	`&#969;`	Small letter omega
θ	`&thetasym;`	`&#977;`	Small letter theta
ϒ	`&upsih;`	`&#978;`	Upsilon with hook
Π	`&piv;`	`&#982;`	Pi

Table 14-3	Special Punctuation		
Char	**Character**	**Numeric**	**Description**
•	`&bull;`	`&#8226;`	Bullet
...	`&hellip;`	`&#8230;`	Horizontal ellipsis
'	`&prime;`	`&#8242;`	Prime
"	`&Prime;`	`&#8243;`	Double prime
–	`&oline;`	`&#8254;`	Overline
/	`&frasl;`	`&#8260;`	Fraction slash

Table 14-4	Letter-Like Characters		
Char	**Character**	**Numeric**	**Description**
℘	`&weierp;`	`&#8472;`	Script capital P
ℑ	`&image;`	`&#8465;`	Blackletter capital I
ℜ	`&real;`	`&#8476;`	Blackletter capital R
™	`&trade;`	`&#8482;`	Trademark
ℵ	`&alefsym;`	`&#8501;`	Alef

Table 14-5		Arrow Characters	
Char	*Character*	*Numeric*	*Description*
←	&larr;	&#8592;	Left arrow
↑	&uarr;	&#8593;	Up arrow
→	&rarr;	&#8594;	Right arrow
↓	&darr;	&#8595;	Down arrow
↔	&harr;	&#8596;	Left-right arrow
↵	&crarr;	&#8629;	Down arrow with corner left
⇐	&lArr;	&#8656;	Left double arrow
⇑	&uArr;	&#8657;	Up double arrow
⇒	&rArr;	&#8658;	Right double arrow
⇓	&dArr;	&#8659;	Down double arrow
⇔	&hArr;	&#8660;	Left-right double arrow

Table 14-6		Mathematical Characters	
Char	*Character*	*Numeric*	*Description*
∀	&forall;	&#8704;	For all
∂	&part;	&#8706;	Partial differential
∃	&exist;	&#8707;	There exists
∅	&empty;	&#8709;	Empty set
∆	&nabla;	&#8711;	Nabla
∈	&isin;	&#8712;	Element of
∉	&notin;	&#8713;	Not an element of
∋	&ni;	&#8715;	Contains as member
π	&prod;	&#8719;	n-ary product
Σ	&sum;	&#8721;	n-ary summation
-	&minus;	&#8722;	Minus

Char	Character	Numeric	Description
*	`&lowast;`	`&#8727;`	Asterisk operator
√	`&radic;`	`&#8730;`	Square root
∝	`&prop;`	`&#8733;`	Proportional to
8	`&infin;`	`&#8734;`	Infinity
∠	`&ang;`	`&#8736;`	Angle
∧	`&and;`	`&#2227;`	Logical and
∨	`&or;`	`&#2228;`	Logical or
∪	`&cup;`	`&#8746;`	Union
∫	`&int;`	`&#8747;`	Integral
∴	`&there4;`	`&#8756;`	Therefore
~	`&sim;`	`&#8764;`	Tilde operator
≅	`&cong;`	`&#8773;`	Approximately equal to
≈	`&asymp;`	`&#8776;`	Almost equal to
≠	`&ne;`	`&#8800;`	Not equal to
≡	`&equiv;`	`&#8801;`	Identical to =
≤	`&le;`	`&#8804;`	Less than or equal to
≥	`&ge;`	`&#8805;`	Greater than or equal to
⊂	`&sub;`	`&#8834;`	Subset of
⊃	`&sup;`	`&#8835;`	Superset of
⊄	`&nsub;`	`&#8836;`	Not a subset of
⊆	`&sube;`	`&#8838;`	Subset of or equal to
⊇	`&supe;`	`&#8839;`	Superset of or equal to
⊕	`&oplus;`	`&#8853;`	Circled plus
⊗	`&otimes;`	`&#8855;`	Circled times
⊥	`&perp;`	`&#8869;`	Up tack
•	`&sdot;`	`&#8901;`	Dot operator

Table 14-7		Technical Characters	
Char	**Character**	**Numeric**	**Description**
⌈	&lceil;	&#8968;	Left ceiling
⌉	&rceil;	&#8969;	Right ceiling
⌊	&lfloor;	&#8970;	Left floor
⌋	&rfloor;	&#8971;	Right floor
⟨	&lang;	&#9001;	Left-pointing angle bracket
⟩	&rang;	&#9002;	Right-pointing angle bracket

Table 14-8		Playing Card Symbols	
Char	**Character**	**Numeric**	**Description**
♠	&spades;	&#9824;	Black spade suit
♣	&clubs;	&#9827;	Black club suit
♥	&hearts;	&#9829;	Black heart suit
♦	&diams;	&#9830;	Black diamond suit

If you find that you frequently work with character or numeric entities in your documents, using some kind of HTML editing tool to handle character replacements automatically is easier than coding them by hand. You can also look for a file-oriented search-and-replace utility that you can use as a post-processing step on your files to turn all special characters into character or numeric entities. You can find a variety of search and replace utilities if you look in the HTML Accessories category at www.tucows.com.

In addition to the various character sets mentioned earlier in this chapter, numerous variants of the ISO-Latin character set have been created, primarily to support developers (and users) who want to read Web pages in languages other than English. As Table 14-9 shows, ten named versions of the ISO-Latin character sets exist, and 15 versions of ISO-Latin itself, each of which is aimed at a separate collection of languages. For those who want to service readers in languages other than English, relief may possibly occur somewhere in this table!

Table 14-9		ISO 8859 Character Sets
Charset	*Script*	*Languages*
ISO-8859-1	Latin-1	ASCII plus most Western European languages, including Albanian, Afrikaans, Basque, Catalan, Danish, Dutch, English, Faroese, Finnish, Flemish, Galician, German, Icelandic, Irish, Italian, Norwegian, Portuguese, Scottish, Spanish, and Swedish. Omits certain Dutch, French, and German characters.
ISO-8859-2	Latin-2	ASCII plus most Central European languages, including Czech, English, German, Hungarian, Polish, Romanian, Croatian, Slovak, Slovene, and Serbian.
ISO-8859-3	Latin-3	ASCII plus characters required for English, Esperanto, German, Maltese, and Galician.
ISO-8859-4	Latin-4	ASCII plus most Baltic languages, including Latvian, Lithuanian, German, Greenlandic, and Lappish; now superseded by ISO-Latin-6.
ISO-8859-5		ASCII plus Cyrillic characters for Slavic languages, including Byelorussian, Bulgarian, Macedonian, Russian, Serbian, and Ukrainian.
ISO-8859-6		ASCII plus Arabic characters.
ISO-8859-7		ASCII plus Greek characters.
ISO-8859-8		ASCII plus Hebrew.
ISO-8859-9	Latin-5	Latin-1 except that some Turkish symbols replace Icelandic ones.
ISO-8859-10	Latin-6	ASCII plus most Nordic languages, including Latvian, Lithuanian, Inuit, non-Skolt Sami, and Icelandic.
ISO-8859-11		ASCII plus Thai.
ISO-8859-12	Latin-7	ASCII plus Celtic.
ISO-8859-13	Latin-8	ASCII plus the Baltic Rim characters.
ISO-8859-14	Latin-9	ASCII plus Sami (Finnish).
ISO-8859-15	Latin-10	Variation on Latin-1 that includes Euro currency sign, plus extra accented Finnish and French characters.

Good HTML, XHTML, and XML development tools all support character and numeric entities. If you don't already have one, you should get one sooner rather than later. If nothing else, it will save you from having to type more ampersands and semi-colons than any sane person should have to. Chapter 6 discusses finding good XHTML tools, and you can always visit `www.tucows.com` to find good HTML tools, and `www.xmlsoftware.com` for good XML tools.

Chapter 15

Using XHTML Tables Effectively

● ●

In This Chapter

▶ Gazing over the table landscape

▶ Deciding to table or not to table

▶ Understanding table elements

▶ Polishing your own custom tables

● ●

*I*n the Web design world, tables are most likely an addiction, and many times even a necessity. This is not always the case. One day, in the perfect world of Web design, you'll use Cascading Style Sheets (CSS) to position all the graphics and text on your page. Until this utopia exists, you can arrange everything from text to images on your pages, efficiently and attractively, in XHTML tables. The 3.0 and later versions of both Netscape and Internet Explorer support tables, as do the more recent versions of other, non-commercial browsers, such as Mosaic and Opera.

If your browser doesn't support tables, it's a sign that upgrade time is here again.

Since the days of HTML 3.2, tables have become standard elements of Web documents. With XHTML 1.0, proprietary extensions from Netscape and Microsoft have given way to official standards. This chapter will have you creating monster tables in no time at all.

Don't Like Tables?

The traditional approach to tabulating data, or organizing content on a page, is the `<table>` element. But before you walk down this road, please ask yourself this question, "Do I really need a table here?" If the answer is no, consider your alternatives:

> ✔ **Lists:** Easy and simple to implement as well as consistently well rendered by every browser available. Lists are sensible alternatives to tables if you want to quickly and easily group information. However, lists don't give you the formatting capabilities of tables, especially for images.

✔ **Images:** You create images in grids with borders and colors, but be warned that these images may become static and difficult to change. Images also can be big and slow!

✔ **Preformatted text:** This choice is the original table markup and an option that will still work in a pinch without causing any concern over browser compatibility. However, most browsers generally display preformatted text in a non-proportional font that looks terrible. If presentation is your goal, this method is not recommended.

✔ **Frames:** These complex constructs may offer an additional dimension to your Web site, but they really aren't replacements for tables.

The preceding alternatives notwithstanding, tables are great for many uses — presenting financial results, organizing lists of related elements (such as dates and birthdays), and giving rowdy elements a defined layout — trust us, there are many rowdy elements!

XHTML <table> Overview

Table markup brings versatility to describing your content. XHTML tables offer virtually limitless description possibilities because you can put almost any XHTML element into a table cell.

The key for right now is to keep it simple. Unless you're developing documents for a private Web server where you *know* your audience is using a particular browser, stick with basic table elements. Sticking to a common denominator (common table elements) is the best way to ensure your Web site gets the most pairs of eyes. As you wander awestruck through the rest of this chapter (well, we can hope), eagerly absorbing the basics (and some nifty uses) of XHTML tables, pay particular attention to how table constructs nest within each other. If you goof up just one nesting order, your information won't display the way you expect it to.

Make your life easier. Every time you add another level to a table, indent the code to offset it from the previous level. Then, when you return to a higher level, decrease your indentation to match previous code at the same level. To demonstrate this healthful and sensible principle, we use this method in all of the examples in this chapter for your rapt perusal.

An obvious-but-important fact is that a table is a visual device that's hard to read aloud to someone who can't see it. If your readership includes users who may be print-handicapped or otherwise visually impaired, provide an alternative form for your table data. Some browsers produce Braille or convert text to speech, but most aren't able to handle the XHTML <table> element for such conversions. As one solution, many Web sites offer text-only implementations for tables as an alternative. You may want to consider doing the same if it's appropriate for your audience. You should also pay attention to the summary attribute discussed later in this chapter.

XHTML Table Markup

Any presentational XHTML body element works in a table cell. You can even nest multiple tables within a single cell — a fun but time-consuming activity that we don't recommend you jump into just now.

The parts of a <table>

The basic parts of a table are the <table> element that surrounds all of a table's contents, the <tr> (table row) element that defines each row within a table, and the <td> (table data) element that defines each cell within each row of a table.

But, that's not all. Optional table elements include:

- ✔ <caption> (caption)
- ✔ <th> (table header)
- ✔ <tbody> (table body)
- ✔ <thead> (table head)
- ✔ <tfoot> (table foot)
- ✔ <colgroup> (column group)
- ✔ <col /> (column)

The following code snippet for a simple XHTML table illustrates the required — and most common — elements, in the most boring way we can imagine. (Hey, ya gotta play some dives before you become a rock star and play the big arenas!)

```
<table>
<caption> Table Caption </caption>
    <tr>
        <th> table header information </th>
        <th> table header information </th>
    </tr>
    <tr>
        <td> column 1, row 1 table data </td>
        <td> column 2, row 1 table data  </td>
    </tr>
```

```
        <tr>
            <td> column 1, row 2 table data </td>
            <td> column 2, row 2 table data </td>
        </tr>
</table>
```

If you put the preceding table code in a Web page and view the result in Internet Explorer, you see something similar to the snazzola table depicted in Figure 15-1 — all bones, no meat. (Bleah!)

Really feeling adventurous? Take our first code sample, replace our less-than-exciting content with some of your own (text, images, or whatever you like), save the new code, and view it in your favorite browser. Voilà! You've created a table.

Regardless of how big or small your table is or what content you choose to include within its cells, always include the following elements in every table you create:

✔ `<table>`
✔ `<tr>`
✔ `<td>`

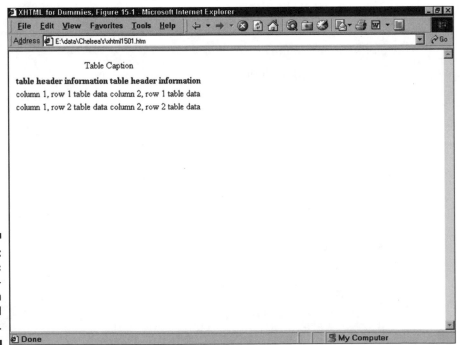

Figure 15-1:
A basic table, complete with caption and headings.

But wait. If you used our example to create your own table, you've already unlocked the basic concepts of table layout and nesting techniques. Now that you have this potent knowledge, you can construct a basic table of your own all by your little lonesome. Before you go forth to rule the world, however, understand each of these elements and their attributes. Say no more.

In the following sections, we define many table elements (such as, `<td>`, `<th>`, and `<tr>`). Because most of these table elements use many of the same attributes, we define all the attributes after you tackle the elements themselves.

`<table>` . . . `</table>` *Table container element*

The `<table>` element is a container element for all other table elements. Even browsers ignore other table elements if they aren't contained by the `<table>` element. The `<table>` element accepts the following unique attributes: `summary`, `align`, `border`, `frame`, `rules`, `cellpadding`, `cellspacing`, `bgcolor`, and `width`.

If you close all elements, without the closing `<table>` tag, your table may not show up at all; invisible tables aren't really very useful. And as a bonus, you get another warning for no cost: The `align` attribute is deprecated, so watch out; it may not be in the next version of XHTML. If you want to position your table, you should consider using Cascading Style Sheets (CSS) instead.

`<tr>` . . . `</tr>` *Table row*

The `<tr>` element contains the information for all cells within a particular table row. Each `<tr>` element represents a single row, no matter how many cells the row contains. The `<tr>` element accepts the `align` and `valign` attributes — which, if you specify them, become default alignments that whip all the contents of all cells in the row into line, as well as `char` and `charoff`.

The `align` attribute is not deprecated in this instance, so if you're dying to use it, it's okay by us (and the W3C).

`<td>` . . . `</td>` *Table data*

The `<td>` element holds the contents of each cell in a table. If those fussbudget browsers are going to recognize cells as cells, you have to put your cell data within this element and then, in turn, nest the table data element within a table row element. The `<td>` element gives your cells some friendly characteristics:

- ✔ You don't have to worry about making each row contain the same number of cells because short rows are completed with blank cells on the right.

- ✔ A cell can contain any XHTML element normally used within the `<body>` element of an XHTML document.

The `<td>` element accepts the following attributes: abbr, align, axis, bgcolor, colspan, headers, scope, height, nowrap, rowspan, valign, **and** width.

`<th>` . . . `</th>` *Table header*

The *table header* element (`<th>`) displays text in boldface with a default center alignment. You can use the `<th>` element within any row of a table, but you most often find and use it in the first row at the top — or head — of a table. Except for its position and egotism, the `<th>` element acts just like `<td>` element.

`<caption>` . . . `</caption>` *Table caption*

The `<caption>` element was designed to exist anywhere inside the `<table>` element, but not inside table rows or cells (because then they wouldn't be *captioning* anything). Similar to table cells, captions accommodate any XHTML elements that can appear in the body of a document (in other words, inline elements), but only those. By default, captions put themselves at horizontal dead center with respect to a table, wrapping their lines to fit within the table's width. Keep in mind that this element is a stickler and can only be used once. The `<caption>` element accepts the align attribute.

Many Web page authors take a short cut and use an `<h*>` tag in place of the `<caption>` tag. Most of us are under the gun and in a hurry to get our projects on the boss' table. But steer clear of this shortcut because it's a no-no according to the W3C's Accessibility Initiative. To read more about the W3C's guidelines, visit www.w3.org/WAI/.

An inline element is any element that controls presentation on an element-by-element basis and an inline element does not denote structure. In other words, it's a text element, for example the `<b>` element is an inline element.

Recent Additions to the Table Family

Recently, the W3C added functionality to tables by introducing the following tags:

- `<tbody>` . . . `</tbody>`
- `<thead>` . . . `</thead>`
- `<tfoot>` . . . `</tfoot>`
- `<colgroup>` . . . `</colgroup>`
- `<col />`

The first three elements allow authors to divide their tables into logical sections; however, in the future, that won't be all. Adding structure is important, but it's not the most fun you can have working with XHTML. Luckily, the W3C has added a little pizzazz to these three elements — now we're just waiting for the browsers to catch up.

After you separate your table into table head, table foot, and table body sections, the table body section is then able to scroll independently of the table head and foot sections. Although this function is not supported yet, we're all keeping our fingers crossed that browsers will provide support on the next go around.

The last two elements (`<colgroup>` and `<col />`) help maintain those pesky columns. With the use of their attributes, you can define uniform behavior for your columns. Another win for tables!

`<tbody>` . . . `</tbody>` *Table body*

Table rows may be grouped into a table body section, using the `<tbody>` element. As a recent addition to the HTML 4 specification, these tags allow for a division that enables browsers to support scrolling of table bodies independently of the table head and table foot (`<tfoot>`). The table body should contain rows of table data. The `<tbody>` element must contain at least one table row.

`<thead>` . . . `</thead>` *Table head*

Table rows may be grouped into a table head section, using the `<thead >` element, which allows for a division that enables browsers to support scrolling of table bodies independently of the table head and table foot. Keep in mind that most browsers don't support the `<thead>` element yet. The table head contains information about the table's columns. The `<thead>` element must contain at least one table row.

If you decide to use one of the logical table dividers — `<tfoot>`, `<thead>`, or `<tbody>` — make sure that all the `<tr>` element are contained by them. Don't leave any out to dry!

`<tfoot>`...`</tfoot>` *Table foot*

Much like the `<thead>` element, table rows may be grouped into a table footer section, using the `<tfoot>` element. This newer element allow for a division that enables user agents to support scrolling of table bodies independently of the table head and table foot. The table foot contains information about the table's columns and must contain at least one table row. If used, you must include your footer information before the first instance of the `<tbody>` element; that way, the browser renders that information before taking a stab at all the content data cells — rules are rules.

When you pull them all together — `<thead>`, `<tbody>` and `<tfoot>` that is — this is what you get:

```
<table border="1">
<caption>The caption.</caption>
<thead>
 <tr>
  <th> Header: row 1, column 1</th>
  <th> Header: row 1, column 2</th>
 </tr>
</thead>
<tfoot>
 <tr>
  <td> Footer: row 1, column 1</th>
  <td> Footer: row 1, column 2</th>
 </tr>
</tfoot>
<tbody>
 <tr>
  <td> Cell: row 2, column 1</td>
  <td> Cell: row 2, column 2</td>
 </tr>
</tbody>
</table>
```

To see a table with a head, foot, and body section, check out Figure 15-2.

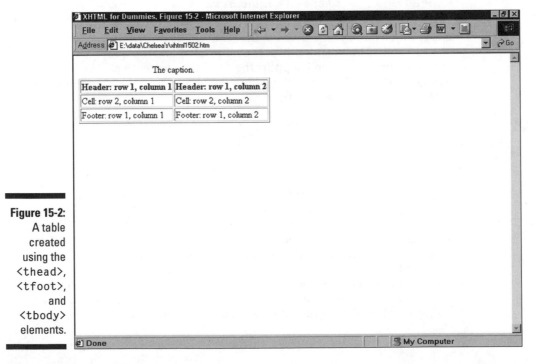

Figure 15-2:
A table created using the `<thead>`, `<tfoot>`, and `<tbody>` elements.

`<colgroup>` . . . `</colgroup>` *Table colgroup*

The `<colgroup>` element creates an explicit column group. The number of columns is specified using the span attribute or using the `<col />` element, which is defined shortly. Using the span attribute allows you to specify a uniform width for a group of columns. The `<colgroup>` element takes two unique attributes:

```
span="number"
```

The span attribute specifies the number of columns in a column group. This attribute is ignored if you specify one or more `<col />` element within the `<colgroup>` element. The default value is 1.

```
width="%" or "pixels" or "n*"
```

The width attribute defines a default width for each column found within the column group. Using "0*" as the default value assigns a relative value, meaning that the width of each column in the column group is the minimum width necessary to contain the column's contents.

Here is an example using the `<colgroup>` element.

```
<table>
<colgroup span="30" width="15">
</colgroup>
<colgroup span="10" width="45">
</colgroup>
</table>
```

The previous code separates 40 columns into two groups. The first column group contains 30 columns, each with a width of 15 pixels. The second column group contains 10 columns, each with a width of 45 pixels. Easy enough, huh?

`<col />` Table column

The `<col />` element is an *empty* element — meaning an end tag is forbidden. All empty elements must follow special syntax: `<empty />`. You use the `<col />` element to further define column structure. The `<col />` element should not be used to group columns — that is a function for the `<colgroup>` element — but rather it should be used as a way to support its attributes. After you define a column group and set a uniform width, you can specify a uniform width for a subset of columns using the `<col />` element. Take a look at our example:

```
<table>
<colgroup>
  <col width="20" />
</colgroup>
<colgroup>
```

```
  <col width="20" />
  <col width="0*" />
</colgroup>
<colgroup>
  <col width="1*" />
  <col width="3*" />
</colgroup>
<thead>
<tr>
...
</tr>
...more rows...
</thead>
...table foot and body sections...
</table>
```

If you're shaking your head and saying, "Huh?," you probably want us to explain the previous code. First, the browser allots 20 pixels to columns one and two. Then, the minimal space required for the third column is reserved. The remaining space is divided into four equal portions. Because $1* + 3* = 4$ portions, column four ($1*$) receives one of the four portions, and column five ($3*$) receives the remaining three.

Add some flair by using CSS to uniformly style your $\langle$col $/\rangle$ groups.

Now that you've toured the new table elements, we get you back to basics by discussing common table attributes.

Basic Table Attributes

Okay, here's where the incantations that create tables get a bit more complicated. You can use several attributes with the different table elements to determine how the table's parts and contents appear on-screen. Get to know these critters, use them innovatively, and they repay your attention by making your tables easier on the eye.

To see a quick overview of table attributes, take a peek at Table 15-1. In the Unique Attributes column, you occasionally notice a big D in parentheses. The D stands for *deprecated*. Anytime you see the term deprecated (or the big D), think style sheets. Deprecated elements are going to be phased out in later versions of XHTML. This is the W3C's polite way to tell you to clean up your act (and your code!) and use style sheets.

Element	Unique Attributes
<caption>	align (D)
<col />	span, width, align, char, charoff, valign
<colgroup>	span, width, align, char, charoff, valign
<table>	summary, align (D), width, bgcolor (D), border, rules, frame, cellspacing, cellpadding
<tbody>	align, char, charoff, valign
<td>	headers, scope, abbr, axis, rowspan, colspan, nowrap (D), width (D), height (D), align, char, charoff, valign, bgcolor (D)
<tfoot>	align, char, charoff, valign
<th>	headers, scope, abbr, axis, rowspan, colspan, nowrap (D), width (D), height (D), align, char, charoff, valign, bgcolor (D)
<thead>	align, char, charoff, valign
<tr>	align, char, charoff, valign, bgcolor (D)

```
align="left" or "center" or "right" or "justify" or "char"
```

There are three different instances of the align attributes. This first instance can be used with the <col />, <colgroup>, <tbody>, <thead>, <tfoot>, <tr>, <td>, or <th> elements. Use align with these elements to define how the content within table cells is aligned. When you set an alignment for a table row tag, the alignment applies to all the contents of all the cells or header cells in that row. When you set an alignment for a single table cell or table header, the alignment only applies to the content in that single cell or header cell. Finally, if you set the alignment for all the cells in a row and then set the alignment for a cell within that row, the setting you add to the cell overrides the setting for the row. Whew! Bet you didn't know one little attribute could do so much.

```
align="left" or "center" or "right"
```

Use align with the <table> element to set the table's alignment relative to the rest of the page. The default alignment for a table is left, so to center the table or force it to justify to the right, set the value of align to center or right. This attribute is deprecated.

```
align="top" or "bottom" or "left" or "right"
```

Use `align` with the `<caption>` element to specify how the table's caption should be aligned relative to the table itself. The default alignment for a caption is `center`. This attribute is deprecated.

```
border="number"
```

The `border` attribute only works with the `<table>` element. Its job is to let the browser know whether you want a border around your table or not, and if so, how big you want that border to be. This attribute takes a numeric value — `border="5"` for example — that indicates how many pixels wide you want the border to be. If you don't want a border around your table, specify `border="0"`. If you don't specify a value, the default value is up to the browser.

If we changed the first line of our plain-Jane table in the "The parts of a `<table>`" section earlier in this chapter to `<table border="5">`, our table is now well outlined, as shown in Figure 15-3.

Tables without borders can provide a clean look and feel and help you control unruly text and graphics, but we've found the business of building tables to be both tedious and exacting. To make things a bit easier, we suggest you set the border on a table to one (1) while it's under construction so you can more easily see how the browser is interpreting your rows and columns. When you're done with construction and like with the results, simply change the 1 to a 0 — and "Bye-bye, border."

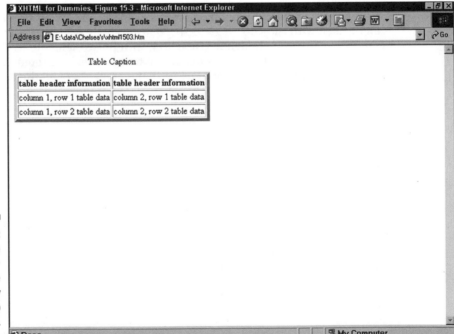

Figure 15-3:
The
border
attribute
can really
box up
a table.

`cellpadding="number"`

Yet another attribute that you only use with the `<table>` element, `cellpadding` specifies the amount of space between a cell's perimeter and its contents. Think, cotton padding in a pillow. The default value for this attribute is 1 pixel but you make the value as large or small as you'd like.

This handy-dandy attribute helps you put some space between the content in your cells, making them easier to read. Combined with cell spacing and a well-sized border, cell padding can enhance the visual impact of your tables.

Once again, working with the basic table from "The parts of a `<table>`" section earlier in this chapter, we add a bit of white space within every cell by changing the opening table tag to `<table cellpadding="10">`. Check out the results for yourself in Figure 15-4. We've added a table cell background color so you see the difference between the `cellpadding` and `cellspacing` attribute.

`cellspacing="number"`

Use the `cellspacing` attribute within the `<table>` element to determine the amount of space inserted between individual cells in a table. The default value is one pixel between cells. If we set the border on our basic table to 5 and change the `cellspacing` attribute to 10 using `<table border="5" cellspacing="10">`, the browser displays the XHTML with a bit more space between the cells, as shown in Figure 15-4. We have added a table cell background color so you see the difference between the `cellpadding` and `cellspacing` attribute.

Unless you have your table border set to more than one pixel or the background colors of your table cells set to different colors — like our example — you won't see a difference in the display of the `cellspacing` and the `cellpadding` attributes.

`summary="text"`

The `summary` attribute is used with the `<table>` element to provide a summary of the table's structure and purpose for users using non-visual media such as Braille. This is a fairly new, yet important attribute to include in all your tables. There's nothing technical here, just in your own words outline what is found in your table.

`width="number" or "percent%"`

When used with `<table>` element, the `width` attribute sets the width of a table in absolute terms (a specific number of pixels) or as a percentage of a browser's display area. You also use this attribute within `<th>` or `<td>` elements — to decree the width of a cell within a table as an absolute number of pixels or else assign it a percentage of the table's width. (Now, that's power!)

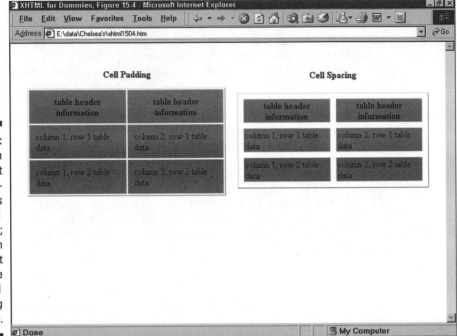

Figure 15-4:
The table on
the left
demon-
strates
`cell
padding`;
the table on
the right
uses the
`cell
spacing`
attribute.

Until now, the display of our basic table has only taken up as much of the browser window as was necessary to show all its content. If we change the opening table tag so its width is `75%` (`<table width="75%">`), the table will take up `75%` of the browser window's width. If we set the width to `600` (for 600 pixels) — `<table width="600">` — the table is forced to be exactly (or absolutely) 600 pixels wide, and the cell contents wrap to fit the specific size.

To create flexible tables that accommodate a wider variety of monitor sizes and browser window widths, we highly recommend that you use relative table widths — percentages instead of pixels. If you absolutely must create a table with an absolute width — pixels instead of percentages — don't make it any larger than 550 or 600 pixels. If you violate this restriction, users with smaller monitors may have to scroll horizontally to read your page. In the Web world, that's sure to chase your users away in hordes.

```
valign="top" or "middle" or "bottom"
```

Tuck the `valign` (*vertical alignment*) attribute within the `<col />`, `<colgroup>`, `<tbody>`, `<thead>`, `<tfoot>`, `<tr>`, `<th>`, or `<td>` tags to vertically align the contents of the table to the top, middle, or bottom of the cell. In general, `valign` is a counterpart to `align`, so you often use them together. The default value for this attribute is `middle`. Ten-hut!

```
nowrap="nowrap"
```

When you use nowrap with a table cell or header (<th> or <td>), Web browsers will try to display all the text for that particular cell on a single line. This sometimes produces weird results. We know if may look funny, but when used, the nowrap attribute must equal itself. This attribute is deprecated.

```
colspan="number"
```

Spanning is a key component of XHTML tables because it helps you over-come one of the most maddening characteristics of tables: their overwhelming desire to be symmetrical. By way of explanation, think about what might happen if you add another <th> element to the first row of our basic table — but not to the second row — using this code:

```
<table border="1">
<caption>The caption.</caption>
  <tr>
    <th> Header: row 1, column 1</th>
    <th> Header: row 1, column 2</th>
    <th> Header: row 1, column 3</th>
  </tr>
  <tr>
    <td> Cell: row 2, column 1</td>
    <td> Cell: row 2, column 2</td>
  </tr>
</table>
```

Tables always want to be symmetrical, so the browser will automatically add an empty cell to our second row to serve as a balance for the new cell we added in the first row, as shown in Figure 15-5.

Not the prettiest picture we've ever seen. What to do, what to do? There's got to be a way to force one cell in a row to act as more than one cell. In fact, there is. Spanning allows you to create a single table cell that spans several rows or columns, depending on your needs. For example, to make the second column of our second row span two columns — act like two cells in one row — we only need change the table data element to:

```
<td colspan="2"> Cell: row 2, column 2</td>
```

Ta-da! As Figure 15-6 shows, the single cell now acts as two cells and spans across two columns, filling in the space where the empty cell created by the browser had previously been. It's not magic; it's XHTML.

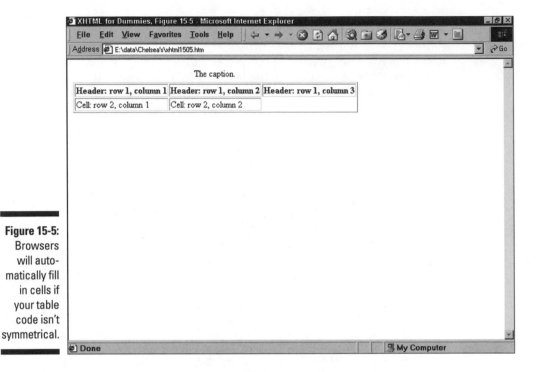

Figure 15-5:
Browsers will automatically fill in cells if your table code isn't symmetrical.

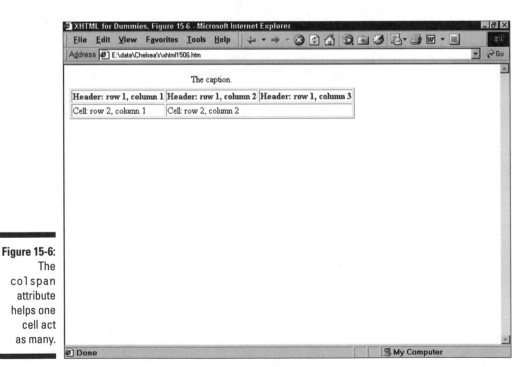

Figure 15-6:
The colspan attribute helps one cell act as many.

```
rowspan="number"
```

The `rowspan` attribute is similar to `colspan` in both form and function — as if their names didn't give that away. When you use `rowspan` with table data (`<td>`) or table header (`<th>`) element, the cell spans multiple rows — as opposed to multiple columns. In the previous section, we used `colspan="2"` to force one cell to act as two in the same row to solve the dilemma created by the unbalanced table code example we used. In the same way, we use `rowspan="2"` with the new table header cell (row 1, column 3) to force the cell to expand down into the second row and make the table symmetrical:

```
<th rowspan="2"> Header: row 1, column 3</th>
```

Check out the results in Figure 15-7.

```
bgcolor="color"
```

Remember the `bgcolor` attribute that goes with the `<body>` element? This is the same attribute, and it affects the background of table cells in the same way it affects the background of your entire XHTML document. Simply add this attribute to any `<table>`, `<td>`, `<th>`, or `<tr>` element to change its background color. This attribute is deprecated.

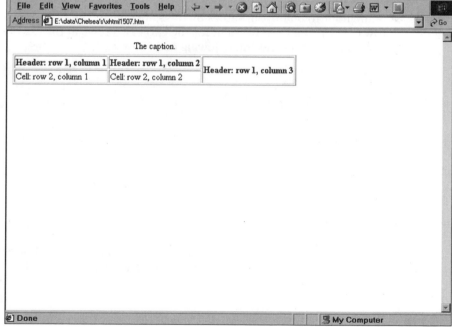

Figure 15-7:
The rowspan attribute causes one cell to expand down several rows.

Build Your Own Tables

Building tables by hand is time-consuming, repetitive work, even if you make them out of data instead of wood. So be sure that a tabular form enhances your content. You can simplify your work by carefully planning the layout of your tabular data and by making use of search, replace, copy, and paste functions in your XHTML/text editor. Before you start tagging your data to make it totally tabular (is there an echo in here?), consider . . .

Laying out tabular data for easy display

First, sketch how you want your table to look (give yourself room; it might be *bigger* than a cocktail napkin). Then create a small XHTML table with only a few rows of data to test your layout; does the table appear the way you envisioned it? If you're using table heads that span multiple columns or rows, you may need to adjust the space they take to fit your data. Finally, test your tables with several browsers to see how they look on each one. Finalize your design before you add the data you want the table to contain.

Multirow and multicolumn spans

Remember to build your tables by rows. If you use rowspan="3" in one table row (<tr>), you must account for the extra two rows in the next two rows. For example, consider the following code morsel:

```
<table border>
  <tr>
    <td rowspan="3">Letters</td>
    <td>A</td>
  </tr>
  <tr>
    <td>B</td>
  </tr>
  <tr>
    <td>C</td>
  </tr>
</table>
```

The idea is to leave out a cell in each row or column that will be assumed ("spanned into," if you prefer) by the rowspan or colspan cell.

Mixing graphics and tables to add interest

If you want to frighten off a visitor to your Web page, just pack a screen full of dense and impenetrable information — especially numbers. A long, unbroken list of numbers quickly drives away all but the truly masochistic. You can stop the pain: Put those numbers into an attractive table (better yet, *several* tables interspersed with a few well-chosen images). Watch your page's attractiveness and readability soar; hear visitors sigh with relief.

Individual table cells can be surprisingly roomy; you can position graphics in them precisely. If you're moved to put graphics in a table, be sure to:

- ✔ Select images that are similar in size and looks.
- ✔ Measure those images to determine their heights and widths in pixels (shareware programs such as Paint Shop Pro and GraphicConverter do this automatically).
- ✔ Use XHTML markup to position these images within their table cells.

A short and sweet table keeps the graphics in check and guarantees that the text will always sit nicely to its right.

Two more handy graphics-placement tips: (1) size your rows and columns of cells that contain images to accommodate the largest graphic, and (2) center all graphics in each cell (vertically and horizontally). The result is a consistent, coherent image layout.

Tools automate tedious markup

Most decent/recent XHTML editors build tables for you — we tend to be addicted to Dreamweaver at the moment! Many have table wizards that ask you how many rows and columns you'd like and then automatically generate the necessary XHTML markup. In these same editors, you also find tools that make adding new rows, columns, spans, and background colors as easy as pie.

Likewise, Microsoft Excel now offers a Save as Web Page option in the File menu. You can create your table in Excel — or easily transfer an existing Excel table to XHTML — and then use this nifty function to make Excel create the necessary markup automatically.

Three cheers for progress! So how come we made you learn the details of XHTML table markup? Well, what can we say — we're sadists (just kidding).

Actually, none of these tools *fully* automates all the details that appear within a table. Your artistic touch is still needed to create borders, cell padding, cell spacing, and so on. Besides, no automatic process really understands how to position graphics as precisely as a human designer (take *that,* soulless machines!). Still, these tools simplify the initial and often tedious creation of table markup. Because you're going to have to tweak your tables by hand anyway, we figured the best way to get started was with a little "manual labor." (You'll thank us later. Honest.)

Using CSS with Tables

Many — more like most — presentation attributes are deprecated. There's a very good reason for this madness and it's all about semantics. XHTML should define structure — that's been its purpose since the very first version of HTML (XHTML's predecessor). Over the years, presentation elements have crept their way into the various specifications as browsers continued to introduce their own proprietary stylish elements. The W3C is not putting their foot down and bellowing from the roof tops..."Enough is enough!" Style has its place in Web design — in fact, is has an entire specification to it.

To keep on top of the learning curve, start to learn CSS now. Your first stop should be Chapter 8 of this book. Your next stop should be the W3C Cascading Style Sheet Specification found at `www.w3.org/TR/REC-CSS2/`.

However, before you go flipping pages, browse through the following example of an XHTML table styled with CSS:

```
<!DOCTYPE html PUBLIC "-//W3C//DTD XHTML 1.0
          Transitional//EN"
          "DTD/xhtml1-transitional.dtd">
<html xmlns="http://www.w3.org/1999/xhtml">
<head>
    <title>XHTML Table</title>
    <style type="text/css">
      p.intro {color:grey; font-weight:normal; text-align:
          left}
      p.last {color:black; font-weight:normal; text-align:
          left}
      caption {text-align: left; font-weight:bold}
      td {border: double black}
      th {background: pink}
    </style>
</head>

<!-- This starts the body of the document. -->

<body>
<p class="intro">What property-value pair works in place of
          deprecated table attributes? Take a look at a
```

```
couple examples!</p>
<table>
<caption>CSS Property-Value Pairs</caption>
    <tr>
        <th> Deprecated Attribute </th>
        <th> CSS Property-Value Pair </th>
    </tr>
    <tr>
        <td>align="center"</td>
        <td>text-align:center</td>
    </tr>
    <tr>
        <td>bgcolor="pink"</td>
        <td>background:pink</td>
    </tr>
</table>
<p class="last">To read more about CSS, please see Chapter
        8.<p>
</body>
</html>
```

Make sense? Now take a look at Figure 15-8 to see how it might look in a browser. Remember, CSS is not fully supported yet, but Netscape Navigator 6 and Internet Explorer 5 do a pretty good job!

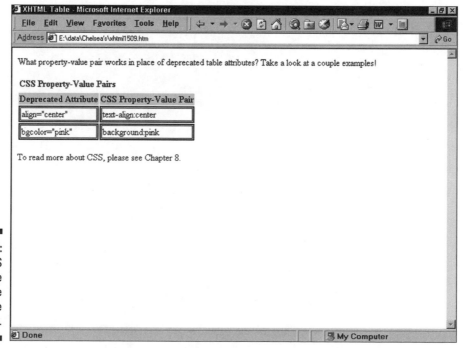

Figure 15-8:
Using CSS
to add style
makes the
folks at the
W3C smile.

Some Stunning Table Examples

To find the best uses of tables on the Web . . . well, look around the Web.

We think these popular sites make excellent use of tables in their design:

- ✔ **CNET** — This entire site uses tables for all the complex layout. Often, tables are within tables within tables: www.cnet.com.

- ✔ **Yahoo!** — The most popular search engine on the Web uses tables to display their front page and all of the navigation items on all results pages: www.yahoo.com.

- ✔ **Dilbert Zone** — The only engineer on the planet to publicly disparage his boss and still keep his job (wait a minute — didn't he quit and become a cartoonist?). This daily dose of Dilbert is presented entirely by means of tables: www.unitedmedia.com/comics/dilbert/.

After you load these documents into your Web browser, take a look at each one's XHTML source code (try View⇨Source from your menu bar). Observe how complex the markup is, and mark ye well when the markup looks haphazardly arranged (alas, if only they'd asked us . . .).

Part IV
Taking XHTML to the Next Level

The 5th Wave   By Rich Tennant

"Before the Internet, we were only bustin'
chops locally. But now, with our Web site,
we're bustin' chops all over the world."

In this part . . .

Here, we cover some of the more interesting and complicated aspects of Web page design. To start, you learn the ins and outs of building and using tables in your Web pages, for effects that can combine text and graphics in all kinds of interesting ways. After tables come image maps, where you find how to turn an ordinary digital image into a Website navigation tool. Next, it's your turn to fabricate forms, so you can solicit and handle user input on your Web pages. After that, it's time to tackle the joys and sorrows of HTML frames, and what multiple frames can do to your Web site. Finally, you conclude with a lightning tour of what adding code to your Web pages — including Java programs, inline scripts, and multimedia data streams — can do for your content (and your users). In short, it's a whirlwind tour of some really snazzy Web stuff!

Chapter 16

Map It Up!

In This Chapter
▶ Using clickable maps
▶ Using image map alternatives
▶ Deciphering the differences between server-side and client-side maps
▶ Mapping from the client side

*Y*ou want to create a groovy navigational graphic. You already know how to insert graphics into XHTML documents using the `<img />` element (if not, see Chapter 12). So it's time to turn your graphics into hypertext links with image maps. In this chapter, we show you how to treat a graphic as a collection of hot spots, each pointing to a different hypertext resource.

One Step at a Time

Don't create an image map for a graphic that is all text. If your graphic image is textual navigation, you can achieve the same effect using plain text and the *anchor* element. Not only is it easier to use plain text, but your pages download quicker!

If you use plain text, you need to be familiar with the `<a>` element. Here's how it looks in action:

```
<a href="url.here">plain-jane text here</a>
```

If you are not familiar with the `<a>` element, follow the path of enlightenment in Chapter 12.

If your boss wants you to use a specific font for your hyperlink text that most browsers don't support, you must use a graphic. We feel your pain. Your boss is forcing you to use graphics when all you want to do is throw in some text and hyperlinks. If you must use graphics as hyperlinks, you have two options:

- ✔ Use an image map
- ✔ Break your images into smaller pieces

Breaking images into smaller pieces keeps your image file sizes down. If you break your image into smaller pieces, forget the image map. This code is all you need:

```
<a href="url.here"><img src="file.gif" /></a>
```

Mapping out the Territory

The geographical maps we're accustomed to identify landmasses and divide them along boundaries into named regions — countries, counties, office parks, and so on. You can use graphics the same way on the Web, divvying an image so its regions activate different hyperlinks.

Users familiar with graphical interfaces have no trouble interacting with buttons, icons, and other kinds of interface controls. Graphical maps add this capability to a single image displayed on a Web page — in Web-speak, an *image map,* or *clickable map*. We prefer *clickable map* because it suggests both the nature of these graphical elements and how they're used, as follows:

- **Their nature:** Clickable maps break a graphic into discrete regions that function as a collection of individual hyperlinks. Normally, the regional boundaries are obvious; users simply select whatever portion of the graphic attracts their interest.

- **Their use:** Users select regions by putting the cursor inside the desired region and clicking the mouse. Then it's *bon voyage!*

Those who have bossed a computer from a command prompt, word by word, are hip to a fundamental limitation of clickable maps: They absolutely require a GUI browser. Clickable maps don't work if you can't click 'em (or even see 'em). The image that represents the map isn't visible in a character-mode browser. Therefore, as a friendly gesture to users with text-only browsers, supplement your clickable maps by implementing alternate navigation methods that don't need pictures.

Breeds Apart

If you decided that creating an image map is the solution, you must make one more decision before you talk in x, y and z's: Which *type* of image map you want to use:

- **Client-side:** A user activates a region of the map with his or her pointing device, such as a mouse.

   When the mouse is over an active region, the browser interprets the pixel coordinates and reacts accordingly (normally by linking to another page).

✔ **Server-side:** The work is done on the server. A user activates a region of the map with a mouse click. Once clicked, the pixel coordinates are sent to the server. The server then interprets the coordinates and performs the corresponding action.

We (and the W3C) suggest that you always use client-side image maps instead of server-side image maps. There are two reasons to keep your hands off server-side maps:

✔ Server-side image maps are not accessible to people using non-graphical browsers (think accessibility!).

✔ Server-side image maps don't let a user know whether the mouse is over a link. Client-side image maps do.

This chapter focuses on client-side maps. For the straight story on server-side maps, see `www.wdvl.com/Authoring/HTML/Tutorial/defining_image_maps.html`.

Map It Out

A client-side image map is a graphical navigation tool that runs within a user's browser and requires neither a server nor a CGI map file to operate. (Whoa! No visible means of support! How do they do that?) Both Netscape and Microsoft Web browsers support client-side image maps. Because a clickable map is a mode of cybertransportation as well as a nifty picture, building one requires three different processes:

1. **Create (or selecting) a usable image.**

   This image is an existing graphic or one you make on your own. (If you create your own graphics, be forewarned that a lack of sleep may result.)

2. **Define the hot-spot areas of the image.**

   This task requires a step-by-step investigation of the image file inside a graphics program that gives you the pixel addresses (coordinates) of each point on the boundary that separates the regions you want to create. (The impatient and efficient among you can use a map-building utility such as Mapedit, which we describe later in this chapter.)

   Here's an example. You create a five-button image in which all the buttons are about the same size. Working through this process of creating an image map is easy: The image starts in the upper-left corner of the button bar (at vertical location 142, or about the middle of this 285-pixel-high image) and is consistently 143 pixels high. The individual buttons vary slightly in width, producing the following set of coordinates:

```
(0,142)—(99,142)—(199,142)—(299,142)—(399,142)—(499,142)
  button 1 | button 2 | button 3 | button 4 | button 5
(0,285)—(99,285)—(199,285)—(299,285)—(399,285)—(499,285)
```

Just that easy, just that simple.

Unfortunately, the only way to produce this collection of numbers is inside a graphics program that shows *pixel coordinates* (we use Adobe Photoshop, but you can use Paint Shop Pro, a widely available shareware graphics program for Windows). The alternative, of course, is to use an *image-map construction program.* (You haven't peeked ahead, have you?)

An image-map tool generates a map after you tell the tool which shapes you're outlining. One example is Tom Boutell's excellent program, Mapedit, which builds map files at your command. Mapedit is available for Mac, DOS/Windows, and UNIX. Go to `www.boutell.com/mapedit/` to find Mapedit.

3. **Embed the coordinates and link information in an XHTML document.**

   This is what provides the browser with the information for each active region.

4. **Define the shape of your map.**

   Defining the shape of your map allows you to use coordinates. A rectangle is not a circle — at least not in our book!

<map>...</map> Client-side map

The `<map>` element contains information for the client-side map.

Unique Attributes:

```
name="text"
```

The `name` attribute assigns a name to the image map.

When you name your element, you must also associate that name with the corresponding image, using the `usemap` attribute — or how else would the browser know which map goes with which image on your page. To see the `usemap` attribute in action, see the "Learning by Example" section with a full example.

<area /> *Client-side image map area*

The <area /> element defines each individual region, providing the shape, coordinates and hyperlink.

Unique Attributes:

```
nohref="nohref"
```

When used, this attribute specifies that a region has no associated link.

```
shape= "default" or "rect" or "circle" or "poly"
```

Defines the shape for the region. See the following bulleted list for detailed descriptions.

```
coords= "coordinates"
```

Defines the *coordinates* — position — for a region. Format for defining coordinates differ for each shape.

Possible area definitions and coordinates as defined in the shape and coords attributes are

- default: (Specifies the entire region and does not require coordinates). Easy enough, eh? Specifying an entire region sounds rather silly. Why not just use the anchor element to create a link. Good point. You can do just that. However, if you want to use the default attribute value, it takes the form <area shape="default" href="url.htm" />. Note that when you use the default attribute, you don't have to define coordinates because you're selecting the entire area.

- rectangle: (Specified by the coordinates for the upper-left and lower-right corners.) Use this to select a square or rectangular region in your image. (We use this style in our button-bar map.) To define a rectangle, provide locations for the upper-left and lower-right corners. Defining a rectangle usually takes the form of <area shape="rect" coords= "left-x,top-y,right-x,bottom-y" href="url.htm" /> where rectangle is a keyword that denotes the shape, left-x, top-y denotes the upper-left corner, and *right*-x, bottom-y denotes the lower right corner. Here again, the URL identifies the Web document where a click in this region takes the user.

- circle: (Specified by the coordinates for a point at the center and the number of pixels for the radius.) Use this to select a circular (or nearly circular) region within an image. To define a circle, you specify where its center is located and its radius. This usually takes the form of something such as `<area shape="circle" coords="center-x,center-y, radius" href="url.htm" />` where `circle` is a keyword that denotes the shape and the values for `center-x`, `center-y`, and `radius` are numbers. The URL identifies the Web document where a click in this region takes the user.

✔ `polygon`: (Specified by the coordinates for the point at the vertex of each edge. You remember *vertex* from geometry? We didn't either, but vertex sounds more exotic than *corner* or *intersection of endpoints*.) Simply put, vertices define the points where lines in a polygon come together to define a shape. Creating a polygon usually takes the form `<area shape="poly" coords="x,y,x2,y2,x3,y3, . . ." href="url.htm" />` where one pair of `xn`, `yn` values is necessary for each vertex in the polygon. Once again, `URL` plays the same role: It identifies the Web document where a click in this region takes the user.

Use vertices to outline the boundaries of regularly or irregularly shaped regions that aren't circular or rectangular. Although it takes more effort, the more points you pick to define an outline, the more a region behaves as users expect when clicking inside or outside its borders.

You probably recognize all these types except for `circle`. A circle's area is defined by a central point and a point on the circle's edge (which, as we all fondly remember, is the circle's radius — and you thought you'd never use geometry). Circle coordinates are grouped, separated by commas. But what is that `<area />` element all about? What's that `<map>` thing?

Learning by Example

Creating a client-side map is easy. Slam a set of `area` elements inside a `map` element associated with a properly labeled `<img />` element, and you've built a client-side image map. Notice that we name a client-side image map using the `name` attribute of the `map` element and reference it with the `usemap` attribute in the `<img />` element. Here's an example:

```
<img src="xhtmlfdmemu.gif" usemap="#xfdmap" />
<map name="xfdmap">
<area shape="rect" coords="0,142,98,285" href="http://www.
        domain.com/xhtmlfd/ftpstuff.htm" alt="files" />
<area shape="rect" coords="99,142,198,285" href="http://www.
        domain.com/xhtmlfd/contents.htm" alt="contents" />
<area shape="rect" coords="199,142,298,285" href="http://
        www.domain.com/xhtmlfd/search4d.htm" alt="search" />
<area shape="rect" coords="299,142,398,285" href="http://
        www.domain.com/xhtmlfd/contact.htm" alt="contact" />
<area shape="rect" coords="399,142,499,285" href="http://
        www.domain.com/xhtmlfd/whatsnew.htm" alt="what's
        new" />
```

```
<area shape="default" href="http://www.domain.com/xhtmlfd/
        contents.htm" alt="contents" />
</map>
```

Given all this flexibility, why do we use server-side image maps? Only one reason: Progress is never uniform. Which is to say, not all browsers support client-side image maps. However, any graphical browser that calls a CGI can use a server-side image map. So be wary and au courant if you're switching to the client side of the street.

Character-mode browsers (or GUI browsers with graphics turned off) can't handle image maps of any kind. So, even if you do take the plunge into client-side image maps, always provide a text alternative, just as you do with a server-side equivalent. Either way, the graphically disadvantaged compensate in another way!

Chapter 17

Formulating Forms

• •

• •

At first glance, the Web may look like a one-way street — that is, an environment in which Webmasters communicate aplenty with Web users, without much interaction from users. But it doesn't have to be that way. XHTML forms provide you with the tools for Web pages that allow your users to talk back to you (but without getting their mouths washed out with soap).

The Many Uses of XHTML Forms

An XHTML form is nothing more than a collection of controls that help users pass information from a Web page back to your Web server. The business of building forms involves not only writing markup to make the form widgets appear on the screen, but also looking long and hard at the information you want to collect from your users. Before you build a form to gather information, you must figure out what kind of information you want to gather. XHTML forms have countless uses, two of which are

✔ **Soliciting feedback.** The best judge of the quality of your information is your audience. Wouldn't it be wonderful for your readers to give you feedback on your Web pages? Then, your users tell you which parts they liked, which they didn't like, and what other features they'd like to see on your site. XHTML forms create pages that let your audience communicate with you and share their feedback.

✔ **Deploying applications on the Web.** Who thought that one day you'd be able to check your e-mail from a Web page, or pay your bills or browse store catalogs online? All of these application-like Web services are impossible without forms. The only time an online catalog works is when you find the items you want and then provide billing and address information so your products are shipped to you. Likewise, you can't send e-mail from a Web page without a place to type your message. With the help of forms — and some programming on your Web server — Web pages and Web sites are interactive; interactivity is the key to building Web-based applications and providing Web-based services.

The same form widgets that you can use to build a feedback form can build an online store or other service. The XHTML form doesn't do all of the work on its own — the form simply gives your Web site visitors a way to send information back to you. You must

✔ Receive the data — using form controls, of course

✔ Have a program or other tool that acts on the information you receive

That's what we're going to show you how to do in this chapter.

The behind-the scenes work that makes Web sites respond to information users send via forms is way beyond the scope of this book. You see a bit about it near the end of this chapter.

Before you dive headlong in to a form-building frenzy, take a few moments to find how your Web server supports forms. You save time and effort if you investigate your server situation before you begin the business of form building.

✔ You may need a Web programming guru to build a tool to process your form data.

✔ Your Web server administrator may have tools for you.

What's in a Form?

When adding forms support to a Web page, there are basic components:

✔ Text to prompt user responses

✔ Elements that gather input to your server

Here's how the entire information-gathering process of a form works:

1. You use XHTML elements to set up a form and solicit input from users.

   Users work their way through this material and you provide with the information that you want — in other words they fill out your form.

2. After users fill out your form, they click a button that directs their input to the program running on the Web server that delivered the form.

The click of the button not only sends the users' information to the server, but it also tells the server to start the program that interprets the information.

3. Assuming that the program is available, the program accepts the input information. The program then reads and interprets the contents to get instructions for further actions.

4. After the input is received and interpreted, the program does almost anything you want it to.

   For example, you can instruct the program to build custom Web pages based on the form data.

5. The custom-built document is delivered to the user in response to the form's content.

   At this point, additional interaction occurs (if the "return page" includes another form). Requested information is delivered (in response to requests on the form), a simple acknowledgment is issued, or much more.

Forms not only provide communication from users to servers, but also provide ongoing interaction between users and servers. This interaction adds a lot of value to your Web pages. In addition to using form data to build a custom Web page, the information collected from a form can be

- ✔ E-mailed
- ✔ Submitted to a database
- ✔ Written to a file

Though you can't reach out and touch your users with just input tags, forms-input tags provide you lots of ways to interact with your users by

- ✔ Creating text input fields, called text areas, in which users type whatever they want.

  Designers choose either single or multilane text fields and specify how much text displays on-screen and how much text fits into any text area.

- ✔ Creating labeled checkboxes or radio buttons on-screen that users select to indicate choices.

  Checkboxes allow *multiple* selections. Radio buttons allow *exactly one* selection.

- ✔ Generating drop-down menus that allow a user to make one or more selections from a set of predefined choices.

- ✔ Creating custom buttons and graphical controls for incorporation into forms.

- ✔ Assigning labels and captions to individual fields or buttons, or to groups of fields or buttons, as needed.

Forms involve two-way communication

Most input-catching programs on a Web server rely on an interface between Web browsers and servers called the *Common Gateway Interface (CGI)*. This interface specifies how browsers send information back to servers. CGI specifies formatting for user-supplied input, so forms-handling programs know what to expect and how to deal with what they receive. In a `<form>` element

- ✔ The `action` attribute specifies the URL that indicates a specific CGI script or program that processes the form data that a user entered.
- ✔ The `method` attribute describes how input data is delivered to such a forms-handling program.

These capabilities may sound mild-mannered, but if you combine them with the power to prompt users for input by using surrounding text and graphics, forms are a super way to ask for information on a Web page.

Using Form Elements

Although there are only nine form-related elements in the XHTML Document Type Definition (DTD), these elements allow detailed forms that add complex user interactivity to your pages. The secret to using so few tags to do so much is the plethora of attributes associated with the different form elements (you see this in spades with the `<input>` element). As you use different form elements, pay close attention to how different attributes and values change the functionality of the form.

The majority of form elements are associated with scripts using one attribute or another (`onblur`, `onfocus`, and so on). Chapter 19 discusses scripts and the attributes associated with them in more detail.

<form> . . . </form> Form container

All data-gathering elements in a given form are situated within the `<form>` element. The two head-honcho attributes within the `<form>` element are `method` and `action`. Together, these attributes control how your browser sends information to the Web server and which input-handling program receives the form's content. You don't usually build forms without these attributes. The other attributes discussed in this section (besides the `method` and `action` attributes) provide additional functionality to the form and you may or may not use them from form to form, depending on your needs and preferences.

Unique attributes:

```
method="post" or "get"
```

The `method` attribute indicates how your browser sends information to the server after you submit the form: `post` or `get`. Of these two methods, we prefer `post` because it's meticulous but practical: The `post` attribute causes a form's contents to be parsed one element at a time. On the other hand, the `get` attribute joins field names and their associated values into one string, which works okay if the string of text is a relatively short one. As it happens, UNIX (and most other operating systems) puts a practical, but inconvenient, limit on a single string's length; for UNIX, a single string is limited to 255 characters (this sentence just squeaks by as a single string). It's easy to imagine long strings getting *truncated* (lopped off), losing important information en route.

```
action="url"
```

The `action` attribute points to the CGI script or other input-handling program on the server that works with the form's input. The script's URL is a fully qualified reference or a relative reference. Either way, you must make sure the URL points to the right program, in the right location, to do the job you expect.

```
name="name"
```

The `name` attribute assigns a unique name to the entire form.

```
enctype="content type"
```

The `enctype` attribute specifies which file format the form's input should be submitted to the server as. Usually, the format is a standard text file, which is defined as `text/html`. You can find a list of the most common file types at `ftp://ftp.isi.edu/in-notes/iana/assignments/media-types/`.

```
onsubmit="script"
```

Use the `onsubmit` attribute to point to a script that the browser should execute when a form is submitted.

```
onreset="script"
```

Use the `onreset` attribute to point to a script that the browser should execute if a form is reset.

```
accept="content type"
```

The `accept` attribute identifies what kind of file the form accepts as input in an `<input type="file" />` control (discussed a bit later in the chapter). Remember that you can transfer (not necessarily display) just about any kind of file from one computer to another over the Web, which means a form can accept any many varieties of files, including audio, video, and word processing documents. If you build a form to accept files as input, it's a good idea to specify which types of files you accept so the browser only allows users to upload those kinds of files. Specifying file types can protect you from users trying to upload viruses, large video files, and more.

There's a list of the most common file types at `ftp://ftp.isi.edu/in-notes/iana/assignments/media-types/`.

```
accept-charset="character set"
```

The `accept-charset` attribute specifies which character encoding system the form supports. Visit `ftp://ftp.isi.edu/in-notes/iana/assignments/character-sets` for a complete list of registered character sets. Chapter 14 covers character sets in more detail.

```
target="frame name"
```

The `target` attribute specifies which frame the form's results should be sent to. Use this attribute if your form is part of a set of frames or you want the form results to appear in a new window. Read Chapter 18 for more information on frames and targets.

Example: See the example in the following `<input />` element section.

Example on CD: See files `/xhtmlfd/examples/ch17/input.htm` and `/xhtmlfd/examples/ch17/select_list.htm`.

<input /> Input control

The `<input>` element defines the most basic form element — the one you use to gather input. The `<input>` element usually contains at least two attributes — namely `type` and `name` — although they aren't required. The `type` attribute indicates what kind of element should appear on the form. The `name` attribute assigns, well, a name to go with the input field (or with the `value` that corresponds to the `<input>` tag). Note that the input element is an empty element so don't forget the slash before the greater than sign.

Unique attributes:

```
type="text" or "password" or "checkbox" or "radio" or
         "submit" or "reset" or "file" or "hidden" or
         "image" or "button"
```

As you build XHTML forms, you use the `<input />` element and the `type` attribute over and over again — almost ad nauseam. The `<input />` element is a perfect example of how a single element can have many uses thanks to an attribute or two. The value you assign to the `type` attribute gets you one of the following input controls:

- `text`: Provides a one-line text box. Use this attribute for short fields only. For longer text fields, use the `<textarea>` . . . `</textarea>` tags instead.

- `password`: Same as the `text` type, but the characters a user types in the form field display as asterisks ("****"), or some other masking character, to keep passwords from appearing in clear text.

- `checkbox`: Produces an on-screen checkbox for users to make multiple selections from a list of choices.

- `radio`: Creates a radio button for a range of selections, from which the user may select only one.

- `submit`: Creates a button labeled "submit" (or whatever value you supply for the `value` attribute in the same element) in your form.

  Not as tyrannical as it sounds, a submit button tells the browser to bundle the form data and pass it all to the CGI script indicated by the `action` attribute. To put it simply, this is the button readers use to send the filled-out form; therefore, a form is more or less useless without an `<input type="submit" />` element.

- `reset`: Creates a button labeled "reset" in your form (by default, or whatever value you supply for the `value` attribute in the same element). Include this attribute so users can clear a form's contents and start over (to err is human; to reset, a good thing).

  Be sure to label your reset button clearly — you don't want users to clear the form by accident!

- `file`: Allows users to upload a file, but for `file` to work, you must provide a list of acceptable file types using the `accept` attribute.

- `hidden`: Produces a "stealth" element that has no visible input area but still passes data (set using the `name` and `value` attributes in the same element) to the CGI on the Web server.

- `image`: Designates a graphic as a selectable item in a form. You can use this to include icons or other graphical symbols which users can click on to provide input (you know, which baby is cuter and such).

- `button`: Creates a button that has no specific use, except to call a script when a user clicks the button. The `<button>` element (discussed later in the chapter) performs the same function as the `<input type="button">` element, but it's newer and less supported.

These `type` attribute values provide a wide range of input displays and data types for form input. As you look at HTML forms on the Web (and in this book) with a new — dare we say more trained — eye, you see how effective these attribute values are.

```
name="name"
```

You use the `name` attribute to identify the contents of a field in the form information that is ultimately uploaded to the input-handling Web server. In fact, what the server receives from the form is a series of name/value pairs. The name that identifies the value is the string supplied in the `name="string"` attribute of the `<input>` tag, and the value is what the user enters or selects for that particular field.

```
value="value"
```

Supplies a default value for a text or hidden element or supplies the corresponding value for a radio button or checkbox selection. You can also use this attribute to determine the label of a submit or a reset button (such as `value="Submit this form!"` for a submit button or `value="Wipe it clean!"` for a reset button).

```
checked="checked"
```

Makes sure that a certain radio button or checkbox is checked when the form is either visited for the first time or after it is reset. Use this attribute to create "default" settings for your forms.

```
disabled="disabled"
```

Renders an input element unusable, even though the element still displays on-screen.

```
readonly="readonly"
```

Renders the contents of the control and the control itself unchangeable. Any information already present in this control is automatically submitted with the form.

```
size="number"
```

Sets the number of characters that a text input element can display without scrolling.

```
maxlength="number"
```

Sets the maximum number of characters that a value in a text input element can contain.

```
src="url"
```

Provides a pointer to the source file for an image input element.

```
alt="text"
```

Defines alternative text for an image input element. Every image that you include on a Web page (including images used a form input controls) should have an alternative text description marked with the `alt` attribute. Browsers that don't display graphics use the value of the `alt` attribute to clue a user in on what the image represents. The alternative text should describe the image well, and identify its function in the form.

```
usemap="map name"
```

Identifies a client-side image map used to solicit user input.

```
tabindex="number"
```

Specifies an element's position in the tabbing order so field-to-field transitions after the user strikes the tab key can be explicitly controlled (default is by order of appearance).

```
accesskey="character"
```

Sets a single character to act as a shortcut key for the input control.

```
onfocus="script"
```

Use the `onfocus` attribute to point to a script that the browser should execute when an input element comes into focus.

```
onblur="script"
```

Use the `onblur` attribute to point to a script that the browser should execute when an input element moves out of focus.

```
onselect="script"
```

Use the `onselect` attribute to point to a script that the browser should execute when a user selects an input element (like a checkbox or radio button).

```
onchange="script"
```

Use the onchange attribute to point to a script that the browser should execute when an input element's value is changed.

```
accept="content type"
```

The accept attribute identifies what kind of file the form can accept as input in an <input type="file" /> control.

```
align="top" or "middle" or "bottom" or "left" or "right"
```

Determines how an image input control is aligned on the form, vis-à-vis the accompanying text. This attribute is deprecated.

Example:

```
<?xml version="1.0"?>
<!DOCTYPE html PUBLIC "-//W3C//DTD XHTML 1.0
          Transitional//EN" "DTD/xhtml1-transitional.dtd">

<html xmlns="http://www.w3.org/1999/xhtml">
<head>
 <title> Contact Information</title>
</head>

<body>
 <h3>Reader Contact Information</h3>
 <p>Thank you for buying our book. Please fill out this
    form so we can get in touch with you when new
    information is available.</p>

<form method="post" action="/cgi-bin/usr-inf">
  <p>First name:
     <input name="first" type="text" size="12"/>
     MI:
     <input name ="MI" type="text" size="1" maxlength="1" />
     Last name:
     <input name="last" type="text" size="15" />
  </p>
  <p>Address 1:
     <input name="adr1" type="text" size="45" />
     <br>
     Address 2:
     <input name="adr2" type="text" size="45" />
  </p>
  <p>City:
     <input name="city" type="text" size="15" />
     State:
     <input name="state" type="text" size="2" maxlength="2" />
     ZIP&#47;Postal Code:
```

```
      <input name="zip" type="text" size="11" maxlength="11" />
   </p>
   <p>Country:
      <input name="country" type="text" size="15" />
   </p>
   <p>Thank you!
      <input type="submit" name="submit" value="Send the form" />
      <input type="reset" name="reset" value="Clear the form" />
   </p>
</form>
</body>
</html>
```

Example on CD: See file `/xhtmlfd/examples/ch17/input.htm`.

Figure 17-1 shows how the HTML form in the previous example code is displayed in a browser. Note the positions of the one-line text boxes immediately after field names and how both paragraph and line break elements affect the placement of these boxes on individual lines (as with Address1 and Address2) or together — as with First name, MI, and Last name. Ultimately the final display of your form is impacted by both form elements and the other XHTML elements you throw into the mix (and of course your handy, dandy style sheet).

```
Contact Information - Microsoft Internet Explorer                        _ |8|X|
 File   Edit   View   Favorites   Tools   Help

 Reader Contact Information

 Thank you for buying our book. Please fill out this form so we can get in touch with you when new information is available.

 First name: [        ]   MI: [ ]  Last name: [          ]

 Address 1: [                              ]
 Address 2: [                              ]

 City: [        ]   State: [ ]  ZIP/Postal Code: [        ]

 Country: [        ]

 Thank you!  [ Send the form ]   [ Clear the form ]
```

Figure 17-1:
The Reader
Contact
Information
form as
seen in a
browser.

<select> . . . </select> Drop-down menu group

The `<select>` element works much like a list; except it builds a drop-down list of `<option>` elements instead of list items defined with the `<li>` element.

Unique attributes:

```
name="text"
```

Provides the name in the name/value pair passed to the server.

```
size="number"
```

Controls the number of elements that the drop-down list displays.

```
multiple="multiple"
```

Indicates that multiple selections from a list are possible; if this flag isn't present in a `<select>` element, your users can select only a single element from the drop-down menu.

```
disabled="disabled"
```

Renders an element unusable but still viewable.

```
tabindex="number"
```

Identifies an element's position in the tabbing order defined for the page.

```
onfocus="script"
```

Use the `onfocus` attribute to point to a script that the browser should execute when a select element comes into focus.

```
onblur="script"
```

Use the `onblur` attribute to point to a script that the browser should execute when a `<select>` element moves out of focus.

```
onchange="script"
```

Use the `onchange` attribute to point to a script that the browser should execute when a select element's value is changed.

Example: See the example in the `<option>` element section.

Example on CD: See file `/xhtmlfd/examples/ch17/option.htm`

<optgroup> . . . </optgroup> Drop-down menu item group

The `<optgroup>` element was added to forms in HTML 4.0 so it's relatively new. You can group options in a single drop-down menu. This tag isn't well supported by older browsers.

Unique attributes:

```
disabled="disabled"
```

Renders the entire group unusable but still viewable.

```
label="text"
```

Use this attribute to set a label for the option group.

Example: See the example in the following `<option>` element section.

Example on CD: See file `/xhtmlfd/examples/ch17/option.htm`

<option> . . . </option> Drop-down menu item

The `<option>` element identifies each item in a select drop-down menu.

Unique attributes:

```
selected="selected"
```

Selects a menu item when the form is either visited for the first time or after it is reset. Use this attribute to create "default" settings for your drop-down menu.

```
disabled="disabled"
```

Renders an option unusable but still viewable.

```
value="value"
```

Specifies the value in the name/value pair passed to the server. The name is specified in the select element for the menu. If you don't include a value for this attribute, the text between the option element's start and end tags is passed as the value.

Example:

```
<?xml version="1.0"?>
<!DOCTYPE html PUBLIC "-//W3C//DTD XHTML 1.0
          Transitional//EN" "DTD/xhtml1-transitional.dtd">

<html xmlns="http://www.w3.org/1999/xhtml">
<head>
 <title>Coffee Special</title>
</head>

<body>
 <h3>This Month's Coffee Selections</h3>
 <p>Add a bit of variety to your daily grind. Order from
    this month's special selections.</p>
 <hr>
 <form method="post" action="/cgi/monthly_special.cgi">
 <p>Please choose your selection(s) from the following:<br>
    <select name="coffee" multiple size="3">
    <optgroup label="Special">
     <option>Special Roast</option>
     <option selected>Special Reserve</option>
    </optgroup>
    <optgroup label="Flavored">
     <option>Hazelnut</option>
     <option>Vanilla</option>
    </optgrop>
    <optgroup label="Varietal">
    <option>Kona</option>
    <option>Special Blend</option>
    </optgroup>
    </select>
 </p>
 <p>Please pick a button to indicate how the coffee
    should be delivered: <br>
    <input type="radio" name="grind" value="ground"
     checked="checked" />
    Ground
    <br>
    <input type="radio" name="grind" value="whole" />
    Whole
 </p>
 <p>Thanks for your order!
    <input type="submit" value="Send Order" name="submit" />
    <input type="reset" name="Clear Form" />
 </p>
 </form>

</body>
</html>
```

Example on CD: See the file `/xhtmlfd/examples/ch17/option.htm`.

Figure 17-2 shows what nice results you can get from using `<select>` elements to provide options for your users to pick from. (Coffee, anyone?)

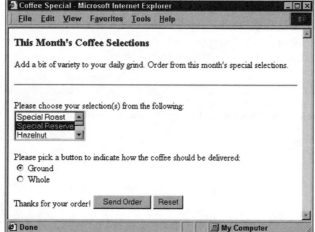

Figure 17-2:
The nice results you can get from using `<select>` elements.

`<textarea>...</textarea>` Large text box

Use the `<textarea>` element to create input elements of nearly any size on a form. Any text that appears between the element's opening and closing tags dutifully appears within the text area you define on-screen. If you leave the text area unmodified, the tags supply the default value delivered by the form — the tags have you covered.

Unique attributes:

```
name="name"
```

Provides the identifier part of the all-important name/value pair delivered to the server.

```
rows="number"
```

Specifies the number of lines of text that the text area contains.

```
cols="number"
```

Specifies the number of characters that fit onto any one row of the text area; this value also sets the width of the text area on-screen.

```
disabled="disabled"
```

Makes the element unusable even though it still displays.

```
readonly="readonly"
```

Prevents users from modifying the text area; any information contained therein automatically is submitted with the form.

```
tabindex="number":
```

Identifies this element's position in the tabbing order defined for fields on the page.

```
accesskey="character"
```

Sets a single character to act as a shortcut key for the input control.

```
onfocus="script"
```

Use the onfocus attribute to point to a script that the browser should execute when a text area element comes into focus.

```
onblur="script"
```

Use the onblur attribute to point to a script that the browser should execute when a text area element moves out of focus.

```
onselect="script"
```

Use the onselect attribute to point to a script that the browser should execute when a user selects text within a text area.

```
onchange="script"
```

Use the onchange attribute to point to a script that the browser should execute when a text area's content is changed.

Example:

```
<?xml version="1.0"?>
<!DOCTYPE html PUBLIC "-//W3C//DTD XHTML 1.0 Transitional//
          EN" "DTD/xhtml1-transitional.dtd">

<html xmlns="http://www.w3.org/1999/xhtml">
<head>
<title>Text area</title>
```

```
<meta http-equiv="Content-Type" content="text/html;
          charset=iso-8859-1">
</head>

<body>
<p>
  <textarea name="recipe" rows="10" cols="65">
  Banana Waffles
  Ingredients:
  2 c. waffle batter (see Widget Waffler cookbook for recipe)
  2 ripe bananas, peeled, sliced 1/4" thick
  1 tsp. cinnamon
  Preparation:
  Mix ingredients together.
  Preheat waffle iron (wait until light goes off).
  Pour 1/2 c. batter in waffle iron (wait until light goes
          off).
  Keep browned waffles warm in oven until ready to serve.
  </textarea>
</p>
</body>
</html>
```

Example on CD: See file `/xhtmlfd/examples/ch17/textarea.htm`

The screen that results from the previous HTML document appears in part in Figure 17-4. May your free-form feedback be at least as delightful. (So what time's breakfast?)

Figure 17-4:
The
`<textarea>`
element in
action.

Coffee Special - Microsoft Internet Explorer

File   Edit   View   Favorites   Tools   Help

This Month's Coffee Selections

Add a bit of variety to your daily grind. Order from this month's special selections.

Please choose your selection(s) from the following:

Special Roast
Special Reserve
Hazelnut

Please pick a button to indicate how the coffee should be delivered:
◉ Ground
○ Whole

Thanks for your order!
Send Order   Reset

Done   My Computer

`<fieldset>` . . . `</fieldset>`
A group of input fields

The `<fieldset>` element groups similar input controls together in a form. This element is relatively new to form markup so it's not well supported by the version 3.0 browsers and older.

Example: See the example in the following `<legend>` element section.

Example on CD: See file `/xhtmlfd/examples/ch17/legend.htm`

`<legend>` . . . `</legend>` Field set descriptor

The `<legend>` element provides a label for each grouping of elements in a form.

Unique attributes:

```
accesskey="number"
```

Sets a single character to act as a shortcut key for the set of controls.

```
align="top" or "bottom" or "left" or "right"
```

Sets the alignment of the legend relative to the group of controls.

Example:

```
<?xml version="1.0"?>
<!DOCTYPE html PUBLIC "-//W3C//DTD XHTML 1.0
          Transitional//EN" "DTD/xhtml1-transitional.dtd">

<html xmlns="http://www.w3.org/1999/xhtml">
<head>
 <title>Coffee Special</title>
</head>

<body>
 <h3>This Month's Coffee Selections</h3>
 <p>Add a bit of variety to your daily grind. Order from
    this month's special selections. </p>

 <form method="post" action="/cgi/monthly_special.cgi">
```

```
<p>
<fieldset>
<legend>Please choose your selection(s) from the
         following:</legend>
  <select name="coffee" multiple size="3">
   <optgroup label="Special">
    <option>Special Roast</option>
    <option selected>Special Reserve</option>
   </optgroup>
   <optgroup label="Flavored">
    <option>Hazelnut</option>
    <option>Vanilla</option>
   </optgrop>
   <optgroup label="Varietal">
   <option>Kona</option>
   <option>Special Blend</option>
   </optgroup>
  </select>
</fieldset>
</p>


<p>
<fieldset>
<legend>Please pick a button to indicate how the coffee
   should be delivered: </legend>
   <input type="radio" name="grind" value="ground" checked=
   "checked">
   Ground
   <br>
   <input type="radio" name="grind" value="whole">
   Whole
</fieldset>
</p>


<p>
<fieldset>
<legend>Thanks for your order!</legend>
  <input type="submit" value="Send Order" name="submit" />
  <input type="reset" name="Clear Form" />
</fieldset>
</p>
</form>

</body>
</html>
```

Example on CD: See file /xhtmlfd/examples/ch17/legend.htm

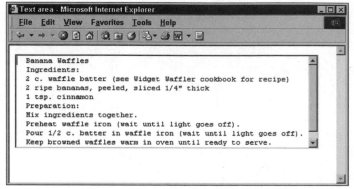

Figure 17-3:
The
`<fieldset>`
and
`<legend>`
tags at
work.

We recommend using the `<fieldset>` and `<legend>` tags to group the differ-ent portions of your form together.

✔ The final visual display helps users know that they are moving from one set of controls to another.

✔ The tags break the monotony of the page without any extra graphics.

<button> . . . </button> Form button

The `<button>` element creates a button on a form. The button is a submit button, a reset button, or a button not linked to any particular action. When a user clicks a button the name/value pair associated with the button — using the `name` and `value` attributes — is sent to the location on the server speci-fied by the `action` attribute of the `<form>` element. This element isn't well supported in browsers, so it's better to use `<input type=button />` to create unique buttons.

Unique attributes:

```
name="name"
```

Provides the name in the name/value pair passed to the server.

```
value="value"
```

Provides the value in the name/value pair passed to the server.

```
type="button" or "submit" or "reset"
```

Specifies the button's type.

```
disabled="disabled"
```

Renders the element unusable even though it's displayed.

```
tabindex="number"
```

Identifies the element's position in the tabbing order defined for fields on the page.

```
accesskey="character"
```

Sets a single character to act as a shortcut key for the input control.

```
onfocus="script"
```

Use the onfocus attribute to point to a script that the browser should execute when a button comes into focus.

```
onblur="script"
```

Use the onblur attribute to point to a script that the browser should execute when button moves out of focus.

So Now What?

Building HTML forms and handling user interaction through Web pages requires action on both sides of the client/server connection. In this book, we concentrate mainly on the client side. However before we go, it's time to slip quietly across the network connection from client side to server side. Here dwells the Common Gateway Interface (CGI). Along the way, we cover the basic details of its design and use. We also introduce you to the issues surrounding your choice of a scripting or programming language for CGI, and we show you how to locate some prime examples of that species.

You ventured to the client side (and come back alive) if you read Chapter 16's account of clickable image-map files. If this present section seems too much like pidgin geekspeak, skip ahead for the skinny on "How to Cheat at CGI."

Specify CGI and gate-a-way with it

A CGI program lets Web pages communicate with applications on the server to provide customized information or to build interactive exchanges between clients and servers.

CGI programs run on the Web server, not on the client side (where you run your browser to access Web-based information). You can't use our CGI programs on your own machine unless it runs Web server software at the same time that it runs your browser, so you're dependant on your Web server to help you out. It's a good idea to look into your CGI options before you delve into forms. Hit your local Web server admin for more info on what your options are.

Gateway *scripts,* or programs, add a powerful capability: true interaction between browsers and servers across the Web. Only your imagination and the tools at hand limit the power. Gateway scripts supply the underlying functions that enable you to work Web magic — search Web documents, parley with databases that accept and process data from your forms, get strategic market intelligence, and customize your Web pages in response to user input.

CGI scripts/programs: Watch your language

Whether you call your server-side creation a program or a script, here's a trade secret: This distinction often describes the tools that you actually use to build the monster. Scripts are built with scripting languages, and programs are built with programming languages. The distinction is useful:

- ✔ A scripting language creates a set of actions and activities that must be performed in the prescribed order each time a script is executed. Like a script read by an actor, scripts are *interpreted*.

- ✔ Statements written in a programming language are transformed, by a special program called a compiler, into equivalent computer instructions in an executable form that the computer can, well, execute.

Both of these approaches work equally well with the Web's Common Gateway Interface (CGI). However, we want to keep it simple — we use CGI programs to mean any code creature you conjure. You can call them whatever you want (although they don't answer to "Fido," "Ralph," or "Hey, you").

You can think of a CGI program as an extension of the core Web server services. In fact, CGI programs are like worker bees that do the dirty work on behalf of the server. The server serves as an intermediary between the client and the CGI program.

Most Web servers are configured to look for CGI programs in a particular directory that's under the server's control. Normal users (including you) probably won't be able to copy CGI scripts into this directory without obtaining help from their friendly neighborhood systems administrator or Webmaster. Before you can install and use any CGI program on a particular server, you want to talk to one of these individuals (if not both), tell them what you want to do, and ask for their help and advice in making it happen.

How to Cheat at CGI

If CGI doesn't exactly give you a warm, fuzzy feeling, you're not alone. CGI can be difficult, especially if you're not a programmer and don't really want to be. But before you throw out the virtual CGI baby with the cyber-bathwater, let us show you how to cheat at CGI! Here, as promised, are the crib notes.

The secret is to use a forms-designing application to create your forms and the background CGIs automatically. O'Reilly's PolyForm is one great application for this. Answer a few simple questions, click a few buttons, follow the instructions of the semi-intelligent program wizard, and poof! Out comes a form and matching CGI application. No messy code lists, no contortions, no infomercials. And the form really, really works!

Find out more about PolyForm by visiting http://polyform.oreilly.com. Unfortunately, for the Apple end of the stick, PolyForm is only available for Windows computers. The good news is many of today's WYSIWYG tools, such as Microsoft FrontPage (www.microsoft.com/frontpage/) and Dreamweaver by Macromedia (www.macromedia.com/software/dreamweaver/), help you build forms and generate the code to work behind the scenes with the form input. Luckily, many of these tools are available for a variety of platforms see the individual Web sites for more information.

Many of the Web-development tools that help you use form input actually use JavaScript or VBScript to process forms on the client-side (the Web browser). Client-side scripting has much to offer but does have its pitfalls. Before you jump right into working with Web scripting, we recommend that you read through WebMonkey's scripting resources at http://hotwired.lycos.com/webmonkey/programming.

We're convinced that anything short of an all-CGI volume barely scratches the surface, but for Pete's sake, we've got other fish to fry here. For more information, consult your favorite search engine and use "CGI" or "CGI script" as your search string. You'll turn up tons of useful references, but we save you at least some hassle by listing some truly useful books and Web sites here:

- Books

    - *Perl For Dummies,* by Paul E. Hoffman (IDG Books Worldwide, Inc.)

    - *Perl and CGI for the World Wide Web: Visual Quickstart Guide,* by Elizabeth Castro. (Addison-Wesley Publishing Company)

- Web sites

    - The CGI Directory: www.cgidir.com

    - Scripting.com: www.scripting.com

    - CGIFiles.com: www.cgifiles.com

Chapter 18

Framing Your Pages

*H*ave you ever known what it's like to be framed? Well, now you do, and you may find you like it. Frames are one of the handier additions to the HTML/XHTML world: They delineate, outline, and give structure to XHTML documents. Frames help move information coherently within and among themselves. But wait, there's more! The big fish (the W3C) decided it liked frames so much that frames became standard in HTML 4.0. The folks who build the XHTML specification even gave frames their own DTD — the XHTML frameset DTD. Best of all, this chapter shows you — step-by-step — how you can use frames to make your Web pages framingly cool.

Many Web Documents, One Web Browser Window

So what are frames anyway and why do you want to use them in your Web pages? A single browser window displays a single document. Technically, the browser window itself is a single, framed display. A browser window, however, isn't limited to just one frame. It can in fact hold several frames. There are actually two different kinds of frames you can use in your XHTML documents:

 ✔ A set of frames that displays several documents at once

 ✔ A floating or inline frame that you add to regular XHTML documents

A *set of frames* uses a whole series of markup to define the set, populate the different frames, and link the frames together. In fact, when you build a set of frames, you create one, specific document that does nothing but define the set. A *floating frame,* on the other hand, is just another element that you add to a good ol' XHTML document. Floating frames are nice because they allow you display more than one document in a browser window at once, but you don't have to create and manage a full frameset to do so. When most resources talk about frames, they focus on sets of frames, rather than floating frames, so we do the same in this chapter.

The exact number and arrangement of frames in a set is defined by the <frameset> element, and each individual frame is defined with a <frame /> element. A set of frames can display several documents at one time. Effectively, each frame functions like a separate browser screen, but all of the frames are displayed together in one window. Imagine having two browser windows open at one time, sitting next to each other on your desktop and you begin to get the picture. What's really cool is that with frames you can connect the different browser windows and have them work together to display your content. And, for the control freak in all of us, depending on the attributes you give it, a frame acts just like a standard browser screen, or it is frozen into Elliot Ness untouchability.

To frame the practical question, "Do I really *need* to use frames?" The answer is no. An alternative to frames is to use a table to format your information into areas, complete with borders, on a single browser screen. But remember that tables are pretty absolute, whereas frames are dynamic — you can scroll through information within frames, and users may find that appealingly easy to deal with. And you can't display several different documents in different table cells, but you can display different documents in different frames.

Because frames didn't become part of the HTML standard until 4.0, there are several older browsers (versions 3.0 and earlier of just about any major browser) that simply cannot handle frames properly. Text-only browsers don't deal well with frames either. To be practical, this means that some of your users may not be able to appreciate the beauty and efficacy of your frames. As long as you're sure users have a frames-compatible browser — the recent versions of both Netscape Navigator and Internet Explorer support frames, as do many of the non-commercial browsers such as Mosaic and Amaya — you can safely use frames on your site. However, if your audience uses a wide variety of browsers, shy away from frames. Another option is to offer a non-framed version of the same materials so users can pick which version of your pages they want to explore (pay close attention to the information on the <noframes> element later in the chapter).

Great frame resources

As you probably guessed, you always have more to learn about the incredible world of XHTML. Frames are no exception; this chapter gives you a basic understanding of how they work, but practicality demands that we stop there. If you like what you see and want to dig around for more down-and-dirty details about using frames, check out the following Web sites:

- ✔ Web Design Group's HTML 4.0 Reference:
  `www.htmlhelp.com/reference/html40`

- ✔ Webmonkey's authoring frames articles:
  `http://hotwired.lycos.com/webmonkey/authoring/frames`

- ✔ WebReference's frame cheat sheet:
  `www.webreference.com/dev/frames/summary.html`

- ✔ XHTML Frameset DTD
  `www.w3.org/TR/xhtml1/DTD/xhtml1-frameset.dtd`

The first three of these references actually teach you how to use HTML frames, not XHTML frames. Luckily, the differences between HTML and XHTML frames are minimal and revolve mostly around creating well-formed XML documents if you're using XHTML. As you work with these resources to learn more about XHTML frames, remember the basic differences between an XML document and an HTML document, as discussed in Chapters 2 and 3.

Frames at work on the Web

You use frames for a whole host of activities, including:

- ✔ A Web page with a fixed logo at the bottom and a scrolling top section

- ✔ A page with a fixed top and bottom, a navigation bar and copyright notice at the top, and a scrolling middle section for displaying page contents

- ✔ A Web page with side-by-side frames that put a table of contents on the left and a scrolling text frame on the right

You find out how to set structures like these a bit later in this chapter. For now, note that frames are flexible without going all rubbery. You use frames to keep constant chunks of information on display — like logos, navigation bars, and copyright notices — while your users scroll happily through large amounts of text or dynamic content. But hold on there. Before you jump ahead and start framing everything in sight, get to know the brass tacks — the XHTML markup elements — that make frames possible.

To see frames at work for yourself check out these two framed Web sites:

- ✔ EverCom's home page (okay, so the whole page is in Norwegian, but hat doesn't stop it from being a great example of frame usage):
  `www.evercom.no`

- ✔ The Internet Garden: `www.internetgarden.co.uk/frameset_1.htm`

XHTML Frame Elements

Welcome to XHTML Elements for Frames Country. Here's where we list 'em, discuss their proper syntax and use, and offer some pointers on their good and better uses. After that, it's up to you and your good taste. Try hanging some nice frames around your Web site and see how your visitors react.

<frameset> . . . </frameset>
A set of frames

The `<frameset>` . . . `</frameset>` element is the main container for any set of frames. Your basic, run-of-the-mill frame document uses the `<frameset>` element instead of the `<body>` element to contain the guts of your main document. Beyond that, there are a few other things you must know about the frameset element:

- The opening `<frameset>` tag follows immediately after the closing `</head>` tag.

- If the `<body>` element appears before the `<frameset>` element, the `<frameset>` element is ignored — not exactly the outcome you're looking for when you're building frames.

- Within the `<frameset>` . . . `</frameset>` element, you only nest three types of elements:

    - Other `<frameset>` elements,

    - `<frame>` elements

    - `<noframes>` elements

Basically, every good set of frames begins with this bit of code:

```
<frameset>
</frameset>
```

And you thought this was going to be hard. That's the skinny on the frameset element. Here are the attributes you put in the frameset element.

Unique attributes:

```
rows="multiple lengths"
```

The rows attribute of the <frameset> element controls two things: (1) the number of frames that appear stacked on top of each other (vertically) in the browser window and (2) the height of each frame. The attribute takes a *multiple length* value, which means it actually takes several values, each separated by a comma. The number of values assigned to the rows attribute determines the number of frames shown up and down the screen. The total height of all the simultaneously displayed frames must equal the height of the browser window; so the browser may adjust the rows attribute's height values to make them all fit. You build your rows using any mixture of the following elements:

- ✔ **An integer:** The direct approach — integer defines a fixed number of pixels (such as 50 or 250) for the row's height. Seems simple, but be careful: Remember that the size of the browser window changes substantially from one user's system to another. If you use integers to set pixel heights for each and every row in a set the measurements are set in stone. You can instead use one or more relative values (described later in this chapter) with a pixel value so your frameset is more flexible. If your combined row heights are more than the browser can display, the integer may override your specified pixel value to ensure that the total height and width of all the frames equals 100 percent of the user's window. You may not want it to do that; a browser doesn't care about eyestrain. All it knows to do is follow orders and *display all defined frames,* even if mercilessly squashed together and crammed with unreadable text.

- ✔ **A percentage:** This value tells the browser, "Size this frame to a percentage of screen area, between 1 and 100." If the percentage total for all frames is greater than 100 percent, the browser reduces all accordingly to fit the frames in the browser window. If the total is less than 100 percent, extra space is added to any relative-sized frames that happen to be hanging around (for example, the next item in this list).

- ✔ **An asterisk:** A single asterisk (*) character identifies a relative-sized frame. Browsers give a frame defined with the asterisk all remaining space left over after the other frames defined with pixels and percentages are laid out on the screen. If you have several frames that take advantage of this flexible system, the remaining space is divided evenly among them.

- ✔ **An integer and asterisk**: If you place a value in front of the *, the frame gets that much more relative space. For instance, an entry such as 5*, * allocates five times as much space to the first frame ($\frac{5}{6}$ of the total on-screen space) as to the second frame (which gets a measly $\frac{1}{6}$).

You don't need a degree in trigonometry to use these different types of values, but you must monitor the on-screen results of your frame work carefully. Give your display extra-severe scrutiny when you mix value types. Following are a couple of examples, each a different way to stack frames on-screen.

Example:

✔ **Two vertically stacked frames:** Both pieces of code achieve the exact same results:

```
<frameset rows="15%,85%">
<frameset rows="15%,*">
```

✔ **Three vertically stacked frames:** A mere snippet of XHTML code creates three vertically stacked frames using a fixed pixel value (125), a relative value (*), and a percentage value (25%):

```
<frameset rows="125,*,25%">
```

```
cols="multiple lengths"
```

The cols (for *columns*) attribute is closely related to the rows attribute; it governs the number of frames that site horizontally across the browser's screen, as well as the width of each frame. Not surprisingly this attribute takes the same kind of values the rows attribute does.

Example:

The following example of XHTML code displays three frames across the screen. The first one (on the left) gets 15 percent of the available space the second (in the middle) is exactly 250 pixels in size, and the third (on the left) gets what ever is left over:

```
<frameset cols="20%,250,*">
```

```
onload="script"
```

Use the onload attribute to point to a script that the browser should execute when the frameset loads. Chapter 19 discusses scripts and the attributes associated with them in more detail.

```
onunload="script"
```

Use the onunload attribute to point to a script that the browser should execute when the browser moves from the frameset to another document. Chapter 19 discusses scripts and the attributes associated with them in more detail.

Examples: To see how a <frameset> element works with <frame> elements to define a complete set of frames, see the examples at the end of the <frame> element discussion.

Example on CD: See file /xhtmlfd/examples/ch18/frame.htm.

<frame /> A single frame

You must define a separate `<frame />` element for each frame on your Web page. Remember that you use the `rows` and `cols` attributes with the `<frameset>` element to set up the number of frames you want on a page. You need one `<frame />` element for each frame defined in the `<frameset>` element.

The `<frame />` element is an empty element so it only has one tag. All by its lonesome, the `<frame />` tag defines the content, a name, and the attributes for each frame. If you want to display four different documents pages in frames, you must create four frames; therefore, you need four `<frame />` elements. The first `<frame />` element defines the top, left-most frame area. The second `<frame />` element defines the frame immediately to the right of the first frame, or if the edge of the browser is reached, the frame in the next row. And it keeps going and going and going, with no end in sight.

You can modify the `<frame />` element using any of eight attributes. And here they are, one by one (we thought you'd never ask):

Unique attributes:

```
src="url"
```

The `src` attribute (short for source) uses a URL value to point at the document you want to appear in the frame. Aforesaid source material may be a document, an image, an audio clip, or any other legal Web resource. If you leave out the `src` attribute or its value, the frame will be empty and may cause the browser to display an error message.

```
name="name"
```

Use the `name` attribute to assign a unique name to a frame. This is particularly important if you want to click on a hyperlink in one frame and have its content appear in another frame. To keep browsers from becoming confused, give each frame a unique name and make sure the name begins with an alphanumeric character.

```
frameborder="1" or "0"
```

Borders add visual definition to a page. Then again, frameborders are annoying when you want a smooth page design. The `frameborder` attribute allows you to decide for yourself if you want borders between your frames or not. Give `frameborder` a value of 1 if you want to see borders and a value of 0 if you do not.

```
marginwidth="number"
```

Give the `marginwidth` attribute a pixel value to specify the exact width of the left and right margins of a frame. Browsers display margins as white space so you can use this attribute to nicely separate the content in one frame from the content in another. The `marginwidth` attribute is optional but there always is a margin of one or two pixels in every frame.

```
marginheight="number"
```

The `marginheight` attribute works like `marginwidth` — you use a pixel value to specify a frame's margins — except this attribute controls the top- and bottom-edge margins of frames instead of the left and right margins. (And the height has to be more than zero — c'mon, you know the rules.)

```
noresize="noresize"
```

Unless you specify otherwise, users resize frames by dragging a frame edge to a new position. You send a message of "Don't touch," when you set the value of the `noresize` attribute to `noresize`. This attribute is not really the killjoy you might think it is; it causes display problems for your users. Also keep in mind that if you set the frame adjacent to the edge of another frame to `noresize`, the edge shared by the two frames can't move. This unmovable edge affects the resizing of any adjacent frames.

```
scrolling="yes" or "no" or "auto"
```

Merrily users scroll along — but you don't want them to if they need to. Conversely, you want them to be able to if they need to. Use the `scrolling` attribute to control a frame's scroll bar. A value of `yes` forces the browser to display a scroll bar on that frame whereas a value of `no` keeps scroll bars invisible. Assign the value of `auto` to set the scroll bar to appear only if more content than fits in the window must be displayed.

Sensibly `auto` is the default value for the `scrolling` attribute, and the wise leave it in place under most circumstances. Remember that you can't always know for sure what size window your users will tack up on their screens to display your framed pages; if you stick with `auto`, you know they get a scroll bar if they need one, nary a one if they don't.

```
longdesc="url"
```

If you need to create a long description for a frame for those who can't view frames, save it in an external file on your site in text or XHTML format and point to it using the `longdesc` attribute.

Example:

```
<?xml version="1.0"?>
<!DOCTYPE html PUBLIC "-//W3C//DTD XHTML 1.0 Frameset//EN"
          "DTD/xhtml1-frameset.dtd">

<html xmlns="http://www.w3.org/1999/xhtml">
<head>
 <title>A Two Frame Set</title>
</head>

 <frameset rows="150, *">

  <frame name="logo" src="/graphics/crop_logo.gif"
    frameborder="0" marginwidth="15" marginheight="15"
    noresize="noresize" scrolling="auto" />

  <frame name="body" src="/home.html"
    frameborder="0" marginwidth="30" marginheight="20"
    noresize="noresize" scrolling="auto" />
 </frameset>

</html>
```

Example on CD: See file /xhtmlfd/examples/ch18/frame.htm.

<noframes> . . . </noframes>
No frame information

So what do you do if you know for a fact that some of your users are surfing
the Web with just the bearskin basics? Version 2.0 browsers and non-graphical
browsers don't support frames. Don't even think about frames and the wireless Web. Give 'em a break. Create some alternative content for users whose
browsers don't support frames. You describe this alternative with the
<noframes> element and presto, users without frames can view your content!
Frame-challenged browsers appreciate at least the text part of your site's
splendor, and frame-cognizant browsers ignore all tags and data within the
<noframes> elment. There are no unique attributes for this element.

Example:

```
<?xml version="1.0"?>
<!DOCTYPE html PUBLIC "-//W3C//DTD XHTML 1.0 Frameset//EN"
          "DTD/xhtml1-frameset.dtd">

<html xmlns="http://www.w3.org/1999/xhtml">
<head>
 <title>A Two Frame Set</title>
</head>
```

```
<frameset rows="150, *">

  <frame name="logo" src="/graphics/crop_logo.gif"
    frameborder="0" marginwidth="15" marginheight="15"
    noresize="noresize" scrolling="auto" />

  <frame name="body" src="/home.html"
    frameborder="0" marginwidth="30" marginheight="20"
    noresize="noresize" scrolling="auto" />
</frameset>

<noframes>

<body>
 <p>
 View our <a href="/home.html">Home Page</a> without
 using frames.
 </p>
</body>

</noframes>

</html>
```

Example on CD: See file /xhtmlfd/examples/ch18/noframes.htm.

<iframe> . . . </iframe> Inline frame

The `<iframe>` element defines a floating frame within a standard Web page. Despite the fact that inline frames are part of the flow of a regular XHTML document and not part of a frameset, they still behave pretty much like every other frame. An inline frame displays a separate Web resource — an XHTML document, image, movie, or other resource with a valid URL. The `<iframe>` element shares most of its attributes with the `<frame>` element.

Unique attributes:

```
src="url"
```

The `src` attribute points to the URL of the resource to be displayed in the floating frame.

```
name="name"
```

Use the `name` attribute to give the frame a unique name.

```
frameborder="1" or "0"
```

Set the frame's border to on (1) or off (0) in the `frameborder` attribute.

```
marginwidth="number"
```

The `marginwidth` attribute takes a pixel value to set the frame's left and right margins.

```
marginheight="number"
```

The `marginheight` attribute takes a pixel value to set the frame's top and bottom margins.

```
scrolling="yes" or "no" or "auto "
```

Specify whether the frame should have a scroll bar or not using the `scrolling` attribute.

```
align="top" or "middle" or "bottom" or "left" or "right"
```

The `align` attribute for a floating frame works exactly like the `align` attribute for an image element. Choose one of the five possible values to specify how the frame should be aligned relative to the rest of the content on the page.

```
height="number"
```

The `height` attribute takes a pixel value to set the frame's height.

```
width="number"
```

The `width` attribute takes a pixel value to set the frame's width.

```
longdesc="url"
```

If you need to create a long description for a frame for those who can't view frames save it in an external file on your site in text or XHTML format and point to it using the `longdesc` attribute.

Example:

```
<?xml version="1.0"?>
<!DOCTYPE html PUBLIC "-//W3C//DTD XHTML 1.0 Frameset//EN"
          "DTD/xhtml1-frameset.dtd">

<html xmlns="http://www.w3.org/1999/xhtml">
<head>
 <title>An Page with a Floating Frame</TITLE>
</head>
<body>

 <iframe src="/news/00000405.html" name="news"
  frameborder="1" marginwidth="25" marginheight="25"
```

```
    scrolling="auto" align="right" height="300"
    width="100"></iframe>

</body>
</html>
```

Example on CD: See file /xhtmlfd/examples/ch18/iframe.htm.

Putting It All Together to Build a Framed Web Site

Your Web pages are like pictures waiting to be framed. Even if you provide pure text for your users, you can still use frames behind the scenes to help them navigate within your site.

One important feature of frames is that they let you keep important information on-screen constantly, while other portions of the screen change to reflect new content.

Okay, back to the drawing board: The first requirement for using frames successfully is to visualize your Web page as a collection of frames. Sketch it on a napkin, the back of an envelope, or whatever's handy (except an old coffee filter). As your rough-and-ready diagram takes shape, remember: You need one XHTML document to define your sketched-out frame page *and* a separate XHTML document for each frame in your sketch.

In frames links have targets

When you click a hyperlink or a navigation button, the document the link is attached to replaces the one that you just clicked in. How do you change the nature of a hyperlink so documents appear in a different frame than where they were started? Believe it or not, the solution is as simple as adding a single attribute to a hyperlink's anchor (`<a>`) element.

The `target` attribute gives you control over where the linked page or other resource appears when a user clicks a link in your documents. Of course, you can use the `target` attribute in other elements — `<area>` and `<form>` to name two — but the attribute really shines when you use it in the `<a>` element in conjunction with frames. To brush up on the anchor element, check out Chapter 12.

So, how exactly does targeting work? Normally, when a user clicks a link, the browser displays the new document in a full browser window. With the `target` attribute, you change that. You assign names to specific frames — remember the `name` attribute? — and decree that certain documents shall duly appear in the frame that bears the targeted name. (Control freaks, rejoice!)

Earlier in this chapter we discuss the attribute `name="name"`, and we explain how to use the `name` attribute to name a frame. Using the `target` attribute to, well, *target* the frame is just as easy: Insert the attribute and its corresponding value (the name of the frame, known inscrutably as the *name*) in the `<a>` element. In the following example, the name of the targeted frame is — you guessed it — `frame_name`:

```
<a href="somepage.html" target="frame_name">
   The page somepage.html will open in the frame named
   frame_name.
</a>
```

The document referenced by this particular anchor element loads in the frame defined by this element:

```
<frame name="frame_name">
```

Do you see a trend here? We thought you might.

Any valid frame name specified in a `target` attribute must begin with an alphanumeric character. Well, okay, the exceptions are a few predefined, special-purpose target names that begin with the underscore character. Any targeted frame name that begins with an underscore or a non-alphanumeric character (and *isn't* a special-purpose name) is ignored.

Special-purpose target names include `_self`, `_blank`, `_parent`, and `_top`. Use these different names to determine where the user sees a Web resource after that fateful click selects the linked document:

- `target= "_self"`: Specify a `_self` target to force the linked document to load inside the frame that holds the linking document. By default, all links act this way. It's like every regular anchor element has an invisible `target="_self"` attached to it. Aren't you glad you don't have to type that every time?

- `target="_blank"`: Specify a `_blank` target to force the linked document to load inside a new browser window, which is an easy way to force the user's browser to launch another window. The `_blank` value for the `target` attribute is useful if you want to link to someone else's site but still make sure that your site is immediately available to users in the first browser window that never went away. Don't over use `_blank` targets. Visitors to your site won't appreciate new browser windows popping up all the time.

- `target="_parent"`: Specify a `_parent` target to force the linked document load in the immediate frameset parent of the document. If the current document in which the `_parent` target appears has no parent, this attribute behaves like the `_self` value.

✔ `target="_top"`: Specify a `_top` target to force the linked document to load in the full body of the window — overwriting any frames that may be hanging around. If the current document is already at the top of the document hierarchy, the `_top` target name behaves like `_self`. You can use this attribute to escape from a deeply nested frame.

If you get carried away using frames nested within frames nested within frames, or you link to someone else's framed site only to find their frames loading inside of yours — what a headache — you can use `target="_top"` to cancel out your frameset and revert back to a nice, simple, regular page.

A sample three-frame Web page

Earlier in this chapter, you find out that whenever you build a set of frames, you need several documents to get started. You have the XHTML document that specifies the frameset and then one document for each and every frame in the set. Therefore, if you build a three-frame Web page, you need four documents: the frameset document and three frame documents. Figure 18-1 shows a pretty simple three-frame Web page that really uses four documents to make it display properly.

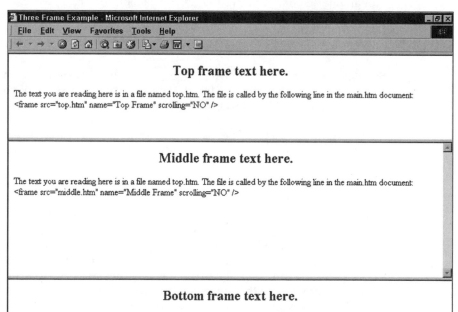

Figure 18-1:
A simple three-frame Web page.

If you'd like to use this sample page to get started building your own frame-sets and apply the different frame techniques you read about in this chapter, you can find the files we used to build the page on the CD-ROM. You need all four of these files:

- ✔ **3frame.html**: This document defines the frameset.
- ✔ **top.html**: This document appears in the top frame.
- ✔ **middle.html**: This document appears in the middle frame.
- ✔ **bottom.html**: This document appears in the bottom frame.

As you tweak our frame example, remember that your job as a Web page author is to make sure that any information you put in a frame is compact or short enough to fit the specified frame space, even if users resize their entire browser screens. If you can't make the information fit the frame, use relative values for the frame height and allow your users to resize as needed.

Chapter 19

Java, Multimedia, and Scripting

In This Chapter

▶ Embedding Java and multimedia in XHTML documents

▶ Using `<applet>`, `<object>`, and `<param>` elements

▶ Integrating client-side scripts in XHTML documents

*W*e need to face facts: Using only text and graphics on a Web site is perfectly acceptable and possible; however, it's hard to build a Web site these days without including one of the many technologies available, such as Java, client-side scripting, or other forms of multimedia. In the end, all you're really doing is embedding files developed using these different technologies in a Web page and letting the Web browser figure out what to do with them. This chapter looks at the XHTML you need to know to integrate other technologies into your Web pages.

Java and Multimedia in XHTML

Java and multimedia share the limelight with other Web buzzwords, such as Extensible Markup Language (XML) and Extensible Hypertext Markup Language (XHTML). However, Java and multimedia precede XML. XML — and consequently XHTML — was designed to work with both Java and multimedia, which give you the ability to extend the functionality of your site and deliver content that XML and XHTML markup doesn't support.

Java is effectively programming for the Web. A *Java applet* is a miniature application that you can embed in and interact with on a Web page. Java applets are comprised of code called *class files,* and your browser must support Java before you view and interact with Java applets. Java applets are used for everything from stock tickers to chat environments. You must be a Java programmer to build a Java applet, but you only need to know a bit of XHTML to include a Java applet in your Web pages.

Multimedia is an all-encompassing term that simply means different media (such as audio, video, graphics, and text) all lumped together. You can view videos and listen to music on a Web page, even though audio and video data aren't text-based. Although you have to know a bit about digitizing audio and video (and then know how to use software to make your page look or sound impressive), to create your own multimedia, you only have to know a bit of XHTML to include audio and video in your Web pages.

Three XHTML elements exist that you need to know about to include Java applets and multimedia files in your Web pages:

- `<applet>`
- `<object>`
- `<param>`

The following sections bring you up to speed on these elements and show you how to use them to embed applets and multimedia in your documents. It's way beyond the scope of this book to discuss building or acquiring applets and multimedia clips. However, you only need to visit your favorite search engine and type **java** or **multimedia** to find links to thousands of sites that may help you find the files we're about to show you how to embed in your documents.

< applet > . . . </applet> embedded Java applet

The `<applet>` element is the original HTML method for embedding Java applets into Web documents. You simply place the `<applet>` element within the body of the document and the applet appears wherever the element is located. An `<applet>` element can take any number of `<param />` elements to pass information to the applet. The actual number of parameters, their names, and their values, are all part of the applet's design, so you don't make them up on your own. The applet's developer or its documentation tells you which parameters go with the applet and how to use them to affect the applet's functionality. The `<applet>` element is deprecated.

Because the `<applet>` element is deprecated, it takes a back seat to the `<object>` element as a means to include applets in XHTML pages. If you want your documents to work well in older browsers, however, you need to continue to use the `<applet>` element instead of the `<object>` element to describe your Java applets in XHTML documents.

Unique attributes:

```
codebase="url"
```

The codebase attribute points to a URL where all of the files that make up the Java applet live. Browsers use this as a starting point to find and execute the applet's files.

```
code="class file"
```

The code attribute points to a specific Java class file that starts the applet. Any given Java applet may be comprised of several different files, so you need to know which one is the start-up file (hopefully, from the applet's documentation) and include that information in the applet element using the code attribute. You should include that information in the applet element using the code attribute.

```
archive="archive url(s)"
```

The archive attribute points to the location(s) of archived Java class files. Java class files can be stored in archives to make them easier to download from a remote server. The archives must be unpacked before they can be useful in an applet. The most common class file archive is called a *JAR,* or Java Archive. If your applet is stored in a JAR or series of JARs, you can point to the location using the archive attribute.

```
object="serialized applet"
```

A Java applet may be built anew from class files every time it's run or it may be read in as a complete object that was running and then was *serialized* to a file. Sort of like flash freezing a partially cooked meal. After loading from the serialized form, the applet resumes operation where it left off. If an applet uses this approach, you must use the object attribute instead of the code attribute to refer to the applet's starting point. If an applet you're using requires the object attribute, its documentation should tell you. Otherwise, don't sweat it.

```
alt="text"
```

The alt attribute provides alternative text for those whose browsers don't support Java applets or who choose to not access Java applets.

```
name="name"
```

The name attribute provides the name portion of the name/value pair sent to the server with form data (which is data submitted with a form).

```
width="number"
height="number"
```

Use the width and height attributes to specify, in pixels, how much space the applet should take when the page is displayed. These attributes are deprecated.

```
align="top" or "middle" or "bottom" or "left" or "right"
```

The `align` attribute takes a value of `top`, `middle`, `bottom`, `left`, or `right` to specify how the applet should be aligned in relation to the surrounding text. If you use this attribute, aligning an applet is an inexact science. Try style sheets instead for more control options and better results. This attribute is deprecated.

```
hspace="number"
vspace="number"
```

The `hspace` and `vspace` attributes identify how many pixels of white space should be on the left and right (`hspace`) or top and bottom (`vspace`) of the applet. This attribute is deprecated.

Example:

```
<?xml version="1.0"?>
<!DOCTYPE html PUBLIC "-//W3C//DTD XHTML 1.0
          Transitional//EN" "DTD/xhtml1-transitional.dtd">

<html xmlns="http://www.w3.org/1999/xhtml">
<head>
 <title>Java Applet</title>
</head>

<body>
<h2> Discover Java Quiz!</h2>
<p>When the Applet starts, just click on the answer
    or answers.</p>

<applet code="Tester.class" width="540" height="320">
<param name="answerbase" value="a" />
<param name="font" value="TimesRoman 14 BOLD" />
<param name="script" value="Test1.scr" />
<param name="barcolor" VALUE="#FF0033" />
<param name="passlevel" value="75" />
<param name="passhtml" value="Passed.htm" />
<param name="failhtml" value="Failed.htm" />
</applet>
</body>
</html>
```

The previous example of applet code (on the CD: `/xhtmlfd/examples/ch19/applet.htm`) actually powers a real applet on the Web. To see it work, visit `www.lanw.com/java/discover/default.htm`. The CD that accompanies this book uses a Java applet and similar code to power the XHTML Context Applet. View it by loading the page `/xhtmlfd/applet.htm` in your favorite Java-enabled browser.

<object> . . . </object> embedded object

The <object> element is designed to describe any kind of non-XHTML object, including Java applets, audio and video files, and other multimedia presentations. Add the <object> element to your document where you'd like the object to be embedded and the browser replaces the element with the object it describes. Nothing could be simpler. Although you may not want to use this element to describe Java applets just yet (as described in the previous section), you should use it to embed media files and all other non-XHTML files in your Web page.

The <object> element was a later addition to HTML, so it's not well supported in some of the older browsers, if it's supported at all. You should test any document that you use this element in on several different browsers. If the object you embed is crucial to the user's experience on your site or provides information they can't get elsewhere, be sure to provide an alternate download site, such as a File Transfer Protocol (FTP) server or a Web page with hyperlinks. This way, the user can download the object separately. Do this just in case a user's browser doesn't support the <object> element.

Unique attributes:

    codebase="url"

The codebase attribute points to a URL where the file(s) that makes up the embedded object lives. Browsers use this as a starting point to find and execute the object.

    data="url"

The data attribute points to the object itself, much as the src attribute of an image points to the image's location on a server.

    classid="url"

The classid attribute points to the startup file for embedded applications, such as Java applets and ActiveX controls. Use the classid attribute in place of the data attribute when you point to embedded applications.

    type="content type"

The type attribute identifies the type of the embedded file. If a browser doesn't know what to do with a particular file type, it may choose to ignore the file or ask the user what to do with the file (usually, you can save it to disk or open it with some other piece of software). For the browser to recognize a file type and decide how to deal with the object, you have to use a correct file type, as discussed earlier in the chapter.

    codetype="content type"

The codetype attribute works with the classid attribute to specify what kind of application is embedded in the document. The discussion of file types at the beginning of the chapter includes some common application types and the example at the end of the section shows the application/java code type at work.

```
archive="archive url(s)"
```

The archive attribute points to the location(s) of archived Java class files.

```
standby="text"
```

The standby attribute specifies a short text message to display while the object is loading.

```
height="length"
width="length"
```

Use the width and height attributes to specify, in pixels, how much space the object should occupy when the page is displayed. These attributes are deprecated.

```
usemap="url"
```

The usemap attribute points to a client-side image map file that defines areas in a clickable map. You can use the <object> element along with the <map> element to build a client-side image map.

Using usemap to build image maps isn't well-supported among most browsers, so you may have better results building image maps using the <img> and <map> elements. See Chapter 16 for more information on <img> and <map> elements.

```
name="name"
```

The name attribute provides the name portion of the name/value pair sent to the server with form data.

```
tabindex="number"
```

The tabindex attribute specifies an element's position in the tabbing order, which allows field-to-field transitions to be explicitly controlled when the user strikes the tab key. (The default is by order of appearance.)

```
align="top" or "middle" or "bottom" or "left" or "right"
```

The align attribute takes a value of top, middle, bottom, left, or right to specify how the applet should be aligned in relation to the surrounding text. This attribute is deprecated.

```
border="number"
```

The border attribute sets a border of number pixels around the object. This attribute is deprecated.

```
hspace="number"
vspace="number"
```

The hspace and vspace attributes identify how many pixels of white space should be on the left and right (hspace) or top and bottom (vspace) of the applet. This attribute is deprecated.

```
declare="declare"
```

The declare attribute allows you to include an object in an XHTML document but not have it immediately start until someone clicks a hyperlink that sets it in motion. Without the declare attribute, an embedded object starts immediately — in other words, starts playing, running, or whatever other activity it might be designed to perform — when the page is loaded. If you want the user to initiate the object by clicking on a link, you need to give the object a unique identifier using the id attribute and reference that ID in the hyperlink. (Check out the following example to see how this works, in practice.)

Example:

```
<?xml version="1.0"?>
<!DOCTYPE html PUBLIC "-//W3C//DTD XHTML 1.0
          Transitional//EN" "DTD/xhtml1-transitional.dtd">

<html xmlns="http://www.w3.org/1999/xhtml">
<head>
 <title>A Java Object</title>
</head>

<body>
<object classid="java:stock_ticker.class" id="ticker"
 codetype="application/java" with="400" height="50"
 standby="The ticker is loading" >
 <p>Stock Ticker</p>
</object>

<p>Start your <a href="#ticker">stock ticker</a></p>
</body>
</html>
```

The previous example is on the CD in /xhtmlfd/examples/ch19/object.htm.

‹param /› object or applet parameter

Many Java developers make their applets reusable and easy to configure by building them to accept several different parameters. In the applet example shown earlier in this chapter, the applet — a testing tool — could take one of several parameters, including the following:

- ✔ name="font" value="TimesRoman 14 BOLD": Specifies in which font the test questions and answers should appear

- ✔ name="script" value="Test1.scr": Identifies the location of the test questions that the applet displays

- ✔ name="barcolor" VALUE="#FF0033": Specifies the color of the button bar on the bottom of the applet

- ✔ name="passlevel" value="75": Indicates the percentage of questions a student must answer correctly to pass a test

- ✔ name="passhtml" value="Passed.htm": Points to a URL for a "test passed" message

- ✔ name="failhtml" value="Failed.htm": Points to a URL for a "test failed" message

Java applets and other applications, such as ActiveX components, can take parameters using the ‹param /› element nested within the ‹applet› or ‹object› element. Some multimedia plug-ins, such as the QuickTime plug-in, also take parameters. Of course, a parameter only works with an application if the application has been set up to know what to do with the parameter. Check your documentation — or talk to the application developer if he or she is available — to find out what parameters you can use with the applications and what values they take.

Unique attributes:

```
id="unique id"
```

The id attribute assigns a unique identifier to the parameter.

```
name="name"
```

The name attribute specifies the name of the parameter.

```
value="value"
```

The value attribute specifies the parameter's value.

```
valuetype="data" or "ref" or "object"
```

The valuetype attribute specifies the kind of value the parameter passes to the applet or object. The default value is data because most of the time, you pass data to the applet or object. However, you can also use the `ref` value to pass URLs, and the `object` value to pass the IDs of other objects in the document to the applet or object.

```
type="content type"
```

Use the `type` attribute in conjunction with `valuetype="ref"` to specify the kind of file to which the parameter is pointing.

Example: Refer to the example in the section "< applet > . . . </applet> embedded Java applet."

Example on CD: See file `/xhtmlfd/examples/ch19/applet.htm`.

All about file types

Once upon a time, the Web consisted only of text and graphics, but that was short-lived. Today, you can find just about any kind of file — from a Java applet to a QuickTime video — embedded in Web pages. As a developer, you can also embed just about any kind of file in your documents, but how the browser handles the file has much to do with the file type you assign to it. The majority of browsers know what to do with most files saved as common file types — even if it involves sending the file to a different application. Some common text file types include the following:

- text/html
- text/css
- text/xml
- text/rtf
- text/javascript
- text/vbscript

You can also include different kinds of images in your documents (no surprise there). What may surprise you is that each of these images has its own file type, just like text files. The most widely supported image types are the following:

- image/jpg
- image/gif
- image/png

Audio and video files also have files types. Some common ones are the following:

- ✔ audio/mp3
- ✔ video/quicktime
- ✔ video/mpeg

Of course, you can embed applications, such as Java applets and ActiveX controls, directly in your documents. Different Web browsers support different applications, and many browsers may not display something they don't support. Letting the browsers know what kinds of applications are included in the file prevents them from spitting errors at your users. Also, if the browser has a plug-in or associated application (such as the Adobe Acrobat Reader for PDF files) that can process the application, it immediately passes the embedded file to that application. Some frequently used applications are the following:

- ✔ application/java
- ✔ application/pdf
- ✔ application/zip
- ✔ application/x-python
- ✔ application/msword
- ✔ application/activex

The `<applet>`, `<object>`, and `<param />` elements discussed earlier in this chapter frequently use content types, as do form elements, and other XHTML elements discussed in the book.

If you're concerned about a file's type, you can always check its documentation, look at someone else's working example to see what type he or she has assigned to it, or e-mail the creator to find out how to reference it correctly.

Script Fans, Rejoice!

As common and prolific in Web pages as Java and multimedia are, client-side scripting ranks right up there with them. Those cute graphics that change when you move your mouse on and off a Web icon are made possible by scripting. Pop-up boxes on Web forms that warn you when you forget to fill out required fields are also a courtesy of scripting. And, of course, expanding and collapsing menus wouldn't be possible without scripting.

Client-side scripts are simply instructions added to Web pages that tell the browser how to react when a user performs a particular action, such as moving a mouse or clicking a button. The instructions aren't written in

XHTML or any other markup language, but are written in a scripting language, usually JavaScript or VBScript. A client-side script only works if a Web browser understands its commands and can execute them correctly. Using the `<script>` element to house scripts is the primary role of XHTML in adding scripting to a Web page.

Events are the key

Client-side scripts work in response to user actions, such as the following:

- Rolling a mouse over an image and rolling it off
- Selecting a radio button in a form
- Submitting a form
- Clicking a hyperlink

What a short list, but you can see a trend. User interaction on a Web page is described as a series of events (mouse moving, clicking, and so on), and XHTML has attributes that define the most common events. You can use these attributes with XHTML tags to specify a script or a part of a script that the browser should run if and when the user performs that action. If the user doesn't perform the action, the script doesn't run. Throughout this book, you've seen event attributes, such as `onselect` and `onload`, associated with different elements. Table 19-1 lists all the events that XHTML supports with a brief description of each.

 The concepts of `focus` and `blur` are about as clear as mud if you haven't spent years building user interfaces. To put it simply, a *page element* (form control, hyperlink, frame, and so on) comes into focus when a user begins to do something with it, such as selecting, changing, or clicking it. The element goes out of focus when a user moves onto another element. If a user is tabbing from place to place in a page, an element is in focus when the user tabs to it.

Table 19-1	JavaScript Events Supported in XHTML 1.0
Event	*Description*
onblur	The user changes focus from one element to another.
onchange	The user changes the value of an element.
ondblclick	The user double-clicks an element.
onfocus	The user focuses on an element.

(continued)

Table 19-1 *(continued)*	
Event	*Description*
onkeydown	The user presses a key.
onkeypress	The user presses a key and holds it.
onkeyup	The user releases a key.
onload	The user opens a Web page.
onmousedown	The user clicks the mouse button.
onmousemove	The user moves the mouse.
onmouseout	The user moves the mouse off of an element.
onmouseover	The user moves the mouse on an element.
onmouseup	The user releases the mouse button.
onreset	The user resets a form.
onselect	The user selects an element.
onsubmit	The user submits a form.
onunload	The user exits the page.

To use these events to orchestrate interactivity on your Web pages, you need to know something about scripting. The last section of the chapter offers you some pointers.

All about content types

If you used scripting with your HTML pages and skimmed — or maybe even skipped — the last couple of sections, you definitely want to stop and read this section because referencing scripts in XHTML documents is a bit different from referencing them in HTML documents.

XML recognizes that an element may have several different kinds of content including, but not limited to, the following:

✔ Other elements

✔ Other elements and text

✔ Just text that the processor should process as XML

✔ Text that may be mistaken for markup that the processor shouldn't process as XML

Client-side scripts fall into the last category. They are illegal XML, but they may contain some markup elements, such as less than and greater than signs, which the parser may try to interrupt. However, you can't use entities in your scripts because the script wouldn't work. In general, you don't necessarily want your XML processor trying to process you scripts. A good example of this is a processor that checks your document for well-formedness or for validity. If your XML processor is a browser that recognizes the `<script>` element — described in the following section — it knows to treat the element content as a script and not as XML. Otherwise, you really just want your processor to ignore it and forge ahead.

XML's container for text that needs to be kept from the XML processor is

```
<![CDATA[ content here ]]>
```

For your XHTML documents to be well-formed and include scripts, you need to place all scripts within a CDATA section, as in this example:

```
<script type="text/javascript language="JavaScript1.1"
   xml:space="preserve">

   <![CDATA[

     script goes here

   ]]>

</script>
```

Although this method produces a well-formed and valid XHTML document, it's not handled well by older browsers. Before you convert pages that use scripts to XHTML and CDATA sections, test your pages on a variety of browsers to see how they deal with the CDATA markup.

Aside from the need to mark your scripts as CDATA, the `<script>` element in XHTML isn't much different from the one in HTML 4.01. The following section includes details about the element and its attributes.

<script> . . . </script> client-side script

The `<script>` element holds client-sides scripts that affect the elements on the page. You can include the `<script>` element within the document's `<head>` element or `<body>` element. The books and Web sites listed at the end of this section discuss the techniques for placement of scripts in a document in more detail.

Unique attributes:

```
charset="character set"
```

The `charset` attribute specifies which character encoding system the form supports. Visit `ftp://ftp.isi.edu/in-notes/iana/assignments/character-sets` for a complete list of registered character sets. Chapter 14 covers character sets in more detail.

```
type="content type"
```

The `type` attribute specifies which scripting language the script is written in, such as text/javascript or text/vbscript.

```
language="language"
```

The `language` attribute is a better-supported alternative to the `type` attribute, and specifies, by name, in which scripting language and version the script is written. The most commonly supported options are JavaScript, JavaScript1.1, JavaScript1.2, and VBScript. If a browser doesn't recognize the language identifier, it may ignore the script altogether.

```
src="url"
```

The `src` attribute points to an external file that contains the script. If you plan on using one script multiple times, it's good practice to store it in a separate file and reference it in different documents using the `src` attribute.

```
defer="defer"
```

The `defer` attribute prevents the browser from processing the script until the entire document is downloaded.

```
xml:space="preserve"
```

The `xml:space` attribute with a value of `preserve` indicates to browsers that they should preserve the white space in the script. Changes in white space may affect a script and cause errors, so this attribute prevents those changes. This is a fixed attribute.

Example:

```
<?xml version="1.0"?>
<!DOCTYPE html PUBLIC "-//W3C//DTD XHTML 1.0
          Transitional//EN" "DTD/xhtml1-transitional.dtd">

<html xmlns="http://www.w3.org/1999/xhtml">
<head>
 <title>A Script Sampler</title>
 <script src="/scripts/navigation.scr"
  type="text/javascript" language="JavaScript1.1"
  xml:space="preserve"></script>
</head>
```

```
<body>

</body>
</html>
```

The previous example is on the CD: /xhtmlfd/examples/ch19/script.htm.

<noscript> . . . </noscript> information in lieu of scripts

If a page depends heavily on scripts for navigation or other important content, you may want to include text, markup, and graphics within the <noscript> element to provide information for those users whose browsers don't support scripts, or who may have turned off scripting support. Browsers that support scripts ignore this information.

Unique attributes: None

Example:

```
<?xml version="1.0"?>
<!DOCTYPE html PUBLIC "-//W3C//DTD XHTML 1.0
          Transitional//EN" "DTD/xhtml1-transitional.dtd">

<html xmlns="http://www.w3.org/1999/xhtml">
<head>
 <title>A Script Sampler</title>
 <script src="/scripts/navigation.scr"
   type="text/javascript language="JavaScript1.1"
   xml:space="preserve"></script>
</head>

<body>

<noscript>
<p>Your browser doesn't seem to support the scripts
   we are using to build the navigation system for our
   pages. Please visit our
   <a href="/ns/default.html">non-scripted site</a>.
</p>

</body>
</html>
```

The previous example is on the CD: /xhtmlfd/examples/ch19/script.htm.

Scripting resources abound

You can visit hundreds of Web sites that devote some or all their space to the discussion of scripting — and most include script repositories where you can download scripts to plug into your own Web pages. Check out these three exceptional sites:

- ✔ **Scripts.com:** www.scripts.com
- ✔ **Scripting.com:** www.scripting.com
- ✔ **WebCoder.com:** www.webcoder.com

A number of good books about scripting are also available. If you're serious about using scripts extensively on your pages and building them yourself, you need a good scripting reference. We suggest the following books:

- ✔ *JavaScript Bible*, Third Edition. Danny Goodman. IDG Books Worldwide. ISBN: 0-7645-3188-3.

- ✔ *JavaScript : The Definitive Reference*. David Flanagan. O'Reilly & Associates. ISBN: 1-5659-2392-8.

Part V

Advanced XHTML Topics

The 5th Wave   By Rich Tennant

"It says, 'Thank you for downloading Gumpton's Compression Utility shareware. Should you decide to purchase this product, send a check to the address shown and your PC will be uncompressed and restored to its original size.'"

In this part . . .

Part V is where we dare you to venture beyond the limits of accepted standards and tried-and-true technologies, to take a look at what gonzo Web artists work with every day — only they do it without a safety net! Here's where you find what modularizing XHTML means and how it can make your Web pages stand up and bark, how to extend basic XHTML markup to capture your own unique data structures and organization, how to use events and objects to keep track of where users are in your XHTML documents and what they're doing with them, and how to put all this whiz-bang technology to work to solve real-world application requirements. By the time you peruse this part of the book, you should be ready to take your company's database and bring it to life on the Web!

Chapter 20

Modularizing XHTML

. . . .

. . . .

*O*ne of the driving forces behind the introduction of XHTML is that it allows easy *modularization* of HTML. Modularization breaks the large XHTML Document Type Definition (DTD) into smaller element sets that can be recombined to meet the needs of different communities.

If you read previous chapters of this book or are already familiar with XHTML, you know XHTML as it's described by the XHTML 1.0 family of DTDs. If you want to validate your XHTML document, you run your document against one of the XHTML 1.0 DTDs. If your document is a large document that uses all of the elements and attributes of XHTML, that's fine; however, what happens if your document is a simple one? In fact, what happens if all your documents use only a simple subset of XHTML? Must you run your documents against the DTD?

The answer to this question is *yes*. You must run your documents against the DTD. If you run your document against the large DTD, this means that your software has to do a lot of extra work. Not a problem if you're using a big, powerful desktop computer. But what if you're browsing on your cell phone, which can't render images, objects, or tables? It seems ridiculous to waste all the power that is needed to validate the document. Wouldn't it be nice to use a simpler subset of XHTML? Aha! You can! There's a *modular* XHTML 1.1 document!

XHTML Modules

The *modular XHTML 1.1 document* is the DTD code from XHTML version 1.0 broken into at least 17 discrete modules. The current modules are Structure, Basic Text, Hypertext, List, Applet, Presentation, Edit, BDO, Forms, Tables, Image, Image Map, Intrinsic Events, Metainformation, Scripting, Stylesheet, and Link. Generally, their names describe the content they contain. As DTD authors, we can use these modules in any way we want.

The Modularization specification may be subject to change.

You can access the latest modules and their content on the CD included with this book from the `xhtmlfd/examples/ch20/default.htm` file.

Why Modules?

Modularization of XHTML brings revolutionary benefits to the world of documents and information interchange.

Before modules, if you wanted to make a new document type you had to write a whole new DTD from scratch. For anything but a non-trivial DTD, this is a laborious (and expensive) task. With XHTML modules, you just take a module containing the markup you want off the shelf and plug it into your own DTD, knowing that it's already been debugged and thoroughly tested in real-world situations.

On the other hand, if XHTML does not meet all your needs, you can write your own custom module into the XHTML document. To read more about customizing your XHTML, see Chapter 21.

The Road to Modularization

As we mention earlier in this chapter, XHTML will be hacked into 17 pieces (at least). These pieces, or *modules,* don't require you to learn much more than you already know (if you know XHTML that is). Of those 17 proposed modules, two are on their way to becoming full-fledged specifications.

What can you expect with a new set of specifications? Take a spin through the proposals currently on the table. And keep your eyes peeled for coming attractions.

XHTML 1.1 is almost here

At the time of this writing, XHTML 1.1 is not quite ready. But, that doesn't mean you should not learn a little bit about it now. Although nothing is written in stone, the goals are set and you should be aware a few of them. XHTML allows for the following:

- ✔ Subset XHTML into smaller pieces
- ✔ Easy extension of the XHTML DTD
- ✔ Easy construction of new document types

With XHTML 1.1, you won't be sitting at your desk memorizing a bunch of new elements or attributes. As a matter of fact, only a few elements and attributes will be changed from XHTML 1.0, whereas some others get the boot.

If you've followed the last few HTML specifications (or XHTML 1.0), you'll notice the use of the word deprecated. Many elements and attributes have been *deprecated* with the last few iterations of the HTML family of specifications. Deprecated mean that the W3C is warning you that one day these deprecated elements and attributes will be deleted from the specification.

If all goes as planned, the next generation of XHTML will clean up those pesky — and once deprecated — elements and attributes. See Table 20-1 for the proposed element changes.

Table 20-1	List of XHTML Elements and Proposed Changes	
Element	*Supported*	*Deleted Unique Attributes*
ALL	Yes	lang
a	Yes	accesskey, name, tabindex, target
abbr	Yes	None
acronym	Yes	None
address	Yes	None
applet	Yes	
area	Yes	target
b	Yes	None
base	No	

(continued)

Table 20-1 *(continued)*

Element	Supported	Deleted Unique Attributes
basefont	No	
bdo	Yes	None
big	Yes	None
blockquote	Yes	None
body	Yes	background, bgcolor, text, link, vlink, alink
br	Yes	clear
button	Yes	None
caption	Yes	align
center	No	all
cite	Yes	None
code	Yes	None
col	Yes	None
colgroup	Yes	None
dd	Yes	None
del	Yes	None
dfn	Yes	None
dir	Yes	None
div	Yes	align
dl	Yes	None
dt	Yes	None
em	Yes	None
fieldset	Yes	None
font	No	all
form	Yes	None
frame	No	all
frameset	No	all
h1-h6	Yes	align

Element	Supported	Deleted Unique Attributes
head	Yes	None
hr	Yes	align, noshade, size, width
html	Yes	None
i	Yes	None
iframe	No	all
img	Yes	align, border, hspace, vspace
input	Yes	align
ins	Yes	None
isindex	No	all
kbd	Yes	None
label	Yes	None
legend	Yes	align
li	Yes	type, value
link	Yes	target
map	Yes	name
menu	No	all
meta	Yes	None
noframes	No	all
noscript	Yes	None
object	No	all
ol	Yes	compact, start, type
optgroup	Yes	None
option	Yes	None
p	Yes	align
param	Yes	None
pre	Yes	width
q	Yes	None
s	No	all

(continued)

Table 20-1 *(continued)*

Element	Supported	Deleted Unique Attributes
samp	Yes	None
script	language	
select	Yes	None
small	Yes	None
span	Yes	None
strike	No	all
strong	Yes	None
style	Yes	None
sub	Yes	None
sup	Yes	None
table	Yes	align, bgcolor
tbody	Yes	None
td	Yes	bgcolor, height, nowrap, width
textarea	Yes	None
tfoot	Yes	None
th	Yes	bgcolor, height, nowrap, width
thead	Yes	None
title	Yes	None
tr	Yes	bgcolor
tt	Yes	None
u	No	all
ul	Yes	compact, type
var	Yes	None

Those are the proposed element changes — every last darn one of them. Keep in mind that the XHTML 1.1 is not complete. This means that we don't expect any hexes if the W3C change its mind.

XForms marks the spot

In 1993, HTML added a much needed component — form elements. When forms were first introduced, no one expected them to take off. Now, Web sites ranging from Amazon.com to small mom-and-pop shops take advantage of forms. (See Chapter 17 for more information on forms.) The problem is that we — the general public — are too darn demanding.

While the existing mechanisms for forms have become dated, the W3C has been scripting a new specification to heed our demands: XForms.

The next generation of Web forms is not a signed and sealed deal yet, but the goals are well established and support the following:

- ✔ multiple browsers (for example, hand held devices)
- ✔ the ability to suspend and resume forms
- ✔ multiple forms per page
- ✔ sophisticated form logic
- ✔ structured data

If you're salivating now, get ready to lick your chops because there's even talk about allowing users to print forms, fill them out by hand, and submit them using a scanner. More importantly, XForms will be designed to mix and mingle with XML related languages, such as XHTML, Scalable Vector Graphics (SVG), and Synchronized Multimedia Integration Language (SMIL).

XForms has its own dedicated Web page at the W3C. Visit it to keep yourself informed: www.w3.org/MarkUp/Forms/.

XHTML Basic goes wireless

XHTML Basic does not contain much mystery. Simply put, XHTML Basic is basic XHTML. As a subset of the coming XHTML 1.1, XHTML Basic includes the necessities for a Web page, and leaves out the fluff.

The world is being taken over by cell phones. Many of the cell phones on the market today are Web ready. One day soon, you'll swerve to miss a driver who is buying a sofa online from a cell phone. Although we don't encourage you to surf the Net from the driver's seat, we are excited to see that we won't be forced to create multiple pages for every browser imaginable. XHTML Basic takes over for us.

XHTML Basic caters to browsers that can't handle the fluff. No one wants to wait as a cell phone browser downloads a bulky page loaded with graphics.

At the least, XHTML Basic is proposed to cover:

- ✔ Text structure
- ✔ Images
- ✔ Basic forms
- ✔ Basic tables

If you wanted to get back to basics, you can have your way!

What about the rest?

Undoubtedly, more specifications will be introduced. There are a lot of walking brains out there inventing methods for better Web surfing. Although keeping up with the times may seem like a daunting task, just keep in mind that all these modules and specifications are really kid's stuff. You can tackle it.

Chapter 21

Extending Markup

● ●

In This Chapter

▶ Understanding modularization

▶ Adding an XHTML module to an XML DTD

▶ Custom building an XML module and adding it to XHTML

● ●

*F*or a while now, many camps have been salivating at the chops for a way to extend the HTML, now XHTML, element set. As the general public — that's us — begins to move from desktop machines to palm pilots and cell phones, the need to accommodate smaller, simpler devices has increased. The folks at the World Wide Web Consortium (W3C) decided that the best way to accomplish this was to define a framework that would set the stage for how to develop XHTML-derived markup languages. This has been done in a new specification called XHTML Modularization, which can be found at `www.w3.org/TR/xhtml-modularization/`. Although XHTML Modularization is still just a lonely Working Draft, this specification is about to make a lot of noise. Now authors will be able to create their own versions of XHTML! To join the salivation party, read on.

What the Heck is Modularization?

The first step to modularization is the *framework* — a blueprint for how these mini-XHTML markup languages work. This blueprint allows an author to use any of the existing XHTML modules. If you feel as though you've finally blown a gasket and have no idea what these module things are, read Chapter 20 for the lowdown.

What makes most Web designers do pirouettes is the simple nature of the XHTML Modularization specification. The possibilities are limitless. You must use a basic framework (you know, all those elements that define an XHTML page `<body>`, `<head>`, and so on); however, after you've developed the framework, you can use one of the many XHTML modules, other W3C modules (think XML), or any modules that you create yourself! The wonderful news is that these modules come with this new blueprint to define a customized markup language for the task at hand. The added bonus is that most of the customized creations will work in existing HTML 4 browsers.

Now, if you're waiting to learn just how to add your own markup, keep on readin'.

Adding XHTML to XML

Your boss asks you to write a DTD to use to mark up books. After much head-scratching and burning the midnight oil, you decide that you can really keep this simple. All you need is a chapter element, a title element, and a paragraph element. You produce the following DTD (see Chapter 4 for more information on DTDs):

On the CD, you can find all the code used in the following examples in the xhtmlfd/examples/ch21 folder, including the code to build the simple XML parser. This parser runs only on any version of Internet Explorer 5.

```
<!--This is xbook dtd-->
<!ELEMENT xbook (chapter)*>
<!ELEMENT chapter (title?,(para)*)>
<!ELEMENT title (#PCDATA)*>
<!ELEMENT para (#PCDATA)*>
<!--end of xbook dtd-->
```

Here's an example of a document that conforms to this DTD:

```
<?xml version="1.0"?>
<!DOCTYPE xbook SYSTEM "xbook.dtd">
<xbook>
<!--This is a basic XML document-->
<chapter>
<title>Chapter1</title>
<para>Here is a paragraph from a chapter for a book.</para>
</chapter>
</xbook>
```

You're happy, your boss is happy, you're in line for a big bonus and well-deserved promotion, you're basking in the light of your colleagues' praise and plaudits, and you're about to leave on a well earned vacation. Suddenly, your boss calls you. "Knuckle head!" he screams (the PICS rating on this book prevents us from using the boss's full, and even more descriptive language), "This stupid DTD of yours does not even allow lists! I want lists! Do it and do it now or you're fired!"

Gulp, no vacation, or no job!

Luckily, you remember something you read about XHTML modules (you see buying that *For Dummies* book really did pay off) and go lickety-split to your bookshelf!

The XHTML 1.1 lists module seems to provide all the granularity that you need, and it should also keep you boss happy. The first thing you do is load the lists.mod file into the same folder as your xbook dtd file. You now make the following addition to your DTD and rename it as xbook2.dtd:

```
<!ENTITY % listmod SYSTEM "lists.mod">
%listmod;
<!--This is xbook dtd-->
<!ELEMENT xbook (chapter)*>
<!ELEMENT chapter (title?,(para)*)>
<!ELEMENT title (#PCDATA)*>
<!ELEMENT para (#PCDATA)*>
<!--end of xbook dtd-->
```

In the previous code, we used a parameter entity declaration, <!ENTITY % listmod SYSTEM "lists.mod"> to link to the DTD material contained in lists.mod.

When we reference this declaration with the entity reference %listmod;, it's as if the complete module has been included in our DTD at this point. A parameter entity works the same way as a regular entity, except parameter entities only work in DTDs, and they use an % instead of an &.

SYSTEM is the keyword that tells your parser to look for an external entity or file, and, of course, lists.mod is the address of that file.

The lists.mod file is included on the CD.

So, after you include the lists.mod file in your DTD and add some lists to the file, the code now looks something like this:

```
<?xml version="1.0"?>
<!DOCTYPE xbook SYSTEM "xbook2.dtd">
<xbook>
<!--This is a basic XML document-->
<chapter>
<title>Chapter1</title>
<para>Here is a paragraph from a chapter for a book.</para>
<para>We want to add a few lists to our book.</para>
<ul>
  <li>First Item</li>
  <li>Second Item</li>
  <li>Third item</li>
</ul>
</chapter>
</xbook>
```

However, when you run this file on your parser, you get the following error message:

```
Parameter entity must be defined before it is used.
```

The complete error message is shown in Figure 21-1.

The code to build this parser, plus an explanatory `readme.txt` file is included on the CD in the xhtmlfd/examples/ch21 folder.

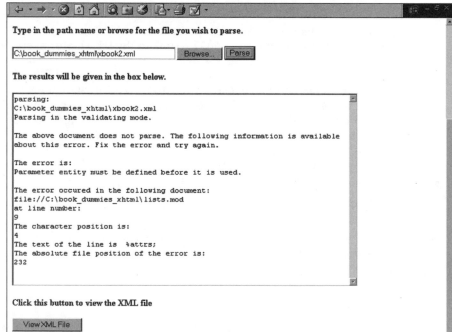

Figure 21-1:
The complete error message shown in a parser when the new code is entered.

Whoops! What's happened is that the lists module declares some entities that have not been defined. If you look inside the lists module (you can open lists.mod file using any text editor), you find the following entities aren't defined in your original document:

- %attrs;
- %inline;
- %flow;

You must define parameter entities in a declaration before you can use them. Therefore, you need to declare the entities at the top of your DTD. Referring back to the previous example, you decide that you don't need any of the common XHTML attributes on your list elements; that the inline objects just need to be text; and that the flow objects that li elements can contain need to be the title and para elements from your DTD. In addition, you need the ul, ol, and dl elements from the lists module. For more information on parameter entities, see Appendix B.

Your xbook2.dtd now looks like this:

```
<!ENTITY % attrs "">
<!ENTITY % inline "#PCDATA">
<!ENTITY % flow "#PCDATA|title|para|ul|ol|dl">
<!ENTITY % listmod SYSTEM "lists.mod">
%listmod;
<!--This is xbook dtd-->

<!ELEMENT xbook (chapter)*>
<!ELEMENT chapter (title?,(para)*)>
<!ELEMENT title (#PCDATA)*>
<!ELEMENT para (#PCDATA)*>

<!--end of xbook dtd-->
```

In most programming languages, the last declared value of something is the value that is used. In XML and SGML entities, the first declared value is used, which provides you with an easy way to override existing entities.

So, you run the program through the parser again, and you get another error message (shown in Figure 21-2):

```
Element model is invalid according to the DTD/Schema.
```

Figure 21-2:
Another
error
message
shown in a
parser when
the code is
entered.

Now, you have to alter the content model of the chapter element. You do this using another parameter entity, so your DTD now looks like this:

```
<!ENTITY % attrs "">
<!ENTITY % inline "#PCDATA">
<!ENTITY % flow "#PCDATA|title|para|ul|ol|dl">


<!ENTITY % listmod SYSTEM "lists.mod">
%listmod;
<!--This is xbook dtd-->

<!ENTITY % listels "|ul|ol|dl">
<!ELEMENT xbook (chapter)*>
<!ELEMENT chapter (title?,(para %listels;)*)>
<!ELEMENT title (#PCDATA)*>
<!ELEMENT para (#PCDATA)*>

<!--end of xbook dtd-->
```

Now, when you run the parser, everything's just fine, as shown in Figure 21-3.

Figure 21-3:
A correctly
parsed
document.

Adding XML to XHTML

In this section, we look at adding an XML module to the XMTML DTD. In fact, we use a simple subset of HTML, called XHTML-lite, which is designed specifically for use in medical records. Medical records need a simple formatting DTD, and they also need to include multiple, specialized documents. XHTML-lite is an ideal module for formatting the purely text part of medical documents. Note that XHTML-lite is not an official W3C recommendation, although it's a family member because it conforms in every way to the definition of a family member.

In this section, for reasons of space and simplicity, we use a cut-down version of XHTML called XHTML-lite. This is a simplified version of XHTML that, in fact, is useful and is used by one of the authors of this book in everyday work.

XHTML-lite.dtd and XHTML-lite.mod can be accessed on the CD from the xhtmlfd/examples/ch21/default.htm file.

A matter of record

In this section, we start with a semi-real-world example of a doctor using XHTML-lite: The names have been changed to protect the innocent. Dr. A. Quack M.D. uses XHTML-lite to write his medical records and he uses a custom DTD to record all the prescriptions he writes. Currently, he keeps the two documents types separate. He approaches you about the possibility of combining the two document types into a single one.

Here's a typical medical record of Dr. A. Quack's:

```
<!DOCTYPE html
     PUBLIC "-//PRIMAHEALTH//DTD XHTML-LITE 1.0//EN"
            "xhtml-lite.dtd">
<html>
<head>
<title>A medical record</title>
</head>
<body>
<div class="note">
<h1>Office Note</h1>
<div class="date"><h3>Apr 01 2000</h3></div>
<div class="ptname"><h3>John Doe</h3></div>
<p>John came in today complaining of back pain. Exam showed
          some spasm but otherwise was normal. I gave him a
          prescription for Indocin. </p>
<p>He will call if he hasn't improved in four days.</p>
<p>A.Quack M.D.</p>
</div><!--end of note-->
</body>
</html>
```

And here is the file that has been developed to record the prescriptions he writes:

```
<!DOCTYPE prerecord SYSTEM "prerecord1.dtd">
<prerecord>
   <ptname>John Doe</ptname>
   <drugname>Indocin</drugname>
   <dose>50mg TID</dose>
   <send>50</send>
   <directions>Take one tablet three times a day while symp-
          toms last.</directions>
   <subgen>Yes </subgen>
   <refills>3</refills>
   <diagnosis>Backpain</diagnosis>
   <delivery>Written Prescription to patient.</delivery>
   <note>Patient has no GI problems. Usual warnings
          given.</note>
</prerecord>
```

Luckily for you, the XHTML-lite DTD was developed for just this (extensibility), so you really don't have to do much work at all. This is obviously a job where you want to quote a flat rate rather than asking to be paid by the hour.

Conning the DTD

So you want to combine the XHTML-lite DTD and the doctor's custom DTD. Where do you start? First, here is the XHTML-lite DTD:

```
<!--This is XHTML-lite DTD-->

<!--redeclare these parameter entities to override
the core dtd's parameter entities.
Remember to rename the DTD with your own name.

<!ENTITY % custom.atts "">
<!ENTITY % custom.inline "">
<!ENTITY % custom.block "">
<!ENTITY % custom.body "">
-->
<!--declare the core dtd-->
<!ENTITY % coredtd SYSTEM "xhtml-lite.mod">
%coredtd;

<!--declare or reference a custom dtd here-->
<!ENTITY % custom.dtd "">
%custom.dtd;

<!--end of file-->
```

The actual DTD itself is short and sweet; the rest of the text is comments. (We've bolded the code that isn't comments so you can easily tell which is which.)

The following two lines import the XHTML-lite module (which contains all the element and attribute declarations) into the DTD by defining a parameter entity declaration, and then referencing it:

```
<!--declare the core dtd-->
<!ENTITY % coredtd SYSTEM "xhtml-lite.mod">
%coredtd;
```

Tada! This DTD is just waiting to be partnered with another module!

Now, here's the DTD of the module that we want to partner the XHTML-lite DTD with:

```
<!--this is prerecord DTD-->
<!ELEMENT prerecord
          (ptname,drugname,dose,send,dir,subgen?,refills,dia
          gnosis,delivery,note*)>
<!ELEMENT ptname (#PCDATA)*>
<!ELEMENT drugname (#PCDATA)*>
<!ELEMENT dose      (#PCDATA)*>
<!ELEMENT send      (#PCDATA)*>
<!ELEMENT dir (#PCDATA)*>
<!ELEMENT subgen (#PCDATA)*>
<!ELEMENT refills (#PCDATA)*>
<!ELEMENT diagnosis (#PCDATA)*>
<!ELEMENT delivery (#PCDATA)*>
<!ELEMENT note (#PCDATA)*>

<!-- end of prerecord DTD-->
```

The next thing you want to do is combine the DTDs.

Checking out the partner

The first thing you have to do before merging the DTDs is to ensure that the two DTDs are compatible, mainly that there is no namespace clash. In other words, you have to make sure that all the element names in the new DTD are different from those of XHTML-lite. If the two DTDs have elements that share the same element name, there will be a family quarrel, and we don't want that. In fact, if you validate the new document type after merging the DTDs, the parser will let you know if there's a namespace clash.

In this case, there's indeed no clash of names. If there was, you would have to alter the names of the clashing elements before merging the documents, which can sometimes be quite a tricky and labor-intensive task.

As you can see, the HTML-lite DTD even provides a space for importing the markup of the new module:

```
<!--declare or reference a custom dtd here-->
<!ENTITY % custom.dtd "">
%custom.dtd;
```

You should now make sure that your new module is in the same folder as the DTD and then simply declare it as an entity declaration and reference it, as follows:

```
<!--declare or reference a custom dtd here-->
<!ENTITY % custom.dtd SYSTEM "prerecord1.dtd">
%custom.dtd;
```

Note how the keyword SYSTEM is followed by an address and used to import the external file.

After you declare the prerecord1.dtd as a declaration, it's as if you took all the declarations in the prerecord DTD and placed them in your HTML-lite DTD.

Next, you need to indicate where you can place the markup from the new DTD. You only want the prerecord markup instance to appear as a child of the body element, so you need to do the following:

```
<!--add prerecord to allowed content in body element-->
<!ENTITY % custom.body "|prerecord">
```

If you peek inside the XHTML-lite module, you see that this effectively adds "prerecord" to the allowed content of body. Here's the entity declaration for custom.body:

```
<!ENTITY % custom.body "">
<!ENTITY % body.class "h1|h2|h3|h4|div|p|ul  %custom.body;">
```

Note how in the original module, the entity custom.body was declared as an empty entity. This means that when you declare it here, your redeclaration overrides the empty declaration.

Later on in the DTD, you get to the element declaration for body:

```
<!ELEMENT body (%body.class;)*>
```

When you un-reference all the entities, it's the same as if the new element declaration for body is:

```
<!ELEMENT body  (h1|h2|h3|h4|div|p|ul|prerecord)*>
```

This is now a new DTD; it's no longer HTML-lite, so you must change the name of the DTD, for example, you could call it HTML-lite-mod.

Because this DTD now has non-XHTML element names in it, HTML and XHTML browsers will not know how to display the new document. Therefore, you should also serve up any compound documents as XML documents and supply a style sheet.

Actually, it's possible, with a bit more juggling, to declare all the elements of the new DTD as allowed content of all the block elements of XHTML. Then, it would be possible to do the following:

```
<h3><ptname>John Doe</ptname></h3>
```

HTML browsers would ignore the `ptname` tags and display John Doe as a level 3 heading. As an old professor of ours put it though, this would probably be "A triumph of technique over reason." It's better just to serve it up as XML with a CSS style sheet!

In fact, you can use this technique to add as many custom modules as you want to XHTML-lite. You just have to make sure that there's not a namespace clash. This applies not only to the XHTML-lite DTD, but also to any other modules you add.

Of course, if you need the power of the full XHTML DTD, you follow a similar process as this. Full details on how to use the main DTD modules can be found at `www.w3.org/TR/xhtml-modularization`.

Building Modules for Different Media

In Chapter 23, you learn that similar modular markup is being used in real life situations all over the Internet. One example is the Wireless Markup Language (WML), which uses XHTML modules to build a markup language suitable for use on cell phones and other wireless transmitting devices. What this means for you, the author of a Web page, is that you can write one set of pages in XHTML and be confident that it can be seen on all different types of media!

Chapter 22

DOMinate Dynamic Web Pages

XHTML 1.0 allows for some pretty darn fascinating stuff. Fans of the cutting edge see some exciting Web functionality that's an everyday occurrence on the Web in the last couple of years: Dynamic pages (also known as Dynamic HTML).

Say it with us:

✔ Dynamic means interactive

✔ Interactive means dynamic

The Web design world loves acronyms as much as catchy key phrases. When interactive pages first took off, it had the catch name, Dynamic HTML (DHTML). It didn't catch on as much as some would have liked, so now you also will hear "interactive pages" or "dynamic pages" and occasionally still "DHTML." All three terms mean the same thing: a Web page that responds to a user's action.

Why Create Dynamic Pages?

The essence of dynamic pages seems simple enough at first: You can create Web pages that can change — almost as if by magic — after they have been sent to the browser from the server. How is this amazing feat accomplished? In a nutshell, scripting (combined with regular XHTML) provides the Web browser with the instructions it needs to *automagically* alter a Web page on the client side — without extra help from the server — according to user activities.

Unfortunately, this new frontier isn't all roses. In the past, Microsoft and Netscape Communications had different visions of DHTML. It's not difficult to create functional dynamic pages for the most current versions of the major browsers, but older browsers may be less cooperative.

You can coax your Web pages into performing all kinds of nifty tricks using dynamic pages, including

- **Menus.** Dynamic pages support hierarchical menus (clicking a selection on one menu pops up another submenu).

- **At your service.** Users can interact with Web documents more quickly; plus, they don't have to request a new page from a server across the Internet and wait for it to arrive. Users get what they need quickly, like it, and spread the word.

- **Styles galore.** Because XHTML supports style sheets, and dynamic pages can operate with style sheets as well as XHTML documents, page designers can even change styles dynamically. Font selections, sizes, and text color can change in response to user actions on a Web page. For example, the contents of a Website map can be presented in small type to fit as much information as possible onto a single screen. When a user selects an item, that item can change to a larger type, perhaps in multiple festive colors. As viewers move from page to page, text can reflow around each new focal point, keeping it at the current center of attention. (Imagine the possibilities that spring from applying such handling to whatever focuses a user's attention. Magic lamps, anyone?)

That's just a small chunk of the dynamic possibilities.

XHTML Turns Interactive

Dynamic doesn't equal magic, which means that it takes more than XHTML elements to make a Web page dynamic. The three main technologies that help your pages along are:

- **Scripting commands** tell a browser how to change a document dynamically.

- **A document object model (DOM)** helps the browser recognize the many different elements in a document (elements refer to individual tags and their content) — and change those elements as directed by scripting commands.

- **Style sheets** help a browser figure out how to display the many iterations possible any dynamic document can go through. To read more about style sheets, be sure to visit Chapter 8.

Scripting your pages

Just as a movie script (with assistance from the director, of course) dictates action in a film, scripts included in dynamic Web pages direct a page's dynamic activities. Even the simplest rollover requires a short, sweet script.

In Web parlance, a *rollover* is a common Web-page addition that swaps one image for another when a user rolls the mouse pointer over the original image. To make the switch, the underlying script must include specific instructions to do the following in this order:

1. Detect when a user rolls the mouse pointer over a specific image.

2. Rewrite the value for the src= attribute for the <img /> element that defines the graphic so the new value points to the location of a new image.

3. Detect when a user moves the mouse off that image.

4. Rewrite the value of scr= to point back to the location of the original image.

The code that passes all these instructions to the computer can't be written in just any language. The browser needs its instructions written in a special computer scripting language. (Is that why they're called scripts? Eureka!)

The most common scripting language used are JavaScript — also called ECMAScript — and VBScript.

To enable as many browsers as possible — on the widest range of platforms — to view your pages, use JavaScript. Both Navigator and Internet Explorer support JavaScript. Only Internet Explorer also supports VBScript.

Both JavaScript and VBScript are complete programming languages. If you want to learn to write your own scripts, you'll need to learn the semantics for one or both languages. (Don't make that face. What if it freezes that way?) Admittedly, it takes some time to learn how to script — but it's not impossible by a long shot. Besides, we know a couple of really great books to help you learn how to script dynamic pages. Try the *JavaScript Bible,* 3rd Edition, by Danny Goodman (IDG Books Worldwide, Inc., 1998) and *JavaScript For Dummies,* 2nd Edition, by Emily Vander Veer (IDG Books Worldwide, Inc., 1997).

If you don't really need another hobby but you want to run with the big dogs, we've got the answer. You can use canned scripts — scripts written by others that you can plug right into your pages and use. Various Web sites offer hundreds — if not thousands — of scripts just waiting for you to pick them up and use them on your pages. (Don't worry, it's legal!) Three chock-full sites also are good learning resources:

✔ www.scripting.com

✔ www.webcoder.com

✔ http://javascript.internet.com/

Behind the scenes

We're not talking about the Oscars. This is a whole different event. Events transform pages into interactive stacks of goodness. Ever moved your mouse over an image and seen another image magically appear? That is what many Web designers call a *rollover,* also known as a *mouseover.* The names make sense, right?

You must be asking yourself, *How does the browser know when a user acts on a Web page?* Well, the browser isn't psychic, but it is "smart" in many ways. Browsers that understand and implement scripts are smart enough to recognize events.

An *event* can represent a user action or response. Events act as triggers for scripts, telling them when to run. When Web developers create a named set of events, they can instruct a Web document to respond in a specific way when the browser recognizes an event. In fact, without events a browser doesn't know when it should run any script on a Web page.

Web-page developers can associate any kind of script with a user event, which means all kinds of crazy things can happen when the browser recognizes those events. Imagine your page showing explanatory messages, looking up terms in a glossary and displaying them elsewhere on-screen (or in a pop-up window), opening a text-entry box to solicit and handle user input, or making a rude noise. All this happens purely on the client side of the Web connection. Your Web page acts like any other local application — which can open a whole other box of delights (or can of worms, depending on whom you ask).

PG-Rated DOM

The DOM is the defining word for how items on a Web page are represented. The DOM is a component of a Web browser that allows the browser to recognize the elements in a page as entities that can be manipulated by a script.

Imagine, for example, loading a Web page from a browser's point of view. As the browser starts to load the page, the browser sees elements as more than switches that turn formatting *on* or *off.* Instead, the browser organizes each element and its content into a miniature database that contains all the pieces and parts of that page. These elements are the objects in the document; the browser's database is a model for how they all fit together. Hence the name — Document Object Model. (It's like a model kit that contains all the parts and instructions that the browser needs to snap the page together, just like that.)

Once a browser stores a DOM a Web page, that browser is able to follow the instructions in a script to recognize and change anything about the different elements on the page — for example:

- ✔ Element attributes and their values
- ✔ Element content
- ✔ Actual elements themselves

Therefore, the script that drives a rollover to switch `image1.gif` with `image1a.gif` tells the browser to find the first image element in its database — usually by assigning that image a unique identifier using the `id=` attribute. Next, the script tells the browser to rewrite the element that reads `<img id="rollover" src="image1.gif" />` to read `<img id="rollover" src="image1a.gif" />`. When the browser rewrites the element, it knows it must then display a specific change to the page — namely, `image1a.gif` rendered in place of `image1.gif`.

History teaches us that the major problems associated with creating dynamic pages stem from differences in the way Internet Explorer and Netscape Navigator implement the DOM. Internet Explorer incorporates built-in support for all the elements in XHTML 1.0 so it can recognize and change anything about any element in a page. But at the time of this writing, the Netscape Navigator DOM recognizes a smaller subset of the elements in XHTML 1.0, so it can only access and change the elements that belong to that subset (not all elements, as Internet Explorer can). A dynamic page that works fine in Internet Explorer sometimes isn't so fine in Netscape Navigator. (This will change with the introduction of Netscape 6. The current beta version boasts full support for the DOM.)

DOM specifications on the rise

The previous section covers the DOM according to the W3C (DOM Level 1), and Netscape and Microsoft 's proprietary versions to-date. With the push to standardize Web-related languages and technologies, it's important that you keep your eyes peeled for the next version of the DOM coming soon from the W3C (DOM Level 2). What's the deal with all the levels? Well, much like markup languages, the W3C continues to update and expand the DOM. This doesn't mean that they scrap the first one and start fresh. Instead, the W3C enhances the earlier version (taking out dated material and adding the new stuff).

At the time this book is going to print, DOM Level 2 is a Candidate Recommendation, which means that it's on the last leg of approval before becoming a state-of-the-art specification. Level 1 focused on the HTML (and now XHTML) and XML document navigation and manipulation. Level 2 introduces a style sheet object model, adding support for manipulation of style information attached to a document.

Here's what the W3C has planned for you:

- Any element generates events
- Various types of events will be supported
- The event delivery mechanism overrides default behavior
- Event definitions are platform independent and language neutral
- Style sheets are represented in the object model.
- Selectors, rules, and properties of individual style sheets can be manipulated (see Chapter 8 for more information on stylesheets).
- All CSS elements can be manipulated in the object model, including
  - Linked style sheets
  - Imported style sheets
  - Alternative style sheets
  - CSS pseudo-classes and pseudo-elements
  - Contextual selectors
  - Inline styles
  - CSS properties

Believe it or not, there are already plans for a level 3 DOM!

The moral of this story is

- Always keep on top of your homework.
- Visit `www.w3.org/DOM/` for updates information.

Chapter 23

Real-World XHTML Solutions

● ●

In This Chapter

▶ Understanding plain-vanilla XHTML

▶ Converting between languauges

▶ Using XHTML modules

● ●

Using the XHTML Namespace

Nothing's better than plain vanilla ice cream on a hot day. And when all is said and done, the best use for XHTML is to write Web pages that can be read on millions of browsers, from cell phones and TVs to your high-powered desktop computer.

Because XHTML is XML and because it can use all those wonderful tools available for XML, there's a guarantee that all you have to do is write one set of pages and people everywhere will be able to read your pages no matter which kind of platform they're using.

How is this minor miracle accomplished? The answer is *proxy servers.* Proxy servers intercept your XHTML pages, and with a minimum of fuss, convert your XHTML pages into a form suitable for rendering on the platform they're serving. You are shown a little more about this conversion process in the following section.

For a good look at a set of pages written entirely in XHTML go to `www.hwg.org/opcenter/gutenberg`. These pages are written in XHTML and rely on Cascading Style Sheets (CSS) for their styling. However, the pages in this Web site still look good when viewed on Mosaic 1, the original Web browser that started it all.

Conversions

Hundreds of different XML document types are out there. For those document types to be useful to everyone, they need to be easily translated from one form to another. By far, the most common document type (if we include the HTML pages that are soon going to be converted to XHTML) is the XHTML document type. The following section shows you how to convert documents from one type to another. First and foremost, you should seriously consider converting all your old HTML pages to XHTML.

Converting HTML to XHTML

How do you go about converting your legacy HTML files to XHTML so that you can get the benefits of XHTML? You can read all about how to do it manually in Chapter 3 of this book (which we suggest you do anyway), or you can use a tool to convert your HTML to XHTML. For those of you who are desperate for a good conversion tool, there's an excellent one available that was designed by Dave Raggett, the technology lead for the XHTML working group. The best news is that this tool is free! It's called HTML Tidy. You can download HTML Tidy from `www.w3.org/People/Raggett/tidy/`.

The bad news is that this tool has to be run from a command line (command line, what's that?). But not to worry, because we show you how to do this right now!

What is your command?

Those of you who are UNIX or DOS whizzes can probably skip this section. If you're a Mac user, go to the end of this section and find out where to get the Mac version of Tidy. (No command lines necessary for Mac users!)

If you're one of those PC users who thinks a command line is what a Marine Master Sergeant barks at his recruits, read on. In the bad old days, before Windows, if you were running a PC, you had to type terse commands at a command line called the DOS prompt to get your computer to do anything. You can still do this if you so desire. If you're running Windows, go to Start➪Programs➪MS-DOS Prompt. The prompt opens at the folder C:\Windows.

The first thing you have to do is navigate to the folder to which you've downloaded HTML Tidy. In our case, the folder is `C:\FRANK`. To navigate to this folder, I had to type the following at the command line:

```
cd ..\frank
```

To change folders in DOS, I used the `cd` command. Then we used `..\` to take us back to the root folder. After that, we typed `frank` to open the FRANK folder. Note there must be a space between `cd` and `..\` but there's no space between `..\` and `frank`.

You're now ready to use Tidy. Your mission is (should you accept) to change the following rather ugly HTML file (note the unclosed <h1> and many other XHTML no-no's) to beautiful XHTML:

```
<HTML>
<Title>An HTML file</Title>
<H1>Untidy HTML file<h1>
<P>This is a rather untidy HTML file
<p>We will use HTML TIDY to convert this to an XHTML file
</HTML>
```

The previous HTML file is located in the following directory:

```
c:\book_dummies_xhtml\ch23\tidy.html
```

Remember folks; this is *just* an example. This directory doesn't exist on your computer unless you create it.

Now, to use Tidy, you type the following at the command line, right after the c:\frank> text:

```
tidy -asxml -m  c:\book_dummies_xhtml\ch23\tidy.htm
```

Here's how this code breaks down:

- ✔ tidy is, of course, the name of the exe file

- ✔ -asxml is an instruction to tidy to convert the file to XHTML

- ✔ -m is an instruction to modify the file where it is currently located

- ✔ c:\book_dummies_xhtml\ch23\tidy.htm is the address of the file to be modified

Figure 23-1 shows the output created by HTML Tidy.

Figure 23-1:
The output created by using HTML Tidy from a DOS prompt.

Now when you open up the file, you find that your ugly HTML has all been converted to perfect XHTML, which should now look something like this:

```
<?xml version="1.0"?>
<!DOCTYPE html PUBLIC "-//W3C//DTD XHTML 1.0 Strict//EN"
    "http://www.w3.org/TR/xhtml1/DTD/xhtml1-strict.dtd">
<html xmlns="http://www.w3.org/1999/xhtml">
<head>
<meta name="generator" content="HTML Tidy, see www.w3.org" />
<title>An HTML file</title>
</head>
<body>
<h1>Untidy HTML file</h1>

<p>This is a rather untidy HTML file</p>

<p>We will use HTML TIDY to convert this to an XHTML file</p>
</body>
</html>
```

If you want to preserve the original file and put the modified HTML in a new file, (instead of replacing the old one as instructed with the -m command) you need to type the following at the command line:

```
tidy -asxhtml  [path of file to be tidied]  >[path of tidied
            file]
```

Tidy can do all kinds of other things to your HTML file. Full documentation is available on the Tidy site at www.w3.org/People/Raggett/tidy/#help.

Even more exciting is the fact that the nice people at WebReview have put a version of HTML Tidy online so that all you have to do is enter your URL into a text box and it checks your page for you. Check it out at www.webreview.com/1999/07/16/feature/xhtml.cgi. See Chapter 26 for a little more info on this online utility.

Macs and other breeds

If you're running a Mac, go to www.geocities.com/siliconvalley/1057/tidy.html, to find a version of Tidy that runs on your Macintosh.

If you're using other platforms, you may have to build a copy of Tidy from the source code, but then again if you're using other platforms, you probably get some kind of perverse pleasure from doing this kind of stuff anyway.

The full documentation for other platforms is available on the Tidy site.

Converting XHTML to XHTML

Have you ever accessed a Web page from a cell phone or a palm pilot? If not, you may be surprised to hear that according to the marketing Gurus, accessing the Web through unconventional means is where the action is going to be within the next two years. According to these oracles, 75 percent of all Web pages will be viewed on platforms other than conventional computers by the end of the year 2002 (there is no spoon)! Because of these changes, your server will have to convert tables to lists and provide an alternative for graphics.

It's likely that most cell phone companies will provide some kind of proxy server for their clients that can automatically route your XHTML page through a conversion device. Figure 23-2 shows how this conversion process may be done.

Figure 23-2:
The conversion process of an XHTML document.

On the other hand, you may be very particular about how your pages are viewed, and you may want to write your own code to convert your pages. In this case, when you get the request from the proxy server, you'll have the opportunity to send pages that you have designed especially for the medium requesting the service. In either case, the fact that your pages are written in well-formed XHTML will simplify whichever process you choose. For the programmers among you, I've included some code that shows you how to do this on the CD.

The code is ASP code. seetransform1.asp, test1.htm, and longdesc1.txt. To run this code, you must have Microsoft Personal Web Server (PWS) installed. PWS is not installed by default on Windows 98 platforms. You need to install it using the Add/Remove Programs applet in the Control Panel. (See Start⇨ Settings⇨Control Panel⇨Add/Remove Programs). For other breeds of Windows, go to the Microsoft site and do a search on PWS. Doing so lets you download a version suitable for your platform.

Converting XML to XHTML

More and more people are storing information as XML and then converting the XML to XHTML for display. This can be done either on the fly every time an XHTML page is downloaded or at set intervals. It can be done either by proprietary software or by scripts using W3C technology.

Proprietary software

If you navigate to `www.hwg.org/opcenter/gutenberg/checkdoc1.html`, you find a table of books that have been marked up in XHTML. If you go to View⇨Source in Internet Explorer or View⇨Page Source in Navigator, you see an XHTML file that, for all intents and purposes, looks like it has been lovingly crafted in a text editor. However, it wasn't created in a text editor. The information in this XHTML file starts as an XML file. The resulting XHTML file was automatically generated by a simple piece of software. Here's a typical entry in the XML file:

```
<xdoc pgnum="690">
    <fname>rfree10.xml</fname>
    <date>16-Feb-00</date>
    <fsize>347k</fsize>
    <docname>Proposed Roads to Freedom</docname>
    <docauth>
        <first>Bertrand</first>
        <middle></middle>
        <last>Russell</last>
    </docauth>
        <marker>Elias Hantzakos</marker>
        <email show="no">ilias@email.com</email>
        <dtd>gutbook1.dtd</dtd>
        <ss>darwin.css</ss>
        <note></note>
    </xdoc>
```

A similar entry is made for every book on the list, and this XML file is used to generate numerous XHTML documents. The XML file indexes by author name, date, or by title, just to mention a few. The XHTML file that you viewed (which is a list of books indexed by author) is automatically generated every evening and it only takes about .02 seconds to generate. Imagine how much time it would take if the whole page had to be coded by hand!

The code of the software that generates the page took about half a day to write and debug. Without going into details, the reason it took such a short time is because it relies heavily on XML processing tools that are available off the shelf. It's estimated that if these tools had not been available it would have taken two to three weeks to write and debug the utility.

Using XSLT

If there's a need for your page to be right up to the minute, you'll probably want to create it every time a request is made to download the page. Doing so is called authoring a page on the fly. If you decide to do this, you can use some kind of scripting language to author the page. Extensible Stylesheet Language Transformations (XSLT) is a syntax developed by the W3C to allow easy transformations from one document type to another. XSLT has just become a W3C recommendation, and already there are numerous tools available that you can use. See the W3C site at `www.w3.org/TR/1999/PR-xslt-19991008` for more information.

Using XHTML Modules

You may be surprised to learn that the vast majority of Internet documents in the real world are not Web documents. Web pages only comprise a minute proportion of all the documents that are written. All over the world, people are communicating. When they communicate, there's a need to record and store what has been said, and increasingly the format that is used is XML. Here are just a few examples of projects that use that XML.

Maintenance manuals

The next time you take a plane and arrive safely at your destination, thank XML. The maintenance manual for the average plane is about 4,000 pages, and at least a third of the manual is updated every year. This enormous task is now made easier by using XML as the markup language to store and catalog the information.

Program documentation

While you're thanking XML for the safe plane ride that resulted from an updated maintenance manual, you may want to thank the computer program that ran the guidance system that helped your pilot to make that (almost) flawless landing at night or in bad weather. These incredibly complex programs must be absolutely fail-safe and require even more complex commenting and documentation. In a typical guidance system program, there are typically three lines of comment for every line of code. And these comments are written in, you've guessed it, XML!

Medical records

The U.S. federal government has passed legislation that by the year 2002 all medical records must be available in electronic form, and guess what language is being used to mark-up these records? XML and XHTML.

Book editing

Book publishers belong to one of the most conservative groups of people in the world, but even this group under the pressure of competition is moving into the modern age. The chances are that the *For Dummies* book you buy next year will be written in XML.

Book writing

This chapter is actually being written in XML. Conservative IDG, at present, requires their chapter to be written in Microsoft Word format, but in fact Word 2000 uses, yup, you've guessed it, XML as it's formatting and styling engine. If you don't believe us, just open a Word 2000 document in a text editor!

Ancient and not-so-ancient manuscripts

Oxford University of England, and the University of Virginia in the U.S. both archive over 100,000 books and documents in electronic form. The language these books are marked up in is Text Encoding Initiative (TEI), which was an SGML application (like HTML) but is now an XML application. To download hundreds of texts for your own use, go to `www.hwg.org/opcenter/gutenberg` where you can find documents marked up in both XML and XHTML.

We could go on, but the truth is that XML really has taken the world of documentation and writing by storm. Remember that XML only became a recommendation in February of 1998, and already it's almost universal. Now what has all this got to do with XHTML?

Writing DTDs

All these different uses of XML require the writing of separate DTDs and the creation of new document types. Writing separate DTDs and creating new document types is a difficult, time consuming, and expensive undertaking.

One of the most useful things about XHTML is that the large, monolithic DTD has been broken down into several smaller modules that enable DTD authors to select chunks of it for use in their own DTDs. Why bother creating a new

DTD for lists or tables when there's one available right off the shelf? Not to mention that price is right — it's free!

More and more custom document authors are now incorporating units of XHTML in their structure with the knowledge that the XHTML module has been thoroughly debugged and tested. (See Chapter 20 for a full account of using modules.)

Converting one document type to another

The second kind of problem arises when there's a need to convert one XML document type into another document type. How do you do this? Well you could do one of two things: You could write special software to convert your XML document into the XML format of the entity you want to communicate with, or you could simply convert it into XHTML. Then your correspondent could either read the XHTML, the universal language of the Web, or you can bet that they already have software to convert XHTML into their document type. The conversion process might looks something like Figure 23-3. It Is rather like a Russian and an Arab talking to each other in English.

Figure 23-3:
XML converted to XHTML and back to XML.

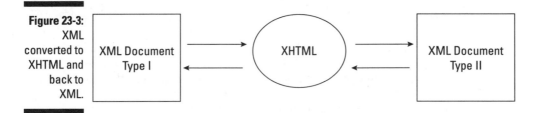

Using XHTML as the universal language of the Web promises to be one of the most common uses for it in behind-the-scenes applications.

Using the XHTML namespace

What happens if you want to make use of XHTML without going to all the trouble of creating a new document type? The answer is that you can use namespaces.

What am I?

One of the prerequisites of marrying two modules is that there should be no namespace clash (see Chapter 20 for more details). In other words, the names of the elements in both modules should be unique. If they aren't unique, the parsing software and the rendering software won't know which element to deal with.

Consider the following two documents. The first document type is from the `xbook.dtd` we use in Chapter 20:

```
<xbook>
<!--This is a basic XML document-->
  <chapter>
  <title>Chapter1</title>
  <para>Here is a paragraph from a chapter for a book.</para>
  </chapter>
</xbook>
```

The second document is an XHTML document with almost identical content.

```
<html>
<head>
<title>A trial document</title>
</head>
<body>
<div class= "chapter">
<h1> Chapter1</h1>
<p>Here is a paragraph from a chapter for a book.</p>
</div>
</body>
</html>
```

If you look through these two documents, you notice that they both contain the `title` element; however, the `title` element is used for a different purpose in each document. In xbook, it's used to describe the title of a chapter in a book; in XHTML, it's used to describe the title of a document. In "Geek-Speak" we say that they have different semantics.

Here's a fragment from another document (called "personal") in which the element type `title` has yet another different semantic meaning:

```
<name>
<title>Dr.</title><first>A.</first><last>Quack</last>
</name>
```

If you want to combine these documents, how would you distinguish between the different uses of the word `title`? Indeed, how would you distinguish which element came from which document?

Luckily, there is a W3C recommendation that enables us to do just that. It's called the namespaces recommendation, and you can find it at `www.w3.org/TR/REC-xml-names`.

Here's an example. You want to mix all these document types up in a document called `mixedbag`. How does this recommendation enable you to do this?

Where do I come from?

The best way to show how the namespace recommendation works is by way of an example. In the following XML file, we've included examples of titles from all the document types from the previous section in a document called mixedbag. For the record, mixedbag can contain one element of its own: a para element.

```
<mixedbag
xmlns="http://www.lanw.com/mixedbag"
xmlns:html="http://www.w3.org/1999/xhtml"
xmlns:xbook="http://www.somedom.com/xbook"
xmlns:personal="http://www.hypermedic.com/personal"
>
<!--This title element belongs to the 'html' namespace-->
<html:title>A very mixed bag of documents</html:title>
<!--This para element belongs to the 'mixedbag' namespace-->
<para>An example of elements from several document types.
        Here is a title from a book chapter.</para>
<!--This title element belongs to the 'xbook' namespace-->
<xbook:title>Cheaper by the dozen</xbook:title>
<para>Written by </para>
<!-- all the following are from the 'personal' name space-->
<personal:name>
<personal:title>Professor</personal:title><personal:first>Joh
        n</personal:first><personal:last>Blowhard</per-
        sonal:last>
</personal:name>
</mixedbag>
```

What's going on here?

The first thing to notice is that mixedbag contains an xmlns attribute. (Every legal XHTML document should contain an xmlns attribute.) This attribute is used to declare namespaces and is one of the W3C reserved attributes. It's illegal for you to use it for any other purpose than to declare a namespace.

The value of this attribute must be given a unique name. A sure way to guarantee that the name is unique is to use a URL. The lanw domain name is under the control of LANWrights.Inc, so it can't legally be used by anyone else. Therefore, you make up a composite URL that contains the lanw domain so that the URL is unique.

Theoretically, you can give this attribute any value that you think may be unique, for example, Supercalifragilisticexpialidociousfromlanwrights is probably unique. However, there's a convention that's developed that states that this value should be a URL. Note that just because the value takes the form of a URL, there is no guarantee that there should be anything at the other end. Indeed, it is best if there isn't.

What this uncolonized `xmlns` attribute tells us, and more importantly tells the processing software, is that unless otherwise indicated, all elements in the following document belong to the `http://www.lanw.com/mixedbag` namespace.

```
<mixedbag
xmlns='http://www.lanw.com/mixedbag'
```

This attribute is followed by three more `xmlns` attributes, one for each type of document we're going to include in `mixedbag`. This time `xmlns` is followed by a colon and a suffix. The first colonized attribute is `xmlns:html`. The value given to this attribute should be familiar; it is the `xhtml` namespace. What this declaration tells both us and the processing software, is that any element that is prefixed by html belongs in the xhtml namespace.

```
xmlns:html='http://www.w3.org/1999/xhtml'
```

Similarly the next two declarations assign the `xbook` prefixed elements and the `personal` prefixed elements to the `xbook` and `personal` namespaces, respectively.

Note that the prefix does not have to be the same name as the document type, although, in practice, this is a good idea.

```
xmlns:xbook="http://www.somedom.com/xbook"
xmlns:personal="http://www.hypermedic.com/personal"
>
```

Now we assign prefixes to all the elements. Those that we don't assign prefixes to belong to the default `mixedbag` namespace.

```
<!--This title element belongs to the 'html' namespace-->
<html:title>A very mixed bag of documents</html:title>
<!--This para element belongs to the 'mixedbag' namespace-->
<para>An example of elements from several document types.
          Here is a title from a book chapter.</para>
<!--This title element belongs to the 'xbook' namespace-->
<xbook:title>Cheaper by the dozen</xbook:title>
<para>Writen by </para>
<!-- all the following are from the 'personal' name space-->
<personal:name>
<personal:title>Professor</personal:title><personal:first>Joh
          n</personal:first><personal:last>Blowhard</persona
          l:last>
</personal:name>
</mixedbag>
```

What we have done in the previous code is disambiguate all these different title elements. We've also clearly distinguished which element comes from which namespace. What this means for XHTML is that we have a way to simply add XHTML elements to our XML documents.

Because XHTML is by far the most common of the XML element types, many XML browsers recognize the prefix html as belonging to the XHTML namespace and render the html document in an appropriate manner, even without a style sheet.

Don't cry for me, XHTML; I never left you

All the old, faithful HTML browsers that now do XML recognize the html namespace. For example, the Internet Explorer 5 browser recognizes the html namespace in the following XML file:

```
<?xml version="1.0"?>
<?xml-stylesheet type="text/css" href="xbook.css"?>
<xbook
xmlns="http://www.somedom.com/xbook"
xmlns:html="http://www.w3.org/1999/xhtml">
<!--This is a basic XML document-->
<chapter>
<title>Chapter1</title>
<para>Here is a paragraph from a chapter for a book.</para>
</chapter>
<html:table border="1">
<html:tr><html:td>Cell 1</html:td><html:td>Cell
        2</html:td></html:tr>
<html:tr><html:td>Cell 3</html:td><html:td>Cell
        4</html:td></html:tr>
</html:table>
</xbook>
```

The resulting code looks like Figure 23-4 when rendered in Internet Explorer 5.

The early versions of the Mozilla browser also recognize the html namespace; however, the preview of Netscape 6 only gives spotty recognition. In fact, the XML rendering of Netscape 6 is problematic at best. Hopefully, the problems are sorted out by the time the beta and the final version of version 6 is released.

Namespaces give you an easy way to introduce all the semantics and functionality of XHTML into your XML documents. Not only does the XHTML namespace work for tables — it also works for images, forms, and hyperlinks.

The rendering of namespaces is characteristic of the individual browsers. There's no recommendation that requires browsers to behave in this manner. It's just nice that they do.

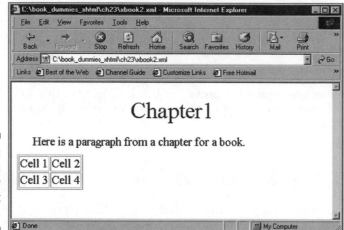

Figure 23-4:
The code as
rendered by
Internet
Explorer 5.

Part VI
The Part of Tens

TARZAN - LORD of the WEB

@RICHTENNANT

Maybe you write memos too long — last one make server traffic move like hippo through mud pit.

What your problem? No can swing link to link? Try going "ahAHahAHahAHah!" real loud next time you click — ahhahahaha.

This guy real interesting. Wonder how long it take to call in elephant stampede?

Why you say this not elegant interface? Tarzan work hard to design warthog icons!

In this part . . .

Here, we cover the do's and don'ts for XHTML markup, help you rethink your views on document design, explore some "best of breed" XHTML tools and programs, and identify the cream of the crop in the many XHTML resources available online. Enjoy!

Chapter 24

Ten XHTML Do's and Don'ts

In This Chapter
- ▶ Concentrating on content
- ▶ Going easy on the graphics, bells, whistles, and hungry T-Rexes
- ▶ Creating well-formulated XHTML and then testing, testing, testing
- ▶ Finishing the work after the building is done

*B*y itself, XHTML is neither excessively complex nor overwhelmingly difficult. As some high-tech wags (including a few rocket scientists) have put it, "This ain't rocket science!" Nevertheless, a few important do's and don'ts can make or break the Web pages you build with XHTML. Consider these humble admonishments as guidelines to help you make the most of XHTML without losing touch with your users or watching your pages blow up on the launch pad.

If some of the fundamental points that we made throughout this book seem to be cropping up here too (especially regarding proper and improper use of XHTML), it's no accident. Heed ye well the prescriptions and avoid ye the maledictions. But hey, we know they're your pages and you can do what you want with them. Your users decide the ultimate outcome. (We'd *never* say, "We told you so!" Nope. Not us.)

Never Lose Sight of Your Content

So we return to the crucial question of payload: the content of your page. Why? Well, as Darrell Royal (legendary football coach of the University of Texas Longhorns) is rumored to have said to his players, "Dance with who brung ya." In normal English (as opposed to Texan), we think this means that you should *stick with the people who've supported you all along* and give your loyalty to those who've given it to you.

We're not sure what this means for football, but for Web pages it means keeping faith with your users and keeping content paramount. If you don't have strong, solid, informative content, users quickly get that empty feeling that starts to gnaw when a Web page is content-free. Then they're off to richer hunting grounds on the Web, looking for content. To satisfy their hunger

- ✔ Place your most important content on your site's front pages.
- ✔ Save the frills and supplementary materials for secondary pages.

The short statement of this principle for XHTML is "Tags are important, but *what's between the tags* — the content — really counts." For a refresher course on making your content the very best it can possibly be, take a look at Chapter 2.

Structure Your Documents and Your Site

Providing users with a clear road map and guiding them through your content is as important for a single home page as it is for an online encyclopedia. When longer or more complex documents grow into a full-fledged Web site, a road map becomes even more important. This map ideally takes the form of (yep, you guessed it) a flow chart that shows page organization and links. If you like pictures with a purpose, the chart could appear in graphic form on an orientation page for your site. You may also want to place information on individual Web pages that shows users where their pages fit into the overall site hierarchy. (This technique is called *breadcrumbs,* after the story of Hansel and Gretel, and is covered in more detail in Chapter 12.)

Good content flows from good organization. It helps you stay on track during page design, testing, delivery, and maintenance. And organization helps your users find their way through your site.

We're strong advocates of top-down page design: Don't start writing content or placing tags until you understand what you want to say and how you want to organize your materials. Then start the construction of any XHTML document or collection of documents with a paper and pencil (or whatever modeling tool you like best). Sketch out the relationships within the content and the relationships among your pages. Know where you're building before you roll out the heavy equipment.

Need we say more? Well, yes: Don't forget that *organization changes with time.* Revisit and critique your organization and structure on a regular basis and don't be afraid to change either one to keep up with changes in your content or focus.

Keep Track of Those Tags

If you're building documents by hand, forgetting to use closing tags is easy, even when they're required (for example, the $</a>$ tag that closes the opening anchor tag, $<a>$). Therefore, when you're testing your pages, make sure you perform the requisite syntax checks to determine that your documents are well formed (that is, that they meet the syntax rules of XHTML). Badly formed XHTML documents are broken and won't work properly — unlike HTML, which lets you get away with (tag) murder!

Vendors of XHTML authoring tools make some outrageous claims ("You don't even have to know any markup!"). Your authors politely differ:

- ✔ XHTML and HTML code is what makes Web pages work; if you understand it, you can troubleshoot with a minimum amount of fuss.

- ✔ Ensuring that your page's inner workings are correct and complete is an important step in ensuring the quality of the documents your produce, whether you build them by hand or a program builds them for you.

We could go on ad infinitum about this, but we'll exercise some mercy and confine our remarks to the most pertinent:

- ✔ **Keep track of elements yourself while you write or edit XHTML by hand.** If you open a tag — be it an anchor, a text area, or whatever — create the closing tag for it right then and there, even if you haven't added the content. All XHTML editors do this for you.

- ✔ **Use a syntax-checker to validate your work during the testing process.** Syntax-checkers are automatic tools that find missing tags. Use these whether you build pages by hand or with software assistance.

- ✔ **Obtain and use as many browsers as you can when testing pages.** Doing so can point out potential design flaws or browser dependencies (especially important if you need to rely on XHTML's backward compatibility with HTML). This exercise also emphasizes the importance of alternate text information. That's why we always check our pages with Lynx, which is a character-only browser (in other words, it's a nongraphical, words-only browser).

Although XHTML isn't exactly a programming language, it still makes sense to treat it as one. Therefore, using an editing tool to make sure you follow required formats and syntax helps avoid trouble. Likewise, careful testing and rechecking of your work — especially when you make "a few changes" by hand, as often happens during the maintenance phases — ensures a high degree of quality, compliance with standards, and a relatively trouble-free Web site.

Make the Most from the Least

More is not always better, especially when taking about Web pages.

- ✔ Design and build your pages using simple layouts and minimal ornaments.

  Don't overload pages with graphics; add only as many levels of headings as you absolutely need and make sure your content is easy to read and follow.

- ✔ Make sure any hyperlinks you include connect your users to useful information that adds value to your site.

  Gratuitous links are nobody's friend; if you're tempted to link to a WebCam that shows a "growing" houseplant, resist, resist.

Structure and images exist to *highlight* content. The more elaborate your structure — or the more bells, whistles, and dinosaur growls dominate a page — the more they distract visitors from your content. Therefore, use structure and graphics sparingly, wisely, and as carefully as possible. Anything more can be an obstacle to content delivery. Go easy on the animations, links, and layout elements, or risk having your message (even your page) devoured by a hungry T-Rex.

Build Attractive Pages

When users visit Web pages with a consistent framework that focuses on content — and supplements (but doesn't trample) that content with graphics and links — they're likely to feel welcome. Making those Web pages pretty and easy to navigate only adds to a site's basic appeal and makes your cyber-campers even happier.

If you need inspiration, cruise the Web and look for layouts and graphics that work for you. If you take the time to analyze what you like, you can work from other people's design principles without having to steal details from their layouts or looks (which isn't a good idea anyway).

When you design your Web documents, try out the following helpful hints:

- ✔ Start with a functional page layout.
- ✔ Pick a small, but interesting, set of graphical symbols or icons and adopt a consistent navigation style.
- ✔ Use graphics sparingly (yes, you've heard this before) and make them as small as possible, reducing size, number of colors, shading, and so on, while retaining visual appeal.
- ✔ Work up simple, consistent navigation tools for your site, label them clearly, and use them throughout.

Avoid Unneeded Extensions

As you know, the *X* in XHTML means that your XMTHL markup is *extensible*. As a wise person once remarked to us, "Just because you *can* do something doesn't mean you *should!*" This is as true for XML-derived extensions to your Web documents as it is for anything else in life (or art).

By adding extensions to your Web pages, you automatically deprive whatever portion of your audience depends on backward compatibility with HTML of whatever benefits those extensions confer on XML-capable Web browsers. In the early 21st Century, we can't help but think that old-fashioned HTML compatibility is going to be important for years to come. That's why you must think long and hard before you abandon the confines of the markup in XHTML that works with older Web browsers to add the kinds of structure and functions that newer-fangled XML-based markup can deliver.

If several pages on your site use the same XML extensions, create a consistent wrapper around that markup and use it in your pages if you must. Be sure to offer alternate text to other readers who can't see the results of those extensions — even if that means creating text-only replacements that they must download to read (ouch!).

Think Evolution, Not Revolution

Over time, Web pages change and grow. Keep a fresh eye on your work and keep recruiting fresh eyes from the ranks of those who haven't seen your work before, to avoid what we call *organic acceptance.*

This concept is best explained by the analogy of your face and the mirror: You see it every day; you know it intimately, so you aren't as sensitive as someone else to the impact of changes over time. Then you see yourself on video, or in a photograph, or through the eyes of an old friend. At that point, changes obvious to the world are obvious to you as you exclaim, "I've gone completely gray!" or "My spare tire could mount on a semi!" or "Who the heck is *that?*"

As with the rest of life, changes to Web pages are usually evolutionary, not revolutionary. These changes should occur in small, daily steps; big radical leaps are rare. Nevertheless, you must stay sensitive to the supporting infrastructure and readability of your content as pages evolve. Maybe the lack of on-screen links to each section of your Product Catalog didn't matter when you had only three products, but now that you have 25, it's a different story. Maybe you've heard the phrase *form follows function;* in Web terms, the structure of your site needs to follow changes in its content. If you regularly reevaluate your site's effectiveness at communicating its contents, you'll know when you need to make changes, whether large or small.

Knowing when to make changes is where user feedback is crucial. If you don't get feedback through forms or other means of communication, go out and aggressively solicit info from your users. If you're not sure how you're doing, consider the following: If you don't ask, how can you tell?

Navigating Your Wild and Woolly Web

Users who view the splendor of your site don't want to be told "You can't get there from here." Navigational aids are vital amenities on a quality Web site. In Chapter 12, for example, we introduce the concept of a *navigation bar* (a consistent graphical place to put buttons that help users get from A to B). By judicious use of links and careful observation of what constitutes a *screenful* of text, you can help your users minimize (or even avoid) scrolling. Text anchors make it easy to move to *previous* or *next* screens, as well as to *top*, *index,* and *bottom* in any document. Just that easy, just that simple, or so it appears to the user.

We believe pretty strongly in the *low scroll* rule — that is, users should have to scroll *no more than one screenful* in either direction from a point of focus or entry without encountering a navigation aid to let them jump (not scroll) to the next point of interest.

Not having to scroll at all — ever — is even better!

We don't believe that navigation bars are required or that the names for controls should always be the same. We do believe, however, that the more control you give users over their reading, the better they like it. The longer a document gets, the more important such controls become.

Navigation bars work best if they occur about every thirty lines in longer documents (or in an always visible navigation widget, if you take the time to build one or find somebody else's that you can use).

Beat the Two-Dimensional Text Trap

Conditioned by centuries of printed material and the linear nature of books, our mind-sets can always use adjustment. The nonlinear potentials of hypermedia give the Web a new definition of what constitutes a document. Of course, the temptation is to pack your page full of these capabilities until it resembles a Pony Express dynamite shipment and gallops off in all directions at once. To avoid this, judge your hypermedia according to whether it does the following:

> ✔ Adds interest
>
> ✔ Expands on your content
>
> ✔ Makes a serious — and relevant — impact on the user

Within these constraints, hypermedia can vastly improve any user's experience on your site.

Stepping intelligently outside old-fashioned linear thinking can improve your users' experience on your site and make your information more accessible to your audience. That's why we encourage careful use of document indexes, cross-references, links to related documents, breadcrumbs, and other tools to help users navigate within your site. Keep thinking about the impact of links as you look at other people's Web materials; it's the quickest way to shake free of the linear text trap. (The printing press was high-tech for its day, but that *was* 500 years ago!) If you're looking for a model for your site's behavior, don't think about your new trifold, four-color brochure, however eye-popping; think about how your customer-service people interact with new customers on the telephone. (*What can I do to help you today?*)

Overcome Inertia through Constant Vigilance

When dealing with your Web site after you publish it, remember that goofing off after finishing any big job is only human. Maintenance is not nearly as heroic, inspiring, or remarkable as creation, but it represents most of the activity that's needed to keep a Web site alive and well. Sites that aren't maintained often become ghost sites; users stop visiting when developers stop working on them. Never fear — a little work and attention to detail can keep the mold from growing on your pages.

If you start with something valuable and keep adding value, a site appreciates over time. Start with something valuable and leave it alone, and it soon becomes stale and loses value. Consider your site from the viewpoint of a master aircraft mechanic: Correct maintenance is a real, vital, and ongoing accomplishment, without which you risk a crash. A Web site, as a vehicle for important information, deserves the same regular attention. The maintenance work requires discipline and respect.

Chapter 25

Top Ten Design Tips

*Y*ou've heard this familiar refrain from other chapters: Before you can design and build a Web site that works, you have to know exactly what (the content) and to whom (the audience) you want to communicate. Remember that content is your site's king, queen, and big kahuna. To help keep the crown steady, we suggest a bevy of design tips to consider as you lay out your Web pages.

Consider the principles in this chapter to be the Big Kahuna Content's court and cabinet: As long as these principles play a supporting, not a starring, role, they add value and appeal without getting you into too much trouble. Let one of these hams take over the stage, and you may be in for some trouble!

Create Standard Layout Elements

As you build or renovate a site, focus your design efforts on a common layout for your pages. The elements of a common layout may include text links, graphical controls, or a combination of both, as well as frequently used icons (or other graphical conventions, such as logos) and styles for page headings and footers.

- ✔ Savvy designers should build style sheets to keep everything straight; regardless of complexity; you have to govern layout and typography for your site's pages. If you choose to use frames, establish a set of framing rules to lay out common page areas and elements.

- ✔ Headings can incorporate text, navigation, graphics, and other information that works best if it's consistent on all pages.

- ✔ Footers should include contact information and a unique URL for reference, preceded by a horizontal rule or graphical line (or packaged in their own compact frames).

✔ Use a consistent navigation mechanism throughout — be it an interactive tool or just breadcrumbs — to show users where they are in your site's hierarchy, and make jumping around in your Web site easy. (See Chapter 12 for more navigational details.)

Whatever your final layout looks like, make it as attractive as you can (without making it distracting) and apply it consistently. Such reassuring touches help create a welcome feeling of familiarity across your pages and make it easier for users to find their way around your site.

For some solid examples of good-looking, consistent site layouts, look at the family of CNET sites, including `www.cnet.com`, `http://home.cnet.com/webbuilding/0-3880.html`, and `www.news.com`.

Build a Graphical Vocabulary

Web sites speak in pictures partly because they save a lot of words. If you use graphics for navigation, keep icons or buttons small and simple. The smaller a graphic (in file size and number of colors), the faster it downloads. Speed your users to your content!

A small, consistent set of graphical symbols (also called a *vocabulary*) also improves browser efficiency: Most browsers cache graphics so they don't have to download them after they first appear in a particular session.

✔ Reusing an existing graphic is much faster than downloading a new one.

✔ Users don't have to make sense of a new set of graphics for each page.

Supply `alt` text definitions for graphical elements for users with character-mode browsers (or users who surf with graphics turned off). With simple graphical elements, a word or short phrase can substitute for — and deliver — the same meaning and impact as the graphic itself. Supplying the `alt` text definitions is very important because of the accessibility guidelines for visually impaired users. See `www.w3.org/WAI/` for more details on the W3C's accessibility guidelines.

Use White Space!

Although content may be the true big kahuna of Web pages, you can have too much of a good thing. Nothing obscures text more than too much other text. Even though you should limit scrolling on your pages, don't muddle the text by eliminating headings and paragraph breaks; try dropping in a little white space.

White space is the term that page designers use to describe the real estate on a page that's unoccupied by graphics or text. Even if your background is navy blue, you still have "white" space (well, okay, blue space in this case). The human eye needs to rest now and then; a certain amount of white space is needed for it to function well. In general, the more complex your images or content, the more positive the effect of white space on a page.

Be sure to give your content and images room to breathe by leaving at least 20 percent of any screen unoccupied. You can build white space into your documents by doing the following:

- ✔ Use alignment attributes to place your graphics. (See Chapter 7 for details on the `align=` attribute.)
- ✔ Divide regions of text and graphics with headings.
- ✔ Build a style sheet to control line spacing and white space for all kinds of tags (strongly recommended).

Whichever method you use, give readers plenty of room to follow your lead through your pages!

Format for Impact

XHTML includes a variety of descriptive character tags, such as `<em>`, `<strong>`, and `<cite>`. These tools give you ways to set particular words apart from other words in a sentence or a paragraph. You can also use styles to invoke larger fonts and alternate type treatments (such as bold and italic) to make such text dramatically different from ordinary text.

In the wake of Cascading Style Sheets (CSS), we think working with style attributes makes great sense to achieve a consistent look throughout your site. The tags work best if you have a unique-but-relevant item to include — for example, a snippet of text that mimics a newspaper:

```
900 Bags of T-Rex Chow Missing from Local Warehouse
City officials were stunned Tuesday to find the Hungry
    Dino Pet Food Store's main distribution center
        opened like a sardine can. . . .
```

Character-handling can create nice effects, whether descriptive or stylistic — but overusing it can blunt any document's overall impact. Be sure to use such controls only where impact is critical. Remember that too much **boldfaced,** *italicized,* or underlined text is hard to read on a computer screen. Be kind to your users (and their eyes) by limiting your use of character formatting. Keep It Simple, Sillyhead.

While you're deciding how to emphasize your chosen text elements, be aware that some browsers provide wider options for descriptive tags than others, and that style definitions have the widest latitude of all. Browsers often display descriptive tags (such as <b>) the same way they display other tags (such as <strong>) — in fact, those two particular tags produce the same effect in most browsers: boldfaced text. Some browsers (especially the graphical ones) provide other options for representing descriptive tags, such as different fonts or text colors. Style tags give designers complete control over text appearance and layout, but these tags can be overridden by savvy users or may not be supported by older browsers.

Bottom line: Consider which aspect of your text — appearance or emphasis — is more important to your message.

- ✔ For *appearance,* use a physical style.
- ✔ For *emphasis,* use a logical style or a style sheet.

Enhance (Don't Curb) Content with Graphics

If a picture is worth a thousand words, are a thousand words worth a picture? (All together, now: "Which thousand words? What picture?") When you combine text and graphics in your Web pages, emphasize the relationship between them. Graphics are useful for diagramming complex ideas, representing physical objects or other tangible phenomena, and compressing large amounts of content into a small space. However, text that surrounds a graphic needs to play off the image, to use it as a point of reference, and to refer back to key elements or components as they're discussed.

The methods you use to identify graphical elements — such as labels and captions — are almost as important as the graphic itself. Careful integration of text and graphics enhances content. (Take another look at that "newspaper" snippet in the "Format for Impact" section earlier in this chapter. Imagine it illustrated with a simple graphic — say, a Volkswagen half squashed by a reptilian footprint. . . .)

Graphics can pull double duty, both enhancing the look and feel of your page and adding significant content. Some graphics that work overtime to play both roles include navigational aids (such as buttons and arrows) as well as diagrams and charts. If you use a graphic to provide content as well as splash of color, include the appropriate alternative text as well.

Rules for using graphics also apply to any other hypermedia on your Web pages. Beyond their novelty, effects such as sound (including music), animation, or video can deliver striking content. To create great impact without distraction, integrate them carefully — and sparingly — with your text.

If you plan to quote the creative work of others in your Web site, make sure you know — and heed — any applicable copyright restrictions. Getting written permission is often a good idea. Assuming you can use a creative work without asking is a bad idea.

Make Effective Use of Hypermedia

The key ingredients in effective use of hypermedia (linked pages, graphics, and other Web elements) are *relevance* and *bottlenecks.*

✔ How well does the linked document relate to the content on the page that links to it?

If you make a link to the Dallas Cowboys Web page from a page about the Wild West because both mention cowboys, you lose your readers in a heartbeat. A link to a site about Buffalo Bill or Jesse James, on the other hand, is right on target. (Moral: Rein in those free associations, pardner.)

✔ How is every potential user equipped to view your page?

The more computer performance users need to appreciate a page, the fewer users are equipped to get the whole point. Effective use of hypermedia, therefore, implies asking your users for informed consent before inflicting the whole cornucopia of effects on them.

For graphics, this means preparing thumbnails of large images, labeling them with file sizes, and using the miniature on-screen versions as hyperlinks so users can request to download a full-sized image. Users who decide to pull down a full-color image of The Last Supper cannot complain when they already know it's a 1.2MB file that may take several minutes to download. By the same token, "decorating" your Web page by putting 2 megabytes worth of photorealistic T-Rex smack in the middle of every visitor's screen — without asking permission — means committing every visitor to a long wait, even those who merely wanted information. (Irritating? You ain't seen ferocious yet.) This applies equally to sounds, video, and other kinds of hypermedia that travel in very large files and very slowly over phone lines.

The Web offers unprecedented expressive options — for example, educators have new ways to engage students' interest. Instead of using pure text to explain, say, a leitmotif (a musical phrase with a specific referent), a teacher could define, and then discuss, a musical phrase from a symphony or string quartet as a leitmotif, setting up a hyperlink that plays the phrase on command. (A beginner's version could highlight the sequence of notes on a musical staff as the file plays.) Likewise, a discussion of film-editing techniques (such as dissolves) could include examples taken from the work of classic directors.

Aid Navigation Wherever Possible

The Web can be a confusing place for new or infrequent visitors. The more you can do to help out your users, the more likely they are to return to your pages time and time again. Put some steering gear on that Web page so your users can not only find their way around your stuff, but also recognize your site as friendly territory:

- Outlines
- Tables of contents
- Indexes
- Site maps
- Search engines

Form Good Opinions

No Web site is complete without an interactive form to ask users for feedback. This is akin to asking for directions when you're lost.

Feedback not only gives you a chance to see your work from somebody else's perspective, it also serves as a valuable source of input and ideas to enhance and improve your content.

Remember:

- Assuming isn't knowing.
- Nothing beats knowing.
- You won't know if you don't ask.

Know When to Split

As pages get larger, or as your content grows, you may come to a point where a single, long document functions better as a collection of smaller documents.

How do you decide when to split things up? Weigh the convenience of a single page against the lengthy download that may tag along with it. A single, long document takes longer to download and read than any individual smaller one, but each time a user requests an individual document, it may have to be downloaded on the spot. The question then becomes "One long wait or several short ones?"

✔ If your document is something that's touched quickly and then exited immediately, delivering information in small chunks makes sense. The only people who experience delays are those who choose to read many pages; in-and-outers don't have to wait long.

✔ If your document is something designed to be downloaded and perused in detail, you may want to keep large amounts of information within a single document — and to let your readers know you set it up that way.

Test your site over a slow link as well as a fast one, and ask users for feedback, to strike a happy medium between long and short pages. The happier the medium, the happier the users — and the more receptive they may be to your content.

Add Value for Value

Obtaining feedback from users is incredibly valuable and makes Web-based forms all the more worthwhile. But you're missing half the benefit if it's good only for you; responding to feedback in a visible, obvious way makes the experience as good for respondents as it should be for you.

Publicly acknowledge any feedback that causes change, whether for reasons good or ill. On many sites (and maybe on yours, too), a *What's New* page that links to the home page is a good place to make such acknowledgments public. We also believe in acknowledging strong opinions by e-mail or letter — it's often a relatively flame-retardant way to let respondents know that you heard what they said and to thank them for their input.

If you cultivate your users as allies and confederates, they can help improve and enhance your content. Such improvements, in turn, can lead to improved business relationships, or maybe just to improved communications. Either way, by delivering valuable information and acknowledging the value of other people's contributions, you create a superior site.

Chapter 26

Cool XHTML Tools

In This Chapter

▶ Tidying up your HTML

▶ Creating XHTML documents using XML tools

▶ Validating with an XML parser

▶ Viewing XML documents

*G*iven XHTML's somewhat schizophrenic nature, you can tackle the topic of tools to help you create XHTML documents in one of two ways:

✔ You can use regular Hypertext Markup Language (HTML) tools to create HTML documents — many such tools can't "do" XHTML as we write this book — and then apply post-processing to turn them into perfect XHTML documents.

✔ You can take advantage of the many Extensible Markup Language (XML) tools already available. Then, simply feed them one of the formal Document Type Definitions (DTDs) for XHTML to turn general-purpose XML tools into more special-purpose XHTML tools.

The approach you use depends on what you're most comfortable with. For those already familiar with HTML and don't have a compelling reason to learn XML, the first approach probably makes the most sense. For those who already know XML or who are motivated enough to climb its sometimes steep learning curve, the second approach is probably best.

In this chapter, so you can take either approach, we collect a list of some of our favorite tools for authoring, checking, and viewing both HTML and XML (and therefore XHTML) documents. If your resources or your time are limited, these are the tools you absolutely must check out!

Unfortunately, we can't cover all the wonderful XML tools available. To find a complete guide on XML software, check out www.xmlsoftware.com.

Start with HTML, Convert to XHTML

Dave Raggett, of W3C fame (he's one of the geniuses behind many flavors of HTML, XHTML, and XML), has created a snazzy software tool called HTML Tidy. As its name suggests, it cleans up HTML source code to produce something even a validator can love (or approve of, anyway). One of its bewildering arrays of options is turning HTML into XHTML, which is, of course, the one we like best for the purposes of this book!

To learn more about this tool, visit the HTML Tidy page at the W3C's Web site:

```
www.w3.org/People/Raggett/tidy/
```

Unfortunately, Raggett built HTML Tidy in the mold of those powerful, but arcane, command-line tools so beloved by Internet veterans and UNIX-heads everywhere. In plain English, this means HTML Tidy takes some serious study and thought to learn.

Fortunately, for Web-heads everywhere, others were not content to work with HTML Tidy as is. In fact, the folks at WebReview have reduced the requirements to use HTML Tidy to create XHTML to its most basic essence. Just visit this Web page

```
www.webreview.com/1999/07/16/feature/xhtml.cgi
```

and you can convert your HTML documents to XHTML one at a time by entering the URL for each page in the text box. What could be easier than that? (See Chapter 3 for more details on using HTML Tidy.)

Stay Tuned for Late-Breaking News

Today, you can find lots of great tools for creating HTML documents, some of which can even help you manage your Web sites. These include well-known tools such as Dreamweaver, FrontPage 2000, HoTMetaL, HotDog Professional, and many, many more. As we write this book, most of these vendors are starting to talk about XHTML. We think it's only a matter of time before these tools support XHTML and continue the grand tradition of HTML. That's why you should check in at the vendors' Web sites regularly to find out when they're going to be ready to handle XHTML as part of their toolsets.

For the vendors mentioned in the preceding paragraph, visit the following URLs to keep in touch with late-breaking news on the XHTML front:

- Macromedia Dreamweaver at
  www.macromedia.com/software/dreamweaver/
- Microsoft FrontPage at www.microsoft.com/frontpage/

  ✔ SoftQuad HoTMetaL at `www.hotmetalpro.com/products/index.htm`

  ✔ Sausage Software's HotDog Professional at
    `www.sausage.com/hotdog5/overview_hdpro5.html`

Take the XML Tool Route

Throughout the rest of this chapter, we tell you a bit about each tool. Table 26-1 provides you with a quick reference that outlines each product.

Table 26-1		Summary of Cool XML Tools		
Product Name	**Tool Type**	**URL**	**Price**	**Free Demonstration Copy**
Clip! XML Editor v1.5	Authoring	`www.t2000-usa.com`	$99	Yes
XMetaL	Authoring	`www.xmetal.com`	Less than $199	Yes
XML Pro v2.0	Authoring	`www.vervet.com`	Less than $199	Yes
SP v1.3	Validating parser	`www.jclark.com`	Free	N/A
LARK	Nonvalidating parser	`www.texuality.com`	Free	N/A
XML4J Parser	Validating parser	`www.alphaworks.ibm.com`	Free	N/A
Amaya	Browser	`www.w3.org/Amaya/`	Free	N/A

If You Build It, They Will Come

Well, we don't know exactly who *they* are, but we do know you must build your XHTML documents whether anyone visits them or not. To help you get them under construction, here's a list of some of the best XML authoring tools available that you can use for XHTML documents, too.

If you're familiar with HTML and you're anything like us, you probably used your trusty old text editor to create your first XML documents. XML supports some full-featured editors that may convince you to change your habits.

Clip! XML Editor v1.5

Techno2000's new editor, Clip!, supports many easy-to-use features, such as multiple authoring environment support, subdocument editing, DTD structure view, guided editing, real-time validation, and DTD creation. Clip!'s ability to generate DTDs from the XML documents you create makes this editor one of the most helpful tools available today.

At a pocketbook-friendly price of $99 (in the United States), Techno2000's editor is definitely worth trying out. You may also download an evaluation copy. Check out Clip! at www.t2000-usa.com. Figure 26-1 shows an XML document and a DTD generated using Clip!

XMetaL

SoftQuad Software, Inc. — best known for its popular HTML editor, HoTMetaL PRO — also built XMetaL. Its low price ($199 in the United States) is one of the reasons it's attractive for creating XHTML documents the XML way.

Like many XML editors, XMetaL offers a familiar, easy-to-use word processing environment. XMetaL also anticipates the next generation of browsers by offering the ability to edit Cascading Style Sheets (CSS). XMetaL conforms to numerous standards, including Standard Generalized Markup Language (SGML), XML, CALS tables, Document Object Model (DOM), CSS, and HTML. For more information, check out www.xmetal.com.

XML Pro v2.0

A more basic product — and a less expensive alternative to XMetaL — XML Pro comes from Vervet Logic. XML Pro sure can edit, but doesn't claim to do much more.

You can create and edit XML documents while using a clean and easy interface (see Figure 26-2). The newest release claims to be fully W3C XML 1.0 compliant and features IBM's XML4J parser. Currently, XML Pro does not support document conversion, DTD creation, or style sheet design. You can read more at www.vervet.com.

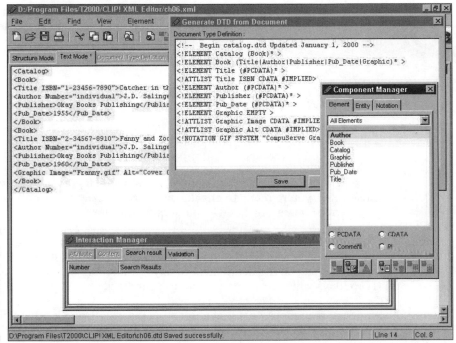

Figure 26-1:
An XML document and a DTD generated using Clip!

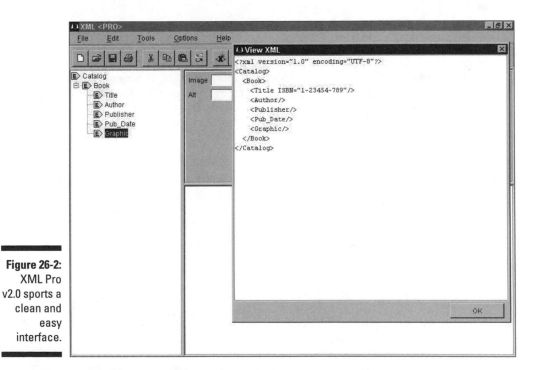

Figure 26-2:
XML Pro v2.0 sports a clean and easy interface.

Because many of the editors listed come at a hefty price, we recommend that you test drive demo versions when available. You can download demos from most vendors' product pages.

Valid and Well-Formed Documents Always Get Along

An XHTML document must be carefully crafted and adhere to one of the three XHTML DTDs available at the W3C Web site. If you believe you followed those rules, you're ready to check your work. Luckily, you don't have to check each element by hand — parsers do that for you!

A parser ensures that XML (and XHTML) documents are well formed and, if linked to a DTD, valid. Parsing is a basic, but important, step in XML publishing. Errors can be the death knell to any XML document. Forget those old HTML days when browsers picked up your slack.

Some parsers check only that a document is well formed; others check for validity as well. Make sure you examine the parser's capabilities when you select one.

SP v1.3

James Clark is a legend in the SGML community because of his amazing collection of tools that support all kinds of cool functionality. Most of his software is in the form of freeware that works like the dickens. His state-of-the-art SP parser, SP v1.3, can be configured to parse and validate XML (and XHTML) as well as SGML, and it makes a dandy tool for that very reason. Download this free parser at www.jclark.com.

Clark's Jade tool adds support for an SGML view of document style as defined in the Document Style Semantics and Specification Language (DSSSL, pronounced *distle,* to rhyme with *whistle*).

XML4J

IBM created an XML parser written in Java that's available to users for free. This parser is the subject of a lot of buzz and seems to lead the pack in online reviews. Tools like this help to explain IBM's stellar reputation in the tool development department. "Big Blue" seems to be creating many XML tools, technologies, and resources as it expands its technology arsenal. Find more information about XML4J and other tools at www.alphaworks.ibm.com.

Lark

Tim Bray has been a member of the W3C's XML Working Group since long before it operated under that name. (It all started as a special interest group within the SGML cadre at the W3C.) His work on XML is widely recognized and deservedly renowned. Among other things, Bray was the co-editor of the XML specification.

Bray also created a Java-based XML processor called Lark, which he built as a way to sanity-check (in other words, to make sure the XML specification does what it's supposed to) the XML design requirement that "it shall be easy to write programs that process XML documents." The fruits of Bray's labor are available for download at `www.textuality.com/Lark/`. Lark does the job for XHTML, too!

Much of the software listed in this chapter is free to download. The only payment you're asked to give is feedback. XML tools are still pretty green, which means you must watch out for bugs. Make sure that you report any bugs you find to the responsible parties. They'll thank you for it!

View It with Amaya

According to most Web designers, XML can revolutionize the way people look at — and transfer — information across the Web. However, before XML can start that revolution, browsers must provide support. Microsoft Internet Explorer and Netscape Navigator do not currently support XML fully. A few other browsers, however, do provide such support. We found the browser covered in this section to be noteworthy.

Amaya is the W3C's browser and authoring tool and may be used to demonstrate and test many new developments in Web protocols and data formats. See Figure 26-3 for an example of Amaya in action.

Amaya is versatile and extensible, which makes adding new features easy. Along with support for XML, Amaya supports HTML and XHTML. If it's good enough for the W3C, it may be good enough for you! Read more at `www.w3.org/Amaya/` and then download the software.

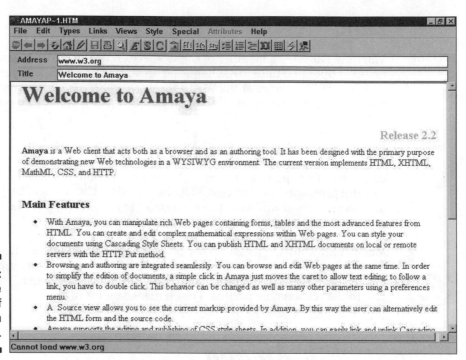

Figure 26-3:
A sample
view of
Amaya in
action.

Chapter 27

Ten Opulent Online XHTML Resources

*B*ecause of the ever-changing nature of cutting-edge technologies such as XHTML, it's probably not surprising that the best resources for up-to-the-minute information reside online. In this chapter of the Parts of Tens, we take you on a quick tour of the electronic landscape for XHTML — stopping only at sites of sufficient depth or breadth to tempt even hardened information miners to dig for a nugget or two while passing through.

It All Starts at the W3C

By now, you've probably figured out that the ultimate source of markup language information, if not wisdom, resides at the World Wide Web Consortium's (W3C's) Web site. Where XHTML is concerned, this site is no exception to the rule. For one of the best sets of pointers to XHTML stuff (including the XHTML specification itself), visit the W3C's markup home page.

You'll find this nonpareil of XML resources at:

```
www.w3.org/MarkUp/Overview.html
```

Be sure to check out the section entitled "Useful Information for HTML Authors" on that same Web page.

Also be sure to visit the XHTML 1.0 specification at:

```
www.w3.org/TR/xhtml1/
```

Nuthin' but the FAQs

On the Internet, creating and maintaining a list of frequently-asked questions — and more importantly, the answers that go with them — is part of the "standard method" for helping newcomers find their way into any subject area. Here again, XHTML is no exception. The nice folks at Internet Related Technologies (IRT) have lovingly compiled and maintained a series of HTML-related FAQs, which include coverage of XHTML and related topics. You can find this information at:

```
http://developer.irt.org/script/html.htm
```

Remember that the ultimate adage when considering asking for help on any topic in the Internet world is to "read the FAQ" before asking. Follow this advice and you'll never get embarrassed by rehashing old, timeworn topics.

Robin's Got It Covered

Robin Cover is a well-known expert on matters related to SGML and XML, including copious coverage of XHTML. His Web sites are widely renowned and heavily used. Visit his SGML/XML Web page at:

```
www.oasis-open.org/cover/
```

to find pointers to all kinds of interesting — and sometimes, highly relevant — information about XML, including coverage of and pointers to XHTML resources.

What's Up at the Web Developer's Library?

When it comes to things related to Web development, one of the best online resources of all time is the Web Developer's Library. If you can name a current topic of interest to Web developers, chance are good you'll find outstanding coverage of that topic somewhere on the `www.wdvl.com` site. XHTML is no exception; check out their coverage called "Introduction to XHTML, with eXamples" at:

```
www.wdvl.com/Authoring/Languages/XML/XHTML/
```

Their front-page list "XHTML in a nutshell" covers all the XHTML basics in one short paragraph!

Microsoft Makes XML Part of Its Game

Despite its reputation as a "dog in the manger" when it comes to standards versus proprietary technologies, Microsoft offers plenty of information about XML and XHTML to go along with its software offerings that support these technologies. For more information about Microsoft's XHTML information and offerings, use "XHTML" as a search term from the company's home page at:

```
www.microsoft.com
```

We think you'll be surprised by how much coverage XHTML gets from the boys and girls in Redmond!

Look It Up in EncycloZine

EncycloZine is a short, sharp source for descriptive and explanatory information online. Its coverage of XHTML is worth perusing for all of those reasons. You'll find a sequence of articles related to XHTML on its Web site, starting with a document that talks about DTDs and XHTML, at:

```
http://encyclozine.com/WD/XHTML/dtd.html
```

Be sure to follow the "Next" link from this page (and thereafter) for still more useful stuff about XHTML.

DevX Marks the (XHTML) Spot!

DevX is an abbreviation for the Developer's Exchange, a collection of online magazines that cover Web development topics from A to Z. More importantly, they cover HTML- and XML-related issues, which means they do a nice job with XHTML, among a bunch of other useful topics.

For a terrific introduction on XHTML that includes lots of useful information and many more useful pointers to online stuff, visit their e-magazine at:

```
www.devx.com/upload/free/features/webbuilder/2000/wb0300/
                    kc0300/kc0300-1.asp
```

More News from the Standards Gang

The folks on the W3C's XHTML Working Group — you know, the people who wrote the XHTML specification, and who continue to work on related extensions, improvements, and enhancements — have put together a separate Web site devoted exclusively to XHTML topics. Because it's easy to get lost at the W3C's main site, this site provides a useful alternative to help you zoom straight into the latest skinny on XHTML. Check it out at:

```
www.xhtml.org/
```

You'll find pointers galore to all kinds of useful stuff, both on and off the W3C site (including lots of e-zine articles, papers, proceedings, and presentations from professional events that cover XML and XHTML).

XML.com Does XHTML, Too

XML.com offers a cornucopia of XML-related articles and information, including good coverage of XHTML-related standards and discussions at the W3C. You can visit this site's XHTML page at:

```
www.xml.com/pub/Guide/XHTML
```

Searching for XHTML Satisfaction

In an area as new and active as XHTML, there's no way we can catch all the good resources on the subject. Some are likely to pop up at a moment's notice; alas, many are likely to emerge after this book goes to print. When in doubt (or to double-check what you find in print here), visit your favorite search engine to get the latest scoop on XHTML. We found Yahoo! (www.yahoo.com), Excite (www.excite.com), AltaVista (www.altavista.com), and AskJeeves (www.askjeeves.com) all quite helpful in locating XHTML resources of many kinds. Although the details will change by the time you try this technique for yourself, the results should be no less rewarding for you. As the old ad ran: "Try it — you'll like it!" Search on XHTML at your favorite search engine (or refine your search in whatever way makes sense for your precise information needs), and you'll find plenty of good information online to peruse.

Part VII

Appendixes

The 5th Wave   By Rich Tennant

"OK, I think I forgot to mention this, but we now have a Web management function that automatically alerts us when there's a broken link on The Aquarium's Web site."

In this part . . .

The appendixes in this part are multifarious and magnificent. In Appendix A, you find a concise overview of XHTML terminology accessible in alphabetical order. Its worthy successor, Appendix B, details all the keen programs and examples that appear on the CD-ROM that accompanies this book. These appendixes are like the instructions that come with a Christmas present for your kids (or yourself, who knows . . .): you don't always have to read them, but they're handy to keep around if you should ever need them! Just remember, when it comes to building your own Web pages, "some assembly is required!" Have fun!

Appendix A

Glossary

• •

absolute: When used to modify pathnames or URLs, a full and complete file specification (as opposed to a relative one). An absolute specification includes a host identifier, a complete volume, and path specification.

anchor: In XHTML, an anchor is tagged text or a graphic element that acts as a link to another location inside or outside a given document, or an anchor may be a location in a document that acts as the destination for an incoming link. The latter definition is how we commonly use it in this book.

ASCII (American Standard Code for Information Interchange): A coding method to translate characters, such as numbers, text, and symbols, into digital form. ASCII includes only 127 characters, and is only really useful for English (okay, and Latin, but nothing else really).

attribute: In XHTML elements, an attribute is a named characteristic associated with a specific element. Some attributes are required, whereas others are optional. In XHTML, all attributes must have a value, which takes the form `attribute="value"`.

browser: A Web access program that can request documents from Web servers and render such documents on a user's display device.

cache: When used in reference to Web pages, cache is a process performed by a computer system that stores frequently accessed Web pages in memory so the computer doesn't have to reload the page every time you visit it.

case sensitive: Means that the way you type computer input is significant; for instance, XHTML elements must be written in lowercase.

CERN (Conseil Européen pour la Recherche Nucléaire): Agency that established the High-Energy Physics Laboratory in Geneva, Switzerland, now known as the birthplace of the World Wide Web. CERN is commonly used as a name for the laboratory itself.

CGI (Common Gateway Interface): A standard that allows CGI programs of various types to interact with Web servers, usually to provide interactive response to user input from a browser.

character entity: A string of characters that represents other characters; for example, `&lt;` and `&quot;` shows a string of characters (`lt` and `Egrave`) that stand for other characters (< and È).

character entity: A way of reproducing strange and wonderful characters within XHTML, character entities take the form &`string`; where the ampersand (&) and semicolon are mandatory metacharacters, and `string` names the character to be reproduced in the browser. Because character entities are case sensitive, the string between the ampersand and the semicolon must be reproduced exactly as written in Chapter 14 of this book.

character set: When referring to script, a character set represents a collection of values that maps to some specific symbol set or alphabet.

clickable map: An image in an XHTML file that offers graphical Web navigation. The file contains linked regions that point to specific URLs after a user clicks them.

client/server: A model for computing that divides computing into two separate roles, usually connected by a network. The client works on the end-user's side of the connection and manages user interaction and display (input, output, and related processing); the server works elsewhere on the network and manages data-intensive or shared-processing activities, such as serving up the collections of documents and programs that a Web server typically manages.

client: The end-user side of the client/server arrangement; typically, "client" refers to a consumer (rather than a provider) of network services; a Web browser is therefore a client program that talks to Web servers.

client-side image map: The same as a server-side image map, except that the hot-spot definitions are stored within the XHTML document on the client side, rather than in a map file stored on the server.

content model: Defines what components may make up a certain part of a document.

content: For XHTML, content is its raison d'être; although form is important. Content is why users access Web documents and why they come back for more.

convention: An agreed-upon set of rules and approaches that allows systems to communicate with each other and work together.

CSS (Cascading Style Sheets): A method of coding that allows users to define how certain HTML, XHTML, or XML structural elements, such as paragraphs and headings, should be displayed using style rules instead of additional markup. The versions of CSS are *CSS1* and CSS2, with *CSS2* being the most recent version.

CSS1 (Cascading Style Sheets Level 1): A style sheet standard that lets authors attach preferred style sheets to Web documents, while allowing readers to associate their own personal styles to those same documents.

CSS2 (Cascading Style Sheets Level 2): The second version of CSS. See also *CSS1 (Cascading Style Sheets Level 1)*.

default: In general computer-speak, a selection made automatically in a program if the user specifies no explicit selection. For XHTML, the default is the value assigned to an attribute if none is supplied.

deprecated: The term used to earmark an XHTML element or attribute that is to be left for dead by future versions of XHTML.

directory path: Device and directory names needed to locate a particular file in a given file system.

DocBook: A heavy-duty XML DTD designed and implemented by HaL Computer Systems and O'Reilly & Associates in approximately 1991. It's used for authoring books, articles, and manuals, particularly those of a technical nature.

document headings: The class of XHTML elements that we refer to as <h*>. Document headings allow authors to insert headings of various sizes and weights (from one to six) to add structure to a document's content. As structural elements, headings identify the beginning of a new concept or idea.

document reference: In XHTML, the document reference is used to indicate that the destination of a link is in another document.

document type declaration: Tells the processor where the DTD is located and contains declarations for the particular document.

document: The basic unit of XHTML information, a document refers to the entire contents of any single XHTML file. Because this definition doesn't always correspond to normal notions of a document, we refer to what can formally be called XHTML documents more or less interchangeably with Web pages, which is how browsers render such documents for display.

DOCTYPE declaration (document type declaration): In XML documents, it's the code used to reference the document's DTD.

DOM (Document Object Model): A platform- and language-neutral programming interface that allows programs and scripts to access and update the content, structure, and style of documents in a standard way.

DOS (Disk Operating System): The underlying control program used to make some Intel-based PCs run. MS-DOS by Microsoft is the most widely used implementation of DOS and provides the scaffolding atop which its 3.x versions of Windows run. See also *operating system.*

DSSSL (Document Style Semantics and Specification Language): A superset of XSL. DSSSL is a document style language used primarily with SGML (Standard Generalized Markup Language) files.

DTD (Document Type Definition): A formal SGML specification for a document, a DTD lays out the structural elements and markup definitions to be used to create instances of documents.

element declaration: Provides a description of an element type and its content within the DTD.

element type: A specific — or named — element, such as `<Book>` or `<Title>`.

element: A section of a document defined by an opening- and closing-tag or an empty tag and its content. In this book, we use the term element, when referring to the opening tag, the content of the tag, and the closing tag (or in the case of empty elements, just the empty tag and its content).

e-mail: An abbreviation for electronic mail, e-mail is the preferred method for exchanging information between users on the Internet (and other networked systems).

empty element: An element used in markup languages that does not require a closing tag. In XML, an empty element must be identified with a slash (/) before the closing greater than sign (>). In XHTML, for backward compatibility, an empty element is identified with a space before the closing slash, for example `<img />`. Occasionally called singleton tags.

entity declaration: Defines a named set of information that can be referenced by a name as an entity within a document or DTD.

entity: A character string that represents another string of characters.

error message: Information delivered by a program to a user, usually to inform him or her that the process hasn't worked properly, if at all. Error messages are an ill-appreciated art form and contain some of the funniest and most opaque language we've ever seen (also, the most tragic for their unfortunate recipients).

event: In reference to scripting, represents a user's action or response.

external style sheet: A style sheet that resides outside of the Web document in a separate, external file.

external subset: The portion of a DTD that is stored in an external file. Also called an *external DTD* and an *external DTD subset*.

footer: The concluding part of an XHTML document, the footer should contain contact, version, date, and attribution information to help identify a document and its authors. Most people use the `<address>` . . . `</address>` element to identify this information.

forms: In XHTML, forms are built on special markup that lets browsers solicit data from users and then deliver that data to specially designated input-handling programs on a Web server. Briefly, forms provide a mechanism to let users interact with servers on the Web.

freeware: Software offered by companies at no charge.

FTP (File Transfer Protocol): An Internet file transfer service based on TCP/IP protocols. FTP provides a way to copy files to and from FTP servers elsewhere on a network.

GIF (Graphic Interchange Format): One of a set of commonly used graphics formats within Web documents, because of its compressed format and compact nature.

graphics: In XHTML documents, graphics are files that belong to one of a restricted family of types (usually .GIF or .JPG) that are referenced via URLs for inline display on Web pages.

GUI (Graphical User Interface): A computer interface in which windows, graphics, and a mouse (or trackball) are used to interact with information instead of plain text at a command line.

heading: For HTML, a heading is a markup element used to add document structure. Sometimes the term refers to the initial portion of an HTML document between the `<head>` . . . `</head>` tags, where titles and context definitions are commonly supplied.

hexadecimal: A numbering system composed of six letters and ten numbers that is used to condense binary numbers. In XHTML, hexadecimal numbering is used with elements and their attributes to denote what colors should comprise backgrounds and other items in a Web page.

HTML (Hypertext Markup Language): The SGML-derived markup language used to create Web pages.

HTTP (Hypertext Transfer Protocol): The Internet protocol used to manage communication between Web clients (browsers) and servers.

hyperlink: A shorthand term for hypertext link. (See also *hypertext link.*)

hypermedia: Any of a variety of computer media — including text, graphics, video, sound, and so on — available through hypertext links on the Web.

hypertext link: In XHTML, a hypertext link is defined by special markup that creates a user-selectable document element that can be selected to change the user's focus from one document (or part of a document) to another.

hypertext: A method of organizing text, graphics, and other kinds of data for computer use that lets individual data elements point to one another; a non-linear method of organizing information, especially text.

image map: A synonym for clickable image, which refers to an overlaid collection of pixel coordinates for a graphic that can be used to locate a user's selection of a region on a graphic, in turn used to select a related hypertext link for further Web navigation.

inheritance: When an element (the child or sibling) takes on, or inherits, the characteristics assigned to a higher-level element (the parent).

inline style: A style that applies to an element within the XML document itself.

input-handling program: For Web services, a program that runs on a Web server designated by the action attribute of an XHTML <form> tag; its job is to field, interpret, and respond to user input from a browser, typically by custom-building an HTML document in response to some user request.

internal anchor: A type of link that connects within the same document.

internal entity: An entity that contains the content directly within the declaration.

internal style sheet: A style sheet that resides inside of the Web document in which you're working.

Internet: A worldwide collection of networks that began with technology and equipment funded by the U.S. Department of Defense in the 1970s. Today, it links users in nearly every country, speaking nearly every known language.

IP (Internet Protocol): IP is the specific networking protocol of the same name used to tie computers together over the Internet; IP is also used as a synonym for the TCP/IP protocol suite.

ISO (International Organization of Standardization): The granddaddy of standards organizations worldwide, the ISO is made up of standards bodies from countries all over the world. Most important communications and computing standards — such as the telecommunications and character code standards mentioned in this book — are the subject of ISO standards.

ISO-Latin-1: Also known as ISO 8859-1 (the numeric equivalent), it's the default character set used by XML, XHTML, and HTML.

ISP (Internet Service Provider): An organization that provides individuals or other organizations with access to the Internet, usually for a fee. ISPs usually offer a variety of communications options for their customers, ranging from analog telephone lines, to a variety of higher-bandwidth leased lines, to ISDN and other digital communications services.

Java: An object-oriented, platform-independent, secure, and compact programming language designed for Web application deployment. Most system vendors support Java, which was created by Sun Microsystems.

Java applet: A miniature application that you can embed in a Web page and interact with on a Web page.

JPEG (or JPG): JPEG stands for Joint Photographic Experts' Group; an industry association that defined a highly compressible format for images designed for complex color still images (such as photographs). JPEG files take the extension .JPG. Today, JPEG is one of the graphics formats of choice for Web use, particularly for complex images.

layout: The overall arrangement of the elements in a document.

linear text: Shorthand for old-fashioned documents that work like this book: by placing one page after the other, ad infinitum, in a straight line. Even though such books have indexes, pointers, cross-references, and other attempts to add linkage, such devices can be employed only by manipulating the physical book (rather than by clicking your mouse).

link: For XHTML, a link is a pointer in one part of a document that can transport users to another part of the same document, or to another document entirely. This capability puts the "hyper" into hypertext. In other words, a link is a one-to-one relationship/association between two concepts or ideas.

list element: An item in an XHTML list structure tagged with `<li>` (list item) element.

list elements: XHTML elements for a variety of list styles, including ordered lists (`<ol>`), unordered lists (`<ul>`), menus (`<menu>`), definition lists (`<dl>`), or directory lists (`<dir>`).

Lynx: A widely used UNIX-based character-mode Web browser, useful for checking a Web page before "going live" with it.

Macintosh: A type of PC created by Apple Computer in 1984 that first commercially introduced the graphical user interface (GUI), complete with a mouse, icons, and windows. Microsoft Windows uses design elements similar to those of the Macintosh operating system. The Mac operating system is the most popular alternative to Windows.

maintenance: The process of regularly inspecting, testing, and updating the contents of Web pages; also, an attitude that such activities are both inevitable and advisable.

map file: Pixel coordinates that correspond to the boundaries of regions that users may select when using a graphic for Web navigation. This file must be created using a graphics program to determine regions and their boundaries and then stored on the Web server that provides the coordinate translation and URL selection services.

markup language: A formal set of special characters and related capabilities used to define a specific method for handling the display of files that include markup. XHTML, XML, HTML, and SGML are all markup languages.

markup: A sequence of special characters that identifies certain text as part of an XHTML document's description, structure, or behavior, rather than as part of that document's content.

metadata: Specially defined elements that describe a document's structure, content, or rendering, within the document itself or through external references. (Metadata literally means data about data.)

meta-language: A language designed for defining other markup languages. SGML and XML are meta-languages.

MIME (Multipurpose Internet Mail Extension): Extensions that allow e-mail messages to carry multiple types of data (such as binary, audio, video, and graphics) as attachments. MIME types are also used to identify document types during transfers over the Web.

mixed content: Allows your elements to contain character data or character data with child elements.

modular XHTML 1.1 document: The DTD code from XHTML version 1.0 broken into discrete modules.

module: When used in reference to XHTML, a small subset of XHTML elements fall in the same category. Currently, the W3C has proposed that XHTML elements be broken into 17 different modules: Structure, Basic Text, Hypertext, List, Applet, Presentation, Edit, BDO, Forms, Tables, Image, Image Map, Intrinsic Events, Metainformation, Scripting, Stylesheet, and Link.

Mosaic: A powerful, graphical Web browser originally developed at NCSA, now widely licensed and used in several browser implementations.

MPEG: An acronym for Motion Picture Experts' Group, MPEG is a highly compressed format designed for moving pictures or other multiframe-per-second media (such as video). MPEG not only provides high compression ratios (up to 200 to 1), but it also updates only elements that have changed on-screen from one frame to the next, making it extraordinarily efficient. .MPEG is the file extension that denotes files using this format, but .MPG is the three-letter equivalent used on DOS and Windows 3.x systems (which can't handle four-letter file extensions).

multimedia: A method of combining text, sound, graphics, and full-motion or animated video within a single compound computer document.

namespace: See *XML namespace.* Generally speaking, all namespaces used in XML documents are called "XML namespaces." An "XHTML namespace" is a specific XML namespace that uniquely identifies XHTML elements.

navigation bar: A way of arranging a series of hypertext links on a single line of a Web page to provide a set of navigation controls for an XHTML document or a set of XHTML documents.

navigation: In the context of the Web, navigation refers to the use of hyperlinks to move within or between XHTML documents and other Web-accessible resources.

nesting: In computer terms, one structure that occurs within another is said to be nested; in XHTML, nesting happens most commonly with list structures that may be freely nested within one another, regardless of type.

newsgroup: A group of users that discusses issues related to a specific topic. Newsgroups are typically found on Usenet or other news servers.

node: Used in XHTML to denote a piece of the tree structure.

numeric entity: A special markup element that reproduces a particular character from the ISO-Latin-1 character set. A numeric entity takes the form &#nnn; where nnn is the one-, two- or three-digit numeric code that corresponds to a particular character. (Chapter 14 contains a complete list of these codes.)

online: A term that indicates information, activity, or communications located on or taking place in an electronic, networked computing environment (such as the Internet). The opposite of online is offline, which is what your computer is as soon as you disconnect from the Internet.

operating system: The underlying control program on a computer that makes the hardware run and supports the execution of one or more applications. DOS, Windows, UNIX, and OS/2 are all examples of operating systems.

parameter entity: An entity created and used within a DTD.

PDF (Portable Document Format): A graphics file format created by Adobe Systems. To view a PDF file, you must download Adobe Acrobat Reader or have access to an Adobe application such as PageMaker or PhotoShop.

presentation control elements: XHTML markup elements that specifically control character styles — bold (<b>) and italic (<i>) — or typeface (<tt>) for typewriter font.

proxy server: An intermediary server that intercepts server requests from the Web browser. If the proxy server cannot handle request, the request is sent to a main server.

relative: When applied to URLs, a relative address provides an abbreviated document address that may be combined with the <base /> element to create a complete address or is the complete address for a local file found in the same directory

robot: A special Web-traveling program that wanders widely, following and recording URLs and related titles for future reference in search engines.

root element: In XHTML, the element you create that is the equivalent of the <html> element in HTML. It's a single top-level tag. Also called a document element.

schema: A pattern that represents the data's model and defines the elements (or objects), their attributes (or properties), and the relationships between the different elements.

scripting language: A specialized programming language used to create scripts that, when inserted into a Web page, control various elements of the page, such as the user interface, styles, and XHTML markup. JavaScript and VBScript are the primary scripting languages.

search engine: A special Web program that searches the contents of a database of available Web pages and other resources to provide information that relates to specific topics or keywords, which a user supplies.

selector: In CSS, identifies the element to which the style rule applies.

semantics: The science of describing what words mean; it's the opposite of syntax.

SGML (Standard Generalized Markup Language): A metalanguage used to construct markup languages, such as XHTML, HTML, and XML.

shareware: Software, available by various means, that users can run for free for a trial period. After that trial period expires, users must register and purchase the software, or they must discontinue its use.

specification: A formal document that describes the capabilities, functions, and interfaces for a specific piece of software, a markup language, or a communications protocol.

spider: A Web-traversing program that tirelessly investigates Web pages and their links, while storing information about its travels for inclusion in the databases typically used by search engines. Also called Web spider and Webcrawler.

SQL server: A database server that uses the Structured Query Language (SQL) to accept requests for data access. Also, the name of either of two database management products from Sybase and Microsoft.

style rule: A rule in an XHTML document that specifies a pattern and an action that the rule applies when the specified pattern is found.

style sheet: A file that holds the layout settings for a certain category of a document. Style sheets, like templates, contain settings for headers and footers, tabs, margins, fonts, columns, and more.

syntax: Literally, the formal rules for how to speak. But in this book, we use syntax to describe the rules that govern how XHTML markup looks and behaves within XHTML documents.

syntax checker: A program that checks a particular XHTML document's markup against the rules that govern its use; a recommended part of the testing regimen for all XHTML documents.

tag: The formal name for a piece of XHTML markup. In this book, we use the term tag to refer specifically to the opening or closing tag (or just the empty tag) of an element, for example, the `</html>` closing tag.

template: Literally, a model to imitate, we use the term template in this book to describe the skeleton of a Web page, including the XHTML for its heading and footer, and a consistent layout and set of navigation elements.

text controls: Any of a number of XHTML elements, including both physical and logical markup, text controls provide a method of managing the way that text appears within an XHTML document.

thumbnail: A miniature rendering of an image that is used as a link to the full-size version.

title: The text supplied to a Web page's title bar when displayed, used as data in many Web search engines.

UNIX: The operating system of choice for the Internet community at large and the Web community, too, UNIX offers the broadest range of tools, utilities, and programming libraries for Web server use.

URI (Uniform Resource Identifier): Any of a class of objects that identify resources available to the Web.

URL (Uniform Resource Locator): The primary naming scheme used to identify Web resources, URLs define the protocols to use, the domain name of the Web server where a resource resides, the port address to use for communication, and a directory path to access named Web files or resources.

valid: Code that follows all the syntax rules defined in a document type definition, allowing the document to pass through a validator program with no errors.

validating parser: A software utility that compares your XHTML or XML document to a declared DTD.

W3C (World Wide Web Consortium): The organization that develops standards for the Web.

Web pages: We use Web pages in this book to refer to sets of related, interlinked HTML or XHTML documents, usually produced by a single author or organization.

Web server: A computer, usually on the Internet, that plays host to httpd and related Web-service software.

Web site: An addressed location, usually on the Internet, that provides access to the set of Web pages that correspond to the URL for a given site; thus a Web site consists of a Web server and a named collection of Web documents, both accessible through a single URL.

Web: Also called the World Wide Web, WWW, or W3. The complete collection of all Web servers available on the Internet, which comes as close to containing the "sum of human knowledge" as anything we've ever seen.

well-formed document: An XHTML document that adheres to the rules that make it easy for a computer to interpret (see Chapters 2 and 10 for more information on well-formed documents).

white space: The "breathing room" on a page, white space refers to parts of a display or document unoccupied by text or other visual elements. A certain amount of white space is essential to make documents attractive and readable.

XForms: The next generation of Web forms. A new specification that is dedicated to Web form technology.

XHTML (Extensible Hypertext Markup Language): The reformulation of HTML 4 as an application of XML 1.0.

XHTML Basic: A subset of XHTML 1.1, used for Web pages to be displayed with hand held devices. The element subset includes text structure, images, basic forms, and basic tables.

XHTML namespace: A specific XML namespace that uniquely identifies XHTML elements.

XHTML syntax: The rules that govern the construction of intelligible HTML documents or markup fragments.

XML (Extensible Markup Language): A system for defining, validating, and sharing document formats.

XML declaration: The code at the very beginning of an XHTML document that specifies which version of XML the document is written in. (Currently, it must state XML 1.0 because that's the only version available.)

XML namespace: General name for a unique identifier (which is attached through a prefix) that links an XML markup element to a specific DTD. (An XHTML namespace is a specific XML namespace that uniquely identifies XHTML elements.)

XSL (Extensible Stylesheet Language): Defines the specification for an XML document's presentation and appearance. Both CSS and XSL provide a platform-independent method for specifying the document's presentation style.

XSLT (XSL Transformations): An XSL conversion tool that provides a set of rules to convert documents described by one set of elements to documents described by another set of elements.

Appendix B

About the CD-ROM

• •

*I*n this section of the book, we explain what you find on the XHTML For Dummies CD-ROM. We've put together a collection of Web documents built specifically to help you find your way around the book's materials. In a nutshell, it contains these goodies:

- ✔ Lists of all URLs mentioned in the book, organized by chapter, to make it easy for you to access any of the Web resources we mention.
- ✔ Copies of all the XHTML examples, easily accessible by chapter.
- ✔ A hyperlinked table of contents for the book to help you find your way around its many topics and treasures.
- ✔ An XHTML context applet to help you build valid XHTML documents.

In addition the CD contains a sampling of HTML, XHTML, and XML editors — both shareware and trial versions — that you can use to start building your own XHTML documents or convert your existing HTML documents to XHTML.

How to Use the Web Pages and Examples

Regardless of what platform and operating system you run, you can view all of the CD material straight from the CD-ROM. To do so, however, you must have a Web browser installed on your system. We included both Windows and Mac versions of the two mainstream browsers on the CD. Before you try to view the CD content, be sure you have one of these browsers installed if you don't already have a browser of some kind on your system. To browse the CD-ROM contents, just do the following:

1. **Launch your Web browser.**

2. **Using the Open File command in your browser's File menu; open the file** \xhtmlfd\xhtml4dum.htm\ **from the CD-ROM.**

This page serves as the home page for the CD-ROM; it connects you to all other files. Although you won't be able to edit any of the files on the CD itself, you can make changes to them and then save them elsewhere on your hard disk or a floppy disk. If you plan to modify any Web pages, examples, or templates, save them to your local drive before you do so. The simplest way to modify the contents is to copy the entire `xhtmlfd` folder to your hard drive, which transfers the all of the Web documents from the CD-ROM to your computer. (You'll need about 2MB of drive space to accommodate it, so we suggest you check your available disk space before you actually copy the files over to your hard disk.)

The XHTML For Dummies Files

The top level of the *XHTML For Dummies* CD-ROM directory includes these items:

- The `xhtmlfd` folder
- Folders containing installers for shareware, freeware, and trial programs
- A License Agreement text file
- A Read Me text file

The `xhtmlfd` folder contains the Web document collection; the software folders are chock-full of trial versions that introduce you to some of the best tools in the business . License.txt includes some important end-user information that you should read before you install any of the software, and Readme.txt is a text-only version of this appendix (just in case your book grows legs and happens to wander away somewhere).

To give you an idea of what's in each Web documents folder, we cover the files within them according to their home directory — and subdirectory when necessary. The `xhtmlfd` directory contains the majority of *XHTML For Dummies* files. Nearly every file in this directory ends with the extension `.htm`, indicating that it is an XHTML document.

All in all, the best way to explore the *XHTML For Dummies* Web pages is to fire up your browser and point it at the file named `xhtml4dum.htm` (the home page for the whole collection). For a complete, linked, graphical overview of all the files on the CD-ROM, open `menu.htm` and behold! Table B-1 lists and describes the remaining top-level HTML.

Table B-1	The xhtmlfd Directory File Listing
File	**Description**
applet.htm	The XHTML context applet page
contact.htm	List of e-mail and home-page links for the authors
copy.htm	Important copyright information
menu.htm	A bird's-eye view of the entire page collection
wayfind.htm	HTML navigation information
xhtml4dum.htm	The *XHTML For Dummies* home page
xhtml4dum_style.css	The cascading style sheet that controls the presentation of all of the pages in the Web documents collection

The xhtmlfd directory has seven subdirectories whose names indicate what you find within them.

- applet: Contains the class files that make the XHTML context applet tick
- contents: Contains files listing the book contents by chapter
- dtds: Contains the XHTML 1.0 DTDs and other DTDs from the book
- examples: Contains files listing the book examples by chapter
- graphics: Contains all the graphics used with the *XHTML For Dummies* Web pages
- templates: Contains a collection of XHTML templates to get you started
- urls: Contains files that list the book's URLs by chapter

For you list enthusiasts who need to know more about the files lurking within the subdirectories, this list unveils them in greater detail:

- **xhtmlfd/applet:** The files in this directory are behind the XHTML context applet. If you're curious to see what Java code looks like, then view any one of these files in a text editor. We can't promise it will make sense unless you have some programming experience, but at least you'll know what Java code looks like.
- **xhtmlfd/contents:** The file default.htm within the contents of the subdirectory includes a hyperlinked listing of all the chapter titles. Click a chapter title to view a list of its contents. The other files in the subdirectory are named chnncont.htm (where *nn* is a two-digit number between 01 and 27) and are keyed to the chapters of the book. For example, ch01cont.htm contains the contents listing for Chapter 1. The easiest

way to navigate through these pages is to choose a chapter from `default.htm` to view a chapter's contents. To return to the list of chapter titles, choose `"Book Contents"` from the bottom image map (or text provided for navigation).

✔ **xhtmlfd/dtds:** We've included all three of the XHTML DTDs in this folder for you so you can use them with some of the different XML editors on the CD-ROM that read DTDs and help you build documents based on the DTD — such as XMLSpy. We've also thrown in other DTDs and XHTML modules that we think might be of interest or use to you. The file `default.htm` within the contents of the subdirectory includes a hyperlinked listing of all DTDs. The DTDs are saved as text files so when you click on a link your browser should display the DTD in all of its glory. To return to the list of DTDs from any given DTD, click your browser's back button.

✔ **xhtmlfd/examples:** The file `default.htm` within the contents of the sub-directory includes a hyperlinked listing of all the chapter titles. The examples folder is further broken down into subfolders that contain the individual XHTML example documents for each chapter. Click a chapter title in `default.htm` to view a listing of the examples included for the chapter. To view a specific example, click the example name. Each example includes the code listing from the book and shows the final rendering of the example by a Web browser when possible.

Note: The easiest way to navigate through these pages is to choose a chapter from `default.htm` to view a listing of the chapter's examples and select the example you would like to see. When you finish with a particular example, press the Back button in your browser windows to return to the list of examples by chapter. To return to the list of chapter titles, choose `"Book Examples"` from the bottom image map (or text navigation).

✔ **xhtmlfd/graphics:** This is the graphics subdirectory for the graphics used in the XHTML documents for the *XHTML For Dummies* pages themselves. As its name implies, this folder houses all the `gif` image files in our Web documents. If we used an image on a Web page (except in the templates pages) you can find it here.

✔ **xhtmlfd/templates:** For your pleasure and convenience, we include a few simple templates to get you started on your HTML authoring adventures. The folder's main page, `default.htm`, gives you a complete rundown on each template. The `graphics` subdirectory within the `templates` folder contains all the graphics we used in creating the templates. All we can say is, *help yourself!*

✔ **xhtmlfd/urls:** The file `default.htm` within the `urls` subdirectory includes a hyperlinked listing of all the chapter titles. Click a chapter title to view a list the URLs we included in it. The other files in the sub-directory are named `chnnurls.htm` (where *nn* is a number between 01 and 26) and are keyed to the chapters of the book. The easiest way to navigate through these pages is to choose a chapter from `default.htm` to view a chapter's URLs. To return to the listing of chapter titles, choose `"Book URLs"` from the bottom image map or text links.

Working with Templates

Nothing is so simple that it can't benefit from a few well-chosen shortcuts. Building an XHTML document may not be quite like falling off a log, but we've put some template files on this book's CD-ROM to help you get your feet wet. Try using one as a starting point for your own XHTML page design. Simply copy it to your hard drive, give it a few tweaks to reflect your own interests, and then edit it to kick-start the Edit-Review cycle. A couple trips around the block on that cycle and your file will soon look like an XHTML page!

Whenever you want to use a template as a point of departure for your work, save it under a different name as soon as you open it in your text editor. That way, you won't have to recopy the files from the CD-ROM each time you want to reuse the same template.

The Software

In addition to the nifty files, examples, and scripts described in the previous section, we also include a small software collection on the CD-ROM. Heft and try out these evaluation and shareware versions of Webmaster tools that might fit your needs. Fear not the compatibility dragon; the CD is a multiplatform hybrid format. You have access to only those packages that can run on the platform you currently use (clever, eh?). To see the other tools, you must load the CD into a computer that uses a different operating system (of course, it has to be one of the platforms the CD itself supports . . . but you knew that). Table B-2 lists all of the software you can find on the CD-ROM along with information about the vendor that produces it.

Table B-2	Software Included on the CD-ROM	
Software	*Vendor*	*Description*
40tude HTML v3.1	Softwareentwicklung Marcus Moennig	HTML editor
Adept*Editor	ArbortText	XML Editor
Aelfred v1.2	Microstar Software Ltd.	XML Editor
Amaya	W3C	XML-aware Web browser
BBEdit Lite v4.6	BareBones Software, Inc.	HTML Editor
BBEdit 5.1.1	BareBones Software, Inc.	HTML Editor

(continued)

Table B-2 *(continued)*

Software	Vendor	Description
Bobby v3.	CAST (Center for Applied Special Technology)	HTML Validation and Accessibility Check Utility
Clip! XML Editor v1.52	Techno2000 USA, Inc	XML Editor
CoffeeCup HTML Editor v8.1	CoffeeCup Software	HTML Editor
ColdFusion Express	Allaire Corporation	Web application development environment
CSE HTML Validator Lite v2.00	AI Internet Solutions	HTML validation tool
CSE HTML Validator Professional v4.04	AI Internet Solutions	HTML validation tool
Dreamweaver 3.0	Macromedia, Inc	WYSIWYG HTML editor
expat	James Clark	XML Parser
Fusion 5.0	NetObjects	WYSIWYG HTML editor
GoLive	Adobe	WYSIWYG HTML editor
HotDog Professional v5.5	Sausage Software	WYSIWYG HTML editor
HTML (Un)Compress 5.1	Jan Jacobs	HTML editor
HTML Tidy	Dave Ragget	HTML to XTML utility
Internet Explorer 5.0	Microsoft Corporation	Web browser
Netscape Communicator 4.7	Netscape Communications	Web browser
SQA SiteCheck	Rational Software Corporation	HTML validation tool
XMetal v1.0	SoftQuad	XML editor
XML Notepad v1.5	Microsoft Corporation	XML editor
XML Pro v2.01	Vervet Logic	XML editor
XML Style Wizard	Infoteria	XML style sheet editor

Software	Vendor	Description
XML/XSL Viewer	Microsoft Corporation	XML/XSL browser
XSL Lint	Norman Walsh	XSL validator
XT	James Clark	XML parser

System Requirements

Make sure that your computer meets the minimum system requirements listed in this handy section. If your computer doesn't match up to most of these requirements, you may have problems using the contents of the CD-ROM. Avoid the heartbreak of obsolescence; look before you load.

- A PC with a 486 or faster processor, or a Mac OS computer with a 68030 or faster processor.
- Microsoft Windows 3.1 or later, or Mac OS system software 7.5 or later.
- At least 32MB of total RAM installed on your computer. For best performance, we recommend that Windows 95/98/2000-equipped PCs and Mac OS computers with PowerPC processors have at least 60MB of RAM installed.
- At least 20MB of hard drive space available to install all the software from this CD-ROM. (You need less space if you don't install every program.)
- A CD-ROM drive — double speed (2x) or faster.
- A monitor capable of displaying at least 256 colors or grayscale.
- A modem with a speed of at least 33,600 bps.

If you need more information on the basics, check out *PCs For Dummies,* 6th Edition, by Dan Gookin; *Macs For Dummies,* 6th Edition, by David Pogue; *Windows 98 For Dummies, Windows 95 For Dummies,* or *Windows 3.11 For Dummies,* 4th Edition, all by Andy Rathbone (all published by IDG Books Worldwide, Inc.).

If You've Got Problems (Of the CD Kind)

We tried our level best to compile programs that work on most computers with the minimum system requirements. Alas, your computer may differ, and some programs may not work properly for some reason. (Check the label. Was your system reverse-engineered from a UFO?)

The two likeliest problems are

> ✔ You may not have enough memory (RAM) for the programs you want to use.

> ✔ Other running programs interfere with installation or running of a program.

If you get error messages like `Not enough memory` or `Setup cannot continue`, try one or more of these methods and then try using the software again:

> ✔ **Turn off any antivirus software that you have running on your computer.** Installers sometimes mimic virus activity and may make your computer incorrectly believe that it is being infected by a virus.

> ✔ **Close all running programs.** The more programs you're running, the less memory is available to other programs. Installers also typically update files and programs; if you keep other programs running, installation may not work properly.

> ✔ **In Windows, close the CD-ROM interface and run demos or installations directly from Windows Explorer.** The interface itself can tie up system memory or even conflict with certain kinds of interactive demos. Use Windows Explorer to browse the files on the CD-ROM and launch installers or demos.

> ✔ **Have your local computer store add more RAM to your computer.** This is, admittedly, a drastic and somewhat expensive step, but be of good cheer: More RAM is almost always a good thing. However, if you have a Windows 95 PC or a Mac OS computer with a PowerPC chip, adding more memory can really help the speed of your computer and enable more programs to run at the same time.

If you still have trouble installing the items from the CD-ROM, please call the IDG Books Worldwide Customer Service phone number: 800-762-2974 (outside the United States: 317-596-5430).

Index

(continued)

Notes

Notes

Notes

Notes

Notes

IDG Books Worldwide, Inc., End-User License Agreement

READ THIS. You should carefully read these terms and conditions before opening the software packet(s) included with this book ("Book"). This is a license agreement ("Agreement") between you and IDG Books Worldwide, Inc. ("IDGB"). By opening the accompanying software packet(s), you acknowledge that you have read and accept the following terms and conditions. If you do not agree and do not want to be bound by such terms and conditions, promptly return the Book and the unopened software packet(s) to the place you obtained them for a full refund.

1. **License Grant.** IDGB grants to you (either an individual or entity) a nonexclusive license to use one copy of the enclosed software program(s) (collectively, the "Software") solely for your own personal or business purposes on a single computer (whether a standard computer or a workstation component of a multiuser network). The Software is in use on a computer when it is loaded into temporary memory (RAM) or installed into permanent memory (hard disk, CD-ROM, or other storage device). IDGB reserves all rights not expressly granted herein.

2. **Ownership.** IDGB is the owner of all right, title, and interest, including copyright, in and to the compilation of the Software recorded on the CD-ROM ("Software Media"). Copyright to the individual programs recorded on the Software Media is owned by the author or other authorized copyright owner of each program. Ownership of the Software and all proprietary rights relating thereto remain with IDGB and its licensers.

3. **Restrictions on Use and Transfer.**

   (a) You may only (i) make one copy of the Software for backup or archival purposes, or (ii) transfer the Software to a single hard disk, provided that you keep the original for backup or archival purposes. You may not (i) rent or lease the Software, (ii) copy or reproduce the Software through a LAN or other network system or through any computer subscriber system or bulletin-board system, or (iii) modify, adapt, or create derivative works based on the Software.

   (b) You may not reverse engineer, decompile, or disassemble the Software. You may transfer the Software and user documentation on a permanent basis, provided that the transferee agrees to accept the terms and conditions of this Agreement and you retain no copies. If the Software is an update or has been updated, any transfer must include the most recent update and all prior versions.

4. **Restrictions on Use of Individual Programs.** You must follow the individual requirements and restrictions detailed for each individual program in the "About the CD" in this Book. These limitations are also contained in the individual license agreements recorded on the Software Media. These limitations may include a requirement that after using the program for a specified period of time, the user must pay a registration fee or discontinue use. By opening the Software packet(s), you will be agreeing to abide by the licenses and restrictions for these individual programs that are detailed in the "About the CD" and on the Software Media. None of the material on this Software Media or listed in this Book may ever be redistributed, in original or modified form, for commercial purposes.

5. **Limited Warranty.**

   (a) IDGB warrants that the Software and Software Media are free from defects in materials and workmanship under normal use for a period of sixty (60) days from the date of purchase of this Book. If IDGB receives notification within the warranty period of defects in materials or workmanship, IDGB will replace the defective Software Media.

   (b) **IDGB AND THE AUTHOR OF THE BOOK DISCLAIM ALL OTHER WARRANTIES, EXPRESS OR IMPLIED, INCLUDING WITHOUT LIMITATION IMPLIED WARRANTIES OF MERCHANTABILITY AND FITNESS FOR A PARTICULAR PURPOSE, WITH RESPECT TO THE SOFTWARE, THE PROGRAMS, THE SOURCE CODE CONTAINED THEREIN, AND/OR THE TECHNIQUES DESCRIBED IN THIS BOOK. IDGB DOES NOT WARRANT THAT THE FUNCTIONS CONTAINED IN THE SOFTWARE WILL MEET YOUR REQUIREMENTS OR THAT THE OPERATION OF THE SOFTWARE WILL BE ERROR FREE.**

   (c) This limited warranty gives you specific legal rights, and you may have other rights that vary from jurisdiction to jurisdiction.

6. **Remedies.**

   (a) IDGB's entire liability and your exclusive remedy for defects in materials and workmanship shall be limited to replacement of the Software Media, which may be returned to IDGB with a copy of your receipt at the following address: Software Media Fulfillment Department, Attn.: *XHTML For Dummies*, IDG Books Worldwide, Inc., 10475 Crosspoint Boulevard, Indianapolis, IN 46256, or call 800-762-2974. Please allow three to four weeks for delivery. This Limited Warranty is void if failure of the Software Media has resulted from accident, abuse, or misapplication. Any replacement Software Media will be warranted for the remainder of the original warranty period or thirty (30) days, whichever is longer.

   (b) In no event shall IDGB or the author be liable for any damages whatsoever (including without limitation damages for loss of business profits, business interruption, loss of business information, or any other pecuniary loss) arising from the use of or inability to use the Book or the Software, even if IDGB has been advised of the possibility of such damages.

   (c) Because some jurisdictions do not allow the exclusion or limitation of liability for consequential or incidental damages, the above limitation or exclusion may not apply to you.

7. **U.S. Government Restricted Rights.** Use, duplication, or disclosure of the Software by the U.S. Government is subject to restrictions stated in paragraph (c)(1)(ii) of the Rights in Technical Data and Computer Software clause of DFARS 252.227-7013, and in subparagraphs (a) through (d) of the Commercial Computer–Restricted Rights clause at FAR 52.227-19, and in similar clauses in the NASA FAR supplement, when applicable.

8. **General.** This Agreement constitutes the entire understanding of the parties and revokes and supersedes all prior agreements, oral or written, between them and may not be modified or amended except in a writing signed by both parties hereto that specifically refers to this Agreement. This Agreement shall take precedence over any other documents that may be in conflict herewith. If any one or more provisions contained in this Agreement are held by any court or tribunal to be invalid, illegal, or otherwise unenforceable, each and every other provision shall remain in full force and effect.

Installation Instructions

1. **Insert the CD into your computer's CD-ROM drive.**

   Give your computer a moment to take a look at the CD.

2. **When the light on your CD-ROM drive goes out, double click on the My Computer icon (It's probably in the top left corner of your desktop.)**

   This action opens the My Computer window, which shows you all the drives attached to your computer, the Control Panel, and a couple other handy things.

3. **Double click on the icon for your CD-ROM drive.**

   Another window opens, showing you all the folders and files on the CD.

4. **Double click the file called License.txt.**

   This file contains the end-user license that you agree to by using the CD. When you are done reading the license, close the program, most likely NotePad, that displayed the file.

5. **Double click the file called Readme.txt.**

   This file contains instructions about installing the software from this CD. It might be helpful to leave this text file open while you are using the CD.

6. **Double click the folder for the software you are interested in.**

   Be sure to read the descriptions of the programs in the next section of this appendix (much of this information also shows up in the Readme file). These descriptions will give you more precise information about the programs' folder names, and about finding and running the installer program.

7. **Find the file called Setup.exe, or Install.exe, or something similar, and double click on that file.**

   The program's installer will walk you through the process of setting up your new software.

WWW.DUMMIES.COM

Discover Dummies Online!

The Dummies Web Site is your fun and friendly online resource for the latest information about *For Dummies* books and your favorite topics. The Web site is the place to communicate with us, exchange ideas with other *For Dummies* readers, chat with authors, and have fun!

Ten Fun and Useful Things You Can Do at www.dummies.com

1. Win free *For Dummies* books and more!
2. Register your book and be entered in a prize drawing.
3. Meet your favorite authors through the IDG Books Worldwide Author Chat Series.
4. Exchange helpful information with other *For Dummies* readers.
5. Discover other great *For Dummies* books you must have!
6. Purchase Dummieswear® exclusively from our Web site.
7. Buy *For Dummies* books online.
8. Talk to us. Make comments, ask questions, get answers!
9. Download free software.
10. Find additional useful resources from authors.

Link directly to these ten fun and useful things at
http://www.dummies.com/10useful

For other technology titles from IDG Books Worldwide, go to
www.idgbooks.com

Not on the Web yet? It's easy to get started with *Dummies 101*®: *The Internet For Windows*® *98* or *The Internet For Dummies*® at local retailers everywhere.

Find other *For Dummies* books on these topics:

Business • Career • Databases • Food & Beverage • Games • Gardening • Graphics • Hardware
Health & Fitness • Internet and the World Wide Web • Networking • Office Suites
Operating Systems • Personal Finance • Pets • Programming • Recreation • Sports
Spreadsheets • Teacher Resources • Test Prep • Word Processing

IDG BOOKS WORLDWIDE BOOK REGISTRATION

We want to hear from you!

Register This Book and Win!

Visit **http://my2cents.dummies.com** to register this book and tell us how you liked it!

✔ Get entered in our monthly prize giveaway.

✔ Give us feedback about this book — tell us what you like best, what you like least, or maybe what you'd like to ask the author and us to change!

✔ Let us know any other *For Dummies®* topics that interest you.

Your feedback helps us determine what books to publish, tells us what coverage to add as we revise our books, and lets us know whether we're meeting your needs as a *For Dummies* reader. You're our most valuable resource, and what you have to say is important to us!

Not on the Web yet? It's easy to get started with *Dummies 101®: The Internet For Windows® 98* or *The Internet For Dummies®* at local retailers everywhere.

Or let us know what you think by sending us a letter at the following address:

For Dummies Book Registration
Dummies Press
10475 Crosspoint Blvd.
Indianapolis, IN 46256

FOR DUMMIES™

BESTSELLING
BOOK SERIES